AGRARIAN AND OTHER HISTORIES

ESSAYS FOR
BINAY BHUSHAN CHAUDHURI

BINAY BHUSHAN CHAUDHURI was born on 9 May 1932. He attended the Shakpura High School in Chittagong (now in Bangladesh), and studied History at Presidency College and at Calcutta University in the early 1950s. He obtained a doctorate from Calcutta University in 1958, and a second doctorate from Oxford University in 1968. He held the position of Professor of Economic and Social History in the History Department of Calcutta University, where he taught with distinction from 1961 until retirement in 1997.

AGRARIAN AND OTHER HISTORIES

ESSAYS FOR
BINAY BHUSHAN CHAUDHURI

Edited by
SHUBHRA CHAKRABARTI and UTSA PATNAIK

 Tulika Books

Published by
Tulika Books
44 (first floor), Shahpur Jat, New Delhi 110 049, India
www.tulikabooks.in

First edition (hardback) 2017

ISBN: 978-93-82381-95-2

Printed at Chaman Offset, Delhi 110 002

Contents

Preface
SHUBHRA CHAKRABARTI and UTSA PATNAIK   **vii**

Introduction
SHUBHRA CHAKRABARTI   **xiii**

SECTION ONE

Emergence of the Peasant Landlord in India
DIETMAR ROTHERMUND   **1**

Towards an Economic History *for* Bengal in the
Eighteenth Century: A View from Its Villages
RAJAT DATTA   **17**

Rethinking the Bengal Peasantry in History
SHINKICHI TANIGUCHI   **41**

Frontiers of Agrarian Bengal: Sylhet in the 1780s
DAVID LUDDEN   **65**

Promise of Modernity, Antinomies of Development:
Canal Colonies of Punjab (1890s–1940s)
NEELADRI BHATTACHARYA   **90**

SECTION TWO

Dalit–Muslim Relations in the Long History of
Partition in Bengal
SEKHAR BANDYOPADHYAY   **139**

Bengal Famine of 1943 and the Chittagong Nari Samiti
GARGI CHAKRAVARTTY   156

From Cantoobabu to Dwarakanath: Emergence of a
New Commercial Elite in Bengal (1757–1850)
SHUBHRA CHAKRABARTI   172

SECTION THREE

Redeeming the Indian Village: Rabindranath Tagore
and the Sriniketan Experiment
UMA DAS GUPTA   201

Gora and Ghare Baire: The Intractable Problems of
Patriotism, Love and Freedom
TANIKA SARKAR   215

The Best of Nationalism and Beyond:
Rabindranath's Swadesh
ANURADHA ROY   237

SECTION FOUR

The Concept of Poverty in Colonial India
SABYASACHI BHATTACHARYA   263

Revisiting the 'Drain', or Transfer from India to Britain
in the Context of Global Diffusion of Capitalism
UTSA PATNAIK   277

Contributors   319

Publications by Binay Bhushan Chaudhuri   321

Preface

The essays in this volume, divided into four broad sections, are on diverse themes. A number are on different aspects of the agrarian world, the major subject of Binay Bhushan Chaudhuri's academic research. Many other papers discuss aspects of social and cultural history that have always interested and inspired Professor Chaudhuri. There are three essays on Rabindranath Tagore, the towering figure he venerates like most intellectuals of his generation from Bengal, and with whom he also happens to share his own birthday.

The first section of the volume, comprising five essays, begins with an essay by Dietmar Rothermund where he argues that a class he calls 'peasant-landlords' emerged in India after the abolition of zamindari from 1950 onwards, from the rich and middle peasant classes. Rothermund suggests the 'peasant-landlords' emerged from among those who could generate a large agricultural surplus by employing labour to cultivate their land, and that they became 'a kind of agrarian bourgeoisie'. They also used this surplus in the lucrative moneylending business, and in improving agricultural land, thus yielding profits.

Rajat Datta, by choosing the word 'for' rather than 'of' in the title of his essay, directs attention to the inadequacy of earlier scholarship regarding the village in eighteenth-century Bengal. He argues that the putative view has been to regard the village economy as something that lay outside urban mercantilism, money economy and commodity consumption. He urges that this notion of the village and its economy needs to be abandoned since the 'village' saw important changes caused by the shift in political rule, monetization of the economy and urbanization. The village economy in the eighteenth century experienced a high degree of commercialization of production, suggesting the need to re-evaluate the popular view of a poorly monetized rural landscape.

Shinkichi Taniguchi begins his essay with a clear definition of the term 'peasant', and discusses the historical evidence relating to the existence of a rich peasant stratum in most districts of Bengal and not only in its frontier areas. He argues that the relative importance of tribal and semi-Hinduized peoples in the populations of different districts of Bengal, and the continuous process of Hinduization of tribal society, marked the differing paths of transition from shifting cultivation to settled agriculture which was not necessarily completed everywhere. The change from tribal communal land ownership to individual ownership saw local variations and gave rise to specific class structures. Distinguishing between the process in the plains and in the hills, the author cites factors like commercialization of agriculture, reclamation of land and ecological factors as all working to influence peasant differentiation. In certain regions, changing political conditions such as commencement of British colonial rule and introduction of the new land tenure system led to further differentiation among the peasantry.

David Ludden shows how Sylhet – now in northeastern Bangladesh, where tributaries of the mighty Meghna enter deltaic Bengal – became a turbulent eighteenth-century farming frontier under Nawab Murshid Quli Khan and then the English East India Company. The essay presents a picture of Sylhet's topography, and shows how its old mobile communities of Khasias, Garos, Ahoms, Dimasas and Boros were absorbed aggressively into sedentary agrarian Bengal. Ludden's paper unravels the gradual intermingling of Khasias and Bengali cultivators who settled in the southwestern lowlands after clearing the jungles. Their revenue-paying farms became tiny estates owned by small landlords who organized cultivation around clusters of villages. Bengali Khasias thus formed a uniquely mixed ethnic identity, which disappeared as the British government enabled Bengali farmers to control the land and confined Khasias to life in the mountains that later became Meghalaya.

The focus of the next essay, by Neeladri Bhattacharya, is related to the search by colonizers everywhere for open spaces that would allow possibilities of unconstrained transformation. The *bars* (pastoral highlands) beyond the Sutlej, it seemed, was such a space. Colonial officials hoped to mould this space in accordance with their dream, develop it through science, capital and imperial imagination. They saw themselves working on a landscape empty of people, unencumbered by the past, unfettered by social rigidities. As the process of colonization proceeded, this fantasy of freedom from constraint, this imperial desire to create a colonial agrarian society from above unhindered by local rigidities, gradually crumbled. The colonizing projects as they evolved were very different from the constitutive elements of the original idea. Bhattacharya examines both the vision and experience of this agrarian colonization, and looks at the relationship between the founding plan and the executed projects. It explores how spaces become sites of conflict and how the specific mode of their re-figuration is defined by this conflict. Through this exploration the author reflects on the different paths to agrarian conquest, and the different modes of colonial domination.

The second section of the volume comprises three essays that reflect aspects of the social history of Bengal during the colonial and post-colonial period.

Sekhar Bandyopadhyay's essay discusses the participation of Dalit–Muslims in Bengal's Partition politics. He argues that the Dalits were both victims and perpetrators of violence during the Partition. The Dalit–Muslim and Dalit–Hindu relationship has to be seen in the context of heterogeneous political responses to fast-changing historical conjunctures of that time. While some leaders opposed the Partition and collaborated with the Muslim League, aligning with the pan-Indian Dalit movement of the All India Scheduled Caste Federation led by B.R. Ambedkar, others joined hands with the mainstream political parties such as the Congress and the Hindu Mahasabha. After Partition, Dalit peasants were displaced from their ancestral homes by Islamic nationalism in Pakistan, while Hindu militant nationalism in India, though it tried to appropriate them, was not ready to offer them full citizenship. As they were dispersed in various refugee camps throughout the country, organized Dalit voices disappeared from Bengal's public space, leading to that all-powerful political myth that caste does not matter in Bengal.

Gargi Chakravartty situates her essay on the Mahila Atma Raksha Samiti (or MARS, Society for Self-Defence by Women) against the back-drop of the devastating Bengal famine of 1943–44. She argues that this famine was a man-made calamity caused by bureaucratic corruption and the exploitative zamindari system. The famine occurred not owing to a shortage of foodgrains, but due to hoarding and blackmarketeering by wealthy merchants. This was also the period of repeated Japanese air-raids on Chittagong as the Second World War raged, when Subhas Chandra Bose began his march from Singapore, the brunt of which was felt by Chittagong. Amidst this volatile situation the Mahila Atma Raksha Samiti, a patriotic and radical organization, was formed for women's self-protection, to counter Japanese aggression and tackle the famine situation.

The theme of Shubhra Chakrabarti's essay is the social and eco-nomic origins of the founders of Calcutta, who made their fortunes from the trading opportunities created by the advent of European companies, particularly the British. They acted as their collaborators, or as inde-pendent traders. Even after the English East India Company came to rule by acquiring the *diwani* of Bengal in 1765, these indigenous merchants continued to dominate the commercial world, right up to the first two decades of the nineteenth century, after which their dominance gradually ebbed. The period 1757–1850 saw entrepreneurs in Bengal investing large fortunes into the making of Calcutta. Through a case study, Chakrabarti analyses the causes that led to the decline of these commercial magnates from the mid-nineteenth century, after the transfer of the Company's rule to the Crown.

The next three essays, which constitute the third section of this volume, relate to some of the many facets of Rabindranath Tagore's life and genius.

Uma Das Gupta's paper explores Tagore's attempt to inspire the deprived sections of rural society towards self-reliance, and to make them economically independent by setting up Sriniketan as a rural development wing of Visva-Bharati University. The idea was pioneering for its time as an endeavour to improve the condition of the peasants by introducing modern methods of cultivation and cooperative artisanal production. The idea of doing something to uplift the neglected village first came to Tagore when he went to tour and live on his family's estates in East Bengal at the age of 30, sent by his father to manage these estates. He lived in Shelidaha, the estate's headquarters in Nadia district. His work as a caring zamindar is documented in the District Gazetteers of the period. This was his first exposure to the countryside and its stark miseries. The experience played a seminal part in turning him into a man of action. The closer he felt to the masses of his society, the farther he moved from persons of his own class who were indifferent to the masses. Tagore's independent thinking gave him the courage of conviction to work alone with his ideas of rural reconstruction.

Tanika Sarkar looks at three political novels by Rabindranath Tagore which were written over a period of nearly three decades of great political turbulence in the country. Her essay probes the changing historical contexts and forms of nationalism that inspired these novels, and focuses on the shifts and changes that appeared as Tagore moved from one novel to the other. Though the novels are primarily reflections on different phases and faces of nationalism, the contexts of class, gender and caste politics are also explored at some length. The predominant focus, however, is on *Gora*, the first of the three novels, and the two others are brought in largely as counterpoints.

Anuradha Roy shows that despite Tagore's vehement criticism of the idea of nationalism, it is possible to trace the evolution of his own concept of nationalism through his writings. His concept of *swadesh* was not very different from what we term 'nation' today. Roy sees three phases in the evolution of Tagore's nationalism: the formative phase in the late nineteenth century; the phase of enthusiasm at the turn of the twentieth century; and his apprehensive reflections on *swadeshi* nationalism and subsequent search for a new trajectory of the national movement. Roy suggests that the history of Indian nationalism cannot dispense with Rabindranath Tagore whose ideas help us to restore the human essence in our individual lives.

The last section of the volume consists of two essays. The first, by Sabyasachi Bhattacharya, outlines three separate discursive approaches to 'poverty' in colonial India: that of the colonial state, the nationalist view in the writings of Dadabhai Naoroji, and the representation of poverty by the poor themselves. He refers to Jeremy Bentham's 'utilitarian' ideas, which influenced the process of managing the poor in nineteenth-century England and its link with the concerns of the Famine Codes and the Famine Relief Committee reports. The author then moves on to the discussion by Dadabhai Naoroji, R.C. Dutt and others which emphasized the structural conditions that sustained deprivation among the agricultural and working classes in colonial India. In the last section of his essay, Bhattacharya explicates the self-representation of poverty by the poor themselves.

Utsa Patnaik's essay discusses transfers from India to Britain, or the 'drain of wealth' during colonial rule. Three propositions are developed. First, the classical conception of the drain and its measurement as articulated by Dadabhai Naoroji and R.C. Dutt was correct and is easily expressed in terms of modern macroeconomic theory. Their concept turned on the fact that India's global commodity export surplus earnings were entirely appropriated by Britain by 'paying' local producers out of their own taxes, namely not paying them at all, which had a strongly income-deflating impact. Second, from the end of the nineteenth century the drain became very large, with India posting the second largest export surplus earnings in the world for at least four decades before the Depression. Third, the gold and foreign exchange earnings thus appropriated from its colonies, especially from India, allowed Britain to export capital to develop Europe, North America and regions of recent white settlement, thus ensuring the rapid diffusion of capitalism to these regions. Existing series on India's balance of payments are used by the author to estimate the extent of drain.

This volume would not have been possible without the scholarly contributions of all the authors, to whom the editors are immensely indebted. We would like to thank the young scholars of the Centre for

Historical Studies in Jawaharlal Nehru University – Kanad Sinha, Shuvajit
Haldar, Debkumar Jhanjh and Parnisha Sarkar, who read through the
manuscript and raised questions. A special vote of thanks is due to Indira
Chandrasekhar and to her team at Tulika Books for their interest and commitment in publishing this festschrift, which we hope is a worthy addition
to Tulika's existing list of felicitation volumes for distinguished academics.

February 2017   SHUBHRA CHAKRABARTI AND UTSA PATNAIK

Introduction

Shubhra Chakrabarti

There is no area in the agrarian history of eastern India that Binay Bhushan Chaudhuri has not traversed. His journey began with his 1956 contribution in *Bengal Past and Present*, on 'Some Problems of the Peasantry of Bengal after the Permanent Settlement'.[1] His extensive opus surveys the agrarian economy of eastern India and all its protagonists – peasant households, zamindars and the state, non-peasant rural agents such as moneylenders, affluent landholders, farmers and agrarian intermediaries (*jotedars*) – all of whom played their decisive role in the rural agrarian structure. His later research explores the impact of colonial rule on tribes and forest dwellers who were in the process of transition to quasi-peasant communities by the middle of the twentieth century.

In his pioneering work, *The Growth of Commercial Agriculture in Bengal: 1757–1957*, which developed out of his doctoral thesis, Chaudhuri discusses two important phenomena that shaped the contours of the agrarian economy of Bengal – first, the demographic factor, namely population growth combined with a simultaneous growth of agricultural production; and second, the role of external demand that determined peasant production for the market. He places additional value on factors such as climate change, natural disasters, and political instability arising out of wars and invasions, which affected agricultural production in India.

It is difficult to do justice to Chaudhuri's academic work, given its depth and range. An inadequate attempt is made here under four broad heads: (i) his concept of the peasantry; (ii) the growth of commercial agriculture in eastern India; (iii) the process of 'depeasantization' by which small and marginal peasants gradually lost their land and turned into sharecroppers or hired labourers; and finally, (iv) the more or less forcible induction of a large number of tribes and forest dwellers into settled agriculture, resulting in spates of rebellion.

I

Peasants are the main protagonists of Chaudhuri's research. In his magnum opus, *Peasant History of Late Pre-Colonial and Colonial India*,[2] he describes peasants as those 'who are directly or indirectly involved in the cultivation process', and whose major livelihood is derived from agriculture. They are placed vis-à-vis all the major characters in the agrarian world – zamindars, moneylenders, *jotedars* and other village intermediaries. Chaudhuri refutes the popular assumption that only those agriculturists in a position of subservience in a village can be labelled as peasants. He also disagrees with scholars who draw divisions between 'peasants' and 'farmers' on the basis of 'profit-oriented' production for the market. For Chaudhuri, anyone who plays a crucial role in the peasant economy, whether they be sharecroppers (*bhag-chashi* or *adhiyar*), small and big tenant-holders (*raiyats* – *khudkasht* or self-cultivating, *pahikasht/paikasht* or migrant peasant), tenant-farmers (*bargadars*), owner-farmers (*nij-chashi*), agricultural labourers (*jan, majoor* or *begar*) – are all included within the category 'peasant'. He asserts that a subsistence cultivator is as much a peasant as the farmer who grows crops for the market on a substantial part of his holding. He also includes persons with supervisory or decision-making roles among the peasantry as part of peasant society. Even if village society is composed of heterogeneous groups, this non-peasant group that lives off the peasant surplus is very much a part of the agrarian world. As Chaudhuri puts it, 'the question to decide is the functional relationship of the non-peasant groups with the peasant economy'.

Chaudhuri situates peasant history in the wider economic, political and social history of India, showing the different levels of stratification amongst the peasants themselves as well as their relationship with other members of the village community. While analysing these two aspects, he points out that it was the extraction of social surplus from the peasant producers, in the form of rent by revenue-paying landlords and directly as revenue by the state, that forged links among all these groups in rural society. He establishes how caste, clan and religion are important determinants of village life.

The beginning of British rule in Bengal after 1757, and in particular the acquisition of revenue-collecting rights by the East India Company in 1765, had a long-term adverse impact on the fate of Indian peasants. The British introduced far-reaching changes in the structure of tenures and the market orientation of agricultural production, first in Bengal followed by the whole of British India. Chaudhuri explains the manner in which the new land revenue systems, such as the Permanent Settlement in Bengal, the *raiyatwari* (*ryotwari*), *mahalwari*, *sepidari* and *ijaradari* systems elsewhere, affected the peasantry as a whole. His contention is that during early British rule, it was shortage of labour that often stunted agricultural production in eastern India (not surprising given the massive 1770 famine in Bengal which decimated a third of its population). Later, even though the population recovered and production, responding to the decisive role of market forces, rose significantly, the condition of the ordinary peasants did not see any noticeable improvement. Technological innovations such as new irrigation systems introduced by the British, did not transform traditional agriculture or enable the ordinary peasants to reap real benefits. The bulk of economic surplus, as always, continued to be extracted by the state in the form of revenue, or as rent by the zamindars who in turn paid revenue to the colonial state. Chaudhuri points out that from about the second quarter of the nineteenth century, the state tended to integrate the regional economy more closely with the metropolitan economy, a process that became even more pronounced during the twentieth century and was a primary reason for the suffering of the poor peasants. The inter-war Great Depression was a culmination of this process.

II

Chaudhuri's in-depth study of the peasant economy leads to his seminal contribution to agrarian studies: the commercialization of agriculture in the colonial context. He draws from archival records, the evidence that helps us conceptualize the adverse effect forced commercialization had on Bengal peasants. He argues that while the Mughal rulers had also encouraged cultivation of cash crops, it was not in the manner of or to the extent that the British did. We may note that the unique feature of British rule, as distinct from any earlier system, was that a large part of the tax revenues – mostly comprising land revenue – was used by the East India Company to purchase export goods (textiles and crops), and this part of the revenues was thus dropped from normal budgetary spending. Moreover, while these export goods earned sterling for the Company, the peasants and artisans were not actually paid since their own tax contributions were being used to 'purchase' the goods from them. This meant very high profits for the Company, since its outlay in purchasing the goods had become zero. Driven by greed for ever-more profit, the Company coerced the peasants into producing crops such as indigo and opium for export in the early nineteenth century, the government exercising total monopoly over crop production. There was hardly any room for the free play of market forces, and peasants could not voluntarily choose the crops they wanted to produce. Chaudhuri's pioneering analysis based on archival records is a vital input for later scholars who argued that there was forced commercialization.[3] Chaudhuri analyses the role of foreign demand that lay behind the expansion of output of specific crops such as opium, indigo, sugarcane, cotton, jute and tea in India. It was this demand that had to be studied in the specific context of the relations between metropolis and colony.

Commercialization stimulated the growth of agricultural production alongside reorganization of the peasant economy. Chaudhuri argues that rather than 'profit motive', it was the compulsion of payment of revenue and rent along with debt obligations to moneylenders that prompted peasants to undertake cultivation of cash crops. From the mid-eighteenth century until the 1850s, the East India Company had coerced peasants into producing cash crops like opium, indigo and silk – for export not only to England, but to the whole world. After 1858, with the transfer of power from the Company to the British Crown, jute, cotton, wheat and tea (the last produced on plantations) became the most sought after among the cash crops. The demand for these cash crops mostly came from international markets, while cotton and sugarcane also enjoyed a large domestic demand. Chaudhuri points out that increased commercialization took place not only for cash crops, but also for food crops. The peasants marketed staple foods like rice and wheat in order to buy those goods which they themselves did not produce, and also to meet their revenue obligations. He mentions that often the poor were obliged to subsist on inferior food crops, while handing over the superior crops to grain merchants from whom they had taken advances in order to finance their crop cultivation. The entire process of monetization and the crucial role of moneylenders in agricultural production are explored in detail by Chaudhuri.

The fact that international markets during the colonial period primarily influenced commercialization of agriculture introduced new features into trade, compared to the earlier period when goods were procured by merchant middlemen from artisans and producers. There was simultaneously a shift in demand from crops such as indigo, opium and silk, over which the Company had exercised strong control and had generally coerced the peasants to cultivate. The most significant change came after the 1850s, when the kind of direct coercive control that the British exercised in the production of opium and indigo was no longer seen in the case of jute and cotton. Rather, an indirect pressure of increased revenue demand, brought about by the collaboration of local landlords and moneylenders, sufficed to ensure production. Jute, the major cash crop in Bengal after the mid-1850s, was an instance of 'subsistence commercialization' which the peasants cultivated willingly as it did not interfere with their winter rice production. Control continued, however, in one form or the other especially as the rulers invested in new technological devices.

Commercialization, according to Chaudhuri, thus meant growing production for the market of either the traditional subsistence food crop or of a new cash crop. This process was more 'forced' in areas where the peasants were more distressed because they had to meet heavier rent obligations. Often the zamindars encouraged the *raiyats* to grow cash crops so that revenues were ensured. Peasants sold a part of their food crops as well – there was heavy external demand for grain – and this rising demand led to an increase in cultivation. Thus the usual food crops also became cash crops, and the 'two continued side by side'.

III

Chaudhuri's analysis explicates the massive impact of commercialization of agriculture on the existing agrarian society. It is from this perspective that he propounds his theory of 'depeasantization', which may be translated as rural indebtedness. Here, he differs to some extent from scholars such as Elizabeth Whitcombe, Daniel Thorner and Alice Thorner among others, who have argued that although pre-British India was familiar with rural indebtedness, it was the new inflexible demand for cash as land revenue that was the root cause of the new and growing forms of indebtedness. The unsparing colonial system forced the poorer peasants to borrow against land in order to pay their rents and revenues on time. Failure to repay loans led to foreclosure on mortgages or the direct sale of land to creditors. Peasants tried to mitigate this desperate situation by taking recourse to cash-crop cultivation. Eventually, the loss of their holdings degraded the peasants into landless labourers. Chaudhuri has responded to this thesis by arguing that while rural indebtedness was a major factor behind the creation of an army of landless labourers in Indian villages, the question of debt was a more complex and differentiated one. Peasants did sell their land during famines, but all sales were not distress sales. 'Indebtedness was not always a signifier of poverty of the peasants; it often meant an expansion of the credit network, of increased agricultural prices and an expansion of the market for peasant production.'[4] Further, 'debts also occurred during occasions of prosperity in the economy, when peasants were eager to increase their holdings, even by borrowing, as happened before the Great Depression of 1929.'[5]

Chaudhuri has put forward several reasons as underlying the growing rural indebtedness under British rule. First, there was the diminishing land–man ratio, particularly noticeable in the districts of Bihar and eastern Bengal. Population pressure arose from large numbers of migrant peasants settling in areas which showed a negative trend in arable acreage per head. Cultivation often shifted to less fertile areas and whenever there was a crop failure, it increased indebtedness. Second, Chaudhuri has shown how the decadent or 'moribund' river delta system in Bengal upon which agriculture was largely dependent, and the ravages of malaria, hindered cultivation and increased borrowing by poor farmers. Third, he is of the opinion that commercialization of agriculture was not the only reason behind rural indebtedness, as commercial crops were restricted to particular regions; indebtedness was a universal phenomenon. Moneylenders and zamindars often forced peasants to engage in cash crop cultivation in place of food crops, which was not determined by demand in the market. Fourth, Chaudhuri has pointed out the coercive role of the state (East India Company's government before 1857) in making the peasants grow cash crops such as indigo, silk, sugarcane and opium during the late eighteenth and early nineteenth centuries. In most cases it financed production, the bulk of which was not remunerative for the peasants. The government's forceful recovery of the money it had advanced increased the already existent rural indebtedness.

Jute was considered to be a 'money crop' to be widely cultivated after the 1850s, but even this cash crop brought misery to cultivators when either the crop was destroyed or there were severe fluctuations in the market. The peasants ran into indebtedness to meet their subsistence requirements. Fifth, Chaudhuri is of the opinion that the expansion of markets in new places stimulated cultivation, for which peasants had to borrow in the initial days. When cultivation failed in these new lands, peasants either had to enter into fresh borrowings or abandon their projects altogether. But as the prices of commercial crops and the price of land rose over time, moneylenders as well as wealthy peasants, who were earlier hesitant to lend to these cultivators, became more than willing to extend loans. Land became transferable under the new laws and could be seized by creditors when debtors failed to pay up. Thus, rural indebtedness became all the more entrenched.

Sixth, a major reason behind rural indebtedness, as pointed out by Chaudhuri, was related to certain phases of price movement, which impoverished the peasantry. When prices fell due to abundant harvests or due to depression, the peasants suffered a loss. A marginal farmer could never stock up enough foodgrains, like a rich farmer. He was perpetually at the mercy of a *mahajan* (merchant-cum-moneylender), who lent him grain when he needed it only to realize it immediately after the harvest was reaped. The *raiyat* could thus never sell his harvest in the open market and reap a profit. Chaudhuri has emphasized that this trend was more visible in tribal areas where peasants became completely indebted to the *mahajans* as they had to sell their grain in order to buy other necessities like salt, kerosene and cotton cloth. He has drawn our attention to conditions that prevailed before 1928, when prices of agricultural products rose and peasants borrowed more for cultivating cash crops, expecting high returns. Also, when the Sarada Act of 1929 raised the marriage age of minor girls, the peasants borrowed heavily to marry off their growing daughters. Consequently, the moneylenders advanced loans generously, expecting high returns. When this boom period was followed by a price slump during the Great Depression and markets crashed, the rural poor suffered a massive blow. The Depression (1929–36), Chaudhuri argues, did not increase rural indebtedness phenomenally, perhaps because the peasants reduced their expenditure. Very little labour was hired for purposes of cultivation during this period, and cooperative societies, which normally gave huge loans to rich farmers, now reduced them.

The Great Depression did not altogether extinguish the rural credit network, but it brought about a change in the composition of rural creditors, as noticed in large parts of Bengal. Using the *Reports of the Famine Commission* of 1946, Chaudhuri cites how small village moneylenders were wiped out largely due to an accumulation of bad debts. Their place was taken by the *raiyat–mahajans* or *jotedar–mahajans*, a community of rich farmers who began to extend loans. During the Depression years, when professional moneylenders declined to lend, these *raiyat–mahajans* combined agriculture with moneylending and probably acquired the land from the *bargadars* (tenant-farmers), who took to outright sale during famines. During this period a new feature was seen in the village economy. When the creditor discovered that he had failed to recover his loan by selling his debtor's land, which was kept as security, he turned the latter into a *bargadar*, or a farm-hand or sharecropper. The creditor also imposed usufruct mortgages in many parts of Bengal, and retained portions of the debtor's holdings. The most significant change of this period came with the rise in agricultural prices, when land became the only form of security accepted by creditors. As for the peasants, getting fresh loans became extremely tough, and they continued to groan under the weight of loans previously taken, which multiplied each day.

Finally, Chaudhuri portrays how the British Raj played a vital role in accentuating rural indebtedness. In eastern India, as the nineteenth century spilled into the twentieth, the administration took every step to help creditors realize their debts and all legal dues. The most forceful argument forwarded by Chaudhuri for 'depeasantization' was that this process ultimately turned debtors into 'debt-slaves', particularly in aboriginal and tribal areas, where popular resistance was extremely feeble to begin with. After the 1870s, a spate of sale of peasant holdings towards realization of debts became manifest as the price of land continuously increased. During the first three decades of the twentieth century, however, creditors preferred loans against occupancy holdings, partly because the land market had become more secure, and partly because of the rise in agricultural prices. Meanwhile, the Bengal Tenancy Act of 1885 clarified peasants' rights on land by placing a check on the constant increase of rent. The 1885 Act was further modified by the Act of 1928, which legalized the sale of peasant-holdings after the payment of a certain amount to the zamindar. This later became ineffective with the onset of the Depression. Now moneylenders preferred mortgages over sales, as this arrangement brought the *raiyats* completely under their control. It served in two ways: (i) cultivation continued; and (ii) the creditor continued to earn interest on the capital loaned. One should not conjecture that there was a decrease in the sale of land as a result of this process. The actual sales were far greater in number than recorded, as most sales were not registered. When the Amended Tenancy Act of 1938 removed all constraints on the sale of peasant holdings, the number of sales became spectacular. Wartime inflation, food scarcity and inability to meet debt/rent obligations further forced impoverished peasants to sell their land. The situation was even more exacerbated by the dreadful famine of 1943. Increase in the sale of part-holdings became the norm, as peasants resisted the sale of their entire land in all possible ways. Some debtors in Bengal sold a part of their land and mortgaged a part, to save the situation. This alarmed the government so much that it enacted the Land Alienation Act of 1944, which enabled the owner to repurchase his land up to a maximum value of Rs 250. But the Act failed to benefit destitute families that could not even pay the initial instalment. It was only through the Kisan Sabha movements of this time that some lands were restored to the poor peasants.

The most important consequence of these sales was that it expedited the process of depeasantization in eastern India. In certain cases, despite the transfer of legal titles, the peasants remained as sharecroppers or *bargadars* and continued to cultivate the land that they once owned. However, there were large numbers of cases of physical dispossession. In the drastically changed conditions, the *bargadar* was reduced to an infinitely inferior position, both socially and economically.

The sale of land did not immediately have an adverse effect on production, as a great deal depended on the landlord who now became the owner of these holdings. Production was affected mainly in those areas where there was a shift from active cultivation to absentee landlordism. Chaudhuri has observed that such land transfers created a parasitical class that survived on rents from the purchased land but was reluctant to promote agriculture. He identifies certain trends as being responsible for the rapid increase of the *bargadari* system. First, he mentions the diminution in the size of family-holdings – resulting from growth of population and enforcement of inheritance laws – as an important factor. Second, when peasants migrated from overcrowded regions, they were absorbed in the rural economy as *bargadars*. Third, with the increase in land price, wastelands were reclaimed and handed over to the *bargadars* for cultivation. Fourth, when new lands were brought under the plough, the landlords initially depended on the *bargadars* for cultivation. Finally, from about the end of the nineteenth century, a new class of 'gentlemen farmers' or '*bhadralok*' came into existence in Bengal. This class migrated to the cities, appointed sharecroppers to cultivate its lands and depended on produce rent. According to the reports of the Floud Commission, the *bargadari* system steadily gained in strength in Bengal and Bihar due to the 'commercialization of land . . . the appropriation of the most valuable right in the land, the occupancy right by non-agriculturists'. Production, therefore, was affected in many areas where a shift was noticed from active cultivation to absentee landlordism.

From his study of contemporary revenue records, Chaudhuri comes to the conclusion that there was an increase in the *barga* and *khas* (directly owned by the proprietor) lands of the proprietors and tenure-holders, largely at the expense of the *raiyats* who were forced to sell their lands either partially or entirely in order to pay up their debts. As direct supervision over the vast and scattered areas of dispossessed lands became near-impossible, creditors encouraged the *barga* system, which ensured them half the total produce. As for peasants who had lost their land, they preferred becoming *bargadars* rather than agricultural labourers. Chaudhuri's foremost contribution to the agrarian history of eastern India is the manner in which he constructs the story of 'depeasantization' in Bengal, and its direct offshoot, the *bargadari* system.

IV

Chaudhuri has also studied the impact of the *bargadari* system, particularly on the *adivasis* (tribals) and the *aranyakas* (forest dwellers) – people who lived a life of abject poverty and egregious destitution. To him these two were not identical categories. *Aranyakas* often included *adivasis*, but all *adivasis* were not *aranyakas*.[6] *Aranyakas*, according to Chaudhuri, comprised four main communities: settled peasants who lived near the forest and used its resources, including land; tribal groups that took to settled cultivation and used forest resources; pastoralists and nomads; and shifting cultivators. *Adivasis*, who practised settled cultivation, also drew part of their means of subsistence from nearby forests. Chaudhuri's research highlights how the new land relations led to the breakdown of indigenous tribal cultivation and adversely affected their socio-economic structures.

Chaudhuri argues that, unlike in pre-colonial days, British rule restricted *adivasis* and *aranyakas* from freely using the forest resources on which they thrived. The state and other private groups, particularly moneylenders, stepped in to control both the forests and the tribal lands, and tried to turn the tribals into settled, rent-paying agriculturists. The main reasons behind this control of the forests were: (i) generation of more revenue from new cultivation; (ii) need for an increased supply of timber for ship-building and sleepers in railway coaches; (iii) uprooting of rebels and anti-state activists who took refuge in the forests; (iv) enjoyment of hunting, which meant control over a large area abounding in wildlife. Chaudhuri's study shows how the British state tried to turn tribals and forest dwellers into peasants, who subsequently became agricultural labourers when they failed to meet their revenue obligations. Ultimately, they revolted against the draconian laws of the state.

Chaudhuri has analysed the various ways in which the British rulers jeopardized the tribal economy. They imposed monopolies on salt and opium, levied arbitrary taxes on home-made liquor, and tried to control diverse forest products including timber, which compromised the Santhal–Munda–Oraon economy. The *adivasis* and *aranyakas* were clueless about the markets in which their products were sold by the rulers. The situation was further complicated by the establishment of a new currency system in place of the old, local coins. But the worst blow came when the British vehemently opposed shifting cultivation (*curao*), which they considered wasteful. Some tribes, such as the Paharias or hillmen of the Rajmahal Hills in Bihar, were too poor to own ploughs, cattle and other agricultural implements, nor could they afford 'artificial irrigation'. They could not adapt to settled plough cultivation easily and stuck to their old mode of agriculture. Some others, like the Santhals, tried to better their livelihood by borrowing the practices of peasant agriculture. Thus they tried to integrate themselves into the peasant-village organizations, which were distinctly different from the tribal mode of subsistence. This was also the time when the migrant Santhals, skilled in wet cultivation, began to poach on the Paharias, the old inhabitants, and pushed them further up the Rajmahal Hills. Chaudhuri's contention is that this process led to the shrinking of shifting cultivation, on the one hand, and only a marginal increase of settled cultivation, on the other.

Colonial rule, he argues, marked a decisive break with the past, so far as the tribals and forest dwellers were concerned. Only the Munda–

Oraon society was familiar with a centralized political authority under Rajbansi rule before the coming of the British. The colonial state with its new centralized political authority was completely uninformed about the Santhals and others. The tribal world received a jolt as the *adivasi* village community lost its hold over traditional, 'old collective communal enterprise', and the new land settlement compelled most of its members to become paid wage labourers. The communal village organization, which once controlled village resources under the guidance of traditional headmen or *manjhis*, could do nothing to help the poor Santhal peasants.

Chaudhuri's research throws new light on the serious consequences of British control over forest dwellers. The loss of rights over forests and wastelands, the rapid spread of agricultural settlements, the worsening of economic conditions under forced borrowing from moneylenders (*dikus*), extortion of exorbitant rents by the landlords – all kindled the flames of revolt against the state. Radical insurgencies, imbued with 'the vision of an independent polity and the rise of an ideology and organization toward the realization of the vision', flared up. Chaudhuri, in several essays, has analysed the causes behind these socio-political insurgencies which broke out in five major phases.[7]

The first phase was marked by the Munda revolt in Bihar in the 1820s, followed by the Santhal uprisings of 1830–32. The second phase saw the radical Santhal movement known as the *Hool* in 1855, which was an armed retaliation against the alien, tyrannical *dikus* or moneylenders, whom the Santhals considered solely responsible for their miserable plight. The third phase, covering the years 1861–1900, is significant because of the Kherwar movement (1874–82), which was more religious and social in nature than political, as the Santhals, under their leader Bhagirath, revolted against the oppressive rent levied by the zamindars at a time when they had not recovered from the devastating famine of 1865–66. The last decade of the nineteenth century witnessed the fourth phase, the *ulgulan* (revolt) by Birsa Munda of the Munda tribe whose modalities were identical to those of the Santhal movement, i.e. 'creation of a revitalized religious and ethical system as the foundation of a radical organization'. Finally, the radical Tana Bhagat movement of the Oraons in Palamu, Chhotanagpur and Hazaribagh districts, that occurred between 1914 and 1930, primarily due to oppressive rent demands during the First World War, and the escalation of prices of necessities such as kerosene and cloth. The movement witnessed a combination of radical politics with religious factors. The songs of the Tanas reflect their bitterness against the British and glorification of the Germans, who they knew were the enemy of the British. Chaudhuri has read a common trend of radicalism among all these movements, in spite of the unique nature of each. He concludes that severe repression coupled with acute poverty accelerated the process of depeasantization in the tribal world, which was at the root of all resistance.

Chaudhuri's research thus covers all questions connected to the life and modes of subsistence of the *adivasis* and *aranyakas* – the transition from hunting, gathering and shifting cultivation to settled agriculture, the consequences of state intervention leading to loss of land and resources to crafty merchant–moneylenders – all of which culminated in armed insurrections against the British rulers. His many articles throw light on the state's forest policy: the debates around 'scientific forestry' and 'commercial forestry'. The core of Chaudhuri's life-long academic project has been exploration of the extent to which all categories of peasants and other classes of agrarian society, including the *adivasis* and the *aranyakas*, were affected by the major changes introduced as a result of British rule in India.

Notes and References

1 B.B. Chaudhuri, 'Some Problems of the Peasantry of Bengal after the Permanent Settlement', *Bengal Past and Present*, Jubilee Number, July–December 1956.
2 B.B. Chaudhuri, *Peasant History of Late Pre-Colonial and Colonial India*, Project of History of Indian Science, Philosophy and Culture (PHISPC) (General Editor: D.P. Chattopadhyaya), Vol. VIII, Part 2, New Delhi: Pearson Longman India, 2008.
3 See Amit Bhaduri, 'The Evolution of Land Relations in Eastern India under British Rule', *Indian Economic and Social History Review*, 13 (1), January 1976; Utsa Patnaik, 'The Process of Commercialization under Colonial Conditions', in *The Long Transition: Essays on Political Economy*, New Delhi: Tulika Books, 1999.
4 B.B. Chaudhuri, 'The Process of Depeasantization in Bengal and Bihar, 1885–1947', *Indian Historical Review*, July 1975.
5 Ibid., pp. 106–08.
6 See B.B. Chaudhuri, '*Adivasi and Aranyaka*: Reconsidering Some Characterizations of Their Polity and Economy in Pre-Colonial and Colonial India', in B.B. Chaudhuri and Arun Bandopadhyay eds, *Tribes, Forest and Social Formation in Indian History*, New Delhi: Manohar, 2004, pp. 89–107.
7 For details, see B.B. Chaudhuri, 'Radical Adivasi Movements in Colonial Eastern India, 1856–1922: Origins, Ideology and Organization', in *Proceedings of the Indian History Congress*, Patiala session, 2011; 'Tribal Society in Transition: Eastern India 1757–1920', in M. Hasan and N. Gupta, eds, *India's Colonial Encounter*, Delhi: Manohar, 1993; 'Reinterpreting the Santal Insurgency: The Hool of 1855', S.C. Misra Memorial Lecture, Indian History Congress, Maldah session, 2010; 'Agrarian Movements in Bengal and Bihar, 1919–39', in B.R. Nanda, ed., *Socialism in India, 1919–39*, New Delhi: Vikas, 1972; 'The Story of a Peasant Revolt in a Bengal District', *Bengal Past and Present*, July–December 1973; 'The Chotanagpur Tribal Revolt, 1831–32: Some Methodological Issues', *Calcutta Historical Review*, July 1989–June 1990. (Also see the List of Publications at the end of this volume for other essays dealing with tribal movements.)

SECTION ONE

Emergence of the
Peasant Landlord in India

Dietmar Rothermund

Introduction

The reference to a 'peasant landlord' seems to be a contradiction in terms. Usually lord and peasant are juxtaposed as the controller of the land and the tiller of the soil. Barrington Moore's seminal book, *Social Origins of Dictatorship and Democracy: Lord and Peasant in the Making of the Modern World*,[1] highlights the contrast between them. For Moore, the peasant is unable to support a bourgeois democracy, and when he gets involved in a revolution – as in China – he finally loses the game as others come to power who then determine his fate. Moore devotes a large part of his book to India, a country which remains a puzzle to him. He derived his knowledge of India from the literature on colonial India, which conveys the idea that Indian landlords were the support base of British power. The peasantry should have therefore revolted against these lords, and then shared the fate of the Chinese peasantry. Moore did not take note of the fact that the British actually curbed the power of the landlords and established a new social base by protecting the upper strata of the peasantry through legislative and administrative measures. In the field of constitutional reforms, the British followed this up by enfranchising these strata of the peasantry, hoping they would support pro-British parties rather than the 'seditious' Indian National Congress. This could have happened in the 1930s, had the Great Depression not driven the peasants into the arms of the Congress. Under the leadership of Gandhi and Nehru, the Congress became a peasants' party. The limited franchise based on property qualifications meant that only rich peasants could vote. Accordingly, the Congress designed its agrarian programme so as to appeal to the upper strata of the peasantry, which then supported the Congress candidates in the elections of 1936. When provincial Congress ministries returned to power in 1946, the franchise was still limited. The abolition of the rights of landlords (zamindars) corresponded with the interests of the Congress electorate. It encouraged the rise of peasant landlords who appropriated the power that the zamindars had been deprived of. A more radical land reform, along the lines of the 'land to the tiller' slogan, would not have been in the interests of the Congress electorate. By the time adult suffrage was introduced with the first general election of 1952, the new power structure in the Indian countryside had already been consolidated. There was now a kind of 'agrarian bourgeoisie' which provided a base for a democratic state, the base Moore was looking for but failed to locate in India.

In my book *Government, Landlord and Peasant in India: Agrarian Relations under British Rule, 1865–1935*,[2] I studied the tenancy legislation and other British measures that affected the rise of a protected upper strata of the Indian peasantry. I then turned to the impact of the Great Depression on India,[3] and while I was working on this theme, Binay Bhushan Chaudhuri came to my Department of History at the South Asia Institute of Heidelberg University as a visiting professor. We conducted a seminar together, to which I contributed a paper on the peasant landlord in India. He encouraged me to pursue this theme. But then I got busy with a great deal of other work and it was only recently that I thought of returning to this theme once more. I wish I could offer the results of detailed research, but I can only produce an essay in which I can raise some points. I have mostly drawn on the work of others, among them Binay Bhushan Chaudhuri's masterly *Peasant History*.[4]

Who Is a Peasant?

Before turning to the peasant landlord, it is necessary to define the term 'peasant'. It usually refers to a settled agriculturist who tills the soil. However, B.B. Chaudhuri stresses that being a peasant does not necessarily imply ownership of land; tenants and sharecroppers are also peasants.[5] The essential unit of the 'peasant economy' is not the single cultivator but the peasant family. This family will follow different practices if it cultivates land of its own or the land of others as sharecroppers. If the family owns land, it will usually cultivate it intensively so as to maximize the yield per acre; sharecroppers, however, will cultivate the soil extensively in order to maximize the output per labourer. It has been asserted that even a glance at a field can tell the knowledgable observer whether it has been cultivated by its owners or by sharecroppers.[6] This raises the question why a landowner would tolerate the less-than-optimal results of sharecropping. The answer would be that he must accept it unless he has enough family labour of his own or is able to closely supervise hired labour.

The institutional framework is very important for the way in which a peasant lives and works. Crucial elements of this framework are property rights or security of tenure, the availability of credit, the law of contract and, last but not least, the law of inheritance. A peasant holding 10 acres of land and having five sons is likely to be prosperous as he has enough family labour for intensive cultivation. But once he dies and the five sons inherit 2 acres each, they will join the ranks of poor peasants who have to work for others in order to make both ends meet. This could be avoided by a law of primogeniture under which only the first son inherits the land and the others must either work for him, or leave the land and earn a living elsewhere. Since in most parts of India the land is usually divided among all heirs, the prosperity of a peasant could be called an accident – for instance, if there has only been one heir in each generation in a continous sequence. Under conditions of population growth and restricted supply of cultivable land, the natural tendency is a whittling down of the size of landholdings. This has already happened in India to an alarming extent. The number of holdings has about doubled in India from 1970 to 2000, while the total cultivated area has remained the same.

This shows that the law of inheritance is a major element of the institutional framework which conditions the peasant economy. Another important element is the status of the peasant as defined by the state. A good example is the 'occupancy ryot' (*raiyat*) created by the British in India.[7] Under earlier regimes there was a recognition of the rights of the *khudkasht* ryot who cultivated his own land; his rights were defined in relation to his land. The rights of the occupancy ryot, however, were defined in relation to the zamindar under whom he held his land. Since the British had vested land rights in the zamindar in northern India, they could protect tenants, once they decided to do so, only by creating prescriptive rights – usually defined in terms of possession for twelve years. According to the respective legislation, the occupancy ryot could not be evicted by the landlord as long as he paid his rent. Arbitrary enhancement of rent could have driven away the ryot, so the power of enhancing rent also had to be restricted. The tenancy Acts in various provinces limited this on an average to 1 per cent enhancement per year.[8] In a period of rising prices this greatly diminished the rights of the landlord and benefited the occupancy ryot very much. He could even sub-let his land to others, living on the rent paid by them – all the more so since the British did not protect such under-tenants but left them to the tender mercy of the 'peasant landlord'.[9] In the so-called *ryotwari* provinces, the 'government ryot'[10] was the equivalent of the occupancy ryot. He held his land directly from the government and his under-tenants were also not protected. This type of definition of the status of prosperous peasants followed political motives. In independent India too, the government followed such motives in supporting the 'peasant landlord' rather than the rural poor.

Having discussed various determinants affecting the life of the peasantry, we may now turn to the problem of class differentiation in order to locate the 'peasant landlord' in India's rural society.

Pattern of Peasant Class Differentiation

Karl Marx called the peasantry a bag of potatoes. With this drastic expression he wanted to illustrate that the peasants are differentiated at random, and that they cannot be compared to the workers who do not control the means of production and must sell their labour, thus forming a homogenous class. Neverthelesss, Marxist scholars have made attempts to find out about peasant class differentiation. They have, so to speak, sorted the potatoes. Instead of looking at peasants as a homogeneous class, they have sub-divided them according to economic criteria. In India, Utsa Patnaik has presented a convincing scheme of this kind.[11] She has criticized those who have attempted such sub-divisions merely according to the size of landholdings. Since Indian statistics of this kind are available in great detail, it is very tempting for social scientists to resort to them. Utsa Patnaik, however, bases her class analysis on the employment of hired labour over and above the available family labour. Productivity rather than mere size of landholding distinguishes the surplus-generating peasant from others who may hold even more land but where output is meagre. She identifies six classes of landholders altogether, of which the highest and the lowest do not cultivate their land themselves.[12] The highest class consists of landlords who rely exclusively on hired labour, and the lowest of 'petty employers' (such as a widow without family labour or a handicapped person) who may hire just one labourer. In between these two non-cultivating classes lie four classes of peasants – the rich, the middle, the small and the poor peasant. The rich and the middle peasant hire labour, the small peasant relies on family labour only, and the poor peasant must work for others in addition to cultivating his own land.

The peasant landlord could be located among the rich and middle peasants who generate surplus by employing labour. As we shall see later on, the economic behaviour of such peasant landlords may follow different lines. But whatever they may do, they are distinguished by their dominant position in the village. Chaudhuri has pointed out that rich peasants existed in India even before British rule, and although their dominant position in the village did not necessarily give rise to their prosperity, it undoubt-edly helped to consolidate it.[13] However, 'rich peasants' did not form a compact class as did feudal lords whose estates were usually passed on to the next generation in a line of well-defined succession. Teodor Shanin, who analysed Russian studies of the peasantry, has stressed that the 'rich peasant' is an elusive type, an aggregation rather than a class. He cannot be identified easily as patterns of inheritance affect the fate of the peasant family. There is a rise and fall of rich peasants in each generation.[14] The rise and decline of peasant families in India has been studied by Tom Kessinger in his pioneering work on a village in the Punjab for the period 1848 to 1968. Half of the 110 families with landed property which he could identify at the beginning of the period had disappeared by its end. Only six families had just one male heir in each generation and could thus maintain their position.[15]

As has been pointed out earlier, the pattern of inheritance had a tendency to diminish the size of holdings. However, while one family declined, another could rise due to fortuitous circumstances as well as special efforts of the individual peasant who operated his holding well. Presumably, this would lead to a 'fuzzy' class solidarity that would encompass peasant landlords of different economic strata as long as their interests as labour-hiring controllers of land were similar. Even the son of a rich peasant who had sunk to the level of a small peasant when the property had been divided among many brothers would probably still feel an attachment to the class to which his father belonged. The institution of caste would help to preserve such a solidarity across economic sub-divisions.

The peasant landlord who generated surplus by hiring labour had two main options when using this surplus: he might act as a moneylender or as an entrepreneur who invested in land amelioration and crop production. Of course, there may have been peasant landlords who did both. In fact, they may have pre-empted labour by means of moneylending and employed it so as to increase the productivity of their holding, but we may discuss these two options separately as they usually correspond to two different types of economic behaviour.

The Peasant Landlord as Moneylender

Rural moneylending has been a universal activity in India as peasant agriculture was always in need of credit. In general, a distinction has been made in India between professional moneylenders (usually belonging to a caste of traders) and 'agricultural moneylenders' who were landholders in the village. Chaudhuri has discussed the growing power of the agricultural moneylender by looking at the Punjab after 1900.[16] In that year the British had passed a Land Alienation Act specifically for that province. The Act was so designed as to prevent the acquisition of the land of rural debtors by professional moneylenders. This Act was an elaborate exercise in social engineering. Since it was impossible to distinguish between professional and agricultural moneylenders with sufficient legal precision, the

Act contained an enumeration of castes which were supposed to belong to one or the other of these categories. In fact, land alienation was enhanced in this way, because agricultural moneylenders were interested in attaching the land of their debtors whereas non-cultivating professional moneylenders usually exploited their debtors in different ways. However, this did not bother the British. Their motive was a political one. They wanted to strengthen the Punjabi Muslim agriculturists and curb the influence of the professional moneylenders who were generally Hindu traders.[17]

The moneylender is tempted to indulge in usury unless he is restrained by social custom or state intervention. In pre-colonial India the rule of *damdupat* was prevalent, which stipulated that the total debt with compound interest should not exceed double the amount originally borrowed.[18] Under British colonial rule this was replaced by 'freedom of contract', which permitted moneylenders to settle terms with their debtors according to mutual convenience. The debtor usually had to sign a bond which could be enforced in a court of law. The judge was not obliged to examine the debtor and could issue an '*ex-parte* decree' based on the signed bond presented by the creditor.[19] British law supported the creditor against the debtor. This was supposed to ensure that credit was always freely available. British revenue officers were also interested in the ready availability of credit to the revenue payers as they knew that the collection of revenue depended on it. These officers were generally averse to any state intervention aimed at restricting moneylenders.[20] Thus, the moneylending business flourished under British rule. Special communities of moneylenders, such as the Marwaris from Rajasthan, penetrated many regions of India.[21] They competed with the traditional village moneylenders and used the opportunies offered by British law to the utmost. Of course, village moneylenders also learned new tricks of the trade and followed the precedent set by the Marwaris. The Marwaris, however, had a vast network through which they could refinance their operations, whereas the village moneylender had to rely on his own resources.

It was only when riots broke out in the area around Pune, Maharashtra, in 1875 that legislation was introduced which empowered the judge 'to go beyond the bond' and enquire into the origin of the debt, and to find out about unfair practices of the moneylenders.[22] Binay Bhushan Chaudhuri has devoted much attention to these riots and their different interpretations by various scholars.[23] He has highlighted the novelty of the seizure of the creditor's bonds by the rioters, and the fact that the village elite, i.e. the peasant landlords, were organizing the riots. The British realized that these bonds – which had acquired such great importance in British courts and had become powerful instruments of oppression – could undermine the legitimacy of British rule. This caused them to intervene in a matter which they otherwise would not have touched, because the freedom of contract was an article of faith with them.

When the 'Great Depression' of the 1930s hit India, the British were once more impelled to intervene between creditor and debtor. Due to the Depression, the income of the peasants was halved but their debt charges remained the same. Sometimes moneylenders even tried to recover the amount originally lent to the peasant and thus increased his misery. The various Acts passed by the British at that time, which attempted to control the practices of moneylenders and to introduce debt conciliation boards, were not very effective.[24] They only helped to incense the moneylenders who then supported the Congress candidates in the elections of 1936–37.

In independent India, the government made strenuous efforts to extend institutional banking to the countryside so that peasants would have access to credit at reasonable charges and could break the stranglehold of the moneylenders. There was undoubtedly some progress in this field. But the moneylenders survived because their transactions were unbureaucratic and they had the advantage of close local supervision of the credit they granted. Poor peasants, who had very little to offer as security for their loans, would anyhow have no access to institutional banking. On the other hand, the moneylenders could use the new type of rural banking to re-finance their operations – making use of the very institution which had been set up to eliminate their activities. [25]

The reform era after 1991 actually led to a contraction of institutional rural credit.[26] This gave a new lease of life to the traditional moneylenders. The peasant landlord generating the surplus he could invest found much scope in lending money to his needy neighbours. In some instances he could even extract unpaid labour from them if they could not service their debt in any other way.[27]

There is voluminous literature on rural credit in India and on the role of moneylenders, but there are hardly any field studies of the actual transactions of specific moneylenders in Indian villages. This is why the fieldwork of German economist Hans-Dieter Roth in Dhanbad district, Bihar (now in Jharkhand), is of great importance. Before turning to the details of this study, it must be mentioned that agriculture in this district had remained rather backward in spite of the fact that the major Indian coalfield located here provided a market for agricultural produce, and this should have stimulated the production of a variety of foodstuffs in the immediate vicinity of the coalfield. However, because of the insufficiency of supply in the district, traffic by road and rail had linked the coalfield with agricultural production centres in distant places. Often trucks carrying coal over long distances came back with loads of vegetables instead of returning empty. The local villages were literally bypassed, and most of them stuck to traditional rice cultivation at a fairly low level of productivity. Accordingly, the three villages surveyed by Roth showed no traces of any impact of the demand for food by miners in the coalfield. He found out that the two sectors of these villages – the surplus-producing sector of what may be termed the peasant landlords, and the deficit sector of the poor peasantry – maintained a stagnant equilibrium. Neither the rich nor the poor showed an increase in productivity. The rich lent from their surplus in cash and kind to the poor, who then repaid them in cash, kind or labour.

Each of the three villages showed a distinct profile as far as the relations between creditors and debtors were concerned. They were characterized by three rather different types of social structure. Village I was dominated by six families of peasants holding more than 5 acres of land, all of whom were engaged in moneylending. These dominant families belonged to the Kurmi Mahato community, a peasant community very prominent in this area. There were also seven Brahman households but they were economically insignificant. The rest of the households belonged to local tribal groups. There was no institutional credit available in the village. Roth could identify fourteen moneylenders within the village and eighteen outside the village who lent money to the villagers, but only four in each group were genuine moneylenders whereas the rest were what he termed 'amateur' moneylenders who did not lend money regularly. About half the loans in this village were in kind, which clearly showed that consumption needs predominated. If such loans could not be redeemed they could lead to debt bondage.

Village II was dominated by one landholder belonging to a merchant caste (baniya). He was not only the headman (mukhiya) of the village, but also its postmaster, secretary of the cooperative society as well as its only moneylender. While he owned more than 10 acres of land, all the other households owned less than 5 acres, but twenty-seven out of a total of thirty households also had incomes from work other than that of cultivating their land. Accordingly, the need for credit was limited and could be met by the one lender who enjoyed a monopoly in this business. Almost all loan transactions were in cash and not in kind, in this village.

Village III was founded by a family of Hindu landowners (bhumihars) who had moved into this area in the nineteenth century and had held the position of zamindars. These former zamindari families formed the dominant twelve households that owned nearly a quarter of the land in the village. The rest of the land was owned by low-caste smallholders whose ancestors had been settled in this village in order to work for the 'peasant landlords'. The twelve dominant households did lend money to the smallholders in the village, but this was restricted to small amounts lent to those who could also provide labour to the dominant landholders. Usually these were loans in cash; loans in kind were rare in this village. The dominant households also needed credit, and for this they turned to their caste fellows in other villages.

All traditional moneylenders usually charge high nominal interest rates, which are designed to keep the debtor under the moneylender's thumb; but they may, however, adjust effective interest rates according to the actual situation of the debtor. Debt service often takes the form of labour in the creditor's field. Roth found that this prevailed in Villages II and III, while in Village I the interest due on the loans was mostly paid out of the annual income of the peasant cultivating his own land. On the other hand, mortgages were to be found to a much larger extent in Village I than in the other two villages.[28] This was due to rather peculiar circumstances – the cooperative society which had existed in this village, had collapsed as debtors could not repay their loans after a drought. Being nevertheless, forced to repay these loans they had to mortgage their lands to the local moneylenders. In this way a cooperative providing institutional credit to the peasants so as to reduce their dependence on moneylenders finally subjected them to those moneylenders in an emergency.[29]

Most of Roth's moneylenders held moderate areas of land; only one each in villages I and II, and three in village III, held more than 10 acres. There were no entrepreneurs among them, except for the *mukhiya* of village II who owned a small rice mill. Roth's sample is typical for the backward regions of northern India. In order to trace the evidence for peasant landlord entrepreneurs we have to turn to southern India, where there seems to have been a greater tendency to invest agricultural surplus in activities beyond moneylending.

The Peasant Landlord as Entrepreneur

There are numerous options for the investment of agricultural surplus. First of all, there is the cultivation of special cash crops such as tobacco, chillies and sugarcane among others. Then come investments that are immediately related to the processing of agricultural produce – the milling of rice, the decortication of peanuts, the ginning of cotton, etc. The third option is investment in manufacture, such as in textile mills, production of garments, etc.

The growth of commercial agriculture in India has been a subject of intense scholarly debate. Some have argued that it was 'forced', as the peasant was not free in his decision about what to cultivate but responded to a rent-and-credit squeeze; others highlighted the rational response of the peasant to price signals. There was also a tendency to distinguish between subsistence agriculture and production for the market. In summing up these various debates, B.B. Chaudhuri has arrived at a balanced verdict.[30] He has stressed the continuity between production for subsistence and for the market, and accepted the validity of price signals. But he has not ruled out that for certain types of crops, 'forced cultivation' could be noticed. At any rate, production for the market did increase and peasant enterprise did play a role in it.

In Andhra Pradesh, the ascent of what Adapa Satyanarayana has called 'a nascent Peasant-Bourgeoisie' could be noticed already in the 1920s and 1930s.[31] These peasant landlords cultivated garden crops such as turmeric, betel-leaf, plantains, oranges and lemons. This cultivation was expensive and labour-intensive, but much more profitable than rice cultivation. If these Andhra peasant landlords participated in moneylending, they often did this with a view to foreclose mortgages and force their debtors to sell their lands to them.[32] They also practised leasing-in of land so as to increase the economies of scale of their operations. The Kammas, a peasant community of Coastal Andhra, were particularly enterprising as pioneers of commercial agriculture.[33] In Guntur district they pioneered the cultivation of tobacco, which proved to be a very profitable crop.[34] They were also not averse to migrating to distant areas. When the Nizam of Hyderabad's government offered attractive terms of landholding in Telengana, many Kammas went there, sometimes encroaching on tribal lands.[35] Some generations earlier, the Kammas had migrated all the way to Coimbatore district in Tamil Nadu, where they then emerged as cotton growers and, in the 1920s and 1930s, as owners of textile mills.[36]

The Kammas were not the only enterprising peasant community. There were others such as the Gavaras of Vizagapatam district who actually monopolized sugarcane cultivation in this area. Their women participated in cultivation and also looked after the cows.[37] In this way they could sell dairy products which provided additional income to their household. The Gavaras could sell their sugarcane to the local sugar mills at remunerative rates as they belonged to sugarcane growers' cooperative societies.[38]

In Tamil Nadu, the Gounders of Kongunad were a prominent peasant community which eclipsed the great Mirasidars of the coastal valleys. The Mirasidars were mostly Brahman landlords who concentrated on rice cultivation. They employed a large number of low-caste labourers and also relied to a significant extent on sharecroppers. As these Brahmans did not participate in cultivation and gradually turned into absentee landlords, they presided over a stagnant agriculture.[39] In Kongunad, agrarian relations were of a different type. The Gounders, a progressive peasant community, pioneered the well-irrigated cultivation of remunerative cash crops. They also employed labourers, but the 'landlord' would always work in the fields along with his labourers who were often treated like members of the family.[40] Their transition from peasant landlords to manufacturers has been studied by Sharad Chari.[41] The Gounders transferred their style of close collaboration with labourers to the textile workshops they established in Tiruppur. This city was originally a cotton ginning centre.[42] In 1921 it had just about 10,000 inhabitants; today, it has more than 400,000. The Gounders engaged in the production of cotton knitwear for making vests and then added many other types of garments. There are factories of different sizes in Tiruppur, but the Gounders mostly own small workshops. The owner–operator usually sits at the central stitching table. Instead of expanding his workshop the owner often invests his surplus in the workshops of other Gounders. This is what Chari calls 'fraternal capital'. This modest format is in tune with the investment activities of peasant landlords. It is also convenient in view of the fact that government regulations favour small-scale industries. Altogether this beehive of Gounder enterprises nowadays provides 90 per cent of all Indian cotton knitwear exports worth about 1 billion US dollars.

An altogether different story of the transformation of peasant landlords into entreprenenurs has been told by Scarlet Epstein, who studied the contrast between two neighbouring villages in Mysore (Karnataka) around 1960 and again ten years later.[43] One village was a dry one with no scope for irrigated rice cultivation; the other was a wet village with intensive rice cultivation. Initially the wet village seemed to be prosperous with much scope for economic development. Nevertheless, as time went by, the wet village stagnated while the dry village forged ahead. The peasants of this dry village realized that they could not keep up with their prosperous neighbours and found a new way of making a living, by going into the transport business. They owned trucks and specialized in carrying agricultural produce to distant markets. They did so well in this business that they surpassed the wet village in terms of general prosperity.

Suggestions for Further Research

The evidence presented here can be called 'anecdotal'. Much further research would be required to establish the contours of the 'peasant landlord' more firmly. A combination of Utsa Patnaik's synchronic class analysis with Tom Kessinger's diachronic method of reconstructing the fate of peasant families over more than a century, may yield good results.

It should also be backed up by the kind of detailed field survey that distinguishes Hans-Dieter Roth's work.

Rural labour relations also deserve to be studied in detail. In recent times, the ranks of landless labourers have swelled. This has reduced the need for keeping agricultural labourers permanently employed because a large 'reserve army of labour' is readily available. In earlier times landowners had relied on systems of bonded labour in several regions of India.[44] Nowadays they have access to the 'reserve army'. This is also indicated by the increase of 'casualization' of agricultural labour, which means that the employer may hire the labourer for any period of time that suits his convenience.[45] Since work in the fields follows a seasonal cyle which includes long periods of 'leisure', the landless labourer without a permanent contract faces roughly 100 days of unemployment every year. The National Rural Employment Guarantee Scheme was introduced in 2005 to bridge this gap. It has been ably advocated and monitored by the economist Jean Drèze.[46] However, even this bold scheme can only alleviate the poverty of the landless labourers; it cannot change the structure of rural employment. In fact, it may contribute to the survival of this structure.

Ever since W. Arthur Lewis proposed his theory of a dual economy in which the organized sector can draw on the unlimited supply of labour from the unorganized or informal sector, many economists had hoped for a transition of the labour force of developing countries to modern employment and an increase in the productivity of labour. As Ajit K. Ghose has pointed out, this does not happen in India because it is not a dual economy, but two parallel economies which coexist and hardly interfere with each other.[47] They both follow separate patterns of growth. Agriculture, which belongs to one part of this parallel economy, has also improved its performance, but it is still plagued by widespread poverty. This does not affect the other part of the economy, which forges ahead in terms of productivity and its share in the gross domestic product (GDP). The landless labourer is trapped in this sphere of two parallel economies. In fact, this saves Indian cities from being swamped by migrants who desert the countryside. There is evidence that the rate of rural–urban migration has slowed down in India in recent times.[48] This also means that the peasant landlord can continue to exploit underpaid labour. As we have seen, the peasant landlord can also become an entrepreneur, but he will rarely become that type of 'dual landlord' who accumulates capital in agriculture and transfers it to investment in industry. Actually, one can observe the opposite tendency in India where in recent years big industrial firms have tried to organize commercial agriculture.[49] This may generate more

productive employment for rural labour and also encourage entrepreneurial tendencies among peasant landlords. The pioneers in this field are
Mukesh Ambani of Reliance Industries and Sunil Mittal of Bharti Airtel.
Reliance Industries began with contract farming, paying advances to their
peasant partners in order to secure deliveries to Reliance Industries' urban
supermarkets. When they found out that the peasants sometimes used the
advances for other purposes and failed to deliver the goods, they changed
to what Mukesh Ambani calls 'contact farming'.[50] Under this scheme the
peasant receives no advances, but is assured of a stable demand and a
remunerative price when he sells his produce to Reliances Industries. This
has obviously worked well. It has stimulated production for the market
and provided an additional income to the peasants.

Notes and References

[1] G. Barrington Moore, Jr., *Social Origins of Dictatorship and Democracy: Lord and Peasant in the Making of the Modern World*, Boston: Beacon Press, 1966.

[2] D. Rothermund, *Government, Landlord and Peasant in India: Agrarian Relations under British Rule, 1865–1935*, Wiesbaden: Steiner, 1978.

[3] D. Rothermund, *India in the Great Depression, 1929–1939*, Delhi: Manohar, 1992; and D. Rothermund, *The Global Impact of the Great Depression*, London: Routledge, 1996.

[4] B.B. Chaudhuri, *Peasant History of Late Pre-Colonial and Colonial India*, Project of History of Indian Science, Philosophy and Culture (PHISPC) (General Editor: D.P. Chattopadhyaya), Vol. VIII, Part 2, New Delhi: Pearson Education India, 2008.

[5] Ibid., p. 43.

[6] Rothermund, *Government, Landlord and Peasant*, p. 110.

[7] Ibid., pp. 93f., 109f.

[8] Ibid., p. 134.

[9] Ibid., p. 56.

[10] Ibid., p. 86.

[11] Utsa Patnaik, *Peasant Class Differentiation: A Study in Method with Reference to Haryana*, Delhi: Oxford University Press, 1987.

[12] Ibid., pp. 77f.

[13] B.B. Chaudhuri, *Peasant History*, p. 587.

[14] Teodor Shanin, *The Awkward Class: Political Sociology of Peasantry in a Developing Society: Russia, 1910–1925*, Oxford: Clarendon Press, 1972, pp. 96f.

[15] Tom Kessinger, *Vilyatpur, 1848–1968: Social and Economic Change in a North Indian Village*, Berkeley: University of California Press, 1974, pp. 97f., 115f.

[16] B.B. Chaudhuri, *Peasant History*, p. 529.

[17] Rothermund, *Government, Landlord and Peasant*, pp. 76f.

[18] Rothermund, *India in the Great Depression*, p. 124.

[19] Rothermund, *Government, Landlord and Peasant*, pp. 17, 89.

[20] Ibid., p. 39

[21] Ibid., p. 50

[22] Ibid., pp. 63f.

[23] B.B. Chaudhuri, *Peasant History*, pp. 533f.

[24] Rothermund, *India in the Great Depression*, pp. 123f.

[25] Hans-Dieter Roth, *Indian Moneylenders at Work*, Delhi: Manohar, second edition, 2007, p. 26.

[26] Rohini Pande, 'Rural Credit', in Kaushik Basu, ed., *The Oxford Companion to Economics in India*, New Delhi: Oxford University Press, 2007, p. 462.

[27] Roth, *Indian Moneylenders*, p. 83.

[28] Ibid., pp. 66f.

[29] Ibid., p. 82.

[30] B.B. Chaudhuri, *Peasant History*, pp. 403f.

[31] A. Satyanarayana, *Andhra Peasants Under British Rule: Agrarian Relations and the Rural Economy, 1900–1940*, Delhi: Manohar, 1990, pp. 111f.

[32] Ibid., p. 117.

[33] Ibid., pp. 62, 79, 112.

[34] Ibid., p. 86.

[35] B. Janardhan Rao, *Land Alienation in Tribal Areas*, Warangal: Kakatiya University Press, 1987.

[36] Christopher Baker, *An Indian Rural Economy, 1880–1955: The Tamilnadu Countryside*, Delhi: Oxford University Press, 1984, pp. 347, 351f.

[37] Satyanarayana, *Andhra Peasants*, p. 119.

[38] Ibid., p. 85.

[39] Baker, *An Indian Rural Economy*, p. 172.

[40] Ibid., pp. 94f.

[41] Sharad Chari, *Fraternal Capital: Peasant Workers, Self-Made Men and Globalization in Provincial India*, Stanford: Stanford University Press, 2004.

[42] Baker, *An Indian Rural Economy*, pp. 268f.

[43] Scarlett Epstein, *South India: Yesterday, Today and Tomorrow: Mysore villages revisited*, Basingstoke: Macmillan, 1973.

[44] B.B. Chaudhuri, *Peasant History*, pp. 657f.

[45] Amitabh Kundu, 'Changing Agrarian System and Rural–Urban Linkages', in Shovan Ray, ed., *Handbook of Agriculture in India*, New Delhi: Oxford University Press, 2007, p. 190.

[46] Dietmar Rothermund, *India: The Rise of an Asian Giant*, New Haven and London: Yale University Press, 2008, p. 216.

[47] Ajit K. Ghose, 'Informal Labour', in Kaushik Basu, ed., *The Oxford Companion to Economics in India*, p. 291.

[48] Kundu, 'Changing Agrarian System and Rural–Urban Linkages', in Shovan Ray, ed., *Handbook of Agriculture in India*, p. 194.

[49] Rothermund, *India: The Rise of an Asian Giant*, pp. 134f.

[50] Ibid., p. 135 (interview of the author with Mukesh Ambani, February 2007).

Towards an Economic History *for* Bengal in the Eighteenth Century

A View from Its Villages

Rajat Datta

Analysing the economic history of India's villages is a difficult task. A number of things make it so. First, despite the fact that more than 85 per cent of the people then lived in the countryside, historical records for our period do not throw up too many details about life in the village as such. The general slant of these records is towards taxes and revenue, and conditions of life in the countryside are either ignored or referred to only in passing. Second is the problem of inadequate enumeration and quantification regarding both the number of villages and the people living in them at any point of time in the past. Since the demographic component is so vital in economic history, this lacuna is one of the most severe shortcomings with regard to tracking economic fluctuations in India's pre-industrial countryside. The third gap is the absence of macroeconomic indices, such as prices and trade figures, especially those pertaining to internal trade. This is particularly problematic considering that there is very little doubt about the tremendous expansion in India's trade in the early modern period, and that much of this trade, particularly in textiles and foodgrains, has had a direct bearing on the village economy.

Another difficulty happens to be historiographical. Much of what passes as the history of the agrarian economy is at best a history of tenurial relations or at worst a history of land revenue administration. The essential focus is on the quantum of revenue imposed and collected by the state, and not on the actual operation of the agrarian economy. Therefore, what is often characterized as economic history, and this is of particular applicability to eighteenth-century Bengal, is revenue history, or at best a history of changes in the structure of landed property between 1765 and 1793.[1] While there is no denying the important role performed by the revenue squeeze in the provincial economy, there is a pressing need to contextualize that role in the overall framework of economic, mainly agricultural, production. Revenue is a form in which the surplus is appropriated by the state, but the mode in which that surplus gets created is what provides a crucial insight into the domain of production.

It is in this context that the title of this paper, which emphasizes the word *for* instead of what would be the more commonly expected 'of', has to be situated. The reasons for this choice arise from a slightly different perspective I have about the economic history of India in general, and of Bengal in the eighteenth century in particular. My general point critiques what I call a conventional view – conventional because of its long usage – which has tended to divide Indian economic history into two enclaves, one non-agricultural (maritime or urban) and the other agrarian (or rural), without specifying the interconnections between the two. My intention is to indirectly question such binaries by focusing on the processes of agrarian commercialization from the micro-perspective of the village economy in this crucial period of Bengal's history. Another reason why I propose to take a fresh look at the countryside is also specific to Bengal. This is to critique the idea of a structural discontinuity (a breakdown) in the period after 1757.[2] For far too long existing historiography has tended to view the eighteenth century as a period of economic crisis and regression that followed a supposedly prosperous pre-colonial past. This view has turned the regional historiographical focus towards the agrarian sector, but within a monochromatic frame of reference.

To quit this restrictive frame, one needs to situate the village economy as the pivot of economic activity. Though the stereotype of an autarkic village has long been discarded, in its place has been inserted the idea of 'relative self-sufficiency' of the village, caused by the one-way transfer of surplus from the village to the city, the indifferent and sluggish use of money at this level, and the absence of a rural demand for urban or 'industrial' goods. This formulation is problematical and we need to re-examine it in the light of regional evidence. There is no doubt that India (and Bengal) saw a huge expansion of export trade both overseas and overland, an absolute and relative increase in the use of money, and a major densification of the urban networks during the seventeenth and eighteenth centuries.[3] Could the village have remained impervious to such changes? Therefore, we need to identify the numerous village-level commercial impulses. I intend to do so by situating the village as the centre of the dynamics of agrarian commercialism in the early modern period.

The main argument I propose is that early modern Bengal was characterized by an unprecedented degree of commercialization. The main frame of this argument, which I have developed elsewhere,[4] may be recapitulated briefly. The initial conditions of this commercialization were created in three anterior developments which occurred in the seventeenth

century. These were: (i) a shift from spices to textiles by the European trading companies; (ii) the transfer of imperial tribute from Bengal to Delhi
in the form of high-value textiles, among others; and (iii) the export of
primary commodities (particularly rice and sugar) on a regular basis both
by sea and by land. The eighteenth century saw a convergence between
this ongoing process of textile-induced commerce, and the commercialization of the province's *rice-producing small-peasant economy and of
the social relations embedded in it*. The latter process was shaped in this
period by four macro-level reconfigurations. The first two constituents of
this reconfiguration were purely economic: a growing demand for food,
especially in the rural areas, and a secular upward swing in the prices of
agricultural produce. The third element was ecological, and consisted of
the apparently fortuitous clusters of dearth and famine years between
1769 and 1793. The political transition from the middle of the century,
which reoriented the existing nature of relations between the state and the
commercial economy, particularly the market, was the fourth constituent.
What emerged through all these was an integrated provincial economy,
integrated through marketing networks[5] and convergent agricultural
prices (see below). This extended and broadened the range of commercial
production and commercialized transactions initially set into motion by
items like silk and cotton.

      The village was at the centre of this integration. It was in the
eighteenth century that the peasant household, agriculture and trade
structurally integrated with production for the market. I see the social
symptoms of this in the continued expansion of the agricultural frontier,
the rapid proliferation of a sharecropping peasantry and the increasing
intervention of the grain merchant (*byapari*) in agricultural production.[6]
The critical facilitators here were the webs of connected surface and river
communications,[7] and a dense lattice of mercantile networks operating
out of both towns and villages. The integration of peasant households,
both as seller and as producer, was of primary importance because it was
this that determined (despite the many burdens and pressures on it) the
amount of agricultural produce which could *actually* be marketed. It also
shaped the various proprietary, tenurial and sub-tenurial arrangements
that mushroomed in this period.[8] Such were the distinctive features of the
eighteenth-century early modern economy.

The Problem of Numbers

Given the paucity of empirical data, it is very difficult to estimate
the number of people residing in an average Bengali village in the eighteenth
century, though Johnstone's estimate does give us an average of 250 persons

per village in Burdwan in the 1760s.[9] Relatively large villages could have more than 250 households around Murshidabad,[10] whereas in relatively less developed districts in the frontier regions 'the average [was] less than 10 persons [per] village'.[11] However, the idea that most of Bengal was an interlinked chain of 'innumerable villages' interspersed with a few towns was originally put forward by James Rennell in 1765.[12] The same theme recurs when W. Hamilton, writing in 1828, says: 'villages from 100 to 500 inhabitants are astonishingly numerous, and in some parts form a continued chain of many miles along the bank of rivers'.[13]

Obviously, clusters of villages would tend to be greater in areas closer to important commercial and administrative centres. In places like Rajshahi, Burdwan and Nadia, villages could exist within a mile's distance from each other, whereas in more sparse districts like Midnapur, Birbhum or Jessore, villages were separated by greater distances but seldom more than 2 miles from each other.[14] Population data for this period are very scarce and often unreliable, but there is a consensus that Bengal was undergoing a fairly rapid increase in its population despite the severity of the famine of 1769–70 and, to a lesser extent, of 1787. That Bengal's population was steadily growing was 'obvious to [the] common observation' of John Shore in 1789.[15] Contemporary estimates provide the following demographic profile:[16]

Year	Population (in million)	Percentage increase since 1789
1789	22	
1790	24	9.09
1793	25	13.64
1800	27	22.73
1822	37.6	70.91

If we apply the suggested average of 15 per cent people living in towns in seventeenth-century India to Bengal,[17] these numbers are suggestive of rapid rural demographic growth after the famine of 1769–70. They also conform to specific data we get from the early British surveys (including the Amini Commission report of 1778) about the relatively dense village clusters in settled agricultural areas, the growing intensification of settlements in areas of fresh reclamation, and of accretion of village-level markets (*haats*).[18] Of great significance is the impressive density of such markets in some of the districts devastated by the famine of 1769–70. By 1790 Burdwan was being serviced by a chain of 17 *ganjes* (wholesale markets) and 345 *haats*. In Rangpur, the number of listed marketplaces had increased from 321 *c.* 1770 to 591 *c.* 1807, and in Dinajpur the corresponding increase was from 206 to 635.[19] Bengal's countryside was being subjected to frenetic economic activity.

Contextualizing the Village: Three Possible Ways

It is undeniable that these data are indicative, and do not take away from the overall limitations imposed by the paucity of quantitative information. Therefore the question still remains: how does one understand the history of India's villages in the period preceding the era of modern censuses and other quantitative paraphernalia? Much of our understanding has to be based on indirect, qualitative evidence contained in various descriptions and accounts of conditions in the rural society and economy. There are possibly three ways of doing so.

The Constituents of a Village

How do we characterize a typical village of Bengal in this period? The first characterization would be nomenclatural. A village was specifically referred to as a '*gaon*' or '*gram*', denoting a settlement composed principally of *raiyats* who cultivated and paid taxes (*mal*) to government. A *gram* would then be further sub-divided into areas of habitation, areas of cultivation and the village waste. According to a late eighteenth-century Persian manual, the *Risala-i-Zira'at*, a typical village in Bengal would have the following:

- the '*basa*', also called *basti*, which was 'the place of the cultivator's residence;
- the '*audbasa*', or 'the courtyard or cowshed as well as storehouse';
- the '*lal*', or the land under cultivation – 'the varieties and names of this type of land differ widely from one pargana to another';[20]
- '*mat*' (*math*), or a 'meadow which has never been brought under tillage';
- '*patit*', or 'land which was earlier under the plough but [was] left untilled for the [past] two or three years';
- '*banjar*', 'also called *khila* [which was] forest land capable of cultivation'; and
- '*jangal*', or land 'so covered with thickets and intersected with hollows, that it is unfit for cultivation'.[21]

Once the lands had been designated, the *raiyat*, also called *kersans* or *chassis*, were classified into various categories depending on their location in the village and locally prevailing customary usage. Both the Amini Commission (1778) and the *Risala-i-Zira'at* tell us that Bengal's peasantry were divided and classified according to the type of *pattas* (title deeds) they held, and whether or not they were residents of the village in which they cultivated. Resident cultivators were called *khudkashta* or *fasli,* while non-resident peasants were called *paikashta.* In addition were those who cultivated for others, either as agricultural labourers or as sharecroppers. These were variously known as *kaljanah* or *khamar.*[22] By the end of the century two other terms, *bargadar* and *adhiar,* were being used to denote such peasants in northern and northwestern Bengal.[23]

Perceiving a Village

First, we have to proceed by making a difference between the rural (*muffussul*) society and economy, and the village (*deh, gram* or *gaon*) society and economy. Rural society refers to social groups living in the countryside and living off agriculture without participating directly in the processes of agricultural production. These groups comprised landholders, merchants and other service gentry who were managers or owners of critical economic and cultural resources that had a direct bearing on the lives of people inhabiting the same space. Village society, on the other hand, would be composed largely of people who were directly implicated in the production of goods, mainly agricultural and craft, using their own and their domestic labour.

Secondly, rural society – made up of those who did not participate directly in agricultural production but lived off it – would have people of a higher social and ritual status compared to the village population, which would have a greater concentration of people lower down the caste–culture divide. The difference, thus, was both social and locational – the difference between a *deh, palli* or *gaon* and the *muffussul sadr* constituted the difference between living in the countryside but outside the village, and belonging to the countryside but living in a village. The village was situated at the bottom of a countryside-oriented chain of administrative-cum-fiscal markers in the following order: *pargana, taraf* and *deh or gaon,* each constituting the nuclei of distinctive types of social existence. The zamindar and *chaudhuri* would reside in a *pargana,* as would a large grain *byapari*; the *taluqdar* would reside in the *deh* or *taraf* alongside the *paikar* and the zamindar's *gumastha*; while in the village lived the people referred to as *raiyats* in our sources.

Of course, these were not watertight compartments. This brings me to another possible way of perceiving the village: it is explicable by looking at the larger rural social complex of which it was a part. The notion of a self-sufficient village 'republic', so dear to early-colonial ethnographers, is *passé.* No village was closed or isolated. Many factors made it so. There is an argument which says that the sole factor integrating the village with the larger world was 'flow of the surplus to the towns forced by the land-tax'.[24] The importance of the land-tax as an important agent in breaking the isolation of a village is undeniable, but this was one of many other influences working in the same direction. One such element comprised the various non-peasant groups who lived in villages to perform a multiple range of ritual, commercial and administrative functions. These included zamindari officials like the *karmachari* (who collected rents and was generally entrusted with overseeing the affairs of the village), the *patwari* (who was the keeper of accounts but could also double up as a *karmachari* in a smaller village) and the *halshnah* (who measured the peasants' lands and settled new arrivals in the village).[25] These 'outside' groups also comprised the Brahman priest, the *vaidya* (the medical practitioner) and the local moneychanger-cum-trader (the *sarraf*). Large town-based merchants also had their agents (variously called *gumastha* or *faria* or *phiriwala*) who either resided there or came periodically to purchase directly from the peasant at the time of the harvest.[26]

A Bengal village also had a substantial number of people who were artisans or traders or engaged in providing various services to the village folk. Detailed lists that are available show the existence of the *putwa* (silk-worm breeder), *tanti* (weaver), *chotoor* (carpenter), *naphit* (barber), *manjhi* (boatman), *goala* (cowherd), *chassar* (silk weaver), *moochis* (cobbler), *kasari* (brass maker), *moira* (confectioner), *sonar* (goldsmith), *jalia* (fisherman), *pasahri* (provisioner), *dokandar* (shopkeeper) and *bania* (trader).[27]

Then there were a host of privileged people, called *la-kharaji*, *aima* or *baz-izamin* tenure-holders, who constituted a composite religio-cultural elite representing the percolation of dominant religions, whether of Hinduism and its variants, or of Islam and its major derivative Sufism, in the heart of rural Bengal. Documents from various districts in the 1790s tell us that such lands were meant for the support of 'various religious edifices and colleges' whose upkeep was enshrined as one of the bounden duties of the 'Mughal government', and for the upkeep of 'bramins, mohunts, sannasies . . . fakirs, pirs etc.'.[28]

I must refer here to Richard Eaton's important work on medieval Bengal showing that there was a symbiotic link between the rooting of Islam in Bengal's countryside, particularly in eastern Bengal, and the role played by Muslim *pirs* and *fakirs* in the extension of Bengal's agricultural frontier into the Gangetic delta. One of his principal findings – that 'Bengal's eastern zone was not only an agrarian or a political frontier, but also a cultural one, as Islam became locally understood as a civilization-building ideology, a religion of the plough' – indicates the powerful role played by cultural-resource controllers in opening the boundaries of the village to powerful external influences.[29] While Eaton's argument is important, we should also remember that reclamation was being organized by other 'secular' institutional and social arrangements. Bakarganj, for instance, was being actively reclaimed by a landed gentry (specifically identified as *taluqdar*) and the large grain trader (*aratdar*)-cum-merchant combination throughout the eighteenth century.[30]

One must also ask whether this model can be applied to the possible influence of Vaishnavism on changing the agro-commercial context of Bengal's villages. The commercial content of popular monotheistic movements in medieval north India has been highlighted by historians. The popularity of Vaisnavism and its dissemination in later-medieval Bengal was accompanied by the growth of its own gentry variant who were paid for their piety by a variety of revenue-free lands, variously called *debottar*, *brahmottar* and *bishnuwattar*. The papers of the Amini Commission (1778) have enormous information on such grants throughout Bengal.[31] If the Muslim gentry's power revolved around the shrine and the mosque, the power of their Hindu counterpart revolved around the *matha* or the various temples – *chala*, *shikhara* and *ratna* – which were constructed all over Bengal, especially in western Bengal in the same period.[32]

Trade and Its Implications for the Village

The third way of contextualizing the village is by looking at trade as a major factor linking it with the external world. That Bengal's trade increased enormously in the eighteenth and nineteenth centuries is indisputable. This had two major implications for its economy and for its villages. First, Bengal received massive amounts of silver bullion to pay for this trade. On an average, the Dutch brought 4.69 million florins worth of bullion into the Indian economy between 1700 and 1760. The English East India Company imported a total of £8.72 million worth of bullion into India between 1701 and 1721; this went up to £12.9 million between 1733 and 1756.[33] The English victory at Plassey (1757) brought about significant reductions, but these were temporary contractions. The Company imported £2.46 million of treasure between 1758 and 1768, £1.3 million between 1769 and 1779, and £3.83 million between 1779 and 1789; but between 1790 and 1805 the Company pumped in £9.14 million worth of bullion into India, of which Bengal's share was a massive £5.77 million.[34] Bengal had never received such huge supplies in the past. Bullion continued to flow from this time onwards, and it was not before the early 1830s that one got to see a terminal contraction arising out of a drastic fall in the export of manufactures from the province and from India in general. From a peak of Rs 47.5 million in 1818–19, the value of bullion imports dwindled to a mere Rs 5.4 million in 1832–33.[35] Private European trade was responsible for the arrival of £5.2 million worth of silver to Bengal between 1796 and 1806,[36] and despite their trade being on a downward slope, the Dutch still imported 4.24 million florins worth of bullion per year to pay for their merchandise between 1790 and 1794.[37]

Such huge injections of bullion facilitated a massive expansion in the use of money in Bengal's economy. It is therefore no accident that by the time of English ascendancy in the province, the silver *sicca* had become the 'general currency' of Bengal, which was '13 oz. 15 devts or 13 devts better than the English standard', and whose purity was maintained by 'recoinage after every three years'. It is also not surprising that this had 'become the standard of weight throughout Bengal; the seer is composed of so many siccas, and the maund at forty seers'.[38] The loot of Bengal's resources after the Battle of Plassey had not been able to demonetize the economy, and James Grant was of the opinion that notwithstanding the combined financial depredations of Mir Qasim in 1763 and that of the Company between 1763 and 1765, which accounted for a loss of about 10 crores,[39] Bengal still retained '15 krore [£15,000,000] in specie . . . in accumulation of the former stock of provincial wealth'.[40] Grant may have actually erred on the side of understatement as he did not consider the substantial amounts of money continuously entering Bengal through channels of inter-provincial trade to procure its goods, particularly cloth and rice, throughout the eighteenth century.[41]

Use of money and cash transactions were now a fact of daily life all over the province. Even when transactions were in *cowries*, these were done through established rates of exchange between *cowries* and the silver *sicca*. One significant development was the appreciation in the value of the *cowrie* relative to the *sicca* between the sixteenth and eighteenth centuries. From an exchange ratio of 1 rupee : 8,960 *cowries* in 1515, the *cowrie* appreciated to 1:4000 in 1676, and stood at 1:2560 in 1765.[42] This 'inflation' of *cowries* relative to silver up to about 1765 seems to have kept in line with the general depreciation in the price of silver, with an appropriate time-lag, with what James Grant saw as 'the influence of American treasures in reducing the price of [silver] bullion' in India.[43] This constitutes one of the most inconvertible pieces of evidence about the pervasiveness of the cash nexus in Bengal's villages in this period. No rural market was complete without a *shroff* or two who dealt in all 'species most in demand either for the purposes of commerce or revenue payments',[44] 'well knowing the times of the payment of payment & that the cultivator must at all events and at any price have sicca rupees fixes the exchange at his own arbitrary rate and the farmer without resource is obliged to purchase them on any terms'.[45] It is inconceivable to imagine the village as either autarkic or even relatively self-sufficient, given such pervasive webs of monetary expansion and cash transactions.

Commodity requirements for the export market could no longer be handled by urban manufactures. Though towns like Dhaka or Qasimbazar were atypical production centres, the sheer pull of the export market induced a widespread dispersal of production centres across the Bengal countryside. Cotton textiles had moved beyond the established zones of western and eastern Bengal (like Santipur–Nadia or Dhaka–Lakshmipur), and had spread to Chittagong on the eastern fringes, and to Bishnupur and Midnapur in western and southwestern parts of the region. So had the silk production zones expanded, from the Murshidabad–Qasimbazar axis to newer places like Bishnupur and Rajshahi.[46] Such expansion meant that high-end non-agricultural production, often organized under the aegis of urban capital, could now be located in the villages. Evidence indicates that depending on the commercial importance of a locality, between 27 per cent and 15 per cent of the people living in Bengal's villages were artisans producing a variety of 'urban' goods.[47] Moneychangers (shroffs), carpenters (chootor), oil-pressers (teli) and provisioners (moodi) did good business in Bengal's villages. Small wonder that 'in every pergunnah & village there are established bazaars and hauts. Several of the villagers keep shops in them while others hold them in their own houses.'[48] These markets catered to a variety of local needs, both of commodities and services. A purely rural market supplying a few villages (taraf) of Rangamati (with a total of 256 houses in 1776) had thirteen shops, which included four grocers, one tobacconist, three dealers in cowries and two moneychangers (sarrafs).[49] In the floodprone areas of Contai, markets stocked 'thread, coarse weaving cloths, mats made of split bamboos, brass and cassie (tutenag) plates, kodallies (spades), ploughs, plough shares and ruts for winding threads'.[50]

Another noteworthy development in Bengal's commercial expansion was the export of rice from the province throughout the eighteenth and nineteenth centuries – from Bakarganj, Rajshahi, Dinajpur, Rangpur, Burdwan and eastern Bihar.[51] In 1775 Midnapur exported 16 per cent of its rice, whereas Noakhali was exporting 23 per cent of its output around the same time.[52] Bakarganj's exports increased from 28.5 per cent of its produce in 1775 to 33.4 per cent in 1794,[53] and stood at about 28 per cent in 1818.[54] Rangpur and Dinajpur exported 35 per cent and 68.6 per cent of their grain respectively in the early nineteenth century.[55] Bengal's rice was being exported to Madras, and also to places as far away as Britain and Mauritius.[56]

The important point to note is that such expansion was occur-

TABLE 1 *Quinquennial averages of common rice prices, 1701–05 to 1796–1800*
(Rs per maund)

		Index with 1701–5 = 100
1701–05	0.57	100
1706–10	0.49	85.96
1711–15	0.69	121.05
1716–20	0.82	143.86
1721–25	0.89	156.14
1726–30	1.1	192.98
1731–35	1.39	243.86
1736–40	1.13	198.24
1741–45	1.37	240.35
1746–50	1.08	189.47
1751–55	1.47	257.89
1756–60	1.31	229.82
1761–65	1.54	270.17
1766–69[a]	2.36	414.03
1772–75[a]	1.5	263.16
1776–80	2.12	371.93
1781–85	1.37	240.35
1786–90	1.84	322.81
1791–95	1.61	282.46
1796–1800	1.17	205.26

Note: [a] Prices of 1770 and 1771 have not been averaged as these were famine prices.

ring under conditions of rising agricultural prices, as can be seen from the quinquennial averages of rice prices between 1701 and 1800 given in the table above. These figures have been procured from the price data available for the Dutch settlement of Chinsura, adjusted against the prices of provisions near Calcutta. The evidence leaves little doubt about the rise in agricultural prices in eighteenth-century Bengal. One can safely conclude that there was at least a doubling of price through the century, with the price-crest stretching between 1750 and 1795.[57]

The Agricultural Frontier, Mobility, Dynamism and the Village

Rising numbers, coupled with the rising trend of agricultural prices, meant that the agricultural frontier of Bengal was constantly being pushed forward as peasants moved out to colonize new lands still available on the fringes of the settled areas. It has been suggested that most such attempts tended to be concentrated on the eastern frontiers, thereby continuing the process of eastward extension of the agrarian frontier already under way.[58] Such efforts were however not limited to that direction. Despite some slowing down of certain old areas of high agricultural production in western and northern Bengal (like Burdwan and Rajshahi), new areas were being opened up in this period. Evidence regarding the spread of cultivable land suggests that the following districts were undergoing rapid reclamation: Midnapur and 24 Parganas, Jessore, Sylhet and Chittagong.[59] This was the dynamic aspect of peasant production in eighteenth-century Bengal, as a result of which the acreage under cultivation in Bengal Presidency rose from 30 million in 1793 to 70 million in 1857.[60]

The case of Bakarganj illustrates this process well. Favourable agricultural prices and an expanding market for agricultural produce meant that the ongoing agricultural reclamation in this region gained additional momentum,[61] and integrated the region's wet-rice agriculture with the regional and inter-regional demand for foodgrains. Three outcomes followed. First, an entire hierarchy of traders in agricultural produce got constituted. These ranged from the middleman (paikar) to the peddler-cum-agent (faria) in the villages.[62] Second, the Padma estuary was reclaimed with frenetic speed. This was actively patronized by these rice dealers along with the small landed proprietors (taluqdars) and the Muslim 'charismatic pioneers' – sufis, pirs of the estuaries.[63] Third, tenurial and sub-tenurial arrangements proliferated, engineered by the more resourceful cultivators in order to keep the best spots of land under their own control and to attract labour on a permanent basis to lands which were initially often inhospitable.[64]

Jessore also saw massive reclamation of its Sundarbans in the 1780s. This process was slowly coming to a close by the 1870s when the great forests of estuarine Jessore had almost entirely been converted into immense rice tracts.[65] Similar developments occurred in the 24 Parganas. The pull of Calcutta was the major stimulus behind agricultural reclamation in this district. It was also fortunate in escaping the ravages of the famine of 1769–70 and its aftermath.[66] One major indication of reclamation in the district is the data available of villages: in 1778 there were 3,124 villages in this district;[67] less than a century later, in 1872, the number had increased to 4,978.[68]

New villages were constantly in the making, and this explains the remarkable fluidity of village boundaries and the great willingness of Bengal's peasants to move from one place to another at short notice. Though such tendencies were greatest in the newly settled areas, they were not completely absent in the older zones. Reports from Rangpur in

the 1770s noted that 'the poorer riots [were] always constantly desert-
ing from one talook to another'.[69] Such practices apparently continued;
Francis Buchanan, writing in 1807, noted that 'a village . . . is removed 4
or 5 miles with very little inconvenience indeed'.[70] Interestingly, the land
vacated by such migratory peasants seldom went to waste as such lands
'are eagerly seized by a more fortunate neighbour, who includes them in
his own tenure & recalls the absconding ryott or settles a deserter from
some other place to cultivate them for his benefit'.[71]

     While some peasants may have moved out of distress, it would be
wrong to see this as the only reason for such movements. Most moved in
search of better terms of revenue, which an expanding agrarian frontier
and commercial growth brought in their wake. Sometimes the two became
intertwined, and adversity could also be turned into opportunity. The latter
was indeed the case with the *paikasht* peasants of Burdwan and Bishnupur
in the late 1780s. As the river Ajoy breached its embankments and flooded
Burdwan, large numbers of peasants fled to the neighbouring zamindari
of Birbhum which suffered less from the floods in 1787. The zamindar of
Burdwan subsequently demanded the return of these cultivators on grounds
that they were settled resident-cultivators (*khudkasht*) of his zamindari,
and were therefore obliged to cultivate land and pay revenue in Burdwan.
The counterclaim proffered by the zamindar of Birbhum was that these
migrants had acquired the legal status of non-resident peasants (*paikasht*)
in his lands, and were therefore entitled to stay and cultivate land in his
zamindari.[72] In the midst of an expanding population, such mobility meant
a constant accretion in the number of villages in new areas, or a significant
expansion in the numbers residing in the older villages. Expansion of the
agrarian frontier went hand in hand with such mobility.

     While economic dynamism was an ingrained part of the village,
it was far from being an egalitarian place. The fact that sources refer to
agricultural labourers or sharecroppers would indicate that the average
Bengali village was socially quite stratified. In a still land-abundant situation, the existence of peasants with insufficient land who cultivated the
land of others for a share appears paradoxical. While low-caste status (*jati*)
has sometimes been advanced as an explanation for this phenomenon,[73]
we also have evidence of upward mobility amongst the relatively lower
castes both in the agrarian and the artisanal-commercial sectors;[74] and
there would have been a large component of Muslim sharecroppers in
eastern and northern Bengal.

     Also, sharecropping was not an invention of early-colonial Bengal.
Sanjhadars in Burdwan were functioning as such even prior to 1765.[75]
Sharecropping was both widened and deepened because of certain ecologi-

cal occurrences in the latter part of the century. These were the famine of 1769–70, and a cluster of dearth years which struck Bengal's agriculture between 1765 and 1793.[76] Briefly, a famine or a dearth placed immense strain on the already meagre resources at the disposal of the peasants. Additionally, each cycle of adverse weather or harvest failure threw up a fresh crop of uprooted peasants. Land was abundantly available, but the main problem was productive absorption. The urban sector was unable to fruitfully absorb even a fraction of the displaced, thereby giving them no alternative but to stick to the land as sharecroppers or agricultural labourers. Even though absolute landlessness was not a major agrarian problem of the late eighteenth century, the objective constraints on agricultural production nevertheless led to the creation of a sharecropping peasantry on a scale that can only be described as extensive.

Production: Organization, Rationale and Controls

How did production take place in these villages? An estimate made around the time of the Permanent Settlement showed that foodgrains (rice, paddy, etc.) comprised 45.5 per cent of the gross agricultural output, whereas cash crops (cotton, sugar, mulberry and tobacco) contributed 20.5 per cent. Pulses and oilseeds, comprising about 20 per cent of total production, were certainly designed for sale, but they were not at par in terms of exportable and commercial importance to crops like cotton and mulberry, and therefore may be seen as part of the overall production of food.[77] The features of agricultural production as revealed by Colebrooke's estimates are also confirmed by other contemporary observers[78] and from the scattered evidence available from specific districts, from which it would appear that more than 60 to 80 per cent of the cultivated land in Bengal was given over to the cultivation of the primary staples, namely, rice and paddy.[79] Such data certainly suggest that the agricultural landscape in eighteenth-century Bengal was one where oceans of paddy-fields were dotted with a few islands of commercial crops. This situation did not differ substantially even in areas which constituted the core suppliers for Bengal's textile industry. Thus, in the major silk-producing district of Rajshahi, there was hardly a 'Ryott that does not hold grain lands & in greater proportion than Mulberry ones'.[80] What such data reveals is the intense commercialization of the rice-producing economies of these villages.

To the early British observer-cum-administrator, the average peasant in Bengal (in fact, in India) appeared very conservative and hidebound in his decisions regarding the agricultural calendar and different crop-regimes. Cultivators 'seldom engage in extraordinary speculations', was how their initial response to indigo cultivation was described in 1790.[81]

Among the many mistakes and misconceptions perpetrated by the early-colonial rulers, this was perhaps the most fundamental one. One of the key components of peasant production was their perception of risks, and this attitude was entirely reasonable in the context of the ecological uncertainties of erratic rainfall, and the almost continuous threat of famine and dearth which these would bring about. Risk avoidance was certainly an important reason behind the preponderance of rice and paddy in cultivated lands, though that did not prevent the products of these sectors from becoming fully commercialized under the twin influences of rising prices and a buoyant demand.

However, it would be wrong to assume that Bengal's agriculture was entirely a risk prevention enterprise. Under conditions of relative ecological normality, average peasants could be seen trying their hands at cultivating 'dearer' and 'precarious articles' of production. In Jangipur, for instance, cultivators often strove to strike a workable balance on their lands between cash crops and essential staples. Here jute and paddy were sown on the same lands 'adjoining to each other' because '*paat* [jute] will bear a length of Drought which would destroy the Grain, nor does it suffer from excessive rains', so that 'in case of the failure of one, from casualties of weather, the whole together may yield him a profit'. Interestingly, there was very little mulberry grown in Jangipur despite the soil being 'well adapted to the Mulberry plant'; and the reasons for this were that mulberry required relatively larger amounts of capital, and that its cultivation was susceptible to frequent losses caused by weather or by 'disasters to the silk worms'.[82]

At the same time peasants realized the commercial potential of different crops and, circumstances permitting, attempted to cultivate for the market. An enquiry into the agricultural conditions of Baldakhal district in eastern Bengal had the following to say about the peasants' choice of crops: 'cotton in this district is an article of universal cultivation, for the Ryot whose land is not favourable to the produce, provides himself with cotton land in some other place more proper for its growth'.[83] Thus, the average peasant of our period blended an attitude of extreme caution with a healthy regard for commercial profit. But these peasants, like all producers, functioned in a material milieu that was usually beyond their power to control, and the influence of this environment was critical in determining the specific features of agricultural production and its social content.

But production was not a matter of a peasant's autonomous choices. Many extraneous factors exerted an influence. The first of these was ecological. Production was often ruined by drought, especially in the western Bengal, and floods, which destabilized production in the eastern

parts. Apart from the drought-induced famine of 1769–70, Bengal underwent eight instances of severe drought and three instances of major flooding between 1761 and 1793.[84] Shifting river courses also caused havoc.
The eastward shift of the Ganga had already debilitated the economy
of parts of western Bengal in the seventeenth century. In the eighteenth
century, two of the most disastrous shifts occurred in 1770, when the
Damodar river changed its course (causing great damage in Burdwan),
and in 1787 when the Tista shifted its course,[85] causing widespread harm
in northeastern Bengal and playing havoc with the thriving economy of
Dinajpur.[86] Apart from these ecological constraints, other factors like the
high revenue demand of the early-colonial state and the depressed state of
the grain market between 1794 and 1798 have been identified as factors
that introduced a degree of vulnerability among Bengal's peasants.[87] In my
earlier study of dearth and famines I found that such episodes subjected
all social groups to the vicissitudes of the market. A bad agricultural year
was only the beginning of a potential food shortage, but the intensity of
the ensuing deprivation was caused by a decline in per capita food availability because people could not afford to buy food at prevailing prices,
and they had no alternative (i.e. 'traditional') institutional arrangements
of famine relief or agricultural credit open to them.[88]

While ecological uncertainties and tax burdens caused problems,
other factors like demographic growth and rising agricultural prices
(referred to earlier) exerted a positive influence on agricultural life. I have
argued in this essay that a rising demand for food in the province, coupled
with a faster rise in the prices of rice in the eighteenth century relative to
other crops, induced peasants to devote more of their land to the cultivation of rice, encouraged the reclamation of new lands for the purposes of
rice cultivation, and involved the participation of a wider social group.
This group included the zamindars, the *la-kharaj* holder and the grain
merchants, who not only financed such reclamation on a large scale, but
involved themselves actively in the local trade in foodgrains that inevitably
followed.

Agricultural production was highly commercialized. One symptom
was the substantial documentation we have on the increasing participation
of merchants in agricultural production. The connections between the
grain merchants and agricultural production were caused by a combination of factors – a buoyant demand for food both in the towns and in
the countryside, rising agricultural prices, and a recurrence of famine and
semi-famine situations which plagued the province from 1769 onwards.
There is evidence to show that the grain merchants had started getting
involved in the process of agricultural reclamation as a device to ensure

steady supplies in the long run. There is also a large amount of evidence from all over Bengal of merchants providing advances of money, through their agents, to cultivators wanting to reclaim wastes or cultivate their own lands. Almost all the major agricultural products (betel-leaf, sugar, tobacco) were tilled under varying degrees of advance contracts, but the most significant development was the extension of such loans to cover the cultivation of rice in this period. About 50 per cent of the standing crop of rice in Bengal's villages were a product of production loans taken by peasants from the grain merchants.[89] This would certainly have induced a silent transformation of petty production in agriculture.

Into the Nineteenth Century: The Transition to a Colonial Economy

In many fundamental respects, the eighteenth century was a period of transition – which would mean that neither had the earlier system dissolved fully, nor had the later system emerged on its own. Thus, this was a period of fundamental continuities coexisting with equally important changes. One cannot visualize much change in the way a typical Bengali village was organized or the way in which its lands were divided from the way it was described by the *Risala-i-Zira'at* in 1785, though it is likely that the proportion of lands earmarked as '*jangal*' would have shrunk owing to demographic pressures.[90] Agricultural seasons continued unmodified, and village life continued to be dictated by cycles of good and bad weather. A positive aspect of this period was that Bengal did not suffer a famine of the magnitude of 1769–70 till late into the nineteenth century.[91] Many of the commercial processes traditionally assigned to the nineteenth century had already established themselves in the eighteenth century. Cash transactions and commodity production for expanding internal and international markets were as much a feature of the eighteenth century as they were of the nineteenth. Bengal's agriculture continued to be highly commercialized, and with the spread of indigo, opium and jute, the pace of agrarian commercialization speeded up. Since the spread of these commodities intensified from the 1820s, and since these were primarily meant for export, Bengal's villages were now completely under the influence of the fluctuations of the capitalist world market. While this expanded the market opportunities, and helped in enriching many indigenous traders and landed people, it also increased the economic vulnerability of the producers. Therefore, while the early-colonial system widened and deepened the processes already underway, it also introduced changes. The remarkable fluidity of the earlier period seems to have been drawing to a close by the early decades of the nineteenth century.

The early-colonial state was aggressively mercantilist with a

European (specifically, British), not Indian, orientation. State policy was fiscally motivated and all institutions were to be streamlined to ensure this ultimate objective. Anterior institutions were reconstituted. They were not dissolved but were twisted around to cater to the new dispensation. Notwithstanding the great rhetoric that accompanied it, the Permanent Settlement was a feat of mercantilist social engineering to stabilize Bengal's revenues for the purposes of the East India Company's commerce. Under its terms the Mughal right of taxation, traditionally devolved upon the zamindars by the state, was fused to their *milkiyat*, their 'private' domains, both of which could now be sold. The Permanent Settlement gave unprecedented power to the landlords without bothering to protect the interests of the *raiyats* who were supposed to pay the revenue. Regulations 7 (*haftam*) of 1799 and 5 (*panjam*) of 1812 gave to the Bengal zamindar the power to distrain crops for arrears of revenue, and to make whatever terms with his tenants as he wished regardless of custom – if necessary, by evicting old tenants and settling new ones.[92] Using these two weapons, Bengal's landlords went on a rent offensive. Between 1793 and 1880, the gross rental increased almost twofold in some parts of Bengal, whereas in Bihar they tripled or even quadrupled.[93]

However, the older idea that the revenue pressures after the Permanent Settlement resulted in the break-up of zamindaris and their consolidation in the hands of moneyed people from outside is no longer tenable. The principal buyers of such lands were the established zamindars themselves.[94] Though this enlarged the 'rule' of private property in Bengal's countryside, the dip in agricultural prices for about five years after 1790 exacerbated matters and left the ordinary cultivator to receive the rough end of the stick. There is no doubt that agrarian distress in Bengal's villages increased considerably in the immediate aftermath of the Permanent Settlement.

Despite these interventions, notions of universal agrarian distress and a devastated peasantry in the post-1793 world of Bengal's villages would be over-pessimistic. The situation on the ground was more complex. As B.B. Chaudhuri says, the zamindars' rent offensive 'was far from a continuous or automatic process'; 'increases of rent only rarely involved eviction of peasants on any considerable scale, except in certain cases, and rising agricultural prices reduced, at least partly, the actual rent burden of the peasants'.[95] Agricultural reclamation along the northern edges of the province and along its estuaries continued robustly till the middle of the nineteenth century. In Burdwan large areas had been brought under the plough by the middle of the nineteenth century, 'especially in the western part of the district, which a hundred years ago was an unpeopled wilderness of *sal* forest and jungle'.[96] Between 1850 and 1874, the area of rice-growing land had increased by 50 per cent in Midnapur.[97] By the middle of the nineteenth century, Bengal's peasants had exhausted the extensive margins at the current low level of technology and begun to exploit new intensive strategies. Some open spaces still remained in east Bengal, which both invited and challenged hardy Muslim and Namasudra peasants.[98]

The fruits of this expansion were mopped up by the zamindars, grain merchants and *jotedars*. Their positions were becoming stronger in relation to the smaller peasantries, sharecroppers, tenants and day labourers. Large zamindaris continued to exert a great influence on the village economies of western Bengal, whereas in east Bengal, where the zamindaris were smaller, another landed category, the *taluqdars*, emerged dominant on the rural landscape. Some historians believe that the *jotedars* on the northern fringes behaved like 'kulak-landlords': providing credit and engaging in agricultural trade over short distances.[99] While there is very little evidence for this for the eighteenth century, there is little doubt that *jotedari* had become unassailable in northern and some parts of southwestern Bengal by the middle of the nineteenth century.[100] Merchants continued to finance cultivation as they had in the eighteenth century through a combination of production and consumption loans to cultivators. These loans defined the changing commercial context of production in Bengal's villages and enabled the intrusion of merchant capital into the very core of Bengal's economy. Famines still affected everyone but not equally adversely. Compared to the reports of universal distress in the worst-affected villages during the famine of 1769–70,[101] reports of the 1866 famine in Midnapur showed that while 'the labouring population died in large numbers', 'the superior classes of cultivators suffered very little'.[102] On the whole, the pace of stratification in Bengal's villages and the vulnerability of the poorer sections living in them considerably increased in the nineteenth century, as did the gap between the rich and the poor.

Notes and References

1. The literature on this subject is vast and well-known. The classic example of this is N.K. Sinha, *The Economic History of Bengal: From Plassey to Permanent Settlement*, Vol. 2, Calcutta: Firma K.L. Mukhopadhyay, 1965.
2. See Sushil Chaudhury, *From Prosperity to Decline: Eighteenth Century Bengal*, Delhi: Manohar, 1995.
3. The literature on these issues is vast and well known.
4. Rajat Datta, *Society, Economy and the Market: Commercialization in Rural Bengal, c. 1760–1800*, Delhi: Manohar, 2000.
5. In a recent essay, Tilottama Mukherjee has reinforced this picture of market integration in the eighteenth century; see her 'Markets in Eighteenth Century Bengal Economy', *The Indian Economic and Social History Review*, Vol. 48 (2), 2011.

[6] For details, see Datta, *Society, Economy and the Market.*

[7] Tilottama Mukherjee, 'Of Rivers and Roads: Transport Networks and Economy in Eighteenth-Century Bengal', in Yogesh Sharma, ed., *Coastal Histories: Society and Economy in Pre-Modern India*, New Delhi: Primus, 2010.

[8] On this, see B.B. Chaudhuri, *Peasant History of Late Pre-Colonial and Colonial India*, Project of History of Indian Science, Philosophy and Culture (PHISPC) (General Editor: D.P. Chattopadhyaya), Vol. VIII, Part 2, New Delhi: Pearson Education India, 2008.

[9] *Letter to the Proprietors of the East India Stock*, 1776, *Tracts*, vol. 50, India Office Library (IOL), p. 6.

[10] Proceedings of the Provincial Council of Revenue (PCR), Murshidabad, vol. 8, 15 February 1776, West Bengal State Archives (WBSA).

[11] Proceedings of the Board of Revenue (BRP), P/70/48, 7 November 1788, Oriental and India Office Collections (OIOC).

[12] Home Miscellaneous (HM), vol. 765, India Office Records (IOR), p. 146.

[13] Cited in P.J. Marshall, *Bengal: The British Bridgehead, Eastern India 1740–1828*, The New Cambridge History of India, Vol. II, Cambridge: Cambridge University Press, 1987, p. 151.

[14] Datta, *Economy, Society and the Market*, p. 189.

[15] W.K. Firminger, ed., *The Fifth Report on East India Company Affairs*, Vol. 2, Calcutta, 1917, p. 31.

[16] W.W. Hunter, *The Annals of Rural Bengal*, London: Smith, Elder & Co., 1868, pp. 32–34; H.T. Colebrooke, *Remarks on the Husbandry and Internal Commerce of Bengal, 1793*, Calcutta, 1804, p. xii; Sugata Bose, *Peasant Labour and Colonial Capital: Rural Bengal since 1770*, Cambridge: Cambridge University Press, 1993, p. 20.

[17] Shireen Moosvi, *People, Taxation and Trade in Mughal India*, Delhi: Oxford University Press, 2008.

[18] Datta, *Society, Economy and the Market.*

[19] Ibid., pp. 207–08.

[20] The Bengali equivalent of this would be '*jote*'.

[21] This tract, written in 1785, was translated by Harbans Mukhia in his *Perspectives on Medieval History*, Delhi: Vikas, 1993, pp. 264–80; a detailed substance of this treatise, entitled 'Substance of a Treatise on the Revenues of Bengal, Translated from Persian in 1785', is also available in Home Miscellaneous, vol. 68, OIOC. I have merged both in this study.

[22] Ibid., p. 269; for the main report of the Amini Commission, see R.B. Ramsbotham, *Studies in the Land Revenue History of Bengal, 1769–1787*, London: Oxford University Press, 1926, p. 106.

[23] See Datta, *Economy, Society and Market*, chapter 2.

[24] Irfan Habib, 'The Peasant in Indian History', in *Essays in Indian Indian History: Towards a Marxist Perspective*, New Delhi: Tulika Books, 1995, p. 154.

[25] Papers Relative to the 'Aumeen' (Amini) Commission, 1778, British Museum (BM), Add. Mss., 29086 to 29088.

[26] Datta, *Society, Economy and Market*, chapter 4.

[27] Ibid., pp. 189–90.

[28] Ibid., pp. 147–48.

[29] Richard Eaton, *The Rise of Islam and the Bengal Frontier, 1204–1760*, Delhi: Oxford University Press, 1997, p. 308.

[30] H.R. Beveridge, *The District of Bakarganj: Its History and Statistics*, Calcutta: Bengal Secretariat Book Depot, 1876; Rajat Datta, 'Merchants and Peasants: A Study of the Structure of Local Trade in Grain in Late Eighteenth Century

Bengal', in Sanjay Subrahmanyam, ed., *Merchants, Markets and State in Early Modern India*, Delhi: Oxford University Press, 1990.

31 Papers Relative to the 'Aumeen' (Amini) Commission, 1778.

32 On these, see David J. McCutchion, *Late Medieval Temples of Bengal*, Calcutta: The Asiatic Society, 1973; H. Sanyal, 'Temple Building in Bengal from the Fifteenth to the Nineteenth Centuries', in Barun De, ed., *Perspectives in Social Sciences: Historical Dimensions*, Calcutta: Oxford University Press, 1977; Hitesranjan Sanyal, 'Bangalir Dharmiya Sthapatya Charcha' (Bengali), in Aniruddha Ray and Indrani Chattterjee, eds, *Madhyayuge Banglar Samaj o Sanskriti*, Kolkata, 1992; David Curley, 'Maharaja Krisnacandra, Hinduism, and Kingship in the Contact Zone of Bengal', in Richard Barnett, ed., *Rethinking Early Modern India*, Delhi: Manohar, 2002.

33 For Dutch imports of bullion into Bengal, see Om Prakash, *European Commercial Enterprise in Pre-Colonial India*, Cambridge: Cambridge University Press, 1998; for imports by the English East India Company, see Datta, *Society, Economy and the Market*, pp. 344–46.

34 Calculated from General Ledgers and Account Books, L/AG/10/2/2, OIOC, pp. 84, 211–13, 235–36, and L/AG/10/2/4, OIOC, p. 148.

35 B.B. Chowdhury, *Growth of Commercial Agriculture in Bengal, 1757–1900*, Vol. 1, Calcutta: Indian Studies Past and Present, 1964, p. 81.

36 HM, vol. 68, IOR, pp. 898, 901; Mss. Eur. G. 33, fol. 139, IOL.

37 Om Prakash, *European Commercial Enterprise in Pre-colonial India*, p. 87.

38 John Shore's Minute on The Coinage of Bengal, 28 October 1789, in BRC, P/51/50, 28 October 1789, OIOC.

39 The amount of wealth looted by the Company's officials and soldiers between 1757 and 1765 – famously known as the Plassey plunder – was £5,940,498. *Parliamentary Papers, Third Report, 1773*, pp. 311–12.

40 Firminger, ed., *Fifth Report*, p. 274.

41 Witness the following description of this phenomenon recorded in 1777 from Lakhipur, a major cotton textile-producing centre in eastern Bengal: 'The weavers and other manufacturers in this district as well as in the other interior parts of [Dhaka] refuse to receive the Sicca rupee according to its intrinsic value. . . . The Arcot rupee is and has been the only specie of general currency in this province time out of mind. It does not appear to have arisen from the mint at Dacca since no other rupee was coined there except the sicca. The only reason we can ascribe is the nature of a considerable part of the produce and manufacture of this province: viz., rice and cloths. Rice having been an article of exportation to the coast of Coromandel and the latter to Bombay and Surat in order to be disposed of to merchants coming from the Gulf of Persia. It admits of a possibility that many years ago Arcot rupees were immediately brought from the Peninsula of India into this province for the purchase of them [and] the balance of trade being then considerably in its favour that this originally established them [as] the current specie.' PCR, Dhaka, vol. 27, 3 to 31 July 1777, 21 July 1777.

42 Tome Pires, *The Suma Oriental of Tome Pires, 1512–1515*, Vol. 1, Indian reprint, New Delhi: Asian Educational Services, 2005, p. 93; Memorandum of J. Herklotts, Fiscal of Chinsura, in *Gleanings in Science*, Vol. I, Calcutta: Baptist Mission Press, 1829, p. 369.

43 James Grant, 'Historical and Comparative Analysis of the Finances of Bengal; chronologically arranged in different periods, from the Mogul Conquest to the present Time: Extracted from a Political Survey of the British Dominions and Tributary Dependencies in India' (original, 1789) in Firminger, ed., *Fifth Report*, p. 378.

[44] PCR, Dhaka, vol. 12, 1 July – 30 September 1776, WBSA.

[45] PCR, Dhaka, vol. 5, 30 March 1775, WBSA. A classic description of such a person was provided by the French traveller Jean-Baptiste Tavernier in 1676 in the following words: 'In India a village must be very small indeed if it has not a money-changer called a shroff, who acts as a banker to make remittances in money and issue letters of exchange [hundi]. As is general, these Changers have an understanding with the Governors of the Provinces, they enhance the rupee as they please for paisa and the paisa for these [cowrie] shells. See Jean-Baptiste Tavernier, Travels in India, 1676, translated by V. Ball, edited by William Crooke, Indian edition, Delhi: Asian Educational Services, 2007, p. 24.

[46] Based on Irfan Habib, An Atlas of the Mughal Empire: Political and Economic Maps with Detailed Notes, Bibliography and Index, Delhi: Oxford University Press, 1982, p. 46; and Om Prakash, European Commercial Enterprise in Pre-Colonial India, map 7, p. 197.

[47] Datta, Economy, Society and the Market, pp. 189–91.

[48] BRP, P/71/25, 17 May 1790, OIOC. The account is from Rajshahi, but would apply for every corner of Bengal.

[49] PCR, Murshidabad, Vol. 8, 15 February 1776, WBSA.

[50] Proceedings of the Board of Revenue, Miscellaneous, Sayar (hereafter, BRMS), P/89/41, 15 April 1794, OIOC.

[51] Miki Sayako, 'The English East India Company and Indigenous Trading System: The Grain Trade in Early Colonial Bengal', in S. Sugiyama and Linda Grove, eds, Commercial Networks in Modern Asia, London: Curzon Press, 2001, p. 215.

[52] PCR, Dacca, Vol. 8, 18 September 1775, WBSA; P.J. Marshall, East Indian Fortunes: The British in Bengal in the Eighteenth Century, Oxford: Clarendon Press, 1976, pp. 106–07.

[53] PCR, Dacca, Vol. 8, 18 September 1775, WBSA; and Grain, Vol. 1, 10 October 1794, WBSA.

[54] Sayako, 'The English East India Company and Indigenous Trading System', p. 217.

[55] Ibid.

[56] Ibid, pp. 217, 232.

[57] These prices have been derived by averaging the prices of rice contained in the Journal and Ledgers of the Company with the ones given by J. Herklotts, Fiscal of Chinsura, in Gleanings in Science (Calcutta, 1829). Writing in 1769, H. Verelst noted that prices of 'provisions' had 'considerably advanced within these twenty years' (Verelst Papers, Mss. Eur. F 281/6-10/9, f. 279, OIOC). In 1776, Warren Hastings also noted that 'the price of coarse rice which forms the principal consumption of the people was 5½ times cheaper in the time of Shuja Cawn [1728] than it is now' (BRC, P/49/66, 29 November – 31 December 1776, 29 November 1776, OIOC). In 1789, it was noted how the rise in prices of the 'necessaries of life' had pushed up the prices of 'every article of manufacture' in the textile producing centres (Bengal Commercial and Shipping Consultations, P/155/74, 28 March 1789, OIOC). Such descriptions are strong enough in themselves to show a general rise in price levels.

[58] Dicussed in Eaton, The Rise of Islam and the Bengal Frontier.

[59] For details, see Datta, Economy, Society and the Market, pp. 68–75.

[60] Bose, Peasant Labour and Colonial Capital, pp. 23–24.

[61] See Eaton, Bengal Frontier, for an account of agricultural reclamation in these regions, among many others, in the Bengal delta.

[62] Datta, *Economy, Society and the Market*, pp. 385, 397.

[63] The term is Eaton's; see his *Bengal Frontier*.

[64] Beveridge, *The History of Bakarganj*, pp. 194–203.

[65] J. Westland, *A Report on the District of Jessore: its antiquities, its history and its commerce*, Calcutta: Bengal Secretariat Office, 1871, p. 135.

[66] Datta, *Economy, Society and the Market*, chapter 5.

[67] Ibid., p. 187, Table 34.

[68] W.W. Hunter, *A Statistical Account of Bengal, Volume 1: 24-Parganas and the Sundarbans*, London: Trubner & Co., 1875; reprint, Delhi: D.K. Publishing House, 1973, p. 77.

[69] BRC, P/49/39, 26 March 1773, OIOC.

[70] 'Rongoppur', Mss. Eur. D.74, f. 110, OIOC.

[71] Board of Revenue Proceedings, P/71/28, 7 July 1790, OIOC.

[72] BRC, P/51/21, 4 June 1788, IOR; and BRC, P/51/34, 8 April 1789, IOR.

[73] Ratnalekha Ray, *Change in Bengal Agrarian Society, c. 1760–1850*, Delhi: Manohar, 1979.

[74] See H. Sanyal, 'Continuities of Social Mobility in Traditional and Modern Society in India: Two Case Studies of Caste Mobility in Bengal', *Journal of Asian Studies*, 30 (2), 1971.

[75] Datta, *Economy, Society and Market*, pp. 109–10, 336.

[76] Ibid., chapter 5.

[77] H.T. Colebrooke, *Remarks on the Husbandry and Internal Commerce of Bengal, 1793*, pp. 15–16.

[78] William Tennant, c. 1797, gave a much smaller proportion of the cultivated lands occupied by these cash crops: 'most valuable crops' like 'tobacco, sugar, indigo, cotton, mulberry and poppy' did not occupy more than a 'twentieth part of the land' under cultivation. See William Tennant, *Indian Recreations: Consisting Chiefly of Strictures on the Domestic and Rural Economy of the Mahomedans & Hindoos*, Vol. 2, Edinburgh: Longman, Hurst, Rees and Orme, 1803, p. 11.

[79] Datta, *Society, Economy and the Market*, pp. 55–56.

[80] BRP, P/71/10, 25 June 1789, OIOC.

[81] C. Blume, 'Short Sketch of the Measures Adopted for the Introduction of Indigo and Promotion of Agriculture in Bengal Between 1779 and 1790', HM, vol. 443, OIOC, p. 600.

[82] M. Atkinson, Resident, Jangipur Factory, 21 November 1792, HM, vol. 375, OIOC, p. 318.

[83] 15 June 1789, HM, Vol. 385, IOR, p. 325.

[84] Datta, *Society, Economy and the Market*, pp. 241–48.

[85] Radha Kamal Mukherjee, *The Changing Face of Bengal: A Study in Riverine Economy*, Calcutta: Calcutta University, 1938.

[86] R. Datta, 'Agricultural Production, Social Participation and Domination in Late Eighteenth Century Bengal: Towards an Alternative Explanation', *Journal of Peasant Studies*, Vol. 17, No. 1, October 1989.

[87] Bose, *Peasant Labour and Colonial Capital*, p. 23.

[88] Datta, *Society, Economy and the Market*, chapter 5.

[89] Ibid., pp. 216–20.

[90] This impression is borne out by the way in which forests were being cleared in Jessore and 24 Parganas in this period.

[91] In 1866 there was a famine in Midnapur (Hunter). In 1873 there was an all-Bengal famine (Leela Visaria and Pravin Visaria, 'Population, 1757–1947', in

Dharma Kumar, ed., *The Cambridge Economic History of India, Volume 2: c. 1757–1970*, Indian reprint, Delhi: Cambridge University Press, 1984, pp. 528–31).

[92] Bose, *Peasant Labour and Colonial Capital*, p. 115.

[93] Ibid., p. 118.

[94] Sirajul Islam, *The Permanent Settlement in Bengal: A Study of Its Operations, 1790–1819*, Dhaka: Bangla Academy, 1977; also B.B. Chaudhuri, 'Eastern India', in Dharma Kumar, ed., *The Cambridge Economic History of India, Volume 2: c. 1757–1970*, pp. 117–18.

[95] B.B. Chaudhuri, 'Eastern India', p. 140.

[96] J.C.K. Peterson, *Bengal District Gazetteers: Burdwan*, Calcutta: Bengal Secretariat Book Depot, 1910, reprint 1997, p. 122.

[97] L.S.S. O'Malley, *Bengal District Gazetteers: Midnapore*, Calcutta: Bengal Secretariat Book Depot, 1911, reprint 1955, p. 100.

[98] Bose, *Peasant Labour and Colonial Capital*, pp. 23–24

[99] Rajat and Ratnalekha Ray, 'Zamindars and Jotedars', *Modern Asian Studies*, Vol. 9, No. 1, 1975.

[100] Bose, *Peasant Labour and Colonial Capital*, p. 79.

[101] Datta, *Economy, Society and the Market*, chapter 5.

[102] W.W. Hunter, *A Statistical Account of Bengal: Midnapore*, London: Trubner & Co., 1876; reprint, Calcutta, 1975, p. 124.

Rethinking the Bengal Peasantry in History

Shinkichi Taniguchi

Introduction

We have at the moment conflicting views on the Bengal peasantry, and its differentiation during the pre-colonial and colonial periods. This is unfortunate, because our interpretation of local politics, popular movements, impact of commercialization and so on during the colonial period depends to a great extent on how we understand the Bengal peasantry and the structure of village society of the time.

The conflicting views may be broadly classified into two, although each has differences within that cannot be ignored. The first view asserts that there was a stratum of rich peasants who dominated village society almost all over the Bengal province. The second view argues that rich peasants could be found only in some frontier districts such as Dinajpur, Rangpur, Koch Bihar and Jalpaiguri; elsewhere, small peasant farms were predominant and differentiation of the rural population was slight. The first view is supported by Kalyan Kumar Sen Gupta, Ratnalekha Ray, Rajat Ray and others including the present author; the second view is supported by Partha Chatterjee, Sugata Bose, Rajat Datta and others. Binay Bhushan Chaudhuri, in his latest book, is of the opinion that while the former went a bit too far in asserting that Bengal's village society was totally dominated by rich peasants or *jotedars*, and that traditional landlords or zamindars had scarcely any presence in it, the latter also went too far in claiming that Bengal's village society, except for a few frontier districts, was almost exclusively composed of small peasants and that there was scarcely any differentiation among them. In the last analysis, Chaudhuri admits that there were rich peasants almost all across Bengal.[1]

The peasantry did not emerge all of a sudden but step by step, under a variety of ecological, economic, social and political conditions of their respective regions. This essay tries to trace the various mechanisms of emergence and differentiation of the peasants in Bengal, and, thereby, to offer certain clues to the solution of conflicting views on Bengal peasants.

Definition of Peasant

We first need to define the meaning of the term peasant (*raiyat*) as we use it in this essay.[2] The peasant is a cultivator with a certain degree of freedom in the management of his land. The essential features that characterize a peasant may be summarized as follows. (1) He possesses stable customary or legal usufruct over the plot of land occupied by him, which is heritable but not necessarily mortgageable and transferable. (2) He possesses the power of decision-making as to various matters concerning management of the land, such as the kinds of crops to be produced, timing of harvesting, sale of products, purchase of agricultural implements and so on. (3) He cultivates primarily using family labour, but from time to time he might hire in outside labour or hire out surplus family labour, or work the field in cooperation with neighbours. (4) The land held by him may be rented in or a part of the holding could be rented out.

Agricultural labourers (*majur*, *krishan*, etc.) are evidently not peasants as defined above. Some sharecroppers (*adhiyars*, *bhag-chasi*, *bargadar*, etc.), who hold the same land for many years fall within the category of peasant, but others do not. Tenants-at-will and subordinate *raiyat* (under-tenants, *korfa*) also pose a difficulty. They usually fulfil conditions (2) and (3) above, but not always condition (1). A rich peasant, if he partially or wholly cultivates lands or supervises their cultivation, comes within the definition of a peasant, but a giant *jotedar* who hardly involves himself in the cultivation or management of the field is not a peasant. Similarly, resident *bhadralok* (high-caste Hindus who reside in the villages), resident *ashraf* (elite Muslims living in the villages) and resident *taluqdars* (petty landlords) are not included in the category of peasants because they usually do not cultivate or manage the fields themselves.

The Bengal plains were surrounded by tribal areas where slash-and-burn cultivation (*jhum*) was extensively carried out. Whether the tribal cultivator in these areas is a peasant or not needs special consideration, which we shall reserve for later. Lastly, the peasant as defined above is neither as old as the practice of agriculture nor present everywhere. We argue that the peasant generally emerged out of the break-up of land-controlling village communities, or landholding joint families, or manorial systems, or land-controlling tribal organizations, and so on. It is important to clearly understand the different mechanisms that gave birth to the peasantry in different regions of Bengal.

Prevalence of the Rich Peasant: Some Evidence

As the prevalence of rich peasants in colonial Bengal has been questioned in some recent works, we shall show, first, that they did exist widely in the period under review. We have demonstrated,[3] mostly on the basis of Board of Revenue records, that there existed wealthy peasants in the districts of Dinajpur, Rangpur, Murshidabad, Rajshahi, Bardhaman, Birbhum, Tipperah and Purnea in the late eighteenth century, and, as a corollary, there existed a multitude of very poor cultivators in these districts. Nakazato, analysing the *Indigo Commission Report*, has detected rich peasants in indigo-producing districts such as Nadia, Jessore and Pabna in the middle of the nineteenth century.[4] Taniguchi,[5] on the basis of the statistical data contained in the *Report on the Condition of the Lower Classes of Population in Bengal*, has described highly stratified structures in various districts such as Midnapur, Malda, Murshidabad, Rajshahi, Pabna, Tipperah and Nadia in the late nineteenth century. Sirajul Islam has also shown the existence of a highly stratified structure in some villages in eastern Bengal,[6] and Taniguchi has found a similar structure in the districts of Dhaka, Faridpur and Bakarganj on the basis of survey and settlement reports published in the late nineteenth and early twentieth centuries.[7] Much more evidence can be cited, if needed. Thus, it is not possible to gainsay that there existed a stratified structure of the peasantry almost all over Bengal during the colonial rule.

Emergence of the Peasantry and Regional Characteristics of Peasant Society in Bengal
Emergence of the Peasantry in the Old Settled Areas

A recent work on ancient and early medieval Bengal states, on the basis of the reading of copperplate inscriptions, that the 'peasantry was already . . . highly stratified into *kutumbin, mahattara, mahamahattara, mahapradhana*'.[8] Some researchers further maintain that the 'local society' headed by 'landowning peasants' (*kutumbins*) were very powerful and rivalled the state during the Gupta period, and that subsequently, during the post-Gupta period, the rising local governments and subordinate kings extended their local influence and relegated the local society and the *kutumbins* to a subjugated position.[9] Though these studies show that there existed supra-village organizations (*adhikaranas*), and a certain degree of stratification among the peasantry and powerful traders, they fail to demonstrate the process of formation of the landowning peasant. Thus, to our great frustration, we have no explanation to offer as to when and how the landowning peasant appeared in the Bengal plains in the ancient and medieval periods.

In the absence of historical evidence, we have no other way than to present briefly a theoretical perspective on the emergence of the peasantry in general terms. A number of preconditions are required for a small peasant farm to emerge as a viable economic unit. These are as follows. (1) Protection of life and property, including land, from hostile marauders, with the help of powerful organizations such as tribal organizations, local potentates or the state. However, at the same time, it must be ensured that these protectors do not intervene in the production process. If the tribal organization, village community, local potentate or the state tightly controls the use of the land and other resources within their territories, it is difficult for a small cultivator to lay claim to a plot of land as his separate and independent family farm, or to carry out agriculture as his private undertaking. (2) Technical breakthroughs which enable a small family farm to produce a sufficient amount of food for the family's annual consumption without shifting the site of cultivation every two or three years. Under conditions of mainly rainfed agriculture, as in Bengal, the introduction of transplanted wet-rice cultivation with plough and draught animal is a typical case of such a breakthrough. (3) Existence of markets or any other exchange system through which the family can obtain the necessities of life and those agricultural tools that cannot be produced by the family. Unless these three conditions are fulfilled, it is not possible for a family to carry on settled agriculture on a farm for successive years. These preconditions suggest that the emergence of small peasant farms coincides, to a great extent, with the introduction of wet-rice cultivation, the break-up of the tribal system of production, and the formation of the state.

On the basis of the above theoretical perspective on the emergence of small peasant farms, we may postulate that the establishment of several local governments during the post-Gupta period might have facilitated this transition. And the social reforms vigorously carried out by the Sena dynasty in the twelfth century seem to have firmly positioned the small peasant in the regional caste system in Bengal, and also in the Hindu system of the social division of labour.

Later on, under the Mughal rule in Bengal, both Todar Mal's famous revenue settlement in the second half of the sixteenth century, and a similar but more vigorous attempt by Nawab Murshid Quli Khan at measuring all the cultivated lands in Bengal in the early eighteenth century, may be taken as epoch-making policy measures which officially established the peasants' rights over their holdings. Let us reproduce the invaluable description of Nawab Murshid Quli Khan's attempt from the pen of a near-contemporary:

> When he thus entirely dispossessed the zemindars from the management
> of collections, his aumils and their officers made an actual measurement
> of all the lands in cultivation, as well as of those called benjer (land that

has lain fallow five years and upwards); and obtained information of the ability of every husbandman, in every village throughout the Soobah. To those who were so distressed as to be unable to purchase the necessary implements of husbandry, or grain to sow their land, he advanced tekawy (a loan of money given to the husbandman to enable him to purchase a first stock), and by this humane attention to the wants of individuals, cultivation was increased, and the revenues consequently augmented.

He made an exact hustabood or comparative statement of the collections of former years with present; and conformably thereto, his aumils collected the produce of every harvest immediately from the husbandmen. He resumed all the extra expenses of the zemindars and gave them a nankar (subsistence either in money or land), barely sufficient for a subsistence. Thus, by the augmentation of the revenues, by his attention to the syer or duties, and by considerable retrenchments on the expenses of every department, he brought prodigious sums into the treasury.[10]

In addition to the measurement and assessment made by the Bengal provincial government, the zamindars from time to time conducted measurements in their own estates, and made fresh assessments of the holdings held by each peasant in order to ascertain the taxable assets of the estates.[11] Thus, these administrative measures both by the government and the zamindars must have consolidated the otherwise elusive right of the peasants over their holdings.

Regional Social Characteristics of Bengal: An Analysis of the Preliminary Population Census of 1872

In order to identify the regional social characteristics of peasant society in the old settled areas, we many briefly analyse the distribution of the upper three castes (Brahman, Kayastha and Baidya), the other caste groups, semi-Hinduized tribes, and the tribals, on the basis of the preliminary population census of 1872.

Before going into an analysis of the census data, some remarks are in order about the conversion of Hindus into Muslims. The census classifies 96 per cent of the Muslim population as 'unspecified', as opposed to elite Muslims such as Shaikhs, Mughals, Afghans, etc. Doubtless, most of the 'unspecified' would have been indigenous inhabitants who had accepted the Muslim faith. Though we have no information regarding the breakdown of their previous social identities, we may tentatively suppose that their conversion to Islam took place in proportion to their ratio in the non-Muslim population[12] of each district. Under this hypothesis, we may

TABLE 1 *Percentage share of tribal and semi-Hinduized population in the non-Muslim population*

30–35%	Bogra	Cachar	Murshidabad	Dacca	Bankura
	(30.2%)	(30.6%)	(31.2%)	(32.1%)	(33.1%)
35–40%	Birbhum	Jessore			
	(35.2%)	(37.9%)			
40–50%	Malda	Faridpur	Bakarganj		
	(41.0%)	(41.6%)	(42.1%)		
Over 50%	Rangpur	Darjeeling	Dinajpur	Jalpaiguri	Chittagong Hill
	(59.1%)	(63.2%)	(73.8%)	(82.0%)	Tracts (89.1%)

roughly say that our analysis of the non-Muslim population in each district may be more or less applicable to the whole population of the district.

In 1872, of the total non-Muslim population of Lower Bengal, 30.6 per cent belonged to the tribes and semi-Hinduized tribals, a figure that reveals the significance of the tribal and semi-tribal inhabitants of Bengal. The rates exceeded 30 per cent in fifteen districts, the total of which amounted to 48 per cent of the entire population. Thus, about a half of the people in Bengal lived in areas with dense tribal and semi-tribal populations. It is only natural to presume that this proportion was even higher in earlier times. This strongly suggests that the mixture of the Hindu social system and the tribal social system took place at the grassroots level, and, therefore, the influence of the tribal system on regional social characteristics in these areas could not have been negligible.

Let us very briefly examine the social characteristics of these fifteen districts. In the western district of Bankura, the leading zamindari (Bishnupur Raj) was said to trace its foundation to one of the tribal populations, and in Jangal Mahal of the same district there was a local kingdom of Bagri (Bagdi). Though the king's family claimed a Rajput descent, they controlled the forest peoples.[13] Towards the north, the districts of Dinajpur, Rangpur, Jalpaiguri, Darjeeling and Cachar were ruled by the king of the Koch Bihar, who definitely descended from a Mech man and a Koch lady.[14] The king of Tripura in the southeast also had a tribal origin.[15] There is no denying that the northern districts of Jalpaiguri and Darjeeling were completely tribal areas until the beginning of the nineteenth century. And the kingdoms of Khasi, Jaintia, Manipur and Ahom (Assam) in the northeastern frontier were tribal states with systems largely built on tribal organizations, at least in the beginning. The districts of Malda, Bogra and Murshidabad, adjoining the previous Koch kingdom, had a high proportion of tribal inhabitants such as the Koch, Mech, Palia and others. The large concentration of the Namasudra (previously called Chandala) in the eastern districts of Dacca, Faridpur and Bakarganj explains the existence of a high proportion of tribal inhabitants in these districts. They were concentrated in the interior backwaters of these districts.[16]

What of the other districts on the frontiers of the Bengal province? Take the example of Midnapur district, which is a neighbor to the tribal belt of Orissa and Bihar. The major social groups of this district were the *Kaibartta* (32.1 per cent of the district population, a cultivator caste), Santhal (5.4 per cent, a tribe), Bagdi (5.1 per cent, a semi-Hinduized community), *Sadgop* (4.8 per cent, a cultivator caste), and Brahman (4.1 per cent, a high-ranking Hindu caste). Besides these, Muslims accounted for 6.5 per cent. These social groups were distributed very unevenly in the district. The Bagdis and the Santhals were concentrated in the northern, western and southwestern parts. The *Kaibarttas* occupied the larger part of the eastern and southeastern regions bordering the Hooghly river. Distribution of the *Sadgops* more or less overlapped with that of the Bagdi. Brahman and other functional social groups were distributed relatively evenly all over the district. Thus, while the tribal social elements became thicker towards the northern, western and southwestern parts of the district, the Hindu social groups dominated the eastern and southeastern parts. Though Midnapur district as a whole was not ranked among the top fifteen tribal-majority districts, certain tracts of the district showed a very strong tribal presence.

Significance of the Tribal System for the Emergent Bengal Peasantry

It is now widely accepted that Hinduization of the tribes had been continuously taking place all over India,[17] and that this social transformation almost always involved economic transformation such as changes in agricultural practices and land systems among the tribal people. It is also arguable that the later system could never be completely free from the traits of the previous system, because of path-dependency.

On the frontiers of Bengal, the agricultural system was changing from shifting cultivation to settled cultivation with plough, draught animals and transplanted wet-rice.[18] Shifting cultivation based on communal landownership gave way to individual settled agriculture basically dependent upon family labour. This also implied changes in land ownership from the community to the individual, of course, with plenty of variations from locality to locality and also from tribe to tribe.[19] It needs to be emphasized that this transformation was frequently associated with state formation, or with the advent of powerful outsiders such as an invading army, Hindu merchants, European tea-planters and, finally, cultivators from the old settled plains, attracted by the fertile virgin lands available at advantageous rent.

Binay Bhushan Chaudhuri, on the basis of his researches on tribal societies on the western frontiers of the Bengal plains, says that slash-and-burn cultivation was no more the dominant form of agriculture, and also that even shifting cultivation became basically a family undertaking.[20] However, these statements are not applicable to the eastern frontiers or to the northern bordering areas. We have several monographs and observations on the shifting cultivation in the Tripura Hills, Garo Hills, etc., which almost always reveal that the land did not belong to a particular family but to the village or a small unit of the clan, consisting of ten to fifteen households.[21] When they shifted to a new site, they first cleared the jungle through community labour and then distribution of the cleared land was made either by the village heads or the village elders, or by carrying on a kind of negotiation within the community. Though annual cultivation of their assigned field was mainly conducted by family labour, the respective families were not allowed to claim individual ownership over particular plots of land in the territory. However, changes started taking place with the growth of population and the resultant shortage of land, and/or with the introduction of transplanted wet-rice cultivation that required permanent irrigation facilities.

We may argue that a similar kind of situation as we saw in the tribal areas more or less prevailed even in the Bengal plains at one time in history. Though the transition to settled agriculture was completed much earlier in the Bengal plains, vestiges of the tribal or communal system continued to exist here and there.

Koch Bihar: A Case Study of Transition in Tribal Areas

In the late fifteenth century, on the northern frontiers of Bengal, there appeared a prominent leader of the Koch tribe, Hajo, who successfully united many conflicting chiefs. His two daughters Hira and Jira married one of the leaders of the twelve leading families of the Meches, Hariya Mandal, and gave birth to two sons – Visu by Hira, and Sisu by Jira. Visu grew into a very competent commander who subdued many local chiefs and potentates, and finally established the kingdom of Koch Bihar or Kamarupa in 1522. Visu accepted Hinduism, assumed a Hindu name, Bishwa Singh, and declared himself a descendant of God Shiva in disguise. The other important policy adopted by him was the detribalization of the state administration and the introduction of the labour rent assignment system. Under this system, state officers were given the right to a certain number of obligatory tasks performed by the common people. The kingdom continued to expand during the reign of the second king, Naranarayan (1540–84), who not only conquered nearly the whole of northern Bengal including Sylhet and part of Mymensingh, but also subdued other tribal kingdoms on the northeastern frontiers, such as Ahom (Assam), Manipur, Kachari, Jaintia, Garo Hills, Khasi, Tripura and Lushai.[22] He divided his extensive kingdom into Western Kamarupa (Koch Bihar) and Eastern Kamarupa (Koch Hajo), and gave the latter to the son of his deceased younger brother in 1581.

During the days of Naranarayan, the population of the kingdom consisted of two distinctive groups. People living in areas to the north of the great highway (the Gohain Kamala Road) remained strongly governed by tribal customs and manners, and tribal priests were allowed to hold religious rites, whereas to the south of the highway the influence of traditional tribal institutions among the inhabitants became weaker and Hinduization of the people advanced further. Here, the traditional tribal priests were prohibited from worshipping and, in their stead, Brahmans who were invited by the king exercised religious authority over the inhabitants. The caste system was enforced under royal patronage, and the upper strata of the tribals accepted Hinduism and assumed the title of 'Rajbangshi'. However, it should be noted that even in this part of the country Hinduization of the tribal mass was only half complete, and this in spite of the rapid spread of neo-Vaishnavism under Sankaradeva.[23]

Turning to agricultural production, it is highly likely that the old slash-and-burn type of cultivation was still widely carried out in the northern and eastern regions of the kingdom, while settled agriculture (or transplanted wet-rice cultivation with plough and draught animals) became the dominant form in the southern and western regions during the sixteenth century.[24]

Buchanan found that agricultural change was still taking place near Bijni in the district of Goalpara, located in the central part of greater Kamarupa, in the early nineteenth century. He noted that the cultivators' lands were of three types: transplanted wet-rice land, homesteads, and other fields where crops other than wet-rice were grown. The first two were assigned to the cultivators by the state and they had to pay rent for these. As for the third type, they could hold as much land as they liked. It seems that the inhabitants of this locality had started settled agriculture rather recently. They probably built permanent residences near the wet-rice lands, while carrying out shifting cultivation on the other fields. Their rent was calculated by the number of ploughs (*hal dhari*) they possessed and not according to the size of land occupied by them.[25]

Even as late as the early nineteenth century, Hinduization of the tribal mass remained incomplete. Buchanan identified three types among the Koch tribals: (i) the Gorol who refused to accept the Hindu gods, the Bengali language and plough cultivation, and clung to the tribal religion, their mother tongue and shifting agriculture; (ii) the Koch who accepted both plough cultivation and the Bengali language, but rejected Hindu gods; and (iii) the Rajbangshi who accepted plough cultivation, the Bengali language and Hindu gods. Buchanan also pointed out that the Koches and Meches in Assam, Nepal and Bhutan remained outside the reach of Hinduization.

In 1773, the kingdom of Koch Bihar (West Kamarupa) was merged with British India and became one of the princely states. A new administrative system was introduced on the advice of the British Commissioner, and the state structure underwent great changes. In 1788, reform of the revenue system was implemented, and a kind of survey and settlement operation was carried out.[26] Lands were measured and land revenue was assessed on the land held by each cultivator by applying the newly introduced regulated rates of rent. This change in the land-revenue system implies that at least in the princely state of Koch Bihar (West Kamarupa), settled cultivation by individual cultivators was already predominant. In Patgong and Boda, both belonging to the *sarkar* Koch Bihar in the district of Rangpur, which was the property of the king in his capacity as a zamindar of the English Company, Buchanan found two types of local settlements: one was the *dehabandi* where the village head (*bosneah*) and some village officers collected land revenue (imposed on the village) from the villagers; the other was the *jotedari* where the *jotedar* was responsible for the payment of land revenue of the estates (*mahal*). He also pointed out that the *jotedars* sub-let part of the estate to under-tenants, and the latter to sharecroppers (*adhiyars*). He further recorded that in many *taluqs* there were two to five *taftadars* who were appointed by the king on the recommendation of the inhabitants. The *taftadars* were influential rich peasants held responsible for the payment of land revenue of the villages under their supervision.[27] The wealthier section of the Koch peasants became *jotedars* and *taftadars*, and exercised great influence in the rural area. Thus, there existed a certain form of differentiation within the Koch community by the early nineteenth century.

Ahmuty, the Commissioner appointed in 1797, found that because of the direct collection of land revenue by state officers who were mostly outsiders (Bengalis), the cultivators were oppressed and impoverished. In order to remedy the miserable conditions of the cultivators, he proposed to introduce the farming system (*izaradari*) of land revenue. As a result, the whole kingdom was farmed out to 100 to 125 *izaradars*. These *izara-dars* included the queen, members of the royal family (*kunwars*), high officers of the state who were mostly Bengalis, and the king's spiritual guides (*gurus*). They, in their turn, sub-let their farms to under-farmers (*mustajirs, kutkina-izaradars*) and thus a process of 'sub-infeudation' started soon after, and the oppressions never ceased. Many of the resident *jotedars* were oppressed and deprived of their *jotes* by the *izaradars*, who were often high-caste Bengalis with titles such as Chaudhuri, Sanyal and Lahiri. The *izaradari* system was abolished in 1872 and government revenue was again collected from the *jotedars*. It should be noted that in this process, many of the original inhabitants gave up their *jotedari* rights to the powerful *jotedars* who had connections with the royal court, and became their sub-tenants (*chukanidars*) in consideration of the protection provided by them.[28] At the time of the abolition of *izaradari*, it was found that 54 per cent of the lands were held by foreign *jotedars*, 31 per cent by non-cultivating resident *jotedars* and 15 per cent by cultivating *jotedars*.[29]

By the latter half of the nineteenth century, Koch Bihar became a producer and exporter of highly commercialized crops like jute and tobacco. This gave an impetus to moneyed outsiders (Marwari merchants) to come and settle down in the princely state, where they started to accumulate land rights. The records of the three consecutive survey and settlement operations (in the 1870s, 1890s and 1930s) clearly show the rapid growth of a multi-tier tenure system, and the resultant enhancement of rent payable by the actual cultivators who were mostly of tribal origin.[30]

During this process of rapid transformation of land relations in the princely state of Koch Bihar in the latter half of the nineteenth century and early part of the twentieth century, while Bengali officers and foreign traders, and some of the richer sections of the original inhabitants, acquired land and became big *jotedars*, many of the tribal cultivators were relegated downwards to become subordinate cultivators, sharecroppers (*adhiyars*) and even agricultural labourers. Tribal ties and tribal norms, if any, must have broken down rapidly, and – within a few decades – the tribal society in this locality became a highly stratified peasant society.

Emergence of the Peasantry and Its Differentiation

The emergence of peasants and their differentiation may be better understood if we analyse the process in the Bengal plains and on the Bengal frontiers separately. We will discuss the impact of ecological conditions, commercialization, characteristics of the social groups and reclamation upon the growth and differentiation of the peasantry in areas of settled agriculture.

Agricultural regions

Bengal can be divided into several regions according to their ecological characteristics. The Sundarbans are dense forests along the coastline of southern Bengal, and it requires considerable capital and mobilization of a team of labourers for carrying out any reclamation project here. The term *char* refers to fertile sandbars formed in the river courses, which produce an abundant rice crop. *Char* land is typically found in eastern Bengal. *Dhoba* and *bil* are low swamplands, and produce only deep-water rice of the broadcast type. These too are typically seen in eastern Bengal. The soil types of the different regions also differ: for example, *khyar* is a highly clayey soil which produces only transplanted winter rice of high quality, and is mostly found in the Varendra region spreading over western and northwestern Bengal. The *pali* or *doangsh* is a mixture of clayey and sandy soils, which easily produces two or three crops of various kinds in a year. It is typically seen in northeastern Bengal. And *bali* is sandy soil often found at the riverside, and produces vegetables. These differences lead to the development of different types of agriculture, and, consequently, different kinds of land tenure and peasantry.

Commercialization

Equally important for the formation of particular types of land tenure and peasantry is the extent of commercialization. Extension of indigo cultivation in the first half of the nineteenth century placed many indigo cultivators under the influence of the European indigo planters who advanced large amounts of money in order to secure the supply of indigo to be used in their factories. The forcible expansion of indigo cultivation not only increased indebtedness among the cultivators, but also changed the cropping pattern.[31] A more drastic case was the rapid growth of tea plantations in northern Bengal since the 1850s, which attracted many tribal labourers from Chota Nagpur in Bihar. The immigrant labourers who were given small plots of land started agriculture for their subsistence. Thus, tea production not only promoted the clearing of forestlands for tea plantation, but also resulted in transplanting different types of people and land relations in northern Bengal.[32] As is well known, jute production had a deep and extensive impact on the peasant economy in northern and eastern Bengal since the 1870s. Many cultivators, in view of the greater profitability of jute, changed their rice-lands into jute-lands, thereby creating a demand for marketed rice among jute cultivators. Consequently, this encouraged reclamation of land for rice production outside the jute-growing areas. It is also noteworthy that extension of jute cultivation and population growth have a high positive correlation.[33] It seems that prosperous jute cultivation not only attracted labourers from outside, but also enhanced the birth rate within the regions concerned. The brisk jute trade attracted traders and moneylenders to the jute-growing areas, who advanced money to the jute cultivators in order to secure a stable supply of jute from them. These credit relations, in many cases, eventually resulted in the transfer of lands from the peasants to the moneylenders. The peasants who lost their lands were obliged to cultivate the same lands on a sharecropping basis. Thus, it was reported that the extension of jute cultivation not only attracted professional moneylenders from outside, but also brought about a rapid increase in *barga* cultivation.[34]

Regional characteristics of social groups and functions of the community

The regional characteristics of social groups and communities had an unmistakable influence on the forms of the peasantry and its differentiation.

In eastern Bengal, a high concentration of Hindu *bhadralok*, in the Bikrampur area of Faridpur district, was particularly noticeable. Population density there was as high as 475 persons per square kilometre in 1881, and the locality presented a kind of urban situation.[35] The high concentration of upper-caste Hindus seems to have been a result of land grants made to Brahmans and others by the local Hindu kings. Once the locality became renowned as a place of high-ranking Hindus, many other Brahmans were inclined to purchase small landed properties and came to reside here. As petty resident landlords they could supervise their estates much better than the non-resident bigger landlords. Under the close supervision of so many landlords, it must have been very difficult for the peasants to accumulate holdings through usual malpractices such as the possession of concealed (*chapashi*) lands, reduction of rent rates, etc. Thus, domination by the *bhadralok* is likely to have suppressed the rise and development of rich peasants. If we only look at the cultivating classes, there seems to be less differentiation among them. However, it will be misleading to call this a small peasant-dominant situation, because the cultivating class was not powerful enough to play a leading role in the locality.

Similarly, in the giant estates of the Maharaja of Bardhaman, considerable land was granted to his officers and kinsmen as *aima* lands (a kind of privileged tenure), and to the Brahmans, etc., as *brahmottar* and *debottar* lands. The holders of these petty grants seem to have had a similar effect as did the holders of religious grants in Bikrampur.

We do not have sufficient historical evidence to show the structure and internal workings of the village communities in Bengal. However, some reports testify that village festivals were held in some regions. For example, the 'Final Report of the Survey and Settlement Operations in the District of Nadia' refers to a village festival and village servants who were paid both by the zamindar and the villagers.[36] Buchanan's reports speak of the village-gods (*gramdebota*) that were seen all across the districts he traversed. The term *gramdebota* certainly suggests a popular religion rooted in a belief system at the grassroot level. A document of the 1790s shows the human composition of a colony for reclamation (*gacchibandi*). The organizer of the reclamation (*gacchidar*) rented out the tracts to many sharecroppers after the reclamation work was completed. This colony, which was situated in the forests to the northeast of Purnea district, included a set of artisans and functionaries who were paid a fixed proportion of agricultural produce by the cultivators. Thus the cultivators, the artisans and village functionaries were tightly united to form a colonizers' community. Only with the help of such division of labour, perhaps, could each cultivator carry on produc-tion in sparsely populated forest areas.[37] In the hills of Tripura district, the annual village festival was considered an essential obligation for the tribal villagers to take part in. When they shifted the sites of cultivation after an interval of a few years, as we have seen above, the allotment of land to each family was made either by the village heads or by the council of village elders.[38] These fragmentary and diverse examples suggest the importance of community in agricultural transactions and everyday life in certain areas, especially in the frontier regions.

Reclamation

In almost all the districts of Bengal, more than one-fourth of the area probably remained uncultivated towards the end of the eighteenth century. In the Sundarbans and other forest areas such as Dwar and Terai in the north, this ratio must have been much higher. In the nineteenth century, the speed of the reclamation geared up with the introduction of new commercial crops like indigo, tea and jute, and with the immigra-tion of many labourers from the tribal belts of Orissa and Bihar to the tea plantations in northern Bengal and Assam, and the dense jungles of northern, central and eastern Bengal.

Colebrooke very roughly estimated the population of Bengal at 21 to 22 million[39] at the beginning of the nineteenth century, and the first census of Bengal conducted in 1881 recorded it at about 37 million – an increase of about 15 to 16 million in 80 years. Thus, the population in 1881 was about 70 per cent greater than that at the beginning of the nineteenth century. The additional population had to be supported by an extension of the cultivated area, increase in productivity and intensification of cropping.

As the productivity and cropping intensity of Bengal's agriculture do not seem to have advanced very much until the second half of the nineteenth century, the major portion of the food supply for a 70 per cent increase in population must have come from the increase in area under cultivation.[40] This simple calculation suggests the size as well as the vital importance of reclamation for the sustenance of Bengal's economy during the first 80 years of the nineteenth century.

Thus, we cannot emphasize too strongly the importance of reclamation in the nineteenth-century economic history of Bengal. It is of vital importance for us to enquire into the kind of land system and the characteristics of the peasantry that developed in these newly reclaimed areas. The answer to these questions may be found in the processes of reclamation in the different regions. Of course, it cannot be denied that commercialization and other circumstances following the initial stage of reclamation could have greatly changed the initial structure that had emerged in the process of reclamation. Even so, the later developments could not but be affected by the preceding conditions.

On the basis of information available from various volumes of the Board of Revenue proceedings, reports of survey and settlement operations, and other foregoing researches, we shall briefly examine these aspects of the reclamation in the forests of the Sundarbans, the *char* areas in eastern Bengal, and the *gacchibandi* system of Purnea district.

The Sundarbans[41] lie at the mouth of the great rivers that form the Ganges delta, extending 265 kilometres in length (from east to west) and 130 kilometres in width (from south to north), with a total area of about 19,500 square kilometres that is equal to more than 10 per cent of Lower Bengal. When Rennell prepared his famous *Bengal Atlas* in the 1770s, the Sundarbans were covered by extensive, largely unoccupied forests without a sizeable number of inhabitants. Serious attempts at reclamation of the Sundarbans started only after the late eighteenth century. In spite of the efforts of the colonial government, the pace of reclamation was very slow and the area reclaimed remained less than 10 per cent in 1830, and 30 per cent in 1872. The development of the Sundarbans went into full swing only towards the end of the nineteenth century. The timing coincided with the rapid extension of jute cultivation, a rise in the prices of agricultural products (especially rice) and population growth. The right of reclamation was granted to the applicants either by the government or by the zamindar, as the case might be, on easy terms and conditions. Those who obtained the right were often called the *taluqdars*, more correctly the *jangalbari* or *abadkar taluqdars*. They were government officers using fictitious names, landlords, legal practitioners and traders who managed only a small portion of the permitted land, while the rest was leased out to persons called *haoladars*.[42] *Taluqdars* often provided the initial cost of reclamation to *haoladars*, who employed the labourers and cleared the forests. After constructing dykes and embankments designed to prevent salt water from entering the fields, they rented out the lands to subordinate tenants, and also provided them with the necessary seeds, implements and draught animals so that they could carry out cultivation. Sometimes the *haoladars* reclaimed only a part of their leases, and the rest was sub-leased to the ones inferior (*nim-haoladars*) who undertook exactly the same kind of reclamation but on a smaller scale. It was not rare for the *nim-haoladars* to further create a sub-tenure, called *dar-nim-haola*. In this way, a multi-layered structure of lease relations appeared on the same plot of land. The impact of reclamation of this type on the land tenure system and forms of peasantry in the Sundarbans area has been studied in detail by Sirajul Islam.[43] According to his study, which uses survey and settlement records at the village level, *haoladars* almost always settled the subordinate peasants (*korfa raiyats*) and the sharecroppers (*bargadars*). Thus, he clearly showed that reclamation by *haoladars* resulted in a stratified structure of village society, where the great majority of the peasants belonged to the subordinate class.

Similarly, statistical data given in reports of numerous survey and settlement operations that were conducted in the areas of sandbars or sandbanks (*chars* and *diaras*) in eastern Bengal also clearly show that on the reclaimed lands, almost always a kind of stratified structure of the peasantry was formed with the *haoladars* at the top. It is noteworthy that as the recorded names of the *haoladars* suggest, some of them were upper-caste Hindus or *bhadralok*, and actual cultivation was carried out by the numerous lower-caste Hindu and Muslim cultivators.[44] Therefore, it should be admitted that *haoladar* is an ambiguous term, because it could mean a wealthy peasant or an intermediate landlord who is only interested in receiving rent from subordinate cultivators without bothering about agricultural production conducted on their lands.

We may take one more example from Purnea district in the late eighteenth century. In this district, there was a tenure called *gacchibandi*. The zamindar gave this tenure to a person who proposed to organize reclamation of forestlands, and in such areas we find a handful of wealthy colonizers called *gacchidar* and many poor sharecroppers (*adhia raiyats* or *adhiadars*).[45] This is quite similar in nature to the well-known case of reclamation organized by rich peasants in the northern districts, as reported by Buchanan, and also by *haoladars* in the Sundarbans.

Thus, large-scale reclamations on Bengal's frontiers to the north as well as to the south almost invariably gave birth to a small number of intermediary landlords and rich peasants, and a multitude of subordinate peasants. It is true that small-scale reclamations undertaken by ordinary peasants around their own settled villages, which we may call everyday reclamation, should not be overlooked. However, we are inclined to think that the constraints imposed by the general shortage of agricultural stocks among ordinary peasants put serious limitation on this type of mini-reclamations by them.

The Logic of Peasant Differentiation: Theoretical Considerations

The emergence of peasants in Bengal produced various regional patterns, and recent researches on ancient and early medieval Bengal tell us that a stratified structure developed among the peasants at an early stage. The process and mechanism of peasant differentiation greatly differed according to the regional conditions – ecological, social and political. A theoretical attempt at identifying some of the important logics of peasant differentiation is made below.

It should be clearly understood that peasant differentiation and the formation of a multi-layered land system (sub-infeudation in official jargon) are different. We are concerned here only with the former process.

From 'Jhum' Cultivation to Settled Agriculture

Jhum cultivation required tribal or communal ownership of certain tracts of land within which shifting of fields took place at an interval of a few years. Partial introduction of settled agriculture strengthened the claims of particular families on the fields where settled agriculture was carried out. For some time, the two different modes of agriculture would go side by side. Gradually, however, settled agriculture would extend and supersede *jhum* cultivation, because of its obvious superiority in stability and productivity. This transition meant the break-up of tribal or communal landownership, following which individual ownership of land became the norm. As long as communal ownership was still dominant, the internal inequality among *jhum* cultivators with respect to the size of landholdings was, to some extent, checked by the tribal customary laws. However, after the division of the tribal territory into individual holdings, differentiation among the tribal cultivators began and a highly stratified peasantry emerged in a short time. Such changes started early. For example, in the Koch Bihar kingdom, the process probably began in the fifteenth and sixteenth centuries, and continued even up to the first half of the twentieth century. The break-up of the more or less homogeneous landholding structure into a highly stratified one was pushed ahead by the imposition of the principle of individual landholding by the state, by ordinary processes of growing indebtedness, by the intrusion of outside traders into the tribal regions, and by the establishment of land markets.

Reclamation: The First Clearer's Right

After the formation of the state, which generally recognized the rights of the first clearers, they virtually became landlords of the tracts reclaimed by them and other cultivators became their tenants. Thus, where reclamation took place with the sanction of the state authority, the organizer's right to the cleared lands was protected by a state mechanism and a landlord–tenant relationship that developed within it.

Peasant Differentiation in the Second Half of the Eighteenth Century: Political in Nature

Generally, peasant differentiation is supposed to occur through the sale of land or usufruct by poor peasants. This standard mechanism works only when land or its usufruct is a transferable property of the peasant or, in other words, there is a land market for the peasant. However, in late eighteenth century Bengal, the zamindar's control over his estate was so strong that peasants were not allowed to sell the landholdings or usufruct of lands held by them. In fact, the burden of rent payment was so heavy that it was meaningless for a common peasant to hold more land than he could cultivate with the help of family labour. Therefore, he usually returned the surplus land to the zamindar. It was not land, but the crop or cattle or plough or any other movable property such as silver ring, etc., that were distrained or sold when the *raiyats* could not pay rent to the zamindars or repay loans to the creditors. The land market that existed was for the sale of right to rent from landed property, such as zamindari, *taluqdari, lakhiraj, inam, bazi zamin, debottar, brahmottar*, etc.

However, in spite of the absence of a land market for the peasant, the rich peasants accumulated lands through various means, as a result of which differentiation within the peasantry did take place. The richer peasants, taking advantage of the political confusion, began to organize subordinate labourers for the cultivation of surplus lands amassed by them through various means. (1) The rich peasants often provided their needy neighbours with loans in kind or money. When the borrowers failed to repay the debts, the rich peasants forced them to return the lands held by them to the zamindars, or to abandon the cultivation of land for a few years. The zamindars were then obliged to rent out the returned or abandoned lands to the rich peasants on easier terms. In this way, the rich peasants owned a larger area of land than they could cultivate themselves, and had it cultivated by needy cultivators as their subordinate *raiyats* (*korfa*) or as sharecroppers (*adhiyars, bhagdars, bargadars*). (2) Some of the richer peasants secretly cultivated the fallow-lands or arable wastelands without obtaining permission from the zamindars. These lands then became their 'concealed lands', and they had them cultivated by subordinate labourers or subordinate *raiyats*. (3) Rich peasants were often appointed as village heads (*mandals, pramanikhs, giris, bosneahs, pradhans*, etc.) by zamindars. When the zamindar adopted the village farming system as the method of local rent-settlement (*mofassal* settlement), it was the village heads who were authorized to allot to the respective villagers, the village rent required of them. The village heads assigned smaller sums than they should bear on their own lands, and, in order to make up for the deficiencies thus created, demanded greatly inflated rents from the ordinary peasants. This was camouflaged by creating a complicated list of rent-rates (*nirkh*), and resulted in surprisingly unequal rent-rates within the same locality.[46]

Such manoeuvres by the rich peasants were possible because the zamindars were already greatly weakened by the time the British East India Company acquired the provincial government of Bengal – first, by the extortions of the Mughal provincial ruler, especially Nawab Mir Qasim, who desperately needed money to wage war against the British Company; and secondly, by the new colonial government's demand for higher land revenue. Under these heavy political and economic pressures, the control of the estate by the zamindars was in disarray and they could no longer maintain the regular method of rent settlement with measurement of the lands held by the respective cultivators.

Thus the rich peasants, by exploiting political confusions, extended their landholdings at the cost of the poorer peasants. This was the mechanism of peasant differentiation of a political type that operated in the late eighteenth century.

Peasant Differentiation in the Second Half of the Nineteenth Century: Economic Type

The absence of a peasant land market as explained above continued until the second half of the nineteenth century, though the weakened local control by zamindars was greatly amended by legal and administrative support, including the rent court and police support, provided by the colonial government.

The secular rise of agricultural prices – beginning from the mid-1850s, the enactment of the Rent Act of 1859, the jute boom and the agrarian disturbance in eastern Bengal in the 1870s, the enactment of the Bengal Tenancy Act of 1885, and the remarkable population growth in the

eastern divisions of Dhaka and Chittagong since the 1880s – contributed
to the emergence and growth of the peasant land market.

   After the formation of the peasant land market, even though the
zamindar's right to receive the transfer fee persisted, the mechanism of
peasant differentiation shifted from the political type to a market-mediated
one. As we already have well-documented studies on this type of peasant
differentiation, we need not go into any further details.[47]

Conclusion

   In this essay I have sought to clarify the historical processes of
the emergence of peasants and their differentiation in Bengal. While we
were obliged to fill up the gap by theoretical exercises wherever the paucity of historical records prevents us from taking an empirical approach,
the present exercise raises important issues, some of which had hitherto
remained unasked. Let us now briefly recapitulate some of the major
findings of this essay.

   First, the emergence of the peasant requires certain preconditions,
including freedom from communal landownership of the tribe or clan, the
advancement of productive technology such as wet-rice cultivation with
plough, a protecting body such as the state, and an exchange system such
as the market and a money economy.

   Secondly, differentiation among the peasantry can occur even in
the absence of a land market for peasants, through political processes.
Differentiation has often been accelerated by the intrusion of outsiders
such as European tea planters and Indian traders from the plains, by
the development of commercial agriculture such as jute, as the result of
indebtedness, and by state intervention as we have seen in the case of the
princely state of Koch Bihar.

   Thirdly, there was roughly a 70 per cent increase in population
across entire Lower Bengal for 80 years, since the beginning of the nineteenth century. The food for this additional population was mainly supplied by the extension of cropped areas through reclamation. Wherever
large-scale reclamation took place, it was promoted by similar mechanisms,
that almost universally produced a group of privileged peasants who were
descended from the first clearers, such as the *gacchidar*, *jotedar*, *haoladar*,
grantidar, etc. Thus, the very process of reclamation gave birth to a group
of rich peasants. It is also worth noting that the so-called *bhadralok* often
obtained the right of reclamation from higher authorities at various levels.

   Lastly, the findings of the present essay show that there was a group
of peasants who held large landholdings, cultivation of which could not be

done by family labour alone. In some localities we also found the existence of other privileged groups who held different sizes of landed properties or intermediated tenures. They usually belonged to high-ranking Hindu castes or were elite Muslims who did not cultivate their land themselves, but rented them out to subordinate peasants or sharecroppers. Both these groups occupied privileged positions in rural Bengal, and exercised a considerable influence in the rural society and economy.

Notes and References

1 Kalyan Kumar Sen Gupta, *Pabna Disturbances and the Politics of Rent 1873–1885*, New Delhi: People's Publishing House, 1974; Ratnalekha Ray, *Change in Bengal Agrarian Society*, Delhi: Manohar, 1979; Rajat Kanta Ray, 'The Retreat of the Jotedars?' *The Indian Economic and Social History Review*, Vol. XXV No. 2, 1988; Shinkichi Taniguchi, 'Structure of Agrarian Society in Northern Bengal (1765 to 1800)', unpublished Ph.D. dissertation, 1977; Shinkichi Taniguchi, 'The Peasantry of Northern Bengal in the Late Eighteenth Century', in P. Robb, K. Sugihara and H. Yanagisawa, eds, *Local Agrarian Societies in Colonial India: Japanese Perspectives*, London: Curzon Press, 1996; Partha Chatterjee, 'Agrarian Structure in Pre-partition Bengal', in *Perspectives in Social Sciences 2: Three Studies on the Agrarian Structure in Bengal, 1850–1947*, Delhi: Oxford University Press, 1982; Sugata Bose, *Agrarian Bengal: Economy, Social Structure and Politics, 1919–1947*, Cambridge: Cambridge University Press, 1986; Rajat Datta, *Society, Economy and the Market: Commercialization in Rural Bengal, c. 1760–1800*, Delhi: Manohar, 2000; B.B. Chaudhuri, *Peasant History of Late Pre-Colonial and Colonial India*, Project of History of Indian Science, Philosophy and Culture (PHISPC) (General Editor: D.P. Chattopadhyaya), Vol. VIII, Part 2, New Delhi: Pearson Education India, 2008.

2 For the elusiveness of the concept of *raiyat*, see Sirajul Islam, *Bengal Land Tenure*, Calcutta: K.P. Bagchi, 1988, pp. 94–96, and B.B. Chaudhuri, *Peasant History of Late Pre-Colonial and Colonial India*, chapter 2.

3 Taniguchi, 'Structure of Agrarian Society in Northern Bengal'; Taniguchi, 'The Peasantry of Northern Bengal in the Late Eighteenth Century', in Robb, Sugihara and Yanagisawa, eds, *Local Agrarian Societies in Colonial India*.

4 Nariaki Nakazato, 'Superior Peasants of Central Bengal and Their Land Management in the Late Nineteenth Century', *Journal of the Japanese Association for South Asian Studies*, No. 2, 1990, pp. 96–127.

5 Shinkichi Taniguchi, 'Regional Structure of Bengal Agrarian Societies in the Late Nineteenth Century', in Shinkichi Taniguchi, ed., *Development and Culture in Asia: Comparative Study on Grassroots Solidarity among Peoples in Asian Countries*, Japan: Hitotsubashi University, 2000, pp. 26–61.

6 Sirajul Islam, *Bengal Land Tenure*.

7 Shinkichi Taniguchi, 'Regional Structure of Bengal Agrarian Society during Colonial Rule,' I, II, III–1 and III–2, *Hitotsubashidaigaku-kenkyunenpou Keizaigakukenkyu* (Japanese), 44–47, 2002–05.

8 B.D. Chattopadhyaya, 'State and Economy in North India: Fourth Century to Twelfth Century', in Romila Thapar, ed., *Recent Perspectives of Early Indian History*, Bombay: Popular Prakashan, 1995, pp. 309–46; T. Yamazaki, 'Some Aspects of Land-Sale Inscriptions in Fifth and Sixth Century Bengal', *Acta Asiatica*, No. 43, Tokyo, pp.17–36.

[9] Ryosuke Furui, 'Local Society and State Control as seen in the Copper-Plate Inscriptions of Bengal: 5th to 7th Century' (in Japanese), *The Toyo Gakuho*, 82–4, March 2001, pp. 31–57.

[10] Translated from the original Persian by Francis Gladwin, *A Narrative of the Transactions in Bengal During the Soobahdaries of Azeem-Us-Shan, Jaffar Khan, Shuja Khan, Sirafraz Khan and Allyvardy Khan*, Calcutta: Stuart & Cooper, 1788, reprint 1906, pp. 26–27.

[11] Taniguchi, 'Structure of Agrarian Society in Northern Bengal', chapter 1.

[12] The census of 1872 broadly classified the population into the Hindus, the Semi-Hinduized, the Tribals and the Muslims. We define non-Muslims as the total of the Hindus, the Semi-Hinduized and the Tribals.

[13] W.W. Hunter, *The Annals of Rural Bengal*, London: Smith Elder and Co., 1868, reprint, Calcutta: Indian Studies Past and Present, 1965; Abhaya Pada Mallik, *History of Bishnupur Raj*, Calcutta, 1921; Prabhat Kumar Saha, *Some Aspects of Malla Rule in Bishnupur (1590–1806 AD)*, Calcutta: Ratnabali, 1995; Gouripada Chatterjee, *History of Bagree Rajya (Garhbeta)*, Delhi: Mittal, second and enlarged edition, 1986, p. vii.

[14] E.A. Gait, *History of Assam*, Calcutta: Thacker Spink and Co., 1905, third edition, 1963; D. Nath, *History of the Koch Kingdom (c. 1515–1615)*, Delhi: Mittal, 1989; Rai K.L. Barua Bahadur, *Early History of Kamarupa*, Shillong, 1933, second edition, 1966; S. Rajguru, *Medieval Assamese Society, 1228–1826*, Nagaon: Asami, 1988; Amalendu Guha, *Medieval and Early Colonial Assam*, Calcutta: K. P. Bagchi, 1991.

[15] S.N. Mishra, ed., *Antiquity to Modernity in Tribal India*, Vol. III: *Ownership and Control of Resources among Indian Tribes*, New Delhi: Inter-India Publications, 1998; Law Research Institute, Eastern Region, Gauhati High Court, Gauhati, *A Study of the Land System of Tripura*, 1990; Nalini Ranjan Roychoudhury, *Tripura through the Ages*, Agartala: Bureau of Research & Publilications on Tripura, 1977; J.B. Bhattacharjee, ed., *Studies in the Economic History of North East India*, New Delhi: Har-Anand, 1994; J.B. Ganguly, *Economic Problems of the Jhumias of Tripura*, Calcutta: Bookland, 1968; Law Research Institute, Eastern Region, Gauhati High Court, Gauhati, *A Study of the Land System of Manipur*, 1990; Law Research Institute, Eastern Region, Gauhati High Court, Guwahati, *A Study of the Land System of Mizoram*, 1990; B.B. Dutta and M.N. Karma, eds, *Land Relations in North East India*, New Delhi: People's Publishing House, 1987; Ajay Pratap, *The Hoe and the Axe*, Delhi: Oxford University Press, 2000.

[16] Sekhar Bandyopadhyay, *Caste, Politics and the Raj: Bengal 1872–1937*, Calcutta: K.P. Bagchi, 1990.

[17] N.K. Bose, *The Structure of Hindu Society*, Delhi: Orient Longman, 1975; K.S. Singh, *Tribal Society in India*, Delhi: Manohar, 1988; Dev Nathan, ed., *From Tribe to Caste*, Shimla: Indian Institute of Advanced Study, 1997; Surajit Sinha, *Tribal Polities and State Systems in Pre-Colonial Eastern and North Eastern India*, Calcutta: K.P. Bagchi, 1987; B.B. Chaudhuri and Arun Bandhopadhyay, eds, *Tribes, Forest and Social Formation in Indian History*, Delhi: Manohar, 2004; L.S. Gassah, *Garo Hills: Land and People*, Gauhati: Omsons Publications, 1984.

[18] Amalendu Guha, *Medieval and Early Colonial Assam*, chapter 4.

[19] For example, in Tripura there were several distinctive tribes carrying on shifting cultivation, but the method of land allotment after new clearance of the forests differed from tribe to tribe. Cf. endnote 14.

[20] B.B. Chaudhuri, *Peasant History of Late Pre-Colonial and Colonial India*, chapter 10.

[21] J.B. Ganguly, *Economic Problems of the Jhumias of Tripura*, pp. 25–27.

[22] As shown in a map in Harendra Narayan Chaudhuri, *The Cooch Behar State and Its Land Revenue Settlements*, Cooch Behar, 1903.

[23] S. Rajguru, *Medieval Assamese Society*; M. Neogi, *Early History of the Vaishnava Faith and Movement in Assam: Sankaradeva and His Times*, reprint, Delhi: Indian Bibliographical Bureau, 1980.

[24] See also Amalendu Guha, *Medieval and Early Colonial Assam*, chapter 4.

[25] Francis Buchanan, *Rongpur*, Section 3 of Chapter 7, Book 4 (Agriculture).

[26] Ibid., p. 219.

[27] Ibid., pp. 213–15.

[28] Report by Beckett, *Proceedings of the Revenue Department*, July 1872, No. 210. The process of returning (*istafa*) the land was called *laganee*.

[29] For more detail, see Shinkichi Taniguchi, 'A Perspective into the Changing Agrarian Structure in the Koch Behar Princely State during the 19th Century', in P.K. Bhattacharya, ed., *The Kingdom of Kamata–Koch Behar in Historical Perspective*, Calcutta: Ratna Prakashan, 2000, pp. 179–82.

[30] Ibid., pp. 182–85.

[31] Benoy Chowdhury, *Growth of Commercial Agriculture in Bengal (1757–1900)*, Vol. 1, Calcutta: Indian Studies Past and Present, 1964; Blair B. Kling, *The Blue Mutiny*, Calcutta: Firma K.L. Mukhopadhyay, 1966, reprint 1977.

[32] B.B. Chaudhuri, *Peasant History of Late Pre-Colonial and Colonial India*, pp. 407–08 and 612–15; S. Karotemprel and B. Dutta Roy, eds, *Tea Garden Labourers of North East India*, Shillong: Vendrame Institute, 1990.

[33] Shinkichi Taniguchi, 'Regional Structure of Bengal Agrarian Society during Colonial Rule', II, pp. 20–21.

[34] Shinkichi Taniguchi, 'Regional Structure of Bengal Agrarian Society during Colonial Rule', III–2, pp. 123–24.

[35] Shinkichi Taniguchi, 'Regional Structure of Bengal Agrarian Society during Colonial Rule', III–1, p. 64; Frank Perlin, 'Proto-industrialization and Precolonial South Asia', *Past and Present*, No. 98, 1983, p. 78.

[36] 'Final Report on the Survey and Settlement Operations in the District of Nadia', printed in *The Board of Revenue Proceedings*, P/11800, Nos. 28–33, IOR, August 1929, chapter III; P.M. Robertson, *Final Report on the Survey and Settlement of the Sonthali Villages of Rampurhat and several other Villages in the Rampurhat and Suri subdivisions of the District of Birbhum, 1909 to 1914*, Calcutta, 1915, Part I.

[37] See endnote 42.

[38] J.B. Ganguly, *Economic Problems of the Jhumias of Tripura*.

[39] Henry Thomas Colebrooke, *Remarks on the Husbandry and Internal Commerce of Bengal*, Calcutta, 1804, reprint 1884, pp. 9–11.

[40] No sizeable volume of rice was imported during these 80 years.

[41] On the Sundarbans we have a good number of publications: W.W. Hunter, *A Statistical Account of Bengal*, London: Trubner and Co., Vol. 1, 1875; F.D. Ascoli, *A Revenue History of the Sundarbans from 1870 to 1920*, Calcutta: Bengal Secretariat Book Depot, 1921; F.E. Pargiter, *A Revenue History of the Sundarbans from 1765 to 1870*, Calcutta: Bengal Government Press, 1934; A.K. Mandal and R.K. Ghosh, *Sundarban: A Socio Bio-Ecological Study*, Calcutta: Bookland, 1989.

[42] Sirajul Islam, *Bengal Land Tenure*, pp. 57–59. *Haoladars* were of various types.

Some of them were intermediate tenure-holders, while others might be called rich peasants. This ambiguity poses serious problems in our interpretation of the agrarian structure. Cf. *Proceedings of the Government of Bengal, Revenue Department, Branch-Land Revenue*, August 1899, Nos. 99–100, pp. 677–723. (Final report on Survey and Settlement Operations by Babu Bhupendra Nath Gupta in the Government Estates of Char Badu and Lakhi in the district of Noakhali).

[43] Sirajul Islam, *Bengal Land Tenure.*

[44] *Final Report on the Survey and Settlement Operations in the Riparian Areas of District of Pabna, surveyed in the Course of the Faridpur District Settlement* by B.C. Prance, Late Settlement Officer of Faridpur, 1916; *Final Report on the Diara Operations in the Bakarganj District, 1910–1915,* by Rai Sahib Hara Kishor Biswas, Diara Deputy Collector, Bakarganj, 1916; *Final Report on the Settlement of the Estates Basudeb Roy and Kali Sankar Sen borne on the Revenue-rolls of Backergunge, Dacca and Faridpur 1894–95 to 1900–01* by P.M. Basu, Settlement Officer, Calcutta, 1904; *Survey and Settlement of the Dakhin Shahbazpur Estates in the District of Backergunge, 1889–1895* by P.M. Basu, Settlement Officer, Calcutta:1896.

[45] Shinkichi Taniguchi, 'Structure of Agrarian Society in Northern Bengal (1765 to 1800)', pp. 302–04.

[46] This paragraph is based on ibid.

[47] Karunamoy Mukerji, *The Problems of Land Transfer,* Santiniketan: Visva-Bharati University, 1957; B.B. Chaudhuri, 'The Process of Depeasantization in Bengal and Bihar, 1850–1900', *Indian Historical Review,* 1975; Nariaki Nakazato, 'Regional patterns of land transfer in late colonial Bengal', in Robb, Sugihara and Yanagisawa, eds, *Local Agrarian Societies in Colonial India,* pp. 250–79.

Frontiers of Agrarian Bengal

Sylhet in the 1780s

David Ludden

The Mughals appear to have created the first state authority in Sylhet, when their troops sailed there in 1612, conquered the local Afghans[1] and established Mubariz Khan as Faujdar.[2] But Sylhet remained a remote frontier outpost until Murshid Quli Khan began his career as Nawab (1713–27).[3] In sixty years, after 1658, the Mughals had granted 3,000 acres of forest tax-free to local supporters in Sylhet; and in forty years, after 1719, the Nawabs granted more than ten times that acreage. Almost all forest acres (96 per cent) granted tax-free under Mughal authority in Sarkar Sylhet appear in Nawabi *sanad*s dated after 1719, and (59 per cent) after 1748. Forests given out for extending permanent cultivation – on *Madad-i-Maash* tax-free tenures – represent 59 per cent of all grant acres in Mughal *sanad*s, and most of these acres (68 per cent) appear in Nawabi *sanad*s dated after 1748.[4] Later Nawabs sponsored agricultural expansion in Sylhet by patronizing Muslim investors who would have been the regime's most vital local supporters and also who received the largest grants of tax-free forest. After 1719, 98 per cent of *Madad-i-Maash* forest acres went in big parcels to Muslims; the cumulative Hindu percentage of *Madad-i-Maash* acres granted under Mughal authority declined from 40 per cent in 1719 to 5 per cent in 1759. Brahmans and Hindu temples continued to receive grants, but Muslims who invested in the conversion of forest to farmland received proportionately larger grant subsidies over time. In this context, more new, influential Muslim investors would have settled in Sylhet, setting in motion the gradual increase in the Muslim proportion of the population as may be seen in census returns after 1808.[5]

A Bengal Frontier

Gangetic imperial territorialism moved into Sylhet very slowly and late compared to western parts of northern Bengal.[6] Sylhet's vast inundation is the reason. The Surma and Kushiara are but the biggest of many rivers descending through mountain jungles north and east, in one of the world's highest rainfall regions.[7] Until the Brahmaputra shifted course in 1787, it crossed Mymensingh and emptied into the Meghna at Bhairav Bazar,[8] from which point north a vast freshwater sea covered the land for half of every year.[9] This inland sea deterred settlers from the west, who arrived more frequently after the Afghan conquests of Sena rajas in the thirteenth century. From Mughal times, an accelerating expansion of permanent farming eliminated more and more jungle, and drove more and more shifting '*jhum*' forest cultivators out of the lowlands.[10]

Bengali societies evolved on these moving frontiers, in landscapes inhabited by many non-Bengali peoples in highlands and lowlands, who hunted, farmed and fished without settling down permanently.[11] These mobile people lived in jungle habitats. Their cultural and social practices, including matrilineal kinship, marked them out as primitive aliens for Hindus and Muslims alike; also eventually for Europeans who likewise invested their energies to build territories of permanent cultivation, urbanism; state revenue and state authority. Mughal land grants represent state patronage for local supporters who thus acquired the power to turn forests into farmland and to subdue or expel jungle people.[12]

Sylhet was a farming frontier on river highways up to highlands held by Khasias, Garos, Ahoms, Dimasas, Boros and others,[13] who resisted state incorporation even more than Bengali frontier farmers in the lowlands. In Company correspondence, phrases like 'Sylhet is a frontier province inhabited by a turbulent and disaffected set of people'[14] became standard. In 1779, one land dispute in Sylhet district brought 600 armed local men against Company sepoys, who were 'immediately cut down and shot' before attackers fled into the forest.[15] The highland rulers took over adjacent lowlands. Khasias held most of the land north of the Surma and ruled all the mountains above.[16] Jaintia Khasia rajas held land to the north and east of Sylhet town. Cachar rajas held the Lower Barak Valley. Tripura rajas ruled southern uplands and adjacent plains. North of the Surma, northwest of Sylhet town, ethnic communities of frontier settlers, called Bengali Khasias, had arisen from alliances between mountain Khasias and lowland Bengalis; they had once respected Mughals and Nawabs inside the *jaghir* of Omaid Reza, but they rejected Company Raj.[17]

In the 1780s, Sylhet remained a poor imperial territory. In 1783, the Dinajpur Raja spent more on religious events than Sylhet district paid revenue.[18] In 1785, the Rajshahi Raja's monthly tax (*kist*)[19] exceeded Sylhet's annual tax assessment (*jamma*).[20] Yet the Company increased Sylhet revenue as much as possible, pressing land rights on locals in return for *kists*. The last Nawab collected 3,50,000 *kahans* of *cowries*, all spent locally, mostly on the army. In 1776, Collector Holland more than doubled

Sylhet demand to 8,00,101 *kahans*, and in 1783, the revenue contractor (*waddadar*), raised it again to 9,36,000 *kahans*.[21] Sylhet demand thus tripled in eight years after 1775, a larger increase than in Bengal as a whole.[22] Collections stagnated below 70 per cent of demand until 1788, when they began a steep climb, reaching almost 100 per cent by 1790.[23] In 1785, remittances to Calcutta showed a similar trend. By 1790 – with the addition of the Turruff region around Habiganj,[24] previously in Dacca district – Sylhet began to look like a moneymaker for the Raj, though still a small one compared to other Bengal districts. By 1794, net collections of 8,36,900 *kahans*, available for remittance to Calcutta, surpassed the 1776 Sylhet *jamma*.[25]

The 1780s thus became the decade of Sylhet's incorporation into British Bengal. But this was not easy. Even as more local farmers bought Company land rights, remitting Sylhet revenue posed a difficult problem. For there were no metal coins in Sylhet, no rich merchants or big bankers,[26] and no European Company investments; bills of exchange (*hundi*) were so rare that money moved almost entirely in cash.[27] Nevertheless, local markets thrived. In 1790, Sylhet had over 600 named marketplaces (*haat, ganj* and *bazaar*).[28] Sylhet town included, all markets were small, filled with small transactions.[29] Long-distance commodities, also chains, moved through them, up and down the Meghna, to and from Dhaka, Narayanganj and Bakarganj, and up and down the Barak valley to and from Manipur, Assam and Burma.

In the highlands and lowlands that formed the combined basin of the Barak, Surma and Kushiara rivers, market supply and demand were met in countless transactions among people who lived in economically differentiated localities, where markets received little input from major urban centres.[30] Rice and fish were the only important commodities produced in the lowlands where farms grew almost nothing but rice. The major crop was *boro* rice, planted on flooded lowlands when fields dried out enough to plant, from November to January, and harvested before heavy floods began in April–June. On higher ground, farmers planted *shail* (*aman*) rice under the monsoon rains to harvest from November to January.[31] Lindsay describes the harvest of fish:

> . . . in the months of October and November, when the waters subside, a trade to a great extent carried on the article of fish, which employs many thousands of the inhabitants, and certainly has the effect of drawing more *cowries* into the country than all the other branches of commerce united.[32]

Fish and rice dominated lowland diets; homestead gardens and horticulture at the hem of the hills also produced fruits, vegetables and betel-nut. Lowland rice markets rested on the flood-induced uncertainty of local output. Predictable crop failures sustained rice markets in farming localities, where specialists in fishing, horticulture, hunting, trade, transportation, crafts, finance and administration, all bought rice. As a result, the lowlands fostered a thriving cash economy, whereas the Mughals had received taxation only in cash.[33]

The Sylhet lowlands were part of a commercial geography spanning sites of natural resource utilization, diversified along a topographical continuum running into high mountain forests where shifting *jhum* cultivation prevailed. Lindsay was particularly enthusiastic about the commercial value of the uplands, 'producing sugar, cotton, and other valuable crops . . . wood of various kinds, adapted to boat and ship building, and also iron of a very superior quality . . . silks of coarse quality, called *moongadutties* . . . brought from the frontiers of China, for the Malay trade; and considerable quantities of copper in bars'. He described the hills as 'inexhaustible source of the finest lime, and lower down the river there is abundance of fuel for burning it. . . . The country under the mountains, where the ground undulates, but is not precipitous, furnishes elephants of the best description.'[34] People working everywhere in this diverse topography supplied goods to the markets. Khasias farmed *jhum* on high slopes and grew rice to sell in Lower Jaintia. In high valleys and on low slopes, Khasias grew areca-nut, betel vines and turmeric to sell in the plains, along with honey, wax, gum, ivory, medicinal plants, cloth, 'and, in the fruit season, an inexhaustible quantity of the finest oranges, found growing spontaneously in the mountains'.[35] Mountain Khasias specialized in iron mining and smelting. They would denude whole forest tracts to stoke their cowhide blow-bag iron furnaces before moving on to exploit new fuelwood sites. Khasia iron, steel and metal tools travelled river routes, along with their gold, silver, other metals and ornaments.[36] Khasia merchants carried commodities up and down hills and plains.[37] Elephants, wax, iron, cloth and ivory traveled downhill, as salt[38] and rice moved up the mountains.[39] Lindsay reported that 'at least five hundred elephants were caught annually' in the years he lived in Sylhet.[40] His successor, John Willes, did a brisk business in elephant tusks, and in four years before 1792, bought 480 tusks in Cachar, though they were also available in Jaintia and Pandua.[41] Aloe wood and China-root appear as Sylhet products in the *Ain-i-Akbari*.[42] Timber, sandalwood, cane, ivory, rubber, cotton and silk came from Cachar and Manipur.[43] Cotton came from Tripura.[44]

Cowrie Country

The mountains behind Sunamganj held the finest limestone, and this became a preoccupation for Lindsay in his business ventures. In 1783, he dramatized the commercial value of these mountains by buying off loads of limestone, burnt lime and other mountain products; loading them on six seagoing ships built with forest timber from the mountains; and then sailing the ships on the rising flood down the mountain stream to the Meghna and to Bakarganj, where his agents sold the forest products and bought rice to sell in Madras.[45] His motive was to earn rupees, not only to become rich himself, but also to pay the Sylhet revenue. For Sylhet had no metal coins.

Each region of Bengal had its own distinctive 'money' supply, according to the regional geographies of commodity exchange. Most coins in Rangpur were rupees from Pondichery and Cooch Behar, because Rangpur did heavy trade with Chandernagore and Cooch Behar. English Arcot rupees prevailed in Mymensingh, where merchants sold loads of rice in Calcutta. Specific coins were also attached to individual commodities, as in Dinajpur, where merchants used *sonaut* rupees to buy rice and other grains, but used French and English Arcots to buy ghee and oil, and used only French Arcots to buy hemp and gunny. Locally dominant metal coins in most of Bengal were minted quite far away, mostly in Arcot and Pondichery.[46] Only Sylhet commerce depended entirely on *cowries*, except in the southwestern region of Turruff, around Habiganj.[47] The tiny *cowrie* shells came from the Maldives.[48] They served as the cheapest coin all around the Indian Ocean, Southeast Asia and Africa, and were the first article of British export from the Maldives to India.[49] In the world of *cowrie* trading Bengal was a famous market, but only Sylhet in Bengal had virtually no coin but *cowries*.[50] Gold *mohurs* and silver rupees appeared in ritual offerings. Sylhet people imported almost nothing from downstream except *cowries*, which merchants brought from the Maldives to Chittagong and Calcutta, stored in Dhaka, and carried to Sylhet in boats that returned downstream with rice, fish and such upland products.[51]

The Mughals and Nawabs spent all the Sylhet cash revenue locally. Lindsay faced a new problem: *cowries* needed converting into *sicca* rupees in order to serve the Company. Lindsay had to explain why 'the revenues of the country over which I presided . . . essentially differ from every other part of India'.[52] He believed the Mughals had ruled Sylhet like other regions, so he assumed that standard coins of Bengal would have naturally circulated in Sylhet, if not for local obstacles. He thus concluded that *cowries* reigned in Sylhet because local people could not afford any other coin. The same poverty that explained the *cowrie*'s importance for poor people elsewhere seemed to explain its dominance in Sylhet.[53] However, another explanation seems more appropriate. No ruler had had the means or the need to establish his coin in Sylhet, except for rituals. States never played any significant role in the widespread and thoroughly indigenous pre-modern commercialization of *cowrie* country, which did not include sufficient imports from downstream markets to bring in metal coins. Indeed, copper from the mountains around Sylhet travelled downstream to become coins that did not return to Sylhet. *Cowries* had served Sylhet's commercialization quite well by articulating an indigenous monetary space that did not depend on any state mint, money supply, symbolic authority or transactional hierarchy, all of which entered *cowrie* country only in Habiganj, on the borders of Comilla and Tripura, the area most accessible from the Meghna, where silver rupees did circulate. The geographical extent of *cowrie* country thus coincided with the spatial dispersion of markets connecting uplands and lowlands around the Sylhet basin. The repeated depiction of Sylhet as a 'mountain region' from the fourteenth century onward[54] reinforces the idea that mountains and plains around Sylhet together comprised a diverse yet coherent regional economy, whose *cowrie* coins remained in circulation for many decades after Company coins became prominent in the nineteenth century.[55]

    Lindsay sought to solve the problem of turning Sylhet *cowries* into Company rupees without exporting *cowries* downstream by taking the entire Sylhet district's *cowrie* revenue into his own hands, to finance his own private business ventures.[56] He specialized in limestone trade and in building riverboats armed with swivel-guns, which carried his own goods as well as Company cash, goods, mail, soldiers and officials. By 1781, Lindsay 'had a speculation in hand of very considerable magnitude' and his British agents were selling his cargoes in Calcutta, while 'fleets of boats now covered the rivers and the trade increased so rapidly as to keep five or six hundred men in constant employ'.[57] To generate Sylhet's rupee revenue, Lindsay and his partners also bought Company *cowries* in Sylhet and Dhaka,[58] used them for downstream trades, and delivered drafts payable in rupees to the Company treasury in Calcutta.[59]

    By 1784, Lindsay was rich. He also claimed to have single-handedly ended the 'vast exportation of *cowries*' that attended the Company's rising revenue demand in Sylhet.[60] Lindsay, however, exaggerated the impact of his commercial adventures. He did not actually stop *cowrie* exports. *Cowries* may have left Sylhet in less massive quantities after 1783, but exports remained large and unrequited. *Cowries* still piled up in Calcutta and Dhaka markets, depressing prices and raising the cost of conversion.[61] In the years after 1783 the rupee value of Sylhet *cowries* declined by 25 per cent,[62] which induced more *cowrie* exporters to seek better prices in Dhaka. In 1788 and 1791, Collector Willes again decried the negative impact of *cowrie* exports that attended increasing revenue remittances to Calcutta. As average annual revenue collections almost doubled – from about 6 lakh *kahans* in 1785–88 to nearly 12 lakhs in 1789–92; *cowrie* remittances more than doubled, from 3 lakh *kahans* in 1785–88 to 7.5, in 1789–92.[63] Willes repeated the old refrain that Sylhet did not generate sufficient downstream commerce to bring *cowries* back into the *cowrie* country.[64] Thus, in 1790, the Sylhet basin remained a substantially enclosed economy within the ambit of Bengal Presidency, and its land revenues comprised its most voluminous downstream exports, extracted by the force of state power from its lowland farming villages.

Seasonality and Calamity

Sylhet markets worked in tandem with the rhythm of the seasons. People used markets 'just as sufficient for daily consumption', as rice was never imported, and in the 1780s, annual rice exports fluctuated below 30,000 maunds.[65] Rice prices around Sylhet town moved within a normal range of 1.25–1.5 maunds of rice per rupee.[66] This normal range was breached dramatically during atypically bad years in the mid-1780s: 1779 and 1783, for instance. In 1779, floods came early in March and destroyed much of the standing *boro* crop, raising prices of April rice 50 per cent above normal; but later crops were good, which kept the year's price fluctuations within the normal range.[67] In 1783, insufficient rains reduced the total harvest and the November prices rose rapidly, but stocks from a good *boro* season prevented massive scarcity and rice exports continued.[68]

Local markets coped with bad years by moving large volumes of rice in small batches over long and short distances, among places producing *boro* and *shail* crops, respectively.[69] In such circumstances, grain merchants exercised considerable power and the Company's revenue demand also intervened in market operations. In the bad harvest year of 1783, a severe shortage of *cowries* occurred because of huge *cowrie* exports by revenue farmers, who increased cash revenue demands to meet obligations in Dhaka where *cowrie* prices had declined because of massive Maldives *cowrie* imports.[70] The 1783 *cowrie* crisis crippled Sylhet revenue collection. Tax arrears mounted, along with desertions of land by defaulters. Petitions for remissions multiplied and more litigants came to court to fight for rights to landed property.[71]

As the 1783 bad season and *cowrie* crisis abated, floods in 1784 surpassed traditional limits of seasonal variation by several orders of magnitude; this calamity set a new standard for local assessments of flood destruction. Floods began roughly on schedule, on 7 June, but then became a deluge. Floods dipped in July, peaked again in August, fell 6 inches in September and subsided by December, again roughly on schedule. In June, however, a 'great part of [the] town of Sylhet which sits on one of the highest sites in the whole province [had] been overflowed', and the town of Bangah, 'a large and populous place', was swept away along with many villages.[72] In July, torrents from Jaintia and Cachar forced people to flee to the mountains.[73] Late *boro* harvests and rice stores disappeared with homesteads. Countless cattle drowned and starved.[74] In September, 'all the lower part of the province being totally depopulated', the price of grain was twice the normal.[75] Lindsay described the September scene by reference to normal times, when 'the lowlands tho' always overflowed at this season of the year produced luxurious crops of grain and pasture for cattle'. By contrast, in 1784, 'Both men and women were employed in endeavouring to save the lives of the few cattle that still remained by diving in this open sea and scraping from the bottom roots and grass and weeds for their food, which can prove but temporary relief.'[76] In October 1784, many people 'of the poorer sort [were] daily carried off by famine',[77] and in March 1785, 'a minute survey of the districts' revealed that:

> Two thirds of the cattle have starved to death or [been] swept away by the flood and the few that [remain] are so much exhausted that they are of little use to the Farmers . . . one fourth of the inhabitants have died for want of subsistence . . . one fourth more have deserted the province and the rest are so desperate that there is hardly the sign of cultivation left.[78]

With half the lowland population gone, 'no settlement whatever [was] formed . . . [because] with no deductions authorized, the Zamindars would not settle'.[79] The next year was one of laborious recovery: families returned to rebuild homesteads and farms, and also moved away in large numbers to build new farms elsewhere. In 1786 a massive *boro* harvest ensued, and though people ate well, commerce suffered, because crops were 'so exceedingly plentiful' that rice would 'hardly pay the expense of coolly hire to the Bazar', where five maunds could be had for one rupee, 'and even at that rate there [were] no purchasers'.[80] This plenty prevented Lindsay from collecting revenue. He had actually 'found it a much less severe task to collect any part of the revenue in the year of the [1784] inundation'. In October 1786, he said he could barely raise enough revenue to pay his office salaries,[81] which amounted to 16 per cent of Sylhet's assessment.[82]

The next year, 1787, brought floods that surpassed even 1784. A vast deluge forced the Teesta and Brahmaputra rivers to shift course permanently. Fierce rain began on 22 February and continued, 'without intermission . . . [until] the [Surma] River from being very low [rose] 32 feet perpendicular'. All the standing *boro* rice was lost. By July, lowlands were again a churning sea where cattle drowned, granaries (*golah*) floated away,[83] people starved and the living survived on famine food, 'a small root procured by diving in the middle of the jhills in six or seven feet of water . . . [then] the sole occupation of the inhabitants'.[84] People fled to the hills,[85] but cultivation was impossible even on the highest farms[86] and by November, famine raged in mountains and lowlands alike.[87] In February 1788, rice prices were six times normal. The *boro* planting suffered for lack of seed.[88] Farms on high ground did not get enough April rain to sustain *boro* crops.[89] Cholera and malaria must have killed the prisoners and soldiers who died in Sylhet town of 'disease' and 'violent fevers', amidst a general pestilence from September 1787 through May 1788, which continued until May 1789.[90]

By September 1788, agricultural recovery was well underway. Landowners then settled revenue contracts at a renegotiated median of rates set in 1776 and 1783. Bankers (*shroffs*) provided security for revenue at 40 per cent interest per month.[91] The year 1789 produced a bumper *boro* harvest,[92] but disruptions since 1784 had taken a cumulative toll on profits, savings, livestock and other assets,[93] as well as on state revenue, as Collector Willes[94] explained to his superiors in June 1789, when he petitioned to strike off revenue balances from 1784,[95] saying of the farmers that if 'the Collector [were] rigidly to force the Zemindars to make good . . . the Kistbundy it would either drive them from the country or ruin them by subjecting them to the exorbitant imposition of the Shroffs'.[96]

State Territory and Property Rights

In 1780, tax collections remained a fraction of *jamma* because the Collector had little power to induce tax payments. It seems, in fact, that any determined local resistance could defeat the small force that Lindsay could bring to bear. Many locally powerful men did pay higher taxes, however. They did so primarily, it seems, to maintain and expand their local authority amidst rampant adversity. In six years after 1778, Lindsay claimed to have heard over 2,000 land disputes, involving many of the 'upwards of 4,000 independent proprietors of the soil' who paid him taxes.[97] Company officials then used the term zamindar to denote anyone who paid taxes to acquire property rights under Company authority.[98] Local units of property rights, called *taluqs*, were the domains of small landlords, called *taluqdars*. Sylhet district had only one very big zamindar (whom we shall meet shortly) and none of the big *jotedar* tenants or merchant magnates who controlled so much of rural Bengal.[99] Sylhet was, like Chittagong, a region of small landholders.[100] Yet, in 1784, Sylhet *taluqdars* represented substantial local landed families, whose territories of authority covered as much as 1.5 square miles.[101] Many held the title of Chaudhuri, which the Mughals had used to denote sub-zamindari authority, which spread among the Sylhet gentry who made it a family name.[102] Even poor *taluqdars* employed tenant farmers (*raiyat*) to till their land. To secure their assets against calamity, landed families dispersed their holdings among localities and combined various sources of income including commerce.[103] Ryots were mostly *paikasht*, non-resident tenants, who paid lower rents than *khudkasht* (resident) tenants and received no occupancy rights, but did receive agricultural and subsistence allowance from landowners who needed to attract them to clear and cultivate land.[104] Tenants employed agricultural workers who also lived mobile lives, as a matter of necessity.

All this mobility among local workers, peasants and the lords of the land, combined with the large number of small landholdings in a vast district beset with turbulent seasons, make it most difficult to determine the exact extent of any specific piece of local farm territory or 'private property'. In addition, the local payments that became state revenue moved among various middlemen who used it to acquire rights to land, becoming zamindars owning all or parts of many *taluqs*. Adding further complexity to the property scene, much right to the 'land' escaped taxation and had no official sanction; non-state power was often more effective in securing land rights than a distant Collector's writ, particularly on new farms in the jungle. Zamindars who officially owned *taluqs* under state authority often cleared jungle to create new farms for which they paid nothing, holding land rights outside official view. Thus, though about 4,000 local families and numerous middlemen paid Lindsay in order to bolster their rights to land and its produce, Lindsay described his territory saying, 'there is no place in all the extensive possessions of the Honourable Company where the boundaries of each Individual property of land in general is worse ascertained than in this Province'.[105]

Local people at the lowest end of the state ranks held the knowledge that defined the actual extent of state territory. Village *patwaris* recorded local transactions for *kanungos*, whose records comprised official evidence of local land rights, and local officials had to come personally to Sylhet town to provide evidence to enable the Collector to settle any land dispute. In this context, centralizing state power in order to determine the official boundaries of land property seemed, to Lindsay, the secret to increasing revenues. The more Collectors could define property rights with authoritative information that resided permanently in Sylhet town, the more authority Collectors would have in settling local land disputes, and thus the more effective the Company's tax claims would become.

Higher authorities reached the same conclusion as the British obsession with defining property rights took shape. In the 1780s, a subtle shift occurred in Sylhet in tune with trends in Bengal,[106] moving away from the old transactional definitions of state territory toward a more carto-graphic conception.[107] In 1800, there were still no land maps, no official records of boundaries and no state boundary markers in Sylhet.[108] But by 1791, the idea had been firmly established that the district consisted of all the land inside its geographical boundaries, including a jungle. In 1791, in Sylhet, a cadastral survey, called a *hustabood*, was complete, along with a *bandobast* compilation of all individual land-tax obligations; and together, these two massive official tomes – kept in Sylhet and Calcutta – guided the Decennial Settlement that became the 1793 Permanent Settlement in Bengal Presidency.[109]

The Company's increasing power to define the boundaries of its territory altered the geography of Sylhet by expanding the area open to frontier farming that was protected by the Company, and by providing more secure state authority to support individual claims to property. Markets in state-defined property rights attracted Bengalis, who depended on state power to secure their investments in land. Financial speculation and revenue collection thus formed an economic nexus where investors sank assets into agricultural expansion under state protection, which they paid for with *kists*, as necessary. As people in Sylhet endeavoured to expand cultivation, calamities in 1784 and 1787, especially 'floods', forced them on to the highlands, filled with jungles and non-Bengalis. Thus the interests of local farmers and the Company coalesced around the project of expanding Bengal's agrarian frontiers. Frontier farmers who would pay for Company land rights wanted protection for their claims; the Company wanted to expand the population of people who would pay for that protection.

On the high grounds to the north, east and south of Sylhet, peo-ple attached to the Tripura, Cachar and Jaintia rajas rebuffed Company demands by citing the rajas' claims. The Company sought to erase those claims inside its territory. Thus, when the Rani of Tripura asked the Tipperah Collector to assist her son's succession, the Collector obliged; in return, he secured a new boundary at the base of the hills, inducing the Raja of Tripura to move his capital to Agartala. The raja kept pri-vate landholdings in Tipperah district, but by 1782, his royal authority had officially retreated into mountains east of Comilla.[110] His northern mountain frontiers with Sylhet, behind Moulvi Bazar and Habiganj,

remained indefinite, however, and mountain people there rarely submitted to Calcutta or Tripura. These southern frontiers did not much trouble
early Sylhet Collectors, who worried considerably, however, about the
northern frontiers where, as one explained, 'the lands of the Rajahs of
Chachar and Jointah are blended with those of this District; indeed, the
Rajah of Jointah possesses lands adjacent to the town of Sylhet'.[111] Thus,
it was not in the south, but rather in the north, that transitions to a new
formation of Sylhet territory began. This transition focused on the ethnic
geography of Khasia territory.

The major Khasia figure was the Raja of Jaintia. He held the loyalty of diverse Khasia groups in the northern high mountains, its adjacent
uplands and plains below. He had initially renegotiated his boundaries with
the Company as he would have done with the Mughals: first, he tested the
Company's military with troops armed in the manner of mountain Khasias,
with 'a large shield over the right shoulder, protecting nearly the whole of
the body, the mountain sword, a quiver suspended over the left shoulder,
full of arrows, and a large bamboo bow'.[112] Musket-wielding Company
troops pushed the raja back into a reduced Jaintia territory, but Jaintia
Khasias still settled in what Sylhet Collectors considered Company territory, causing numerous disputes over revenue payments.[113] Jaintia authority did not extend far west of Jaintia, however. The land behind Chhatak
remained an open frontier, 'covered with an impenetrable jungle and so
infested by elephants, tigers, and other wild beasts that . . . clearing and
cultivation [was] attended with great difficulty and expense'.[114] In 1779,
elephants provided the most income for the few forest zamindars who
paid Company revenue.[115] Khasia rajas in the high mountains exercised
sporadic authority among Khasia people in these jungles, and the Company
could no more conquer the mountain Khasias than could the Mughals,
for, as Lindsay explained, 'you might as well attack the inhabitants of the
moon'.[116] Like the Jaintia Raja, Khasia rajas in the northern mountains
conceived Khasia territory as consisting of Khasia people, not land, and in
that sense Khasia territorialism was strictly ethnic even when it included
non-Khasia people, as Jaintia did. Unlike the Jaintia Raja, however, Khasia
rajas in the northern mountains never performed rituals of submission to
lowland rulers; indeed, their families fled the plains to avert submission.

Yet, in 1780, an old formation of Mughal authority did span the
high mountains and jungles below. It comprised the *jaghir* of Omaid Rezah,
whose home was in Bannyachang in southwestern Sylhet, in the lower
floodplain of the Kushiara. Omaid Rezah's family received a Mughal *jaghir*
in return for protecting the Sylhet *sarkar* against Khasia warriors, and he
was last in a line of Mughal frontier commanders called *tankadars*, who

served *faujdars* as a forest vanguard, protecting elite recipients of Nawabi forestland grants. His *jaghir* expanded accordingly[117] and Omaid Rezah became the largest landholder in Sylhet, whom Willes called 'the only true zamindar in the district'.[118] Inside his *jaghir*, a mixture of Khasia and Bengali peoples formed a distinctive ethnic territory. As Willes explained, Khasias who 'inhabit the hills and come down to the plains in search of necessities of life and articles of commerce' engaged in 'intercourse and intermarriages' with lowland Bengalis to produce what he called 'the degenerate Race called Bengalee Cosseahs', who lived mostly inside Omaid Rezah's *jaghir*.[119]

Conflict around Bengali Khasia settlements increased as Omaid Rezah's authority declined. In 1790, Willes described this once commanding figure as 'a respectable old man but entirely incapable', who could not pay his huge *jamma* of 34,665 *kahans*[120] without incurring a debt of more than 1 lakh *kahans* heaped upon him by men who managed his affairs and embezzled his wealth. Willes took the estate under his direct administration and said that insisting on full tax compliance 'would be [an] act of cruelty' that would ruin Omaid Rezah and his family. Willes appointed seven *tahsildars* to replace the eighty or so renters who had claims on the estate,[121] but even so, at Omaid Rezah's death in 1792, his estate was hopelessly in debt, and, to add injury to insult, Bannychang was completely submerged in the 1791 floods.[122] Struggles then ensued over the estate, and litigants even came from London to fight for bits of the old *jaghir* in Calcutta courts. By 1793, the Collector had carved the old *jaghir* into a collection of taxed parcels; sepoys replaced the *tankadar*'s force as protectors of agrarian Sylhet. The Collector's budget came to include an expense of 13,272 *kahans* for defence of the district,[123] raised from revenues from Bannychang land,[124] as *taluqdars* came to Willes 'in a body of some hundreds' to resist claims by Omaid Rezah's heirs and servants.[125]

Omaid Rezah's authority declined as commercial activity increased around Bengali Khasia settlements, around river routes from Sunamganj to Pandua, the river port town in the northern mountains that Lindsay described as being, along with Jaintia, Sylhet's main port for trade with Assam.[126] Conflict attending commercial expansion at Pandua had begun by 1779, when Lindsay received a delegation of Greek, Armenian and 'low European' merchants from Pandua, who complained of 'Hill Rajahs compelling them to dispose of their goods at arbitrary prices'. Lindsay suspected his petitioners had joined with forest zamindars to fight Khasia rajas for control of the mountains; and to keep trade open during their struggles, he stationed a *havildar* at Pandua, explaining to his superiors that because 'trade between Panduah and Calcutta [was] always considered an object worthy of attention . . . to protect merchants a strong force was kept up [at Pandua]'.[127]

By 1781, Lindsay himself controlled the Pandua limestone trade with hordes of Company *cowries* and a handful of troops. In this position, he sought quarry rights from mountain Khasia rajas, and when he arrived at their court, they 'breathed nothing but peace and friendship', resembling in his mind '[Scottish] Highlanders when dressed in the Gaellic costume.'[128] His hosts treated Lindsay to a feast of 'six or eight large hogs . . . roasted in . . . a hole dug in the ground, lined with plantain leaves, and filled with hot stones', and gave him rights to 'a large portion of the mountain, where the quarries are worked . . . including the most favourable situation for access to [his] boats, so as to afford [him] the fullest command of the water-carriage'. Lindsay also received permission to build a fortified villa, which became his personal hill station.[129]

Conflict at Pandua increased as mountain trade increased,[130] as more limestone came down rivers into Sunamganj,[131] more merchants bartered lowland and European products for mountain commodities, and more mountain rajas enriched themselves amidst increasing local competition.[132] Lindsay's Khasia hosts clearly expected him to support them, but Lindsay did not control events at Pandua, where, one day in 1783, a Khasia raja received a personal insult from the Pandua *havildar*, and that same day, 'toward the evening, the shrill war-whoop was heard in every direction, as the Cosseahs retired to the mountains', and 'not a man was seen below for several weeks . . . [until they] descended in considerable force'[133] to attack a fort of copper merchants.[134] Lindsay responded by stationing a 'whole Sebundy corps' at Pandua. In March 1784 he wrote that, 'hill people having collected additional forces, have become more troublesome and . . . more formidable than ever'. By then mountain rajas had 'taken possession of all the neighbouring jungles' and passes leading to Pandua. Lindsay reported ominously that it was 'absolutely necessary to keep that fort for the protection of the whole province',[135] and by September 1784, he had built a new fort at Pandua, to store merchant goods, house troops and free his business from Khasia patrons.[136]

In 1783, when fighting around Pandua forced Lindsay to end his mountain holiday, agrarian investors began moving into the jungles of Bengali Khasias. One prominent investor was Gowar Hari Singh, Sylhet's treasurer (*peshkar*), a banker (*shroff*) and local revenue farmer (*waddadar*), who hailed from Burdwan, where he returned a rich man, in 1791.[137] In 1784, he and other buyers engaged in risky ventures that emerged from Lindsay's desperation to raise cash after the 1783 *cowrie* crisis. They bought land at a government auction paying about twice the *jamma* and twice the arrears; Gowar Hari Singh paid even more. [138] These buyers saw opportunity in government auctions that put land into the hands of well-connected investors, even if this meant bending the rules, as Lindsay did to benefit Gowar Hari Singh at the expense of defaulting zamindars.[139] These transactions and many more indicate the workings of the market in state-authorized property rights that was buoyant even before 1784; in the north it must have benefited from commercial expansion around Sunamganj. John Shore provided a rough contemporary measure of land-market buoyancy when he told the Board of Revenue, in 1791, that he had 'never known of any instance in Bengal in which the price of revenue lands sold, out of Calcutta, exceeded the revenue of two years'.[140] The sale price of four estates sold at auction in Sylhet between 1781 and 1784 exceeded two years' *jamma*. Gowar Hari Singh's two upland purchases in 1784 were for 195 per cent and 282 per cent of the *jamma*, respectively.[141]

Floods in 1784 and 1787 boosted the value of upland jungles, where forest clearance and new *shail* cultivation bolstered the agrarian economy during floods in 1791 and 1793. Observers compared 1791 to 1784.[142] An earthquake occurred on 15 March 1791, followed by torrential storms that destroyed the *boro* crop and submerged Ajmeriganj, Beejoorah and Bannyachung.[143] Yet the overall harvest in 1791 was adequate because of good crops in the second half of the year,[144] which seem to have come from high ground that was not farmed in 1784, whose owners came forward to buy lowland properties destroyed by flood.[145] In 1793, the owners of uplands bought at auctions in 1781–84 could well afford to pay a 43 per cent higher *jamma* (86,715 *kahans*) than the land bore when they bought it (60,485 *kahans*).[146] In 1793, thirty-five small estates in the uplands sold at government auction for an average price that was six times the *jamma*, and all but six of these estates went for more than twice their *jamma*.[147]

The 1787 floods caused new problems on Sylhet's northern frontier, because they ravaged the mountains as well as the lowlands. Famine in the hills drove the Khasias into the plains, and in November 1787, Lindsay emphasized that the military protection of northern frontiers 'against incursions of Hill people' had always been a central concern of the Mughal government. He argued that rapidly increasing revenue demands and indefinite boundaries of landed property aggravated conflict in a region where 'ryots are of unsettled disposition and have no fixed abode or native place like others', moving in 'wretched hordes' as need be from one place to another.[148] In one of his last official letters, he said that floods and Khasia incursions had killed the 1788 revenue. Zamindars had paid him nothing for eight months and would never repay securities advanced by *shroffs*. As remedies, he prescribed lower taxes on insecure farms, fierce protection from Khasia incursions, and a fixing of boundaries for the district and all its landed property.[149]

When Collector Willes took office in February 1788, he only pursued the latter two remedies, and focused first on the mountain Khasias. Problems would arise, he said, 'if Hill people acquire arms' and 'learn the [use] of them from the wandering lowland Europeans, Moguls, Greeks, and Armenians who infest this district'. If this should happen, he feared, 'the Company's territories even as low as Dacca may be subjected to [mountain Khasia] incursions'. He said that Lindsay had 'stopped several foreigners who were going off to the Hills with arms for the purpose of barter', and that 'within these [past] few weeks [in May 1788] a large part of armed Moguls have been stopped and prevented from going off to the Hills to assist in the predatory wars of these inimical Rajahs'.[150] Willes soon discovered, however, that mountain Khasias were not his only problem, or indeed his main problem. In July 1788, as he negotiated with hill rajas to rebuild markets destroyed in battle and bring merchants back to Pandua,[151] conflict erupted among Bengali Khasias.[152] In December, one Bengali Khasia leader, Ganga Singh, 'calling himself the Zemindar of Barrakeah', burned to the ground a neighbouring zamindari and killed its proprietor, also a Bengali Khasia, in a land dispute that became a 'blood feud'.[153] Ganga Singh had captured both banks of a river carrying mountain trade with Sylhet[154] when Willes learned that Pandua had fallen completely to mountain Khasias, while Bengali Khasias under Ganga Singh and his confederate, Aboo Singh, zamindar of Dewallah, expanded control over land below the hills in 'open hostility to the Company', seizing people, goods and boats on the river. [155]

In 1789, Willes proposed that a strict boundary be drawn at the base of northern mountains and requested military force to settle all borders with Khasia rulers,[156] including Jaintia, once and for all.[157] But then, he discovered that territorial ambiguity did not plague only his northern frontiers. Landowners in borderlands between Mymensingh and Sylhet claimed to live in Sylhet to avoid taxation in Dacca district, and claimed to live in Dacca district to avoid Sylhet taxation. As a result, western Sylhet borderland markets boomed as buyers sought strategic sites for evasive investments.[158] To clarify legal property rights, the Company now issued a public notice that *sanads* must be produced for all rent-free land, with the goal of resuming land for which proper *sanads* could not be shown.[159] At the same time, Willes engaged a *hustabood* survey of *jamma* land, and reported that 'about 60,000 Kulbahs of cultivated lands have been measured', despite 'Conungoes and Principal Mussalman Landholders' who had 'combined to retard its operation'.[160]

In April 1789, the Company launched a war against Khasia rajas in the mountains and against Bengali Khasis in the jungles around Sunamganj. The war ended successfully for the Company, in 1791.[161] Bengali farmers proceeded to clear the jungle to expand cultivation, which involved clearing all Bengali Khasias from records of land rights, and expelling them or making them tenants and labourers. In 1793, the Collector reported that he had completed the sale of all the land expropriated from rebellious villagers, except for a 'trifling remainder of Cosseah land'.[162] This frontier land was extremely cheap to buy, because it remained covered with jungles where substantial numbers of Khasias still lived. Even so, tax rates continued to plague investors because demand was pegged to the productivity of cultivated land, and thus to the jungle's potential, rather than its current productivity. Owners of jungle land found it difficult to expand cultivation, in part because property rights rested on state tax demands poorly calibrated to encourage, let alone subsidize, investment. All this did not prevent forest investments, but encouraged investors to concentrate on land already farmed, which they might sell or let go on government auction, where they would reap any excess in the sale price over arrears.[163] Sale proceeds might eventually go into clearing forests for new cultivation, but Collectors complained constantly that investors concentrated attention only on already cultivated land, despite much lower tax rates on forestland.

Sylhet's northern lowlands thus became a settled agrarian territory for new Bengali colonization. More estates than ever before went into auction with settlements in 1792 and 1793, their *jamma* rising as their proportion of jungle land declined; only a very small number attracted no bidders, despite harsh floods in 1791 and 1793. As generally in Sylhet, the profusion of new farms on the northern rim lay in small estates where farmers could clear enough land to pay taxes quickly. In 1783, 4,000 tax payers had held property rights in Sylhet; in 1795, they were 26,000, 'many of these paying from a single Cawn of couries to five hundred and [only] a few any considerable sum above it'.[164] In 1793, 37 per cent of all Sylhet estates owed less than 10 *cawns jamma*, 66 per cent less than 30 *cawns*, and 83 per cent less than 100 *cawns*.[165] Sylhet was changing substantively from a wild frontier to a Bengali agrarian territory filled with small landlord villages organized around family relations. In 1790, its population was about 4,93,000. Official landowners would have comprised a bit more than 5 per cent of the total; and, estimating landowners' immediate families at five persons each, we can imagine that 27 per cent of all people in Sylhet district lived in landowning families. An average village held a tiny population of 67 people and only four landed estates (*taluqs*), each representing about eighteen people, perhaps few more than one family, its dependants and servants.[166] Below the mountains, land rights authorized by the state defined local elites who owned bounded plots of agricultural property, including farms and jungles. Khasias became official aliens in the plains, left to themselves in the mountains. This boundary has ever since defined Bengalis and Khasias as peoples with separate histories, homelands and cultural identities, which mingle in the local history of the borderlands.

Notes and References

[1] *Bar020aristan-i-Ghaybi (A History of the Mughal Wars in Assam, Cooch Behar, Bengal, Bihar and Orissa during the reigns of Jahangir and Shah Jahan, by Mir Nathan)*, translated by M.I. Borah, Gauhati: Government of Assam, 1936, pp. 110–11.

[2] A.B.M. Shamsuddin Ahmed, 'Muslim Administration in Sylhet 1303–1765', in Sharifuddin Ahmed, ed., *Sylhet: History and Heritage*, Dhaka: Bangladesh Itihas Samiti, 1999, p. 342.

[3] See Shirin Akhtar, 'Administration of Sylhet under the Nawabs', in Sharifuddin Ahmed, ed., *Sylhet: History and Heritage*, pp. 347–66; Abdul Karim, 'Suba Bangla: Government and Politics', in Sirajul Islam, ed., *History of Bangladesh, 1704–1971*, Dhaka: Asiatic Society of Bangladesh, second edition, 1997, II, pp. 35–68; Sushil Chaudhury, 'General Economic Conditions under the Nawabs', in Sirajul Islam, ed., *History of Bangladesh*, I, pp. 30–67; Rajat Datta, *Society, Economy and the Market: Commercialization in Rural Bengal, c. 1760–1800*, Delhi: Manohar Publishers, 2000.

[4] Calculated from Richard Eaton, *Rise of Islam and the Bengal Frontier, 1204–1760*, Berkeley: University of California Press, 1993, pp. 260–61. Sylhet District Records (Bangladesh National Archives), Vol. 299, page 22, letter dated 19 October 1789. (Henceforth, references to the Sylhet District Records appear in this format: SDR, 299.22: 19 Oct. 89.)

[5] Md. Mahbubar Rahman, 'Population of Sylhet District During British Period', in Sharifuddin Ahmed, ed., *Sylhet: History and Heritage*, p.115; the statistical summary of Hindu–Muslim proportions is on p. 108.

[6] Abu Imam, 'Ancient Sylhet: History and Tradition', in Sharifuddin Ahmed, ed., *Sylhet: History and Heritage*, pp. 174–85; Barrie Morrison, *Political Centers and Cultural Regions in Early Bengal*, Tucson: University of Arizona Press, 1970.

[7] Dilip K. Chakrabarti, *Ancient Bangladesh: A Study of the Archaeological Sources with an Update on Bangladesh Archaeology, 1990–2000*, Dhaka: The University Press Limited, 2001, pp. 17–21. K. Bagchi, *The Ganges Delta*, Calcutta: Calcutta University Press, 1944. C. Strickland, *Deltaic Formation with Special Reference to the Hydraulic Processes of the Ganges and the Brahmaputra*, Calcutta: Longmans Green & Co., 1940.

[8] M Atharul Islam, 'Population and Environment', in Sirajul Islam, ed., *History of Bangladesh*, II, p. 701.

[9] Haroun er Rashid, *Geography of Bangladesh*, Dhaka: The University Press Ltd, 1977, p. 55.

[10] David Ludden, *An Agrarian History of South Asia*, Cambridge: Cambridge University Press, 1999, pp. 133–40.

[11] Fishing tribes included the Kaivartas. Eaton, *The Rise of Islam*, p. 258, n.78, cit-

ing K.N. Gupta, 'On Some Castes and Caste-Origins in Sylhet', *Indian Historical Quarterly*, 7, 1931, pp. 725–26ff.

[12] See Ludden, *An Agrarian History of South Asia*, pp. 60–129.

[13] *Bararistan-i-Ghaybi*, pp. 158–66, 171–233.

[14] This quotation is from SDR, 294.156: 12 Dec. 86.

[15] SDR, 291.55: 3Nov. 79.

[16] B. Pakem, 'State Formation in Pre-colonial Jaintia', in Surajit Sinha, ed., *Tribal Polities and State Formation in Pre-colonial Eastern and North Eastern India*, Calcutta: K.P. Bagchi, 1984, facing p. 244, also pp. 261–306.

[17] SDR, 298.7: 20 Dec. 88. Ganga Sing, a Bengali Khasia chief 'formerly subject during the Mogul time to Sylhet', launched a fateful revolt in December 1788. SDR, 297.164: 18 Dec. 88. See below.

[18] Expenses for religious occasions were listed as Rs 2,82,842. His total expenses (Rs 5,66,783) were more than double the Sylhet *jamma*. Datta, *Society, Economy and the Market*, p. 171.

[19] A.B.M. Mahmood, *The Revenue Administration of Northern Bengal, 1765–1793*, Dacca: Pakistan National Institute of Public Administration, 1970, p. 28.

[20] The Dinajpur and Rajshahi zamindaris were two of the great estates totally demolished within seven years of the Permanent Settlement. *The Fifth Report from the Select Committee of the House of Commons on the Affairs of the East India Company (dated 28ᵗʰ July, 1812)*, edited with Notes and Introduction by Walter K. Firminger, Calcutta: R. Cambray, 1917, reprint, New York: Augustus M. Kelley, 1969, I, p.103.

[21] SDR, 295.122–30: (n.d.) Nov. 87; SDR, 299.34: 5 Nov. 89.

[22] SDR, 294.53: 31 May 84; SDR, 293: 24 Sept. 84; SDR, 293.156: 1 May 85; SDR, 295.122–30: (n.d.) Nov. 87. Index values for Bengal Presidency *jamma* are 100 in 1767, 137 in 1776 and 164 in 1784. Datta, *Society, Economy and the Market*, p. 334. Revenue demand on Rajshahi zamindari increased only 18 per cent from 1765 to 1784. Mahmood, *The Revenue Administration of Northern Bengal*, pp. 28, 32, 34, 42; and for Sylhet.

[23] SDR, 293.156: 1 May 85; SDR, 306.21–5: 19 Aug. 94.

[24] SDR, 300.106: 30 Dec. 90; SDR, 301.82: 11 Oct. 91.

[25] SDR, 306.21–5: 19 Aug. 94.

[26] Such as lived, for example, in Murshidabad, where, in 1789, the Collector borrowed Rs 41,192 from seven Indian bankers (with the surnames Das, Seth, Mahan, Roy, Singh, Roy and Gopinath) to make good his revenue payment to Calcutta. K.M. Mohsin, 'Mughal Banking System', in Sirajul Islam, ed., *History of Bangladesh*, II, p. 217. For the big picture, see Sanjay Subrahmanyam, ed., *Merchants, Markets and the State in Early Modern India*, Delhi: Oxford University Press, 1990.

[27] SDR, 294.112: 15 Nov. 85. *Comilla District Records*, I, p. 71. Robert Lindsay, 'Anecdotes of an Indian life', in *Lives of the Lindsays; or, A Memoir of the Houses of Crawford and Balcarres'*, by Lord Lindsay (his brother), second edition, London: John Murray, 1858, III, p. 170.

[28] Datta, *Society, Economy and the Market*, p. 208. SDR, 299.128–9: 8 May 90 says 'there are not fewer Ganges and Bazars in Sylhet than six hundred', and that the largest are Ajmeriganj, Bangah and Sylhet town. SDR, 300.89–90: 24 Nov. 90 has a list of thirty-one major *ganjes* and bazaars.

[29] SDR, 299.128–9: 8 May 90 emphasizes the small size of market centres. SDR, 300.89–90: 24 Nov. 90 lists thirty-one major *ganj* and bazaar sites with policemen and superintendents.

[30] On the urban-centered commercialism of eighteenth-century Bengal, see Rajat Datta, *Society, Economy and the Market*. Datta also stresses 'the primacy of the merchant' and urban centres in 'Merchants and Peasants: A study of the structure of local trade in grain in late eighteenth century Bengal', in Subrahmanyam, ed., *Merchants, Markets and the State*, pp. 146–51.

[31] On crops, see Haroun er Rashid, *Geography of Bangladesh*, pp.183–295.

[32] Robert Lindsay, 'Anecdotes of an Indian life', pp. 169–70.

[33] Abul Fazl Allami, *Ain-i-Akbari*, translated by H. Blochman, Delhi: Low Price Publications, 1927, Vol. I, p. 34, says that in rice-growing Bengal (*Bang + Al* = land of hilly mounds), 'people are submissive and pay their rents duly'. Revenue demand is paid 'by installments in eight months, they themselves bring mohars and rupees to the appointed place for the receipt of the revenue, as the division of the grain heap between the government and the husbandmen is not here customary. The harvests are always abundant, measurement is not insisted upon, and the revenue demands are determined by an estimate of the crop. His Majesty in his goodness has confirmed this custom.'

[34] Robert Lindsay, 'Anecdotes of an Indian life', p. 174.

[35] Ibid., p. 176.

[36] Hamlet Bareh, 'Khasia–Jaintia State Formation', in Sinha, ed., *Tribal Polities and State Formation*, pp. 264–67. SDR, 312.141: 7 April 1800: Iron ore in 'immense quantity . . . is extracted and brought down by [Khasias] for sale and compose a principal article of their traffic with the natives in Sylhet'. SDR, 297.48: 29 May 88; SDR, 297.54: 12 May 88.

[37] SDR, 300.56–7: 2 Sept. 90.

[38] Robert Lindsay, 'Anecdotes of an Indian life', p. 164.

[39] SDR, 291.8–9: 2 Dec. 77; SDR, 291.18: Jul 78; SDR 299.101: 21 Feb. 90.

[40] Robert Lindsay, 'Anecdotes of an Indian life', p. 190. Abul Fazl, *Ain-i-Akbari*, Vol. I, p. 295, describes hunting elephants in *khedah*. Lindsay describes *khedah* hunting techniques in 'Anecdotes of an Indian life', pp. 190–97. Elephants suffered high mortality in captivity: SDR, 291.24–5: 15 Oct. 78 reports that of 217 caught, only 112 survived. SDR, 291.18: July 78 reports that of 221 elephants caught from Kartick to Byshack 1187, 106 died.

[41] Other Europeans also did business in tusks, including Henry Raitt, who was also involved in many other Sylhet trades, and reported that the fixed price in Chachar for teeth weighing 13–30 seers was Rs 40/maund, while at other places it was Rs 45–50/maund. SDR, 303.45–7: 26 Oct. 92.

[42] Irfan Habib, *Atlas of Mughal India: Political and Economic Maps with Notes, Bibliography and Index*, Delhi: Oxford University Press, 1982, Map 11B.

[43] Willem van Schendel, *Francis Buchanan in Southeast Bengal*, Dhaka: United Press, 1992, p. 137. J.B. Bhattacharjee, 'Dimasa State Formation', in Sinha, ed., *Tribal Polities and State Formation*, pp. 186, 194.

[44] *Comilla District Records*, I, pp. 49–52.

[45] Robert Lindsay, 'Anecdotes of an Indian life', pp. 198–202. The ships were the *Sylhett* (400 tons), *Highland Green* (260 tons), *Beauty* (160 tons), *Tyger* (150 tons), *Buffalow* (140 tons) and *Rhinoceros* (140 tons), for which Lindsay petitioned to acquire 'the established freight [allowance] for 15000 bags of rice to Madras', which he undertook 'to Purchase at Backergunge from the Honourable Company and load free of all Charges for 1 Rupee per Maund'. SDR, 292.57: 29 Mar. 83.

[46] Debendra Bijoy Mitra, *Monetary System in the Bengal Presidency, 1735–1835*, Calcutta: K.P. Bagchi, 1991, pp. 70–90, provides details.

[47] SDR, 300.106: 30 Dec. 90.

48 See Clarence Maloney, *People of the Maldive Islands*, Bombay: Orient Longman, 1980, pp. 112, 126, 137, 417.

49 Frank Perlin, *Monetary, Administrative, and Popular Infrastructures in Asia and Europe, 1500–1900*, Brookfield VT: Ashgate, 1993, pp. 152–63, 270; Jan Hogendorn and Marion Johnson, *The Shell Money of the Slave Trade*, New York: Cambridge University Press, 1986; Robert S. Wicks, *Money, Markets and Trade in Early Southeast Asia*, Ithaca: Cornell University Press, 1992, pp. 28–72.

50 SDR, 295.108: 30 Oct. 87: 'there are not 500 Rupees in circulation through-out the district and the few that make their appearance are bad Arcots'. SDR, 297.44: 17 May 88: 'there is not above 6 or 700 Rupees to be found in Sylhet and these are bad Arcots . . . no copper coins of any Species passes through the District. The Revenues are paid in *Cowries* and all mercantile transactions are carried on through the same currency.'

51 SDR, 293.126–31: 24 Sept. 84.

52 Robert Lindsay, 'Anecdotes of an Indian life', p. 169.

53 SDR, 293.126–29: 24 Sept. 84.

54 Abul Fazl treats Sylhet as a mountain region. *Ain-i-Akbari*, Vol. I, pp. 136–37: 'In the Sarkar of Sylhet there are nine ranges of hills. It furnished many eunuchs.' He goes on to list only mountain products of Sylhet: Suntarah, orange, China Root, Aloe-wood, Bhangraj and tamed birds.

55 D.B. Mitra, *Monetary System in the Bengal Presidency*, p. 90 indicates that copper prices replaced *cowries* in the 1820s. Montgomery Martin, *The History, Antiquities, Topography, and Statistics of Eastern India (comprising the Districts of Behar, Shahabad, Bhagulpoor, Goruckpoor, Dinajepoor, Puraniya, Ronggopoor, and Assam)*, Delhi: Cosmo Publications, 1976, Vol. III, p. 128 indicates that *cowries* still circulated in Sylhet in the late nineteenth century. I have heard personal accounts of *cowries* circulating in twentieth-century Sylhet.

56 He had begun to combine Company business with personal speculation in Dacca, where he took a large advance from 'a wealthy native' in return for delivering 20,000 pounds of Company salt bought with a Company officer's prerogative at a public auction. Robert Lindsay, 'Anecdotes of an Indian life', pp. 164–65.

57 Ibid., pp. 176–80, 198.

58 To help finance his big shipping venture, in 1783, he pointed out 'to the Honourable Board that there is a very large quantity of couries lying unsaleable in Dacca. The recomporting of these couries will be of infinite service to the Province already drained of this currency by a continual exportation without any visible important [*sic.*] and I will readily accept of them at the Bazar price in payment for the hire of freight.' SDR, 292.57: 29 Mar. 83.

59 For example, in SDR, 292.31: 12 Mar. 83, he reports that his agent in Dacca, Archibald Burnett, transmitted bills of exchange worth 50,000 *sicca* rupees drawn on two other Englishmen, one at sight and one in twenty days. 'These sums being recovered, I request you will give me credit or the same amount the Sylhet Revenue.'

60 SDR, 293.126–31: 24 Sept. 84.

61 SDR, 294.113: 15 Nov. 85.

62 The *cowrie* conversion rate for Company revenue in Sylhet was 4.65 *kahans* per *sicca* rupee in 1781–85 and 5.63 *kahans* per *sicca* rupee in 1785–90. Calculated from District Treasury remission reports. In 1794, the official conversion rate had risen somewhat to 5.25 *kahans* per *sicca* rupee.

63 SDR, 304.9: 20 Apr. 93.

64 SDR, 297.59: 12 May 88.

65 SDR, 301.107: 30 Nov. 91.

66 SDR, 292.56: 22 Mar. 83; SDR, 292.58: 1 Apr. 83.

67 SDR, 291.37: 8 Apr. 79; SDR, 291.57: 20 Dec. 79.

68 SDR, 293.73–75: 4 Nov. 83.

69 SDR, 291.37: 8 Apr. 79; SDR, 293.73–75: 4 Nov. 83.

70 SDR, 292.31: 12 Mar. 83.

71 SDR, 292.61: 29 Apr. 83.

72 SDR, 193.114: 25 June 84.

73 SDR, 293.114–15: 10 July 84.

74 SDR, 293.119: 3 Sept. 84; SDR, 294.64: 3 Sept. 84.

75 Lindsay predicted that prices would 'not considerably fall until the month of May next as the few partial spots of high ground that are now planting will barely produce Rice sufficient for the consumption of the farmer.' SDR, 293.132–33: 28 Sept. 84.

76 SDR, 294.65: 3 Sept. 84.

77 SDR, 293.137–38: 8 Oct. 84.

78 SDR, 293.151–52: 13 Mar. 85.

79 SDR, 295.53: 10 May 87; SDR, 293.124–25: 6 Sept. 84; SDR, 294.102: 20 Jul. 85.

80 SDR, 294.154–55: 2 Oct. 86.

81 Ibid.; SDR, 294.155: 10 Oct. 86; SDR, 294.156: 2 Nov. 86.

82 SDR, 293.147: (n.d.) Dec. 84–Mar. 85; and SDR, 293.151–52: 16 Mar. 85. For 1794 figures, see Appendix 1.

83 SDR, 295.84–88: 11 Jul. 87.

84 SDR, 295.104–05: 23 Oct. 87.

85 SDR, 295.97: 5 Sept. 87.

86 SDR, 295.47: (n.d.) Apr. 87.

87 SDR, 295.136: 16 Nov. 87.

88 SDR, 297.15: 8 Feb. 88.

89 SDR, 297.47: 10 Apr. 88.

90 SDR, 297.131: 19 Sept. 88. In May 1789, twenty-two out of fifty sepoys recently arrived in Sylhet were 'taken with violent fever'. SDR, 298.116–18: 13 June 89.

91 SDR, 297.122: 5 Sept. 88.

92 SDR, 298.172: 1 Sept. 89. One indication of recovery is that in August 1789, the Collector realized 107,533 *kahans* in revenue, as compared to 55,779 *kahans* in August 1788.

93 SDR, 297.70: 12 June 88: 'amongst the Waddadar Farmers, Zemindars, and Ryotts there is no property independent of the produce of the land. . . . In this District whenever inundation or any other calamity occasions a loss of crops on the ground the Company's Revenue will of course suffer. There is no accumulated wealth to supply the temporary deficiency'.

94 SDR, 297.15: 8 Feb. 88 is John Willes' first letter as Collector.

95 The balance was 106,277 *kahans* and the Collector predicted that less than 10,000 *kahans* would ever be collected. SDR, 297.141: 1 Sept. 88. The revenue account for 1195 (1786) was not closed until February 1789. SDR, 298.81–82: 19 Feb. 89.

96 SDR, 298.135–37: 23 June 89.

97 SDR, 293.99–100: 4 Apr. 84.

98 The term 'zamindar' was applied to all landholders paying taxes to the Company at this time, whatever the size of their holdings and their relation to the cultivation process.

99 See especially Rajat Ray, 'The Bengal Zamindars: Local Magnates and the State

Before the Permanent Settlement', *The Indian Economic and Social History Review* 12, 3, 1975, pp. 263–92, and *Change in Bengal Agrarian Society, 1760–1850*, New Delhi: Oxford University Press, 1979; Sugata Bose, *Peasant Labour and Colonial Capital: Rural Bengal Since 1770*, Cambridge: Cambridge University Press, 1993. Rajat Datta, *Society, Economy, and the Market*; and Shinkichi Taniguchi, 'The Peasantry of Northern Bengal in the Late Eighteenth Century', in Peter Robb, Kaoru Sugihara, and Haruka Yanagisawa, eds, *Local Agrarian Society in Colonial India: Japanese Perspectives*, Delhi: Manohar, 1997.

100 For Chittagong, see A.M. Serajud-din, 'The Revenue Administration of Chittagong, from 1761 to 1785', unpublished PhD dissertation, University of London, 1964.

101 Dividing 4,000 tax-payers into the land area of Sylhet in 1783 yields 0.7 per square mile for each landholder; but, as we will see, tax-payers in 1783 did not control nearly the whole land area reported in the *Fifth Report* as comprising Sylhet district.

102 In Mughal *sanad* texts from Chittagong, *shaikh* and *chaudhuri* were the most common titular names. See Eaton, *Rise of Islam*, p. 249.

103 SDR, 297.126: 5 Sept. 88 reports that zamindars typically held lands spread among many *parganas*: 'In example, Chytunnagher is composed of parcels of land lying in eight or ten Pergunnahs.'

104 Datta, *Society, Economy and the Market*, pp. 93–99.

105 SDR, 293.99–100: 4 Apr. 84.

106 For Bengal trends, see Ranajit Guha, *A Rule of Property for Bengal: An Essay on the Idea of Permanent Settlement*, second edition, Delhi: Orient Longman, 1982. Sylhet remained a distinctively different imperial territory, inside Bengal. *Fifth Report*, II describes regional differences among Bengal districts.

107 For an account of contemporary cartographic ideologies and practices, see Matthey H. Edney, *Mapping an Empire: The Geographical Construction of British India, 1765–1843*, Chicago: Chicago University Press, 1997.

108 Contemporary boundaries could often be described in great detail without being mapped, and these descriptions provide data for later maps. See Joseph E. Schwartzberg, ed., *A Historical Atlas of South Asia*, New York: Oxford University Press, 1992, p. 212.

109 SDR, 305.41–42: 30 Nov. 93.

110 *Comilla District Records,* I, pp. 1–49.

111 SDR, 308.150: 22 Feb. 98.

112 Robert Lindsay, 'Anecdotes of an Indian life', p.181.

113 In 1789, Willes estimated the revenue of land taken by Jaintia, Tipperah and Khasias from 1130 to 1195 (1729 to 1784) to be 95,735 *kahans*, of which 69,904 *kahans* went to Jaintia Khasias in thirty named areas (SDR, 298.52: 12 Jan. 89).

114 SDR, 294.126–27: 3 May 86.

115 SDR, 291.48–49: 8 Sept. 79.

116 Robert Lindsay, 'Anecdotes of an Indian life', p. 186.

117 SDR, 304.11–17: 20 Apr. 93.

118 SDR, 299.72–74: 15 Jan. 90.

119 SDR, 298.7: (n.d.) Dec. 88.

120 This was the figure in 1794. SDR, 306.38–43: 10 Oct. 94.

121 SDR, 299.72–74: 15 Jan. 90.

122 SDR, 302.29: 13 Mar. 92; SDR, 301.33: 25 May 91; SDR, 301.15: 13 Apr. 91.

123 See Appendix 1.

[124] See below.

[125] SDR, 304.11–17: 20 Apr. 93; SDR 307.7–12: 10 May and 8 July 95.

[126] SDR, 293.126–29: 24 Sept. 84.

[127] SDR, 291.41: 26 June 79.

[128] '[I]t was evident from their complexion and the war-yell that occasionally escaped their lips, as well as the mode in which they handled their weapons, that their temperament was not dissimilar to that of other mountaineers.' Robert Lindsay, 'Anecdotes of an Indian life', p. 177.

[129] Ibid., pp. 177–78.

[130] SDR, 300.57–59: 2 Sept. 90.

[131] In 1790, seven Europeans owned 120,000 *ferrahs* of *chunam* in Sylhet markets, and fifty Natives owned 50,000 *ferrahs*. (1 *ferrahs* = 1 maund, 10 seers.) SDR, 300.63: 2 Sept. 90.

[132] SDR, 300.57–59: 2 Sept. 90.

[133] Robert Lindsay, 'Anecdotes of an Indian life', p. 186.

[134] SDR, 292.50–51: (n.d.) 1783.

[135] He added, on a personal note, 'I have been in a constant state of warfare with the Cosseahs or Inhabitants of the mountains from whence the [lime]stones are drawn', and 'I have myself sustained considerable loss.' SDR, 293.92–93: 1 Mar. 84; SDR, 293.95: (n.d.) Mar. 84.

[136] SDR, 293.119: 4 Sept. 84.

[137] SDR, 304.38: 30 June 93.

[138] SDR, 294.98: 25 June 85.

[139] SDR, 297.113: 1June 89; SDR, 299.43–45: 28 Nov. 89. In 1792, his personal estate consisted of land in twenty-two *parganas* with 17,678 *kahans jamma*. SDR, 302.43–46: 23 Apr. 92. His purchases were the biggest land purchases at government auction till that time, and his purchases in 1783 and 1784 amounted to 39 per cent of the total sold in the four years after 1781.

[140] India Office Records, Bengal Revenue Consultations, P/52/31, 10 June 1791, quoted in Datta, *Society, Economy and Market*, pp. 146–47. Rajat Datta finds seven estate sales from 1776 to 1793 and 43 per cent purchase prices over 200 per cent *jamma*. He concludes that this sale price pattern 'suggests a buoyant land market in this period' (1724–1793), by the standards of the day.

[141] Collector Willes and Gowar Hari Singh engaged in a lengthy legal battle over the legality of his purchase. SDR, 304.8–17: 20 Apr. 93.

[142] SDR, 301.15: 13 Apr. 91.

[143] Ibid.

[144] SDR, 301.59: 26 July 92.

[145] SDR, 301.29–30: 21 May 91.

[146] SDR, 304.11: 20 Apr. 93.

[147] SDR, 305.8–19: (n.d) Sept. 93. Two more estates were sold in 1793 for 350 per cent their *jamma*. SDR, 306.60–63: 8 Nov. 94. Datta, *Society, Economy and Market*, p. 146, also shows an increase, during the 1780s, in the *jamma*-proportionate sale price of the small number of estates in his sample.

[148] SDR, 295.122–30: (n.d.) Nov. 87.

[149] SDR, 297.17: 1 Feb. 88.

[150] SDR, 297.54–61: 12 May 88.

[151] SDR, 297.93–95: 5 July 88.

[152] Ibid.

[153] SDR, 298.45: 12 Jan. 89.

[154] SDR, 297.154: 15 Dec. 88.

[155] SDR, 297.164: 18 Dec. 88.

[156] SDR, 298.50: 12 Jan. 89.
[157] SDR, 298.49: 12 Jan. 89.
[158] SDR, 298.67–69: 9 Feb. 89.
[159] SDR, 298.64–65: 3 Feb. 89.
[160] SDR, 298.81–82: 19 Feb. 89.
[161] For details and more complete annotation with statistics, see David Ludden, 'The First Boundary of Bangladesh on Sylhet's Northern Frontiers', *Journal of the Asiatic Society of Bangladesh*, 48, 1, June 2003, pp. 1–54.
[162] SDR, 304.38–39: 1 July 93.
[163] SDR, 305.8–19: (n.d.) Sept. 93.
[164] SDR, 306.126–27: 8 Sept. 95.
[165] These figures are from a sample of thirty-five sales in 1793, and exclude atypical cases from the northern frontier in Bunsicoorah and other 'devastated parganas' toured by Willes in 1789.
[166] Willes often asserted that each *taluq* typically belonged to one family: SDR, 297.126: 5 Sept. 88 and SDR, 300.141–44: 24 Oct. 91.

Promise of Modernity, Antinomies of Development

Canal Colonies of Punjab (1890s–1940s)

Neeladri Bhattacharya

In the 1880s, the colonial state in India embarked on one of its grandest projects of social engineering. It proceeded to concretize its dream of creating an ideal agrarian space within the colony. From the beginning of colonial rule, in Punjab and elsewhere, colonial officials were driven by a desire to 'improve' landscapes and modernize agrarian spaces, even as they sought to maximize revenue returns. But they found it impossible to concretize their vision in practice, to transform images into realities. Operating on already inscribed spaces, faced with deeply entrenched social structures, confronted with a maze of customs and practices, and innumerable ecological variations, they had to repeatedly backtrack, rework their conceptions and modify their vision. They had to think of policies that were viable, feasible and workable within given contexts. The imagined ideal was persistently disturbed by politics of the possible.

Colonizers everywhere search for open spaces that allow possibilities of unconstrained transformation. The *bars* (pastoral highlands) beyond the Sutlej, it seemed, were such a space. On these vast scrublands, there were no valuable trees, no populous villages, no settled peasants cultivating their fields, no wheat piled up on threshing floors, no carts carrying local produce to the market. Nomadic pastoralists were the only humans visible, traversing the landscape with their camels and herds, some living on the *bars* through the year, others moving between the riverine tracts and the highlands.[1] The highlands were dry, with water levels sinking to more than 80 feet below the surface. From the earliest days of colonial rule, British officials traversing the region had despaired at the landscape of desolation; at the same time, they had fantasized about reordering this 'wilderness' of their imagination.[2] By the early 1880s the scrublands had been taken over, reclassified as *rakh* (waste), mapped, surveyed and bounded. In subsequent decades, this space was subjected to an even more dramatic process of change.

The first canal colony project was started in Multan in 1886.[3]

Over the next fifty years a vast network of perennial canals spread over the highlands on the interfluves between the Sutlej and Jhelum rivers. The average annual area irrigated by perennial canals boomed: from around 943,000 acres in the five years ending 1985–86, to 4,123,500 acres by the end of the century.[4] Nine colonies were settled around the canals. In the Chenab Colony, settled between 1892 and 1905, over 1.8 million acres were allotted in grants.[5] The area distributed in the other colonies was considerably smaller: in Jhelum Colony about 540,000 acres, in Lower Bari Doab about 900,000 acres,[6] in Nili Bar 800,000 acres. But together these colonies carved up over 4 million acres of pastoral land for agrarian settlement.[7]

The colonial officials hoped to mould this space in accordance with their dream, develop it through science, capital and an imperial imagination. They saw themselves working on a landscape empty of people, unencumbered by the past, unfettered by social rigidities. The high plateau was dry but the soil was good in many places. Once irrigation became available, the Punjab officials were convinced, the land could be cleared, settled and ordered: pioneer settlers were brought in from the densely populated and intensively cultivated tracts of Punjab where the limits of agrarian expansion had been reached. A new society could be founded with the immigrants, the industrious peasants of central Punjab settled in new colonies, a new regime of customs introduced, villages and markets planned, and valuable commercial crops produced. A desolate landscape could thus be covered with cultivating fields, made productive. In the canal colonies, it was assumed, the limits of the possible itself could be redefined.

As the process of colonization proceeded, this fantasy of freedom from constraints, this imperial desire to create a colonial agrarian society from above, unhindered by local rigidities, gradually crumbled. The pastoral landscape was transformed, but the agrarian conquest could not proceed undisturbed, in exact accordance with imperial plans. Embedded landscapes are never erased with ease, emptied of people and reinscribed without a problem. Spaces are not as malleable as modernist minds imagine, the nomads were not as docile as colonial officials desired. The colonizing projects as they evolved were very different from the constitutive elements of the original idea. This essay will examine both the vision and the experience of this agrarian colonization, and look at the relationship between the founding plan and the executed projects. It will explore how spaces become sites of conflict and how the specific mode of their re-figuration is defined by this conflict. Through this exploration I will reflect on the different paths to agrarian conquest, and the different modes of colonial domination.

Canals and the Science of Empire

The construction of the canals was, in a sense, the founding act. The canal colonies were to develop around the canals; they were to derive their identity from the canals. Through the construction of the perennial canals, colonial officials sought to demonstrate their capacity to tame nature, transform wastes into productive landscapes, and create the basis of a new hydraulic order. The canals were to reveal the marvels of western science, and the power of western reason and rationality. They were to mark the transition from the past to the present, from backwardness to progress, from the age of primitive irrigation systems to the birth of the new. They were to announce the advent of modernity and civilization.

In the early years after annexation, Punjab officials were reluctant to directly undertake ambitious projects of irrigation. The potential for irrigation was widely recognized, and the need for irrigating the Bari Doab – the interfluves between the Sutlej and Ravi rivers – was forcefully emphasized. 'No part of the new territory is so important, politically and socially', declared the Board of Administration. 'In no Doab, is there so much high-land susceptible of culture; so many hands to work; so fine a population to be supported.'[8] In the winter of 1849–50, Lieutenant Dyas was deputed to conduct 'scientific investigations' so that a working plan for the irrigation of the Bari Doab could be developed. By the end of the season, officials claimed that the topography of the whole of the Doab had been carefully mapped: level cross-sections were taken, the nature of the ground – its surface, its drainage and its undulations – was 'precisely ascertained', and the capabilities of the existing canals were all carefully examined.[9] Within a few years, the Punjab Administration boasted of having built a canal that was 'second in India only to the great Ganges Canal and equal if not superior to the finest irrigation canals of Europe'.[10]

Yet the Board of Administration was wary of extending the scale of canal operations. Swamped by new proposals for ambitious irrigation schemes and apprehensive of the excessive enthusiasm of the Canal Engineers, the Board, in 1856, urged the need for caution:

> [T]he expediency of multiplying permanent Canals of magnitude is doubtful. On the one hand the outlay is vast, on the other the return is uncertain, until the means of exporting the surplus produce shall have been provided. Until this cardinal and crying want, namely, means of exportations shall have been supplied, a number of great Canals would be in advance of the need of the country. Let the new Baree Doab Canal be fairly tried; let effort for a Railway from Umritsar to Mooltan be made (the first measure will hardly be complete without the second);

and in the meantime Inundation Canals of small size, but large numbers, will suffice.[11]

Nervous about large outlays and unconvinced about secure returns, the Punjab officials stalled new projects and talked of the immense worth of existing inundation systems. They wrote admiringly of the great canals of Multan started by the Pathan rulers and reconstructed under Sawan Mal, and of the value of the Derajat canals that irrigated the parched lands farther west.[12] Initiated and supervised by local chiefs and power-holders, these inundation canals were seemingly constructed without much expense and trouble to the native governments. Local people had combined not only to construct the canals – digging the channels, raising the embankments and constructing bunds where necessary – but also to maintain them, contributing their labour every year to clear the silt. Indeed, if the local people could sustain their own irrigation systems, the officials reasoned, then why should the government intervene? 'In such cases, when the community displays so much aptitude for self-government,' wrote Richard Temple, 'the Board consider non-interference the best policy, while they would always be ready to afford any aid which might be solicited.'

By the 1870s colonial officials in different districts were actively extending the network of inundation canals.[13] The policy was to initiate projects, minimize government expenditure, cajole and force the local inhabitants to build the canal and maintain it with their labour, but take over control of the canal. Colonel Grey, as Commissioner of Ferozepur, got the cultivators on the left bank of the Sutlej to dig ten inundation canals without any pecuniary help from the government.[14] A decade later, while he was Commissioner of Hissar, Grey had three canals constructed. The total length of these canals was 600 miles and the area irrigated annually averaged about 160,000 acres. Initiated by the local government without any outlay from the imperial revenue, the canals were under the supervision of the Deputy Commissioner. The local government was to regulate the supply of water to the fields, ensure the labour contributions of each household towards the annual task of silt clearance and mediate in disputes over water.[15] These canals were not classified in official documents as 'state canals': they were said to belong to the community and were to be maintained by them. What this meant was state control without state investment.

By the 1880s, however, the enthusiasm for inundation canals began to fade as perennial canals were increasingly projected as the embodiment of science, modernity and progress. Even Grey, a great advocate of the inundation system, stated:

[T]he days of inundation canals have passed. The rivers have been or are
being tapped to a degree which much lowers the value of these works
by depriving them of the early and later water which is so important to
irrigation. The method was after all but a makeshift; it has had its day,
and the time has come for arresting the summer floods by weirs, and for
distributing them scientifically over the country to afford a duty of 200
acres to the cusec, instead of the 30 to 40 acres which is the average of
inundation canals.[16]

The pronouncement was unambiguous: inundation canals had come up
against natural barriers to their expansion. A shift to perennial canals
would help overcome these barriers. It would enlarge the total irrigable
area, reduce wastage and optimize utilities, with each cusec of water irrigating a bigger area.

The argument for perennial canals was thus framed within a discourse that played on a set of ideas and themes. There was, first, the idea
that inundation canals epitomized wastage and perennial canals optimized
utilities. The Deputy Commissioner of Dera Ismail Khan recognized that an
inadequate supply of river water made the construction of perennial canals
in the tract difficult and inundation canals the only option. 'However,' he
emphasized,

> as frequently before urged by officers in charge of this district, very
> much of the water supply must be wasted, vast labour be year by year
> rendered fruitless, and the resources of the country remain in a great
> measure undeveloped, until a scientific system of irrigation is applied
> to the river, and the water supply regulated at pleasure, and distrib-
> uted as it might be in quality sufficient for the fertilization of the whole
> country.[17]

This argument, in fact, was official commonsense by the late nineteenth century: inundation systems inevitably meant wastage – of natural
resources, of labour and of productive potential. In the monsoon, when
the rivers were in full flow, vast quantities of water poured into the sea
without being used. The water that inundated the fields at this time was
also in excess of what was necessary. Only western science could optimize
the use of resources, harness natural and human potential for the greatest
common good.

Second: there was the question of variability, continuity and stability. Inundation canals were seasonal. They flowed between April and
September, and were dry in the winter. When the snow in the high mountains began to melt, the water level in the rivers rose and the inundation

canals began to flow. In the monsoon, when the rivers swelled, the channels overflowed, the water spilled over the embankments and inundated the fields. The channels continued to flow for a while after the rains, providing valuable late water for the autumn crop (*kharif*) harvest. But by end-October they ran dry as the river water receded. This seasonality meant excess in one season and shortage in another. During the monsoon there were frequent floods and breaches in the embankments, and in winter there was no water to raise a spring crop (*rabi*).[18]

Beyond these seasonal fluctuations between winter and the monsoon, there were annual variations. The Irrigation Commission of 1901 estimated that in the last two decades of the nineteenth century, the average area irrigated by the seven major inundation canals of Punjab increased by about 19 per cent, from 896,296 to 1,069,606 acres. But the annual figures actually varied enormously. In 1899–1900, for instance, the area irrigated was only 859,981 acres, while in the following year it went up to 1,357,699 acres, an increase of 58 per cent.[19] The annual supply was linked to the level of snowfall, the movement of the barometer, the intensity of summer heat and the level of precipitation during the monsoon. There was no way, so the officials felt, that this supply could be stabilized, the variations eliminated and a continuous flow ensured in the irrigation channels.

To the colonial officials, such instabilities were deeply troubling. Their anxiety derived, first, from an anthropomorphic modernism. To be subject to seasonal rhythms was to be subject to nature, with all its fickleness and unreliability, its capriciousness and unpredictability. To be at the mercy of nature was a quality of the primitive. Modernity announced itself by asserting the human capacity to tame and regulate nature. The perennial canals, British officials believed, would enable them to overcome the dictates of nature and allow them to reshape the landscape in the way they wanted. Inundation canals, on the other hand, embodied nature's constraints.

Third: official anxieties about seasonalities also revealed a bourgeois concern with broken cycles of production. Capitalism strives everywhere to establish a regime of continuous time that can ensure a stable line of production and a continuous flow of commodities. When the logic of capital gets naturalized, seasonality in general appears intolerable and discontinuities cause worry. The fear of uncertainty also pointed to an obsession with fixity and stability that Utilitarianism had transformed into the doxa of nineteenth-century Britain.[20]

Fourth: there was the question of production efficiency. Within the late nineteenth-century colonial discourse, inundation canals came to represent a system of inefficient and slack cultivation. Consider the assessment of C.M. King, penned in 1901, about the canal lands of Ferozepur:

> The type of cultivation on lands irrigated from inundation canals is nec-
> essarily a low one; the supply is limited to one period of the year, and
> is very difficult to control; the consequent flooding prevents the proper
> tilling of the ground, and if kharif crops are sown at all, they are sown
> after a very inefficient preparation of the soil. The results of the annual
> floodings and slack cultivation are very apparent all over the Bet, where
> all the canal irrigated tracts are burdened with heavy growths of weeds,
> and all areas subject to percolation are heavily impregnated with kallar
> . . . Whilst the evils, as far as can be seen, are permanent and progres-
> sive, the extra crops raised by canal irrigation diminish year by year as
> the virgin soil gets worked out, and the position in the Bet is very similar
> to that of a man living on his capital.[21]

It was as if all problems, all evils, flowed from the intrinsic quality of the inundation canal system. It nurtured slack cultivation, allowed
weeds to spread, *kallar* (salinity) to accumulate and unhealthy conditions
to be reproduced. Introduction of the perennial system, it was repeatedly
asserted, would solve all these problems. It would allow water supply to
be controlled, flooding to be regulated, cultivation to be intensive and
productivity to develop. Inscribed with impermanence, associated with
a discontinuous temporality, the beneficial effects of inundation canals
were seen as ephemeral and illusory. Only perennial canals could bring
permanent benefits, ensure continuous growth and progress.

Fifth: there was the issue of control and regulation. Modern perennial canals came to be associated with a regime of precision and regulation,
estimation and survey.[22] Before a canal was constructed, precise surveys
were to be made to determine soil types, gradients, depth of water, velocity
of flow, volume of silting, estimated costs-and projected returns. Cross-
sections were cut to decide the point at which the weir was to be built
and the headwork located. Survey reports were to be written up, schemes
were to be proposed and reviewed, and then, once the schemes were in
operation, regular annual reports were to assess their working. Through
the year, the level of water was to be gauged and its flow regulated from
the headworks. Inundation canals were neither constructed with any such
scientific surveys and careful planning, nor could their operation be as
carefully and scientifically regulated.[23]

Within the official mind, inundation canals in many areas were
synonymous with poor planning, uncontrolled irrigation, waterlogging,
kallar, *reh* and sickness. In 1867 Adam Taylor, a civil surgeon, was asked
to survey the villages around the Western Jumna Canal.[24] In the tracts near

the canal he found stagnant swamps with reeds, vegetation in abundance, a spring level near the surface and widespread sickness. The connection between the inundation canals, marsh miasma and illness was indisputable, he asserted. The canal network and drainage lines were badly aligned. They intersected in such a way that the high banks of the channels blocked the natural drainage of the countryside and created swamps. Percolation from the elevated water courses raised the groundwater level and made the drainage of swamps difficult. Stagnant water on clayey tracts brought the salts to the surface, destroying the fertility of the soil and causing sickness. Some of the problems could of course be solved by lowering the canal level, realigning the channels, draining the swamps, and filling up the hollows and ditches. But could the fundamental engineering flaw of the 'native system' be overcome? Taylor was not entirely sceptical, but other officials were unconvinced.[25]

Jolted by the devastating famines of 1878–79 and persuaded by the Famine Commission of 1880, the Punjab officials gave up their ambiguity towards perennial canals. They had always seen perennial canals as superior to inundation canals, but had hesitated to construct them on any large scale. From the early 1880s new schemes were widely discussed and a series of ambitious projects undertaken. The earlier fiscal over-caution gave way to large outlays. By 1900 a total investment of Rs 92,000,000 had been made on the perennial canals in Punjab, and by 1926 over Rs 158,600,000 were spent on just five of the major canal projects.[26] The total outlay on all irrigation canals in 1926 amounted to about Rs 295,400,000. By the turn of the century it became clear that the fear of low and uncertain returns from investment that had plagued the officials in the 1850s was unfounded. The original capital outlay in most of the canals was recouped with ease. The Lower Chenab Project, started in 1892, proved to be one of the most remunerative. After the first twenty years it brought in an annual net revenue amounting to 35–50 per cent of the capital outlay.[27] This meant that the returns of two to three years paid for the capital costs, estimated in 1927 to be around Rs 35,900,000. In 1917, the accumulated outlay on all 'major works' was Rs 223,305,164, whereas the accumulated net revenue was almost double – Rs 428,026,809.[28] By the twentieth century investment in irrigation had become an appealing financial proposition, and the possibility of high fiscal returns began to attract large investments for ambitious projects of perennial irrigation. The logic of imperial science could unfold without burdening the exchequer.

As imperial science marched forward – cutting through the *bar*, transforming the commons into cultivated fields – the older inundation systems went into decline. While the area irrigated by perennial canals expanded dramatically from the late nineteenth century, the area under inundation canals stagnated, increasing less than 20 per cent in the last two decades of the century.[29] Convinced of the superiority of perennial canals and assured of high returns, the imperial government in the late nineteenth century was willing to make large capital outlays for perennial canals. Inundation canals, on the other hand, were starved of funds. Expenditure on their construction and maintenance was to be met from whatever money could be spared from current revenue, which was rarely adequate even for the maintenance of existing works. The construction of perennial canals, moreover, cut the flow of water in the rivers and squeezed the supply to inundation canals.

The annual maintenance of inundation canals had, in any case, become a general problem from the time the Canal Department began to supervise the clearance. Once *cher* – the collective labour that the community contributed in the pre-British period for the maintenance of collective utilities – was demanded by the state, and the amount of labour to be contributed by each irrigator was specified by the Canal Department rather than regulated by the community, the system began to break down. Cultivators resisted working as *cher*, saw it as coercive and refused to clear the silt. The state reacted by threatening to impose water rates wherever the irrigators were seen as obdurate.[30] When, in the 1870s, an *abiana* (water rate) was imposed at a uniform rate of Rs 5.5 per acre in addition to the demand for *cher* labour, angry zamindars refused to pay and petitioned against the unjust rates.[31] The consequent clashes between the local zamindars and the Irrigation Department paralysed the management of inundation systems.

The Irrigation Commission of 1901, meeting after the terrible famine years at the turn of the century, emphasized once again the protective value of inundation canals in the dry tracts of Punjab.[32] But the ideal agrarian order of British imagination was to be built around the perennial canals that were to stretch through the *bar*, transforming the pastoral tracts, displacing pastoralists and bringing the wilderness into the fold of 'civilization'.

A Regime of Squares
From the beginning of British rule, the colonial officials had despaired at the absence of order within the agrarian landscape. Fields were of irregular shape; plots were splintered into innumerable, scattered small fragments; and meandering village boundaries interlocked in complicated ways. In the canal colonies they could at last hope to impose their own sense of order.

Over the years, colonization became associated with a regime of squares. The entire landscape was plotted within a network of straight lines. In most places, before the construction of the canals, the Canal Department carried out a complete survey of the whole *bar*. A central base-line was laid down the middle of the *bar*, and from this cross-lines were run out at right angles on both sides at distances of 1,100 feet. On these cross-lines bricks were laid at intervals of 1,100 feet. The water courses (*rajbahas*) were designed to run along the sides of the canal squares. This canal survey became the basis of the subsequent field survey on the square system. Permanent pillars were laid at the corner of each square of 27.7 acres, and these were subdivided into twenty-five equal squares.[33] The rectangular plot with straight lines – so important in the modernist imagination – was designated as a *killa*. And the act of enclosing the commons, erecting the demarcating pillars and subdividing the land into smaller squares came to be known as *killabandi*. [34]

Killabandi was seen as an act of mapping order on to space. The early reports on colonization describe with great enthusiasm the annual progress of *killabandi*. We are told of the innumerable obstacles faced and the way each one was surmounted as colonizing officers set about transforming the imperial vision into reality. Apprehensive of surveys, scared of a further loss of their rights over the *bar* and certain that measurement meant taxes, the nomads inevitably resisted *killabandi*. In the existing proprietary villages too, fields had to be remapped, irregular boundaries straightened, ancestral shares transformed into neat rectangular fields and fragmented plots consolidated into uniform large holdings. The task everywhere proved more difficult than was initially visualized. People resented the exchange of lands that was necessary to straighten the boundaries of villages and holdings, and were reluctant to give up their ancient shares. In many places where *killabandi* was completed but irrigation water was yet to reach, people refused to extend cultivation into the waste.[35] And *killa* marks usually disappeared wherever land was not brought under the plough. In the low-lying *chahi* lands irrigated by wells, the old field boundaries were the well-runnels; and when canal officers insisted on demolishing these to construct the new boundaries, the Hithari cultivators refused to oblige.[36] To subdue recalcitrance and counter resistance, canal officers withheld supply of canal water and threatened to impose high taxes. If *killabandi* was essential for the agrarian conquest of the landscape, for the creation of an ideal order, all barriers to it had to be overcome.

Killabandi created a regime of squares – the cartographic grid for an ordered society. It was an image of order that drew upon a long-held western obsession with the straight line. Within this imagination, the straight line signified clarity, confidence, certainty; it reflected the power of man, the order of science. Squares and rectangles represented uniformity, homogeneity, regularity, symmetry, precision and neatness – all essential elements of order. This visual imagination defined itself against an alternative aesthetic that celebrated the curved line, the irregularities of nature, the beauty of the unusual, the strange – an aesthetic that discovered in homogeneity, symmetry and uniformity only a deadening sameness, a numbing monotony.[37] Colonial officials sought to reconcile these opposing aesthetic ideals, appreciating at the same time the beauty of nature and the rationality behind symmetry. They searched for the picturesque, but recognized the need for precise measurements and ordering of space. A regime of squares, it was almost universally felt, would make governance easier and more efficient, the landscape more legible, calculation of revenue demand and crop output simpler. It would affirm the rationality of science as well as the power of the colonizers. The agrarian conquest was not only to extend the arable, but also to civilize the nomad, reorder space and create the basis of an ideal agrarian society.

The map of the *abadi* (residential settlement) operated on the same logic. In contrast to the traditional villages with irregular boundaries, the colony settlements were planned within a grid of straight lines, with a *chowk* in the middle, rows of houses arranged in a series of concentric squares, and residences of the lower castes located on the periphery. Unlike the older settlements which usually came up around wells, the model colony villages were planned around a marketplace. Two sets of broad roads ran through each *abadi* at right angles, with narrower parallel lanes connecting the main roads. Each house was numbered and its location predefined.

The village was enclosed and bounded. It had one entry point and one exit.[38] If this facilitated protection of the village, it equally made possible easy surveillance and policing of inhabitants.

In the long term the order of squares proved to be an elusive ideal. The *killa* (one-twenty-fifth part of a colony square – about 1.1 acres) did become a common measure of distance, but individual fields on the ground could not be demarcated through straight lines separated into neat squares. Sales and mortgages of part holdings made it necessary to re-map field boundaries. In the process the regime of irregular plots reappeared, and the lines on the cadastral maps became messy. As for the model *abadis*, they were simpler to plan than settle. In most places, grantees claimed their right over the residential sites – extending their control over as much land as they could get – but they built their homesteads within their own individual cultivating squares. Location at the centre of their large landholding allowed easy access to fields and management of cultivation.

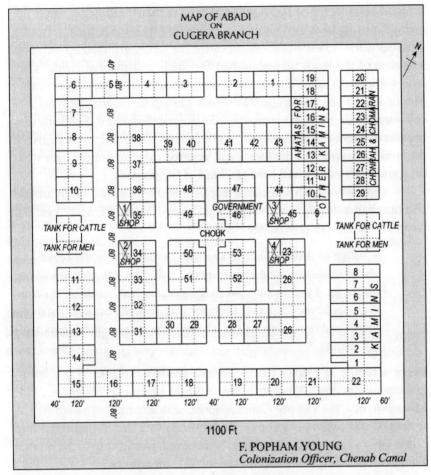

MAP OF ABADI
ON
GUGERA BRANCH

1100 Ft

F. POPHAM YOUNG
Colonization Officer, Chenab Canal

Vision of Order: The Plan of a Canal Colony 'Abadi'

Dismayed officials at first fretted about the intransigence of the grantees and threatened to use punitive measures to enforce compliance to rules. Then, after the plague epidemic of 1907, they persuaded themselves to believe in the virtues of living in isolated houses. Co-residence in compacted settlements, they now declared, increased the possibility of a rapid spread of the epidemic. By 1911 they conceded to a change in the norm itself.

Enclosing the Fields

From the mid-nineteenth century, the pastoralists of the *bar* had found their movements restricted and their grazing lands converted into government *rakhs*. Their ideas of territory and sovereignty were under question, and the authority of their chiefs was radically restructured. Now in the closing years of the century, they saw their land being sliced up, formed into squares and given over to people who descended in hordes from outside.[39] These outsiders cut down the scrub, grubbed up the roots and cleared the land; they ploughed the fields and planted crops. Then fences appeared, marking one field from another and barring the entry of 'outsiders'. The pastoralists were told to stop their cattle straying into cultivated fields, trampling crops and destroying the harvest. Suddenly they became outsiders on land they saw as their own. The immigrants swarmed the land, outnumbered the locals and asserted their monopoly over what till some years earlier had been the land of the nomads.

Stories of enclosures and displacements, however, rarely unfold without drama. In 1919, an exasperated Deputy Commissioner of Lyallpur wrote to the Punjab government in despair:

> A village of Aklake Khurral aborigines exists here in the centre of a nest of villages of Arain immigrant colonists. This village, 9 headstrong janglis, for 4 to 5 months habitually pastured 3000 cattle on the crops of all neighbouring chaks. They never allowed the cattle to get to the pound, and rescued and rioted whenever the immigrant colonists made any seizures.[40]

Every attempt at rescue led to violent confrontations. Many immigrant peasants died. A punitive post was set up in the village, but G.F. Montmorency, the Deputy Commissioner, was sceptical of its efficacy. A system of roll-calls could not tie the Khurrals to a life of innocence and order. Only a heavy communal fine, he believed, would stop such criminal villages from being a nuisance to the settled community.

As reports flowed in from different regions, it became clear that the story of the Khurral villages was being re-enacted elsewhere in the canal colonies. Peasants from central Punjab who had migrated to the colonies and begun cultivation found their enclosed fields regularly invaded by cattle from neighbouring nomad settlements. Cattle rescues led to bloodshed, and official complaints provoked retribution. Cattle belonging to the immigrant peasants were poisoned and harvested crops were burnt.[41] The police were as helpless as the peasants. Unable to check the cattle invasions, officials demanded that the turbulent nomads be classified as a criminal tribe.[42] Severe action had to be taken against those who impeded the progress of colonization and subverted the foundation of a settled agrarian life in the *bars*.

Cattle 'trespass' as a problem was of course not peculiar to the canal colonies. By the mid-nineteenth century, worried officials in different regions of India were debating the need for legislative intervention to stop the evil. The Cattle Trespass Act was passed in 1871, but the clamour for more effective and stringent measures continued for decades. The problem was particularly acute in places where pastoral lands were being taken over for plantations or settled agriculture. In these transitional landscapes, the new order of rights could not be established without the trauma of dispossession, and without negotiation and conflict.

In 1983, the tea planters of Wynad, in Calicut, demanded a modification of the 1871 Act.[43] Trespassing cattle were destroying their plantations, they claimed, and without punitive measures the evil could not be controlled. The existing provisions of the Act were too mild and ineffective, fines were low and impounding of cattle was difficult. It was necessary, they felt, to enhance the fines, punish attempted cattle rescues, brand all cattle over eighteen months old and shoot cattle straying into the plantations.

Sensitive to planter interests and keen on establishing the sanctity of the new regime of rights, Government of India (GoI) began a review of the Act. When, in 1886, the planters petitioned once again, GoI asked local governments for reports on cattle trespass.[44] The need for some amendment was widely recognized, but local officials feared the social implications of harsh measures. With expansion of the arable and contraction of pastures, they conceded, cattle grazing had become a problem. In many areas, villages of pastoralists and peasants were honeycombed together. The boundaries between them were fuzzy and uncertain. Thoroughfares cut through villages, and the paths that cattle had to take on their daily march to grazing grounds ran past cultivated lands. It was difficult to prevent cattle straying on to fields of grain, particularly when the fields were rarely fenced.[45] In such a situation, punitive action against unintentional straying could create needless anger against the administration.[46]

Reports from many regions in fact suggested that it was the cattle owners who needed protection from routine harassment.[47] The Chief Commissioner of Assam asked for legal power to punish planters and landholders for illegitimate seizures and illegal detentions of cattle.[48] They were reportedly seizing any cattle grazing near their land and detaining the animals under their own charge instead of driving them to the official pound.[49] Graziers could not recover their cattle without paying the arbitrary amounts the planters demanded as compensation. Unless the planters were restrained, the Chief Commissioner seemed to say, the legitimacy of the legal regime itself would be subverted. True, trespass had to be controlled and legitimate fines imposed, only then could the new rights of property on common land be legally sanctified. But the efficacy of this legal regime would be undermined if publicly pronounced measures were

persistently violated by planters and landholders, if illegal detentions and
arbitrary and extortionate demands of the planters went unchecked.

The GoI was now caught in a bind. It was willing to deny the
planters the penal powers they were clamouring for, but was reluctant
to grant to local officials the authority to punish the planters under the
Indian Penal Code.[50] A legal regime could not appear to be just unless it
disciplined capital, unless it defined the constraints within which everyone had to operate, but could it be turned brutally against the planters?
The GoI manoeuvred its way out of the fix by refusing at the same time
the demands of both the planters and the Assam Chief Commissioner.
After consultations with the Advocate General of Bengal and Madras,
and a prolonged debate in the Legislative Department, the Assam Chief
Commissioner was told that that his request could have no legal sanction.[51] And in 1888, the planters who had petitioned for greater punitive
powers to stop trespass were informed by the GoI that their request for
amendment of the Trespass Act could not be met.[52]

Trespass was thus a category intimately connected to the new
regime of rights, particularly in transitional zones. At one level, it expressed
the state's desire to settle populations, demarcate fields and define the
spatial limits of mobility. It was a category through which nomadism was
to be restricted and criminalized. It signified a new process of territorialization – a spatialization of rights, the establishment of a regime in which
spaces had to be tied to owners and property was to be deified. At another
level, the outcry of planters against trespass revealed the desire of capital
to appropriate land as the exclusive sphere of its own operation, its refusal
to tolerate any other claims on that land.

In the canal colonies, however, the problem of cattle trespass
had acquired an added dimension. It was the sign of a war between the
nomads and the immigrant colonists. The Khurral cattle did not simply
stray into the fields of the Arain cultivators. They were herded in there. It
was a deliberate and performative act, flamboyantly executed, in defiance
of the new territorialization of space. Before British rule, the *bar* was under
the control of different nomadic groups, each with their distinct areas of
control – spaces within which the sovereignty of each group was exercised,
and the hierarchy of power between the *rat* (leader of the clan) and the
jan (followers) worked out. In the eighteenth century, the Bharwana Sials
controlled the Chenab *bar* in the west, the Khurrals were the masters of
the central *bar*, the Bhattis ruled the Gujranwala *bar* in the northeast, the
Biloches were dominant in the south. Sial power was in decline by the
early nineteenth century, but the Khurrals had pushed further north, helped
the Waghas displace the Bhattis, and consolidated their power over the

entire central *bar*. If the territory defined the limits of pastures, the limits of territory – always ambiguous and fluid – were continuously negotiated through the politics of grazing and raiding.

With British annexation, the *bar* was first taken over as government waste, and then colonized and settled. Faced with the power of the colonial state, the nomadic chiefs were forced to accept their new position as *tirni guzars*, and collected the grazing-tax (*tirni*) for the state. But they hated the loss of their power, their territory, their sovereignty and their grazing lands. In 1857, the great Ravi tribes led by Ahmad Khan, a Khurral chief of Jhamra, rose in rebellion. When the Gugeira revolt was ultimately crushed by the British army, the rebels were cut to pieces, their villages burnt, their cattle tracked down in the jungles and slaughtered.[53] The civilizing state re-enacted in macabre and perverse fashion, the logic of tribal feuds.[54]

The rebellion failed but the war continued. It was a daily, unrelenting war against the new rules and new demarcation of spaces, against the new regime of canals and cultivated fields. Within the political culture of the nomads, outsiders could gain entry into a nomadic territory either through a war or by submitting to the chief who controlled that space. Otherwise the alien presence would subvert the very idea of territoriality. By the late nineteenth century, the cultivated field had appeared as the symbol of the new regime, the visible marks of the radical reterritorialization of space. Hemmed in from all sides and surrounded by Arain villages, the Khurrals were now unable to move freely between their summer and winter pastures, from the uplands to the low lands, or enter the jungles in times of drought when the open pastures withered. The *killas* that demarcated the fields and the *rakhs* marked the lines the nomads could not cross without trespassing. In herding the cattle on to the cultivated fields and allowing them to pasture on the crops, the Khurrals were asserting their right over the space. The Arains were seen as usurpers, outsiders, who had to be displaced. The illegitimacy of their claims had to be visibly and overtly challenged.

If cattle trespass emerged as a major crime within the colonial rule of property and signified a new territorialization of rights, its dramatic persistence reflected the effort of the nomads to question and renegotiate these new notions of rights, property and spatiality. This process of negotiation shaped not only the relations of the nomads with the migrant peasants and the state; it specified the meaning of property. The rights associated with property were not all embedded in the term itself, specified in the grants of land that were given to the colonists.

A New Language of Claims

The war against immigrant colonists continued through the colonial period. Their crops were ruined by invading herds, their harvests burnt by night, their fences demolished, their cattle poisoned with arsenic or carried away in large numbers, their villages regularly raided. Silent resistance enacted off-stage in the anonymity of darkness, away from the eye of power, combined with collective actions, theatrically performed and provocatively executed. This was a war against the new ideas of territoriality and agrarian order, against the new notions of normality and legality, against the colonization of the *bars* by immigrant outsiders, against the new rule of property.

Yet at another level a different process was at work. By the early twentieth century we hear a different language of negotiation, expressed in petitions to officials, articulated in local newspapers and later, by the 1920s, asserted on the floor of legislative assemblies. This was a language of rights that accepted the founding premises of the new order and demanded a space within it. It narrated painful stories of displacement, suffering and distress, and asked for justice. At times it defended the rights of pastoral groups to live in harmony with times past: to be nomads, to retain control over their animals, if not their sovereignty within the spaces they saw as their territory. But more often, it claimed the rights of nomads to a life of dignity within the new set-up. It protested not against colonization as such, but against the specific form in which the project was implemented. Hear Muhammad Khan of Montgomery during a 1929 debate on allotments of grants in the Nili Bar Colony:

> I stick to my old principle that the sons of the soil should get precedence over others in all claims for grants. These are the people who are born and bred there, these are the people who had been earning their bread there and these are the people who have been living there from time immemorial, and now that land is made irrigable, is it fair, is it just and is it equitable that these sons of the soil should be turned out of their holdings, that they should be turned out of their hearths and homes and that they should be sent to some remoter corner, simply because they are not good cultivators? I ask is that a right principle for the Government to follow. Is it right, Sir, that the sons of the soil should be turned out from this place for facilitating people who are much more advanced educationally, economically, and morally, to receive their share in the colonies.[55]

This is no defence of nomadic pastoral life. Mohammad Khan sees irrigation as progress, the expansion of cultivation as desirable, peasants as superior to nomads in every way. He does not celebrate the past against the present, the reason of the nomads against that of a sedentarist state, the trajectory of smooth and open spaces against striated ones. But he questions the principles on which allotments were being granted. Using the language of equity and justice, he pleads for the claims of the *'janglis'* within the new order, and recounts their anguish and misery. Operating through the discourse of indigeneity, he projects the nomads as sons of the soil – tracing their rights back into the mists of time, to the originary mythic moment of creation when the *bars* were supposedly settled. Aware that colonial laws generally recognized the rights of original settlers, Muhammad Khan transforms the nomads into *abadkars* (those who settled the land – original settlers) who, he claims, had cleared the land and settled on it. It was as if nomadism and mobility could not be the basis of any right over space. The critique of government policy was at the same time an affirmation of the colonial agrarian vision. This dialectic between critique and affirmation has a contradictory logic: it transforms as well as naturalizes what it affirms.

Much before this discourse of indigeneity acquired rhetorical power, colonization had become a site of negotiation. By the end of the nineteenth century, as cattle theft and cattle trespass became endemic, and cattle raids led to riots, it was clear that the policy of colonization required rethinking. The original colonization project was based on a radical hostility towards the nomads. They were seen as lazy, rebellious, violent, turbulent, imprudent and thieving. With their dislike of cultivation, love of mobility and proclivity for crime, it was said, they could not be pioneer colonists. They had to be displaced, watched and disciplined.

Gradually, it was reluctantly admitted that the refusal to allot any land to the *janglis* was unjust and unfair: they had to be given grants even if they were bad cultivators. As the Settlement Officer of Chenab Colony said in 1903: 'it was only a bare act of justice to acknowledge their claims'.[56] But once they were given grants, officials found it difficult to sustain the stereotypes through which they perceived the *janglis*. They soon recognized, with a sense of surprise, that the *janglis* were proving to be good colonists.[57] Their lands were carefully cultivated, their were villages clean and well-kept, and their animals were properly groomed. After the success of grants to *'janglis'* in Chenab Colony, the officials decided to replicate the experiment in other colonies that were coming up. But stereotypes are tenacious. And when they become the foundation of a societal vision, they acquire an amazing resilience. Many officials grudgingly accepted the need to accommodate the demands of the nomads, but saw this only as a pragmatic move, necessary for peace and order. The anger of the rebellious nomads could not be controlled without conceding them a space within the new order. But could they be seen as either fine cultivators or good subjects?

Caught in a bind, the officials both accepted and denied the claims of the *janglis*. When Muhammad Hussain declared that the indigenous population, the sons of the soil, had the first claim to colony lands, the Financial Commissioner sneered at the idea:

> I cannot accept the honourable member's proposition that the local peo-
> ple have the first claim on the Crown waste that becomes available after
> colonization. The Government are the trustees of this underdeveloped
> wealth, which is the property of the province as a whole. The first con-
> sideration must be to get the land colonized by the best cultivators in the
> province. Local people in Montgomery and Multan are not, I am afraid,
> particularly famous as good cultivators. In fact many of them are really
> not cultivators at all. However, as I have stated, the Government did
> recognize that it is only fair that the local people should have a certain
> proportion of land and as long ago as 1913 and 1914.[58]

Craik could not entirely reject the claims of the *janglis*, but was unwilling to acknowledge them as ideal colonists. In a familiar move, he deployed the rhetoric of the greatest common good to deny the prerogatives of the indigenous population and justify their displacement as a historically necessary act. If colonization was a collective good and the peasants of central Punjab ideal colonists, then dispossession of the *janglis* was stated to be unavoidable in the general interests of the population.

The developing contradiction within the colonizing project was even more evident in the way service grants were allotted. Worried by the shrinking supply of camels, horses and mules for the army, and the disappearance of pastures with the progress of irrigation, the colonial state had to rework the project of colonization. But how could the supplies of horses and camels be expanded without encouraging nomadic pastoralism? How could dry lands be irrigated and animal stock of the region reproduced at the same time? The idea of service grants proposed by the Horse Breeding Commission provided one seeming solution to the contradiction. It dissociated animal breeding from nomadism, tied breeders to the land, linked animal husbandry to cultivation. In the Jhelum Colonies 402,000 acres out of a total allocable area of 540,000 acres were originally set aside as peasant grants.[59] At the suggestion of the Horse Breeding Commission of 1901, it was decided that this entire area, 74 per cent of the total, would be given out as service grant for horse breeding.[60] Each grantee would be required to cultivate the land as well as maintain a brood mare for every square (28 acres) allotted. The prior claim of the government over animal stock was written into the conditions of the grant.[61] Animal breeders had to be settled just as much as cultivators, confined within bounded governable spaces, subject to observation, survey, enumeration and control.

But who was to get the horse breeding grant? Was it to be the pastoralist who proclaimed his will to settle and cultivate, or the peasant who agreed to maintain a brood mare? The gathering local anger against the influx of immigrants persuaded the state to create more space within the colony for west Punjab inhabitants. But it was still reluctant to open this space to the pastoral nomads. In the months of March, April and May of 1902, J.H.R. Fraser, acting on behalf of the Colonizing Officer of Jhelum Canal, selected the first batch of 1,000 for horse breeding grants. These grantees were all peasants from Shahpur, Gujrat and Gujranwala districts. 'The peasant colonists so far selected', reported Fraser later in the year, 'are nearly all men of the agricultural class, and care has been exercised in taking as far as possible only men who cultivate with their own hands.'[62] Peasants who were willing to buy a mare were given land, though they neither had any experience of breeding nor any real desire to be breeders.[63] Yet, a year after the first round of allotments, the Colonizing Officer criticized the laxity with which the grantees had been selected and underlined the need to be even more vigilant about excluding *janglis* from horse breeding grants.[64] In the ideal colony of colonial imagination, even horse breeding had to be the responsibility of settled peasants. The willingness of nomads to settle was always suspect.[65]

As the clamour for local grants intensified, Settlement Officers had to reduce the area of colony land that was granted to outsiders. But they still discriminated between landowners and nomads, excluding the *janglis* from the best canal lands and favouring the big landowners of west Punjab for the service grants.[66] Allotments to *janglis* were usually smaller in size than those to landowners.[67] They were mostly located on poor-quality land, in marginal areas, at a distance from the perennial canals, or at the end of distributaries where water supply was erratic. The prime land on the perennial canals, near the head, was reserved for 'ideal colonists' – industrious and enterprising peasants from central Punjab. The explosive implication of this politics of discrimination became apparent as the geography of grants came to overlap with the maps of social conflict.

Promise and Betrayal

Awal sain sachche nun saran   First I will remember the true lord
Ik qissa nawan aj joran   I will tell a new tale today.

Bar agge lut khadi choran	Of the old *bar* that was the prey of thieves
Harn, gidar, chuhehan dian ghoran,	A tract where deer, jackals and rats roamed
Sunjan jangal koi nahi raha,	Now no barren jungle is left
Young Sahib diya mulk wasa.	Young Sahib has peopled the land.
Lyallpur da sun hal,	Hear the tale of Lyallpur
Ann jal da kithe sokal,	Where grain and water abound
Nahr wahundi darwaze nal,	The canal runs by gateways
Drakht lawae pal-o-pal	Trees have been planted in rows
Hor pae jamde sawe gha	And green grass comes sprouting up.
Young Sahib diya mulk wasa.	Young sahib has peopled the land.

These are lines from a long ballad of forty-three stanzas that a blind poet, Kana, sang when Captain Popham Young, the Colonizing Officer of Chenab Colony, left Lyallpur in 1899.[68] The ballad tells the tale of a grand agrarian conquest. In language suffused with a sense of wonder and fascination, it describes how a wild and desolate land was turned into a land of plenty, overflowing with grain, well supplied with water, adorned with trees. This extraordinary transformation was made possible only through the incredible, mythopoeic powers of the British. They created the colony, tamed the wilderness and peopled the land: they turned the river aside, dug a canal that was straight as an arrow (*jin dita darya nun chirae, nahr kadhai siddhi tir ae*), built a weir, dammed the river, cleared the brushwood, mapped the *bar*, measured the land, connected the place by railways and telegraph, established markets, and gave land to the Sikhs. They were not only heroic and mighty (*Angrez bahadur bhara bir ae*), but were capable of achieving the impossible. Like saints they could perform miracles: in a moment they could make the jungle disappear (*Eh Angrez aulia zarur, Sach man ozara na kur, Pal wich jangal kita dur*). They made no empty promises: they fulfilled them. They were true to their word (*ikko waida sachchi bat*).

The words of Kana were reassuring to the colonizers' ears. We see them tirelessly reproduced in official records as evidence of 'the impression that the colony made on native minds'.[69] The ballad reaffirmed the self-image of the colonizers as aggressive agents of progress, bringing nature into culture, domesticating the landscape through the application of science and reason. It celebrated both the 'unbelievable transformation' in the canal colonies and the miraculous power of the British. The promise that Kana refers to is the promise of paradise that British officials inevitably made while persuading zamindars from the old districts to migrate to the colonies.

Was Kana capturing the universal experience of those who migrated to the colonies in search of paradise? Barely eight years after Captain Popham Young left, Lyallpur became the centre of an intense social movement that called into question each term of Kana's celebratory narrative of colonization. In December 1906, a Colonization Bill was introduced and hurriedly passed in the Punjab Legislative Council.[70] It sought to amend the Punjab Colonization of Land Act 1893. When Chenab Colony was being settled in the early 1890s, the British were keen to create an ideal agrarian setting free of absentee landlordism, minute plots, unnirrigated fields and unsanitary surroundings. Peasant grantees were given large holdings of 28 to 56 acres, but to ensure a measure of control over them, they were made crown tenants and denied proprietary rights. They were expected to live in the *abadi*, not in their farms, and to maintain clean surroundings; they could not be absent for long periods or leave the colony without prior permission. Within some years the British discovered the difficulty of producing the landscape of their imagination. The colonists were building their homesteads within their farms, resisting living in the *abadi*, disappearing for long periods and transferring their land in accordance with the customary practices of the old districts. When the Colonization Officer began confiscating grants and imposing fines for non-compliance of conditions, angry colonists grumbled and protested, often challenging his actions in court. The Colonization Act of 1906 was to extend the disciplinary reach of the state, legalize the regime of confiscation and fines, and introduce a set of new terms within the old agreements. The colonists were now required to practise primogeniture, plant trees on their farms and maintain a brood mare for supply to the government. The patriarchal power of the Colonization Officer was consolidated by making his actions *sub judice*.

As the terms of the Colonization Bill came to be known, anxious settlers began mobilizing opinion, organizing meetings, drafting memorials and petitioning officials against the Bill. Newspapers carried angry letters and articles detailing the complaints of the settlers and narrating their experience – some written by the colonists, others speaking on their behalf. Energetic mobilization was reflected in the growing numbers at meetings. On 14 January 1907, about 300 zamindars from twenty-four villages met in Samundari *tehsil* and resolved to draft a memorial that was to be submitted to the Legislative Council.[71] Thirteen days later, on 27 January, over 3,000 zamindars assembled at Sangla, protesting against the Bill.[72] At a grand meeting organized at Lyallpur on 3 February, as many as 8,000 zamindars of Chenab Canal collected.[73] The premises of the Arya Samaj, where the meeting was held, overflowed with people sitting on walls and roofs of buildings, clogging the streets and immobilizing traffic. Through the month, the *Bar* Zamindar Association carried on an intense campaign against the Bill, appealing to the *jat* sense of honour and justice, and stirring them to action. On 22 and 23 March, another mammoth meeting was held in Lyallpur in which over 9,000 colonists gathered.[74] By the end of March the agitation spread from Chenab to Jhelum, with nationalist leaders like Lala Lajpat Rai and Ajit Singh addressing meetings, touring the rural areas, and seeking to integrate the movement in the canal colonies into the wider anti-imperialist struggle.[75]

Two different discourses merged and separated in the language of protest that developed around the Colonization Bill. One was a discourse of morality and ethics. Worried and agitated zamindars repeatedly asked: how could the government dishonour its words, its promises and its assurances? Till now, declared one polemicist, everyone had agreed that the British government with all its problems was 'sure to stand firm to an agreement that it has once formally made'.[76] This conviction was now rudely shaken. The government had gone back on its word and violated its commitment; it had subverted the premises of trust and faith. How could the zamindars now rely on the assurances of the government?

Beyond the moral politics of trust and good faith was the question of law. Drawing upon the legal discourse that colonial officials operated with, pedagogues and publicists, lawyers and zamindars warned the government against violating assurances that had been not only verbally stated, but also formally codified, embodied in agreements that were in fact like contracts.[77] Colonial officials, inspired by Benthamite ideals, had emphasized for long that fixed rules and codified laws were the necessary basis of security, stability and rational order, that publicly encoded, determinate and substantive rules allowed the formation of secure expectations and rational calculations. How could they now forget these ideas? In a powerful critique of the Colonization Bill, Harbhajan Singh, a pleader, reminded the government of the meaning of a contract: once a contract was made and its conditions specified, no one party was entitled 'to vary or modify it without the consent of the other party to it'.[78] On what basis, then, could the government arbitrarily and unilaterally change the terms of the colony grants with retrospective effect, modifying the original conditions? The terms could be changed in the future, when fresh grants were given on newly colonized lands – though even these terms ought not to be oppressive – but new clauses could not be written into the conditions of grants that had been already formalized.[79] This was a message forcefully underlined by the *Bar* Zamindar Association that met on 27 January:

> In the opinion of this meeting the Government has no justification to alter, amend or add to the conditions of written agreements under which lands were granted in Colonies; and it is unworthy of Government to make even the slightest alteration in formal agreements entered into with the colonists. . . . Though the Government is at liberty to make any conditions for future grants of Government lands, yet it is desirable that the rules for future colonies be not stringent.[80]

The argument was reiterated with polemical vigour in the pages of the *Zamindar*, a newspaper that claimed to represent the opinions of the rural proprietary body. If the Colonization Bill was to be introduced, declared the *Zamindar*, then government assurances would no longer be believed and contracts would lose their sanctity. The promises of the government would be seen as part of a deliberate strategy of deception.[81] It would appear that the government had seduced the people with false promises, persuading them to migrate to an alien land, leave their families and ancestral homes, bear the expenses and rigours of early colonization, and then changed the terms of settlement once the new colonies came up and the soil began to yield.[82] Such a deception, such a breach of faith, could only create a popular climate of distrust and suspicion, and destroy the authority of the government.[83]

As the theme of deception and bad faith was elaborated, the story of colonization was recast as a narrative of suffering and heroism, of promise and betrayal. When the Chenab Canal Colony was being developed, 150 families from Batala in Gurdaspur were among the first migrants to reach Jhang. Louise Dane had personally told them 'that the land they were going to would be found overflowing with milk and honey'.[84] They were all told that they would get large fields, plenty of water through the year and well-connected markets; taxes would be light, harvests secure and prosperity unbounded. When the migrants reached their destination in 1892 they could see only a vast landscape of aridity, a desolate scrubland covered with wild *farash*, *jand* and *lana*. Water channels were yet to be dug, and for many years the supply of water was erratic and inadequate. The rainfall was good in the first year, and large tracts of the land were cleared and broken up; but by July a cholera epidemic spread and then a malignant fever prostrated the population. In 1891–92, a total of 7,605 peasant grantees received their allotments, 6,453 took possession and of these 914 left, never to return.[85] In the subsequent year, the story was similar: about 151,865 acres were given out to peasant settlers but 47,061 acres – about a third – remained unoccupied.[86] Disappointed migrants, enervated by illness, frightened by the wilderness, unwilling to believe the words of the colonizing officers, returned to the security of familiar surroundings in their home villages.

If we moved from the Chenab to the Jhelum Colony, the story was no different. A migrant settler on Jhelum canal, recounting in 1910 the experience of early years of colonization, replayed the same theme of promise and betrayal. Before the grants were given, we are told, the Colonization Officer 'so highly eulogized the quality of soil that the colonists thought that it was veritable Eldorado'.[87] Only later did the settlers realize that 'the so-called fertile land was no better than a series of mounds of sand with patches of land of worthless quality'. Disenchanted but undeterred, the pioneers cleared and ploughed the land, sparing no pain and hardship to bring it under cultivation, converting the 'once barren and desolate country . . . into a luxuriantly verdant field'.[88] But the problems of the colonists continued. The water supply was so miserable and unpredictable that even in 1910 the standing wheat crops were drying up. Worst affected were lands located at the tail-end of the canal as they rarely got any water. While crops withered and harvests failed revenue officers refused to remit revenue and the state imposed new water rates, adding to the burden the colonists had to bear. In addition to the land revenue and the water rates, the colonists were subjected to a range of levies: unpaid labour for digging channels and dredging canals, arbitrary fines for non-conformity with conditions of grants, tips for the *patwari* and the *tahsildar*.[89] As the protest against the Bill intensified and the catalogue of suffering became ever longer, the canal colonies were re-figured as a place full of danger and trouble. We hear of the constant threat of natural calamities, fear of wild animals and snakes, unrelenting attacks by 'savage *janglis*', and the oppression of the *sahukars*, *patwaris* and *lambardars*.[90]

Narratives of suffering fused with stories of heroism to doubly underline the injustice of British action in altering the terms of the settlement. The pioneer settlers, we are told, faced a hostile environment and suffered immense hardship, but they confronted all the problems and worked hard – living in savage surroundings amidst wild animals and *janglis* – to transform a wilderness into a productive landscape.[91] Many died, many lost links with their families, but the pioneers went ahead, undaunted, to create life in the colonies. It was as if their sacrifices and heroism sanctified their relationship with the land, and made the original contracts doubly sacred. To alter those terms now would be an act of betrayal and treachery.

The image of the canal colonies that these narratives suggest is radically different from the one offered in Kana's ballad. Kana deifies the British, imbues them with creativity, represents them as heroic agents of progress, as resourceful, imaginative and ingenious; in the counter-narrative the settlers appear as the real heroes, the pioneers who tame the wilderness and make it productive with their industry, skill and courage. In one narrative the landscape that the early settlers confront in the canal colonies is a land of promise, bearing all the marks of progress and development – canals, markets, railways, the telegraph; in the other it is a landscape of savagery and desolation, of danger and death. In one story the British appear as benevolent, selfless, honest and trustworthy, always honouring their word, caring about the people; in the other they are seen as violating their promises, dishonouring their commitments, manipulating the poor zamindars. The complicated and tortuous association between these contrary images continued to mediate the relationship between the zamindars and the British in the canal colonies.

The contrary voices that I refer to had one element in common. Both represented the minds of agrarian settlers, whose fortunes were linked to the expansion of the arable, the colonization of the pastoral commons. Dispossessed of their pastures and displaced from their fields, most local inhabitants of the region – pastoralists and peasants – experienced the history of this colonization as a time of violence and repression. Only the power of a small section of landed aristocracy was reaffirmed.[92]

Antinomies of Development
In the *Canal Colonies Report* of 1933 we read the following account of what colonization had meant for the *bar* tracts:

> The year has been one of real progress. The open spaces of the desert have everywhere been portioned out in meticulous rectangles; jungle trees have been felled, and the wandering camel-tracks of the waste have given place to the durable macadam of public roads, running for miles without a curve and without a gradient. The goat-herd's pipe and the quavering love-song of the camel men are mute, and in their place we hear the Klaxon of the motor-lorry and the folding harmonium of the peripatetic preacher. The reed encampments of the nomads, their jhoks and rahnas, open to sun and wind and clean as a dancing-floor, have been replaced by the midden-infested mud-houses of the central Punjab. The nomad himself, once free of the Bar and of his neighbour's cattle, has been pegged out, Prometheus like on his 25 killas, while the vultures of civilization bury their ravenous beaks in his vitals.[93]

A passage that set out to recount a story of progress ends up capturing the pathos of development. The official mind, captivated by the idea of settlement, convinced of the need for agrarian conquest, struggles to free itself from the allure of pastoral imagination. Caught in a bind, it vacillates between two worlds, two visions, which refuse to blend into any coherence. Settlement is celebrated and feared, seen as necessary as well as tragic; it was a civilizing process, but also signified disease and death. Nomadism was a thing of the past, part of a world that had to be transformed; but it was equally a metaphor for freedom. The nostalgia for open spaces and the silence of the desert, the romance of the shepherd's flute and the camel-man's love songs contrast with the cacophony of modern urban spaces. The desire for rational ordering clashes with the romantic's fear of monotony and repetitiveness.

Year after year the *Colonies Reports* catalogued the progress in the colonies. They talked of the problems of measurement and allotment of land, the hitches in distributing water, the difficulties in persuading colonists to cultivate the crops they were contracted to produce; but they also narrated how these problems were all overcome to ensure development. Yet there were times when these narratives broke down, subverted by evidence that resisted explanation within the terms of these heroic teleologies of colonial achievements, questioned by anxious imperial voices that expressed self-doubt. For every official who congratulated the British for their success in creating the landscape of their imagination, there were others who filed reports on increased salinity in waterlogged canal areas and steady fragmentation of the land of the colonists.[94]

Optimists had no problem stitching together a story of unmitigated progress. The creation of canal colonies did lead to a dramatic extension of the area under cultivation. Uncultivated pastoral tracts gave way to verdant fields. In Lyallpur district alone over 1,470,000 acres were brought under the plough by 1916–17. Almost the entire area, about 99 per cent, was irrigated; most of it watered by the new canals. By 1931, a total of 9,929,217 irrigated acres were being cultivated in the canal colonies. Officials could look around with satisfaction and see the irrigated fields covered with wheat in *rabi* (spring harvest) and cotton in *kharif* (autumn harvest). Since the 1860s Britain had been keen on reducing its crippling dependence on America for supplies of wheat and cotton. By the late nineteenth century the expansion of acreage under these crops in India had come up against barriers, and officials desperately looked for 'virgin' lands that these crops could colonize. In the canal colonies they hoped to produce American cotton and American wheat without being dependent on America. As Lyallpur developed, wheat came to occupy 77 per cent of the area under foodgrains in 1904–05 and about 80 per cent in 1939–40.[95] By 1920–21 over 250, 690 acres in Lyallpur were under cotton, accounting for about 15 per cent of the total cropped area, and by 1937–38 the acreage rose by 50 per cent as cotton came to occupy over 25 per cent of the total area under cultivation. The line on the production graph did not dip even during the Great Depression. At a time when world market prices crashed, landowners and tenants expanded production to meet their cash requirements. And as exports shrank, cotton production was reoriented to meet the demands of a growing internal market.

There were, however, disquieting facts that could not be easily incorporated within this story of progress. It is true that in the canal colonies there was a dramatic expansion of total output, and the long-term average rates of growth here were higher than in the central districts, where arable expansion had reached its limits by the end of the nineteenth century.[96] But the figures do not allow us to make a neat contrast between the two zones: the Lyallpur rate is substantially lower than that in other canal colony tracts like Montgomery, and not so different from that in some of the older districts like Ludhiana and Gurdaspur. Moreover, when the annual rates of output growth are plotted on a graph we see a recurring picture. In the years immediately after colonization of a new tract, there was first a phase of growth, followed by stagnation and decline. In tracts like Lyallpur that were colonized in the late nineteenth century, rates of growth plateaued by the second decade of the twentieth century; whereas Montgomery and Multan, colonized between 1915 and 1940, were still showing high growth rates in the 1940s. Clearly, growth in output was driven primarily by a horizontal expansion of the arable.[97] Once this expansion reached its limit, growth of output slowed and ultimately stopped. In the post-1950 period, therefore, the rates of output growth in the canal colony areas slumped.

This picture is doubly confirmed when we look at the figures of productivity per acre. Yields in canal colonies were not unquestionably higher than in the old agricultural districts of central Punjab. In 1916–17, Lyallpur and Montgomery in the canal colonies produced 160–175 lbs per acre of cleaned cotton, while in central Punjab, Jullunder yielded 240 lbs and Ludhiana 160 lbs. The pattern had not changed in the subsequent decades. By 1937–38 Lyallpur and Montgomery cotton fields were yielding 220 lbs, whereas Ludhiana recorded 300 lbs and Jullunder 220 lbs. Wheat figures were no different. If Lyallpur in 1916–17 produced 1,040 lbs of wheat per acre on canal-irrigated lands, Jullunder produced 1,200 lbs on its *chahi* (well-irrigated) lands.[98] Two decades later the picture was very much the same: Lyallpur was yet to catch up with Jullunder.

A shift of focus from absolute yields to rates of productivity growth offers further insights into the antinomies of development. In most canal colonies, after the initial decades the rates of growth first slowed and then turned negative. Not till the 1940s did the lines of the graph turn upwards. Imperial science and capital could not create in the canal colonies a developmental regime powered by high levels of productivity.

What explains this seeming paradox? First: these trends in yield, I will argue, reaffirm the proposition I made in the earlier section about the relationship between decline of pastures and agricultural growth. When permanent pastures of the *bar* were brought under the plough, converted into permanent fields, the soil contained high reserves of nitrogen as is usual in all permanent pastures. This reserve could be tapped over long years to sustain fairly high levels of yield. The nitrogen fixed in pastureland, as we saw, has a very slow release rate. Bound up with organic compounds, it is released gradually as the compounds decompose over time. Continuous cultivation of the *bar* led to declining nitrogen levels and stagnation of yields. The effectivity of any additional nitrogen supply through farmyard manure depends on the existing stock of nitrogen in the soil. As nitrogen reserves dropped, larger quantities of manure were required to sustain existing levels of yield. In the canal colonies, it would appear, nitrogen levels were not continuously and adequately replenished. Available manure per unit of land was lower in the canal colonies than in the older districts (see Table 1).

TABLE 1 *How the farms were cultivated: contrast between older districts and canal colonies*

	Older districts	Canal colonies	Jullunder (central Punjab)	Lyallpur (canal colony)
Days of manual labour per cropped acre (in 8-hour days)	27	19	41	20
Days of bullock labour per cropped acre (in 8-hour days)	13	9	17	9
Intensity of cropping on irrigated land	124	99	142	83
Wages paid to permanent hired labourers (in annas)	4.6	5.2		0–4–8
Expenditure on manure per irrigated acre (in Rs)	1.8	1.06	4.2	1

Source: Farm Account of the Punjab, 1937–38. Estimates based on accounts kept in a set of individual farms in various districts of Punjab. The investigation was carried out by the Board of Economic Enquiry, Punjab.

Second: the official dream of high yields on canal colony lands was based on false assumptions. Officials thought that when industrious peasants were granted large holdings and supplied with plentiful water, the problems of growth would disappear. The steady spread of capitalist farming and scientific agriculture would enhance yields and boost rates of productivity growth. Detailed farm surveys carried out in the late 1920s and the 1930s, however, showed that on the small farms in Jullunder and Ludhiana, intensity of cropping and labour-use, as well as levels of yield per unit of land, were higher than on the larger farms of Lyallpur. Generally, peasants with large families living on small holdings sought to maximize yields to utilize available family labour and increase earnings. They doublecropped the land and prepared the fields with care, ploughing and weeding it many times, applying as much manure as they could pro-cure, and dug wells to irrigate the fields. The number of wells in Jullunder boomed in the early twentieth century. Everyone, it seems, was digging a well to irrigate the intensively cultivated fields. Migrant settlers on the larger farms of the canal colonies, however, could not maximize yields per acre. Family labour was in short supply, agricultural labourers were difficult to find, wages at peak seasons were high, and available manure per unit of land was inadequate. The migrants increased incomes and expanded production by extending the arable rather than intensifying cultivation. As the arable frontier was pushed outward, fields were prepared without adequate ploughing and manuring.

Third: the expansion of the arable frontier came up against ecologi-cal barriers. Driven by self-conceit – arrogance about their own power to reshape all the landscape – colonial officials pushed the frontiers of arable relentlessly outward. When, in 1901–02, allotments in the Jhelum Colony were being planned, it was initially decided that the 'inferior lands' would be given out for 'temporary cultivation', for a stable cycle of production was difficult to sustain on such lands. Within a year the calculations changed. The Colonizing Officer reported that there was 'no need to revert to tem-porary cultivation on the Canal in order to avoid loss of revenue, as the supply of grantees has always been in excess of the land available'.[99] It was as if all lands could be brought under the plough, turned into wheat or cotton fields, and made to yield revenue. This inexorable drive for arable expansion became characteristic of the very process of colonization. In the Chenab Colony, most of the 'culturable' land had been allotted by the end of the nineteenth century. The subsequent opening of the Bhangu Branch created the possibility of another 17,163 acres being allotted. But most of this land was of such poor quality that the Colonization Officer found the selected settlers showing 'much reluctance in taking it up'.[100] This did not deter the officials. They blamed the colonists for being greedy, keen only on the best-quality lands and unwilling to accept what was being offered to them. 'But the land is not as bad as it looks,' the Colonizing Officer declared, 'and if grantees from outside will not take it, plenty can be found here who will.'[101] Settlers continued to complain but the arable frontier marched ahead. The official logic was simple: as long as demand exceeded supply, all land could be allotted and taxed, all spaces could be converted into arable. The quality of land could provide no barrier to expansionary limits. If necessary, the idea of what constituted 'culturable' land itself had to be redefined. This unrestrained expansion of the arable created instabilities, leading to failure of crops and poor yields on these marginal lands.

Fourth: the dramatic march of wheat and cotton in the canal colonies – synonymous with 'progress' in the colonial imagination – created a number of problems. By the 1920s, colony officials were despairing at the fact that cotton cultivation was being extended recklessly without proper preparation of the land. Constrained by a shortage of family labour and high wage costs, in many regions cotton seeds were being sown broadcast, reducing the seed–yield ratio. Extension of cotton also created pressure on fodder crops that fix nitrogen in the soil.[102] Decline of pastures and insufficient supply of fodder inevitably affected animal stock, and this in turn further reduced manure supply. Consequently, nitrogen reserves were not replenished and yields were adversely affected. In contrast, fields in Jullunder and Ludhiana – small parcels that had to sustain large families – were heavily manured and intensively cultivated.[103]

A drive towards uniformity and homogeneity characterizes modernity's search for order. In the field of agriculture this has inevitably meant – whether in the colonies or in the west – a decline of crop diversity. In the canal colonies, the increased predominance of wheat and cotton led to declining area under other crops. Foodgrains like *jowar* and *bajra* counted for a very small proportion of the total cropped area. There was no demand for them in Europe, no incentive to encourage their exports. Obsessed with whiteness, British officials saw these grains as dark and coarse, and associated them with dry cultivation and backward agriculture. They became, in fact, markers of primitivity. The shift from *jowar* and *bajra* to wheat was seen as a sign of progress. In Lyallpur, these two crops together covered only about 6 to 7 per cent of the foodgrain area in the first few years of the twentieth century; and by 1940 the proportion had dipped to less than 3 per cent.[104]

This trend towards crop uniformity was paralleled by a move towards genetic homogeneity. From the beginning of the twentieth century in Punjab, persistent attempts to introduce high-yielding varieties of American wheat and cotton saw the gradual displacement of local *desi* varieties. In 1930, 'improved' strains of wheat were sown on 2.5 million acres in Punjab; within a decade-and-a-half it covered an area of 8.32 million acres, accounting for 80 per cent of the total area under wheat.[105] In response to the Lancashire pressure for long-stapled cotton, the Indian Cotton Association urged Punjab officials to encourage cultivation of American varieties. The F-4, introduced in 1908, came to cover 1,131,800 acres by 1925.[106] In the 1940s, colonial officials in the canal colonies were pointing to the area under improved varieties as a measure of development under colonization.[107]

Few, however, could do this without a measure of doubt. In 1919, zamindars who had planted the F-4 discovered a strange disease that was destroying their crop. In September and October the flowers dropped, the bolls did not open properly, the lint was poor, the seed malformed, and the yields low.[108] The yield did not improve the subsequent year, and in 1921 failure of rain destroyed the cotton crop. Then came a few years of good harvest, followed once again by a cycle of poor ones. Such violent fluctuations of yields were not eliminated even in the 1940s. In 1944–45, for instance, on the government farm at Lyallpur, the yield of American varieties was no more than 25 per cent of what it was just two years earlier. The reason: a heavy infestation of *jassid*, a small, wedge-shaped, greenish-yellow insect, commonly called cotton leaf-hopper (*kohr* or *tela* in Punjabi) that was fond of attacking American cottons.[109]

As vast areas of wheat and cotton continued to be regularly destroyed by pests, the Imperial Council of Agricultural Research began work on resistant varieties. But this did not solve the problems. When immunity was developed against one type of pest, plants still remained susceptible to attacks by other races of pathogens or insects. The problem lay with the move towards monoculture and uniformity. As recent researches have shown, displacement of local varieties and elimination of crop diversity make plant communities particularly vulnerable to recurrent pest invasions.[110] In polycultures, species diversity retards the transfer of viruses by insects, and genetic heterogeneity limits the damage caused by pathogenic organisms – even when they are of virulent strains. In monocultures, the hosts are biologically homogenous, and this enables rapid multiplication and spread of the invading pathogen, transforming every pest attack into a probable epidemic. In the older districts of Punjab, the crop regime that peasants had developed through adaptation with the local environment was genetically more heterogeneous; and the *desi* varieties of wheat and cotton that they grew were less prone to pest attacks. The yield of the *desis* was lower than that of the *amreekan* variety grown under optimal conditions, but the harvests of the former were more stable.

The British had imagined that these optimal conditions would be ensured in the canal colonies; but they were not. By building perennial canals they hoped to irrigate the 'desolate' *bars*, eliminate seasonal fluctuations in supply, regulate the volume of flow in the channels and optimize water utilization. Even as the officials congratulated themselves on their achievements, there were reports that all was not well with the irrigation system. In many areas crops withered due to intermittent flows; elsewhere – particularly at the tail-end of canals – the water supply was woefully short, a problem aggravated by canal breaches at upper levels; in yet other areas excess water clogged the soil. Confident of their dream and arrogant about their capacity to extend the canals over the entire *bar* landscape, the canal engineers had proceeded in a hurry. In some regions they preferred to ignore the compact nature of the clayey soil or the hard rocky substrata that hindered percolation; elsewhere they disregarded the problem of drainage. By the late 1920s the problem became so acute that a Waterlogging Committee had to be appointed to look into the problem.[111]

In waterlogged soils carbon dioxide gets trapped, and nitrogen and oxygen supplies are reduced.[112] Since roots require oxygen for effective nutrient uptake, waterlogging inevitably leads to dwindling yield. Compaction and poor soil aeration also retard root growth, suffocate existing roots and slow nutrient uptake, affecting plant health and leaf activity. Studies have shown that diminished nitrogen uptake restricts the growth of cotton. Nitrogen from older leaves is translocated to the new leaves, causing chlorosis in the older leaves. Lack of potassium, common in waterlogged soils, affects cotton fibre and leaf colour, and a build-up of sodium to toxic levels causes progressive death of shoots and leaves.

The cumulative effect of all this was not only a dramatic decline in levels of yield, but a steady deterioration of the quality of produce. Science could not easily sustain the arrogance of modernity. The promise of modernity crumbled, afflicted by the antinomies of development.

Two Paths of Agrarian Conquest

I would like to end the essay by arguing that development in the canal colonies reveals a pattern that was different to what happened elsewhere in Punjab. Reworking Lenin's famous argument about capitalism, I will distinguish two paths to agrarian conquest under colonialism, two ways of visualizing the constitution of the agrarian modern within the colonial landscape: one that transformed society from below, and the other that sought to impose a structure from above. The way the contradictory dialectic between these two forms worked itself out defined the specific logic of colonial change.

Agrarian conquest from below proceeded slowly, carefully, almost surreptitiously. From the beginning of British rule in Punjab, officials emphasized that the rural order was to be founded on custom and native institutions. The colonial state remapped the landscape, redefined custom, refigured rights, reorganized social relations and reordered agrarian regimes. But this transformation was carried through in the name of preservation. The rhetoric of tradition was a defining element of this mode of agrarian conquest, this mode of shaping the agrarian modern. Within it colonization seemed to work without corroding the social fabric, without demolishing the existing social structures. This appearance of continuity allowed the violence of colonialism to be mis-recognized, and historical ruptures to be read as persistences. When an order is built through the language of custom, when law seeks to encode no more than existing practices, the new order does not appear as radically alien, as severely different. Modernity comes almost surreptitiously, behind the back of tradition.

The language of tradition and custom, however, created constraints. Inhabited landscapes could be reordered, existing practices could be redefined; but there were limits within which this transformation could proceed. Projects of reordering inevitably came up against barriers, social resistance, the rigidities of embedded structures. Imperialism constantly struggles to emancipate itself from these constraints, to discover spaces where the ideal colonial order of their imagination can be built without hindrance. This is what they sought to do in the canal colonies.

The experiment in the canal colonies represented the second path of agrarian conquest. Here the colonial state sought to impose an entire new order from above. It aspired to define everything – the shape of the fields, the lie of the land, the place where the colonist was to reside, the structure of the *abadi*, the mode of irrigation, the crop regimes, the patterns of inheritance, even the attributes of the people who could inhabit the land. It wanted to displace the pastoralists and implant a society of industrious and enterprising zamindars. It imagined that the wilderness of the pastoral landscape would allow the possibility of unconstrained transformation.

This simple difference between the two forms of colonization inevitably broke down. Agrarian conquest from below could not proceed without state initiatives from above. The desire to base British rule on custom and tradition was itself linked to official ideology, a paternalism that was at the same time powerfully influenced by the Benthamite dream of a codifying state.[113] The project of preservation proceeded through processes of enquiry, classification, translation and codification carried out by the colonial government.[114] The intervention of the master defined the way people's customs entered the codes. Yet there were limits to invention. True, codification did not preserve immemorial custom untainted, nor did classification of tenures consolidate ancient coparcenary village brother-hoods, untouched and unchanged. But the discourse of tradition inevitably meant that the state had to operate with caution, enquire into the practices of the people, listen to their voices, see how practices diverged from the code, and change colonial policies in response to social pressures. It had to operate through the inner logic of an agrarian conquest that sought to reorder society from below.

Developments in the colonies similarly showed that conquest from above was not as easy as the state had imagined. It could not produce an ideal agrarian space, unhindered and unconstrained. Villagers reacted to the demarcation of the *rakhs*, and angry pastoralists resisted displacement, carrying away the stock of the immigrant peasant settlers and destroying their crops. They asserted their right to the *rakhs* and opposed the invasion of outsiders. As 1907 showed, even the immigrant peasant settlers were unwilling to accept all the conditions that the state was keen on imposing on the grantees. They grumbled about the canal dues and unreliable water supplies, opposed the new laws of primogeniture, demanded security of rights, and objected to control over their lives, their movements and their economic decisions. Once again the state had to react to these pressures from below, modify the Colonization Bill, change the terms in which grants were given and abolish primogeniture.

This development from above, moreover, was carried through in a language that continued to be paternalist. The development of the canal colonies may have been an attempt to realize an imperial dream of rational reordering of the landscape, establishing a modern agrarian order unconstrained by the heritage of the past and the rigidities of entrenched social institutions. It may have been inspired by an imperial self-conceit: a will to demonstrate that the British could produce in the colonies a model agrarian regime. But colonial officials never tired of emphasizing that they were driven primarily by paternalist concerns, and empathy with the needs and problems of the people. Colonization was said to be necessary to relieve the sufferings of the peasants of central Punjab, ground down by demographic pressure, constrained by fragmented, subdivided miniscule parcels of land. Migration, they repeatedly said, would relieve the pressure on land in the old districts, and ensure for the pioneer settlers wealth and prosperity in the colonies.

Within the developmental regime of the colonies, paternalism and rationalism fused in a curious mixture. As paternal masters, colonial officials in Punjab claimed to know their subjects and realize what was best for them. They had recognized the qualities of the central Punjab peasants, glorified their industry and skill in cultivation, and given them large plots of land. But they were equally certain that development of the colonies could be ensured and the well-being of the settlers guaranteed only if the landscape was rationally ordered; only if colonists followed the rules that had been codified; only if plots were carved out in uniform squares, primogeniture imposed, planting of trees and residence in the model village made binding. What if the colonists thought otherwise – what if they wanted to follow the customs of their home villages, saw partible inheritance as the only basis of equity and residence requirements as oppressive control over their private lives? What if they conceived of the new structure of rights through the prism of the old? What if what appeared as rational to official minds appeared irrational to the zamindars?

At such times paternalism turned perverse. Paternal masters lost the language of empathy: they showed no desire to listen and understand, sit below the banyan tree and hear the complaints of peasants. When, in 1907, the zamindars of the *bar* began to campaign against the Colonization Bill, organize meetings and send petitions to the government, the paternalists reacted with surprising aggression. Unwilling to believe that the complaints of the zamindars could be genuine, they imagined hidden agents at work churning up trouble: the ever-present Russians, seditious nationalists, disloyal lawyers. The police were asked to attend all meetings, track seditious activities and prepare dossiers on the involvement of nationalist leaders in the movement. Governor General Ibbetson, an old patriarch, drew up a picture of the coming catastrophe; foresaw the breakdown of British rule in India; and demanded emergency powers to handle the situation, arrest Lajpat Rai and Ajit Singh, ban all meetings and seal up newspapers. James Wilson, who as Settlement Officer at Sirsa in the early 1870s had empathized with Lalu – a peasant poet who recounted a story of lost rights with the coming of British rule in the countryside – and discovered in his poem the pain and suffering of the dispossessed Sirsa peasants, became, in 1907, the most assertive defender of the Colonization Bill. On investigating the rights of Sirsa peasants, Wilson had argued with passion that those who cleared the waste and made it productive always saw the land as their own; and that denial of their claim was unjust.[115] Now, thirty-five years later and after three years as Settlement Commissioner in the canal colonies, Wilson had forgotten the conviction of his youth. He fumed at the Colonization Committee proposal that colonists be made proprietors of the land they reclaimed. There was no custom, Wilson pronounced, that gave the zamindar a right to the land he cleared.[116]

What accounts for this amnesia, this denial of an idea that Wilson had so fervently espoused? I offer two possible arguments. First, within the official mind, the inner logic of the two forms of colonization differed. In Sirsa, the development was seen as organic, occurring through an evolutionary and natural progression of demographic expansion, pressure on resources, fissioning and separation of households, movement to new areas and reclamation of waste. It was not a process entirely aided or initiated by the state. The state had to recognize the norms, customs and expectations that sustained the process. In the canal colonies, by contrast, the project of reclamation was organized from above. The state initiated the process, brought the colonists, gave them land and water. The immigrant settlers had no moral or ethical claim to the land, no right to expect any more than what they had already got through the generosity of the colonial state.[117]

Second: Wilson's paranoia also revealed the inner contradictions of paternalism. Kindness and concern for the poor was an intimate part of the rhetoric of paternalism, but this humanist empathy was premised on an expectation of deference and obedience. Deeply authoritarian, paternalism could not tolerate a questioning of authority.[118] No doubt could be expressed, no voice raised against the intentions of the filial figure. Every bit of questioning was seen as a possible threat to the bonds of social cohesion that paternalism sought to forge. Benefactors of paternal care could plead but not protest. At times, like in 1907, fears of social breakdown were transformed into visions of apocalypse. When Minto appointed the Canal Colonies Committee, a furious Wilson replayed the images of insurgency that Ibbetson had earlier projected.[119] Plagued by the inner anxieties of his patriarchal ideology, convinced of the illegitimacy of every demand of the colonists, Wilson now had no patience for any language of empathy and concern.

The events that unfolded in the aftermath of 1907 possibly marked the limits of the old paternalistic ideology of Punjab. In order to survive it had to re-adapt itself, become sensitive to a new language of individual rights and allow some space for rebellion of subjects. This was a difficult task in turbulent times.

Notes and References
[1] See the early exploration reports of the different *bars* conducted by the Survey of India, Dehradun Records, 1850–60, Serial No, 625, Old No. Rev/5, 1854–57.
[2] In 1841, Henry Lawrence rode through this region, leaving Ferozepur on 16

December and reaching Peshawar on 28 December. His diary and letters give us his earliest impressions of the terrain. In one of his letters to Mr Clerk he wrote: 'From Kussor to Choong and Rungpoor is a wild waste, and on this side of the Ravi the country is covered with coarse grass; and throughout the 70 miles I have travelled during the last two days, I have been struck with almost the entire absence of inhabitants; seeing very few people in or about the thirty scattered villages, and meeting with scarcely a traveller on the road. Road there is none'. Quoted in Herbert B. Edwardes and Herman Merivale, *Life of Sir Henry Lawrence*, London: Smith, Elder & Co., 1872, p. 288. Writing about these observations of his hero, Herbert Edwards noted many years later: 'Little did Henry think as he marked the desolation through which he marched, that he was only making notes of evils which he himself would have to grapple with in four short years.' Ibid., p. 289. In the colonial imagination the pastoral landscape was not only desolate, it was evil. It had to be transformed into irrigated agrarian countryside, populated with peasants, regulated through laws, and ordered through surveys and maps.

3 Punjab, Revenue and Agriculture (Revenue) [Punjab Rev. and Agr. (Rev.) hereafter], July 1880, A 14; Punjab Rev. and Agr. (Rev.), Nov. 1880 A 3.

4 *Report of the Indian Irrigation Commission*, 1901–03, Part II, Ch. XIV, p. 6.

5 *Annual Report of the Chenab, Jhang and Jhelum Colonies*, 1908, Statement II.

6 *Annual Report of the Lower Bari Doab Canal Colony*, 1916–17.

7 For a discussion of the canal colonies from within a developmentalist paradigm see Imran Ali, *The Punjab Under Imperialism, 1885–1947*, Princeton: Princeton University Press, 1988. For an exploration of some of the ecological implications see David Gilmartin, 'Models of the Hydraulic Environment: Colonial Irrigation, State Power and Community in the Indus Basin', in David Arnold and Ramachandra Guha, eds, *Nature, Culture, Imperialism*, New Delhi: Oxford University Press, 1995; Indu Agnihotri , 'Ecology, Land Use and Colonization', *Indian Economic and Social History Review*, 33.1, 1996; Gilmartin, *Blood and Water: The Indus River Basin in History*, California: University of California Press, 2015.

8 *Report on the Administration of the Punjab* (henceforth *PAR*), 1849–50 to 1851–52; *Selections from the Records of the Government of India* (henceforth *SRGOI*), No. 2, para 351, p. 134.

9 *SRGOI*, para 354, p. 135.

10 *PAR*, 1851–52 to 52–53; *SRGOI*, No. 6, para 424, p. 169.

11 *PAR*, 1854–55 to 1855–56; *SRGOI*, No. 18, para 99, p. 6. On the remodelling of the Bari Doab Canal, see Punjab PWD (Irr.), March 1874, A 17; Punjab, Public Works Department (Irrigation) [Punjab PWD (Irr.) hereafter], July 1894, A 1.

12 *Canals of the Mooltan District*, 1849, in *Selections from the Public Correspondence of the Administration of the Affairs of the Punjab* (henceforth *SPCAAP*), Vol. I, No. 1; F.R. Pullock, *Memorandum on the Dera Ghazi Khan District*, Lahore, 1860, in *SPCAAP*, Vol. 4, No. 4; *Extension of Canal Irrigation in the Dehra Ismail Khan and Dehra Ghazee Khan Districts*, 1868, in *Selections from the Records of the Financial Commissioner of Punjab* (henceforth *SRFCP*), No. 18; Punjab Rev. and Agr. (Rev.), July 1880, A 14; Punjab Rev. and Agr. (Rev.), November 1880, A 3; Punjab PWD (Irr.), August 1874, A 26.

13 Punjab Rev. and Agr. (Irr.), September 1882, A 2. See, in particular, No. 3008–I, 13 August 1875, Sup. Engineer Sirhind Canals to Jt. Sec. Govt. of Punjab (GoP), Irr. Branch; No. 1494–I, 9 June 1875, Sup. Engineer Upper Bari Doab Canal to

Jt. Sec. GoP, Irr. Branch; No. 2990–I, 15 November 1875, Sup. Engineer Bari Doab Canal to Jt. Sec. GoP, Irr. Branch. Also Punjab Rev. and Agr. (Irr.), July 1883, A 2; Punjab Rev. and Agr. (Irr.), December 1883, A 1.

[14] Punjab Rev. and Agr. (Rev.), December 1880, A 4a, pp. 683–88; *Correspondence Relating to Ferozepur and Fazilka Inundation Canals*, 1887, in SRFCP, N.S., No. 61. On the construction and remodelling of inundation canals, see also GoI Land Rev. and Agr. (Rev), May 1881, A 33–34; Punjab PWD (Irr.), May 1891; Punjab PWD (Irr.).

[15] Punjab Rev. and Agr. (Irr.), July 1883, A 1; Punjab Rev. and Agri. (Irr.), July 1884, A 1–3.

[16] Quoted in *Report of the Indian Irrigation Commission*, 1901–03, Part II, p. 15.

[17] Ibid. See *Extension of Canal Irrigation in the Dehra Ismail Khan and Dehra Ghazee Khan Districts*, in SRFCP, No. 18, p. 3.

[18] On variability and uncertainty of water flow in the inundation canals, see Punjab PWD (Irr.), May 1891, A 1; Punjab PWD (Irr.), June 1894, A 1; Punjab PWD (Irr.), June 1873, A 24.

[19] *Report of the Indian Irrigation Commission*, 1901–03, Part II, Ch. XIV.

[20] On the Utilitarian idea of fixity, see Gerald Postema, *Bentham and the Common Law Tradition*, Oxford: Clarendon Press, 1986; Neeladri Bhattacharya, 'The Power of Categories', in *The Great Agrarian Conquest*, Delhi: Permanent Black, forthcoming 2017.

[21] GoI Land Rev. and Agr. (Rev.), January 1914, A 20, 193.

[22] This rhetoric drew upon a wider discourse of precision and quantification that was naturalized in nineteenth-century Europe. See M. Norton Wise, *The Values of Precision*, Princeton: Princeton University Press, 1995; Theodore M. Porter, *The Rise of Statistical Thinking: 1820–1900*, Princeton: Princeton University Press, 1986; Theodore M. Porter, *Trust in Numbers: The Pursuit of Objectivity in Science and Public Life*, Princeton: Princeton University Press, 1995; Ian Hacking, *The Taming of Chance*, Cambridge: Cambridge University Press, 1990.

[23] The British did build headworks in some of the inundation canals they constructed. But the headworks were not as successful in controlling the working of the canals.

[24] Adam Taylor, Civil Surgeon, Ambala, to T.H. Thornton, Sec., GoP, *Sanitary Survey of Villages Watered by the Western Jumna Canal (Report by Taylor and Associated Correspondence, 1867–69)*, in *SRGOP*, NS No 6, para 13.

[25] Ibid. See also Punjab PWD (Irr.), January 1873, No. 15.

[26] *Irrigation Department Report* (henceforth *IDR*), 1926, part II, p. 8.

[27] The actual returns surpassed all expectations. The original Chenab scheme in 1892 had projected a return of about 12 per cent by 1909–10 and 15 per cent by 1914. The actual net revenue (gross revenue – running expenses) in 1915–16 as a proportion of total outlay was 40 per cent, and the net profit (net revenue – interest) was 36 per cent. By 1946, the net revenue had gone up to 50 per cent of the capital outlay. See GoI Rev. & Agr. (Rev.), December 1892, A 16–18; *IDR*, 1915–16, 1945–46. For detailed discussion of the outlays and returns, see Imran Ali, *Punjab under Imperialism, 1885–1947*, Ch. 5; Indu Agnihotri, 'Agrarian Change in the Canal Colonies: Punjab 1890–1935', PhD thesis, Jawaharlal Nehru University, New Delhi, 1987.

[28] *Revenue Report of the Public Works Department (Irrigation Branch), Punjab, 1917–18*.

[29] *Report of the Indian Irrigation Commission*, 1901–03, Part II, Ch. XIV, p. 10.

[30] *Cher* was now defined as water advantage rate paid in the form of labour on the

canals. On *cher*, see App. VI to Fryers, No. 29, 11 February, Punjab Agr. Rev., September 1872, A 15.

[31] On the problem of demanding *cher* labour, see Land Rev. and Agr. (Rev.), A 75–82.

[32] *Report of the Indian Irrigation Commission*, 1901–03, Part II.

[33] For a description of the process of *killabandi* see in particular, *Canal Colonies Report 1902–03*, pp. 21–22.

[34] In tracts where *killabandi* was done, fields were first plotted on maps before they were demarcated on the ground, unlike the cadastral maps of the old districts where fields – of varying sizes and shapes – had to be individually measured before they could be mapped. In 1893–94, while carrying out the *killabandi* of Chenab Canal, F. P. Young realized the need to change the earlier system – seemingly troublesome to both the cultivator and the measuring officer – in the tracts under colonization. 'It therefore occurred to me to take advantage of our unique position, and to reverse the usual process by drawing our maps on paper first, and requiring the zamindars to lay his field out on the ground in accordance therewith afterwards.' 'Report on the Colonization of Government Waste Lands on the Chenab Canal', *Report on the Revenue Administration Report of Punjab and its Dependencies* (henceforth *RRAPD*), 1893–94, appendix, p. XIV. The zamindars were to relate to the land through the spatial framework provided by the colonizers. Maps were not to record the order that pre-existed on the ground, they were to create the ideal order.

[35] E. Joseph, the Colonizing Officer of Lower Bari Doab Canal Colony, recognized the problem: 'you cannot expect people to show much enthusiasm for breaking up the waste area when there are no means of irrigating it or to alter the shapes of their well fields as long as they have to continue using the wells.' *Report of the Lower Bari Doab Canal Colony* (henceforth *RLBDCC*), 1913–14, p. 43.

[36] Ibid.

[37] For an early statement on the aesthetic of the picturesque, see William Gilpin, *Three Essays: On Picturesque Beauty, on Picturesque Travel, and on Sketching Landscape*, London: R. Blamire, 1792. For recent discussions, see David Marshall, 'The Problem of the Picturesque', *Eighteenth-Century Studies*, 35:3, Spring 2002; Dabney Townsend, 'The Picturesque', *The Journal of Aesthetic and Art Criticism*, 55:4, Autumn 1997.

[38] Young criticized the first plan of the village in which there was more than one entry point. In his own model *abadi* he enclosed the village within harder boundary lines. See 'Report on the Colonization of the Government Waste Lands Commanded by the Chenab Canal', 1898, *Report of the Land Revenue Administration of the Punjab, 1898*.

[39] The massive influx of peasants from the densely populated and intensively cultivated regions of central Punjab dramatically transformed the demographic profile of the *bar*. In Lyallpur, one of the major colonies, the population increased from 60,000 in 1891 to 1,167,000. This increase of over a million people was largely due to immigration.

[40] Report of G.F. De Montmorency, Dep. Comm. Lyallpur, Punjab Home (Police), October 1910, A 57.

[41] On cattle poisoning and rick burning in Punjab, see Punjab Home (Police), March 1873, A 11. H.B. Urmstrong, the Deputy Commissioner of Rawalpindi, had reported as early as 1873 : 'To such a pitch has the evil cowardly system now gone that the headmen of the whole country are most anxious to put it down, and have signed a memorial to that effect.' The village headmen demanded that in the case of poisoning the offending party should be made to pay for the cattle.

But the problem was to identify the offender. In the politics of feuding, revenge and retribution had collective support. Most often tribal groups were collectively implicated in the act, and no one gave any evidence against the offender.

42 The nomadic Manes Jats and Vasir tribes residing in village Buddha in Lyallpur were declared to be criminal tribes in 1918. The charge against the Vasirs read: 'The Vasirs, who a generation ago were nomads, own no land but keep large herds of cattle, which are a source of constant annoyance to the neighbouring colonists, in whose fields they trespass with impunity, owing to the dread with which their owners are generally regarded.' The Manes Jats, a community of local nomads, had been given canal land, but they refused to settle, saw agriculture as a subsidiary occupation, and grazed their cattle on the cultivated fields of immigrant colonists. Punjab Home (Police), January 1918, A 285, p. 74. The Dher, Khurrals and Valana Jats of village Bahuman in Lahore district were notified as criminal tribes in 1907. Gazette Notification dated 2 November 1907, Punjab Home (Police), November 1907, A 2. The Biloches in the south were declared criminal tribes.

43 No. 2211, 11 June 1883, C.A. Galton, Acting District Magistrate of Malabar, to the Chief Sec. to Govt. of Madras, GoI, Home (Jud.), December 1883, A 217.

44 Punjab Home (Jud.), September 1886, A 1.

45 No 397, 19 October 1886, A. Anderson, Deputy Comm. Hissar, to the Comm. and Sup., Delhi Div., Punjab Home (Jud.), July 1887, A 8.

46 No 347, 22 April 1887, from R.E. Yonghusband, Sen. Sec. to Fin. Comm. Punjab, to the Sec. to GoP., ibid.

47 For reports from different regions see in particular GoI, Home (Jud.), Jan. 1888, Nos. 66 –132.

48 'Illegal detention of cattle by landholder and tea planters in Assam', Diary No. 1041, the Chief Commissioner of Assam, No. 2338, dated 17 August 1888, Home (Jud.) September 1888, No. 147.

49 According to the rules, the impounded cattle were to be driven to the pound and the fines were to be charged by the pound keeper.

50 In response to the request by the Assam Chief Commissioner for an amendment of the Cattle Trespass Act, 1871, Ch. V, to allow prosecution of 'illegal detention', the Secretary to GoI wrote: 'I am directed to say that the Governor General in Council considers it desirable that it should be placed beyond doubt that the practice referred to ('illegal detention') does not render those who adopt it punishable under the Indian Penal Code.' No. 1499, 17 September 1888, A.P. MacDonnel, Sec., GoI, to the Chief Comm. Assam, GoI, Home Judicial, September 1888, No. 148.

51 See the note, 'Detention by landholders and tea planters in Assam of cattle trespass on their lands', Diary 1422, Home Department, The Solicitor General to Govt., dated 19 December 1888, GoI, Home (Jud.), February 1889, No. 50. See also GoI, Home (Jud.), February 1889, A 51.

52 GoI, Home Judicial, May 1890, A 89.

53 For an account of the Gugeira rebellion see L.F., *The Punjab and Delhi in 1857*. The author was a chaplain of the Punjab Movable Column in 1857. Andrew Major, Return to Empire, PhD thesis, ANU, 1982, Ch. VI. *Mutiny Records: Reports*, Lahore: Punjab Government Press, 1911.

54 A chaplain of the Punjab Movable Column in 1857 tells us that Major Chamberlain, unable to pursue the rebels who retreated across the Ravi, inflicted 'the only punishment that was open to him'. The rebels had driven off their herds, their main source of wealth, into the jungles. Chamberlain employed professional trackers to trace the herds, rounded up over 2,300 cattle and thousands

of sheep and goat, and butchered them. To the chaplain this was undoubtedly a deliberate restaging of a tribal drama: 'Thus in the midst of the Punjab was re-enacted on a gigantic scale the old scene so often performed by the rival lairds of the Scottish borders.' LF, *The Punjab and Delhi in 1857*, Vol. II, p.187. A mimic restaging is, of course, never the same as the original. The violence of a practice within the logic of the feud acquires a new meaning when it becomes part of the politics of counter-insurgency.

55 *Punjab Legislative Council Debates*, 1929.
56 *Chenab Colony Report*, 1903–04.
57 Reviewing the developments in the Jhelum Colony, J. Wilson, the Settlement Commissioner, noted in a marginal comment that the *janglis* had 'in a surprisingly short time, adopted an agricultural mode of life in place of their old wandering pastoral life, and are making very good colonists'. *Jhelum Colony Report*, 1901–02.
58 *Punjab Legislative Council Debates*, 1929.
59 Letter No. 56, dated 11 May 1901, to GoI, in *Jhelum Colony Report*, 1901–02.
60 Financial Commisssioner's Letter No. 7101, dated 23 November 1901, ibid. See also GoP, Letter No., 145 dated 4 September 1902
61 Initially the size of the *ghorapal abadkar* grant was one-and-a-half squares (42 acres); this was soon increased to two squares (56 acres). See No. 793 S, dated 14 July 1902, App. A, *Jhelum Colony Report*, 1901–02. Also GoP Letter No. 471 S, dated 14 July 1902 , *Jhelum Colony Report*, 1902–03, p. 24; GoP letter No. 589 S, dated 23 June 1903 and GoP, No. 1829 S, dated 9 September 1903.
62 *Jhelum Colony Report*, 1901, p. 24. See also Fraser to Settlement Commissioner, No. 134, dated 27 July 1902.
63 The Colonization Officer of course imagined that peasants could be transformed into breeders, but this hope was marked by a deep uncertainty: 'It remains to be seen how this class will prove to be successful horse breeders. As self-cultivating zamindars they are accustomed to dealing with cattle, and know something about live-stock generally, but it will rest with the officers of the Remount Department to teach them the high art of breeding horses.' *Jhelum Colony Report*, 1902–03, p. 27.
64 Ibid.
65 It was as if, inscribed with the marks of a nomadic past, shaped by the culture of mobility, the pastoralists lived forever in an enchanted past of mythic freedom. Even when keen on a space within the new order, they were emotively tied to the old. Carrying out the allotment operation in the Lower Bari Doab, E. Joseph, the Colonization Officer, declared: 'the Janglis while eagerly pressing even for such land as we give, and besieging us for inclusion in the lists, look regretfully back on the days when they were free to follow their camels from place to place and obtained from time to time permission to cultivate a few acres below the *dhaya* (raised ground near the river) in some favourably low ground where, if there was any rain at all, a food crop of wheat could be grown with little labour; the reward was great and the revenue light.' RLBDCC, 1913–14, para 3.
66 In Jhelum Colony, when the allotment policy was rethought after 1901, 74 per cent of the total allocable area, reserved initially for peasant grants, was given out as service grants for horse breeding. But the *janglis* received only 15 per cent of this area. The rest went to powerful local Biloch landowning gentry, and influential local men like the *zaildars*, *haqdars* and *inamdars*. *Jhelum Colony Report*, 1902–03. In Lower Bari Doab, the Janglis and Hitharis were allotted only 26 per cent of the 680,000 acres set aside as horse and mule breeding area. RLBDCC, 1913–14.

67 In Jhelum Colony, for instance, *jangli* grants of cultivated lands were 5 acres of poor-quality land, as opposed to the usual 28 or 56 acres in the case of all peasant grants. As service grants, the Janglis and Hitharis received half a square (14 acres), while the Biloch landowning gentry of agricultural castes were given 2 squares (56 acres) each. *Jhelum Colony Report*, 1902–03.

68 We do not know whether the poet was entirely blind as the record claims, and whether he was translating into poetry the experience of the colony as he had heard others narrate. His name, Kana, suggests he was one-eyed.

69 *Chenab Colony Gaz.*, 1904, pp. 34–35. See also *Chenab Colony SR, 1915; Lyallpur SR, 1925.*

70 For a discussion of the official debate on the Bill, see N.G. Barrier, 'The Punjab Disturbances of 1907: The Response of the British Government in India to Agrarian Unrest', *Modern Asian Studies*, Vol. I, No. 4, 1967, pp. 353–83.

71 *Tribune*, 15 January 1907.

72 The meeting was announced by Hakim Singh, Joint Secretary of the *Bar* Zamindars Association, in the pages of *Zamindar*, 16 January 1907. Also see *Light*, 30 January 1907; *RNP*, 2 February 1907; *Tribune*, 1 February 1907.

73 *Tribune*, 7 February 1907.

74 *Zamindar*, 24 March; *RNP*, 1907; *Punjabee*, 27 March.

75 *Zamindar*, 3 May 1907.

76 *Tribune*, 15 February 1905.

77 *Zamindar*, 8 January 1907; *Tribune*, 12 January 1907; *Siraj-ul-Akhbar* (Jhelum), *RNP*, 5 February 1907.

78 *Tribune*, 15 Febuary 1907.

79 Ibid.

80 *Tribune*, 1 February; *Zamindar*, 30 January 1907; *Light*, 30 January; *RNP*, 2 February 1907. The zamindars' meeting at Lyallpur on 3 February 1907 declared in its resolution that the Bill was improper, unconstitutional, violated contracts and unjustly subjected old grantees to new liabilities. It altered the rules of succession against the provisions of personal and customary law, proposed penal punishments for small offences, provided no check against the offences of officers, and unfairly denied proprietary rights to grantees. *Tribune*, 7 February 1907.

81 *Zamindar*, 12 January 1907.

82 Dwelling on this theme of seduction and deception, one poem published in *Zamindar* explained how the cancellation of 'all previous contracts had frustrated the hopes entertained by the colonists, and created feelings of distrust and suspicion.' *Zamindar*, 8 March 1907; *RNP*, 16 March 1907.

83 One writer in *Tribune* wrote: 'The Bill if passed into law is likely to shake the confidence of the people in the integrity and good faith of official transactions which will be disastrous to the good name of and prestige of the Government.' *Tribune*, 9 February 1907. Another writer declared that it would rudely destroy the implicit faith in the benevolent intentions of the rulers and provoke a massive social conflagration: 'This measure if allowed to stand shall give rise to agitation and irritation through out the whole of Punjab the like of which was never witnessed in this quiet land of the five rivers.' *Tribune*, 15 February 1907.

84 Many years later, in 1910, inaugurating the Punjab Agricultural College at Lyallpur, Dane recounted with pride how he persuaded the colonists to move. *Khalsa Advocate*, 23 December 1910.

85 RCGWCC 1891–92, *LRARP, 1891–92*, App. E.

86 RCGWCC 1892–93, *LRARP, 1892–93*, App. E.

87 *Zamindar*, 8 March 1910.

[88] Ibid.

[89] The *Zamindar* claimed that the settlers had to pay 14 lakhs in fine and four times that amount as tips to the *patwaris*. *Zamindar*, 6 December 1907. This probably was an inflated and arbitrary figure. We are not told of the source and basis of the calculation, nor are we informed about the number of years over which this amount was supposed to have been collected. (Who collected information about tips to the *patwari*!) But such estimates had a rhetorical function. They were meant to underline the enormity of the fiscal burden, concretize the image of suffering and injustice, and create an image of facticity.

[90] One colonist from the Jhelum Canal wrote: 'the poor agriculturists are exposed to all sorts of calamities . . . they have to remain in constant fear of plague, famine, cholera, to say nothing of the pests which ruin crops. The overbearing constable, the meek sahukar, the tahsil orderly, the cringing lambardars and the greedy Zaildar, all vie with one another in putting them to trouble.' *Zamindar*, 8 October 1907.

[91] In pioneering lores of later years, this picture of a hostile landscape recurred, underlining the heroism of the pioneers. In the last years of imperial rule, Malcolm Darling, riding through the canal colonies, asked Maharaja Singh, one of the first 140 migrants to Lyallpur, about his initial impressions of the place. Singh said that the country was 'all waste but dotted with jand trees, snakes lifting angry heads, enormous scorpions, and not a bird to be seen'. In addition to all this was the trouble created by the *janglis*. Michael Darling, *At Freedom's Door*, London: Oxford University Press, 1949, p. 79. These images of danger, fear, poison, death and desolation appeared in most accounts that Darling heard from the colonists.

[92] See Ali, *Punjab under Imperialism*.

[93] *Canal Colonies Report of the Sutlej Valley*, 1933, quoted in *Montgomery, DG*, pp. 58–59.

[94] See *Water-Logging of the Soil in the Vicinity of Punjab Irrigation Canals and Measures for the Prevention of Water-Logging*, produced by Public Works Department Irrigation Branch, 1920; *Report of Waterlogging in Punjab*, 1924; E.S. Lindley, *An Estimate of the Areas Affected By, and Threatened With, Water-Logging with Their Past History, and of the Extent to Which Remedial Measures Will Be Necessary.*

[95] Estimates based on *LRAR* and *Seasons and Crops Reports*.

[96] The semi-log rates of growth of agricultural output between 1906–46 in the canal colonies varied from 5.5 in Montgomery to 4.1 in Multan, 2.0 in Jhang, 1.1 in Shahpur and 1.2 in Lyallpur. In the central districts the rates were: Ludhiana 1.2, Jullunder 0.35, Ferozepur 0.27, Amritsar 0.20. Chander Prabha, 'District-wise Rates of Growth of Agricultural Output in East and West Punjab During the Prepartition and Post-partition Periods', *Indian Economic and Social History Review*, 6.4, 1969, p. 343.

[97] This is a conclusion that is widely accepted. See Raj Krishna, 'Farm supply response in India, Pakistan: a case study of the Punjab region', *Economic Journal*, Vol. 73, No. 291, September 1963; M. Mufakhural Islam, *Bengal Agriculture, 1920–1946*, Cambridge: Cambridge University Press, 1978.

[98] Detailed village surveys suggest even higher yields in the Doaba – the central districts of Punjab – where small holders sustained production on intensively cultivated small parcels. Tehong was a village in Jullunder with about 2,160 acres of cultivated land, parcellized into small holdings of about 3 acres. Forty per cent of the total area was *chahi* (well-irrigated). The Director of Land Records suggested in 1930 that *chahi* lands produced on an average 1,234 lbs of wheat per

acre and 374 lbs of cotton. These figures are higher than those in the *Seasons and Crops Reports* and *Agricultural Statistics of British India*. See *Tehong VS*, p. 180.

[99] *Jhelum Canal Colonies Report*, 1902–03, p. 29.

[100] *Chenab Canal Colonies Report*, 1902–03, p. 3.

[101] Ibid.

[102] The Annual Farm Accounts maintained in selected farms in various districts showed that the proportion of area under fodder crops in the older districts was over 28 per cent, while in the canal colonies it was no more than 13 per cent. See statement IV–A, *Farm Accounts in the Punjab*, 1936–37.

[103] The imputed value of manure used per acre was 80 per cent higher in the older districts: Rs 1.8 compared to Re 1 in the canal colonies. Ibid., Statement VII-A.

[104] *Agricultural Statistics of British India*, relevant years.

[105] Ibid.

[106] Afzal Muhammad, 'American Cottons in India: Their Introduction and Development', *Indian Farming*, Vol. VII, No. 10, October 1946.

[107] Ibid.

[108] D. Milne, *Report on the Causes of the Failure of Cotton Crop in the Punjab in 1919* (1924); D. Milne, *Report on the Complaints of the Abnormal State of the Cotton Crop in 1921*. See also *Review of Agricultural Operation in British India*, 1919–20; *Land Rev. Adm. Rep.*, 1919–20; *Seasons and Crops Report of Punjab*, 1919–20.

[109] Investigations showed that *jassid* attacked two varieties of American cotton – 124F and 289F/K-25, and not others like F-4, LSS and 289f/43. It was, in fact, a pest that usually attacked *guara* (*cyamopsis psoralioides*) and damaged cotton only in the absence of *guara*. This again points to the consequences of species homogeneity. See Muhammad Afzal and Muhammad Abdul Ghani, 'Cotton Jassid in the Punjab', *Indian Farming*, VII: 9, September 1946.

[110] See M.W. Adams, A.H. Ellingboe and E.C. Rossman, 'Biological Uniformity and Disease Epidemics', *BioScience*, 21:21, November 1971; P.A. Matson, W.J. Parton, A.G. Power and M.J. Swift, 'Agricultural Intensification and Ecosystem Properties', *Science*, New Series, 277:5325, July 1997; David Cleveland, Daniel Soleri and E. Smith, 'Do Folk Varieties Have a Role in Sustainable Agriculture?', *BioScience*, 44:11, December 1994.

[111] *Annual Proceedings of the Waterlogging Conference, Punjab*, 1928–38. See also *Waterlogging and Rise of Water Level in Chhaj and Rchna Doabs*, Punjab Irrigation Branch Papers, No. A 20, 1925; Pearson, *Notes on Waterlogging in Punjab*, 1928.

[112] See T.T. Kozlowski, 'Plant Responses to Flooding of Soil', *BioScience*, 34:3, March 1984; R.J. Dowdell and M.H. Mian, 'Fate of Nitrogen Applied to Agricultural Crops with Particular Reference to Denitrification', *Philosophical Transactions of the Royal Society, Series B, Biological Sciences*, 296:1082, *The Nitrogen Cycle*, 27 January 1982.

[113] I have developed this argument elsewhere. See Neeladri Bhattacharya, 'Masculine Paternalism and Colonial Governance', in *The Great Agrarian Conquest*.

[114] See Neeladri Bhattacharya, 'Remaking Custom: The Discourse and Practice of Colonial Codification', in R. Champakalakshmi and S. Gopal, eds, *Tradition, Dissent and Ideology*, New Delhi: Oxford University Press, 1996.

[115] See Neeladri Bhattacharya, 'Remembered Pasts', in *The Great Agrarian Conquest*.

[116] As Financial Commissioner in 1909, Wilson wrote: 'It is not true, so far my experience goes, that in the Punjab the reclamation of waste and unappropriated

land is generally recognized as giving a title to proprietary right. Whether this was even the ancient custom in the older settled parts or not, there has certainly been no general idea of his kind in the minds of the people for the last two generations.' This was an astounding comment from someone who had written the Sirsa Settlement Report and argued so insistently that those who reclaimed the waste expected a permanent right over the land they cleared. In his marginal notes to Wilson's comment Gordon Walker, the Lieutenant Governor, pointed out that the settlers never imagined that their rights over the allotted squares would be similar to tenancies under private landlords: 'The idea that they would stand to Government in the relation which they understood to be that of tenants was so alien to them that they were incapable of realizing it . . . they regarded themselves to all intents and purposes proprietors.' Rev. and Agr. (Rev.), A1, April 1909.

[117] Wilson wrote: 'the colonists . . . it must be remembered, had, most of them formerly no rights, legal or moral, over their land, and who have been brought from narrow poverty in their old homes and placed, by the beneficence of Government, in a position of prosperity, unimaginable in their fondest dreams.' Wilson's Minute, 4 May 1907, GoI, Home (Leg.), June 1907, A 4–8.

[118] On the multiple strands within paternalism and of its authoritarianism, see David Robert, 'Tory Paternalism and Social Reform in Early Victorian England', *The American Historical Review*, 63:2, January 1958; David Roberts, *Paternalism in Early Victorian England*, London: Croom Helm, 1979; P. Thornton, *The Habit of Authority: Paternalism in British Social History*, London: Allen & Unwin, 1966. On the distinction between the paternalism of the eighteenth-century gentry and its mutated, refigured form that became an intimate part of nineteenth-century thought, not just of the Tories, see Peter Mandler, 'The Making of the New Poor Law Redivivas', *Past and Present*, 117, November 1987; Anthony Brundage and David East Wood, 'The Making of the New Poor Law Redivivas: A debate', *Past and Present*, 127, May 1990; Catherine Hall, 'Competing Masculinities: Thomas Carlyle, John Stuart Mill and the Case of Governor Eyre', in Catherine Hall, *White, Male and Middle-Class: Explorations in Feminism and History*, Cambridge: Polity Press, 1992.

[119] The appointment of the committee, Wilson prophesied, would not only weaken the authority of all civil officials, but 'it may prove to be a step towards riot, mutiny and bloodshed, to which troubles in Eastern Bengal are but child's play.' Both Ibbetson and Wilson tapped into imperial fears to argue for the need to discipline the colonists with a strong hand. Minute of Wilson, 3 July 1907, GoI, Rev. and Agr. (Rev.) Oct 1907, A 13–18.

SECTION TWO

Dalit–Muslim Relations in the Long History of Partition in Bengal

Sekhar Bandyopadhyay

Introduction

In the historiography of Partition, the main focus of attention now seems to have shifted from the causes of the great divide to the experiences of its victims, as these had profound consequences for subsequent nation-building processes and communal relations in the South Asian successor states. It is also widely recognized now that the Partition of India was not just an event that occurred in August 1947 – it had a long afterlife.[1] In exploring that aftermath of the Partition, many voices have been recovered, yet many still remain silent. As Urvashi Butalia reminds us: 'In its almost exclusive focus on Hindus and Sikhs and Muslims, Partition history has worked to render many other voices invisible. One such history is that of the Scheduled Castes, or untouchables.'[2] Butalia, Ravinder Kaur and Ramnarayan Rawat have sought to make Dalits visible in the history of Partition in northern India. In eastern India, however, the relative invisibility of Dalits persists, even though we now have a rich literature on Partition. While some of the studies on the aftermath of the Partition and the refugees, particularly by Prafulla Chakrabarti, Tai Yong Tan and Gyanesh Kudaisya, Joya Chatterji, Nilanjana Chatterjee and Haimanti Roy,[3] mention the migration and the struggles of Scheduled Caste peasant refugees, we still have to relate these stories to the questions of their caste disability, self-perception and identity politics. In other words, the Dalits are yet to be made subjects of Partition history in their own right. For that, we need to introduce another layer of analysis into Partition historiography that focuses specifically on Dalit–Muslim relationships.

Butalia and Rawat have claimed that since Dalits in Punjab and Uttar Pradesh did not actively identify with Hindu nationalism or Congress politics, and asserted instead their distinctive social and political identity in the late colonial period, they did not become targets of violence except by accident. Therefore, the Partition did not concern them. In Uttar Pradesh, it is true, the Dalits were not directly affected by the Partition. But in

Punjab, as the works of Ishtiaq Ahmed and Ravinder Kaur suggest, there were greater complexities in the Dalit position. Ahmed has indicated the existence of divisions on the Partition issue within the Scheduled Caste leadership in Punjab.[4] Kaur has shown that 'untouchable groups were neither untouched by nor isolated from the Partition-related events'.[5] In Bengal, as this essay will argue, the Dalits did not remain untouched by Partition politics and violence. But they did not represent a homogeneous community and they responded to the situation in diverse ways. While one group of Dalit leaders was opposed to Partition and believed that a Dalit–Muslim alliance was in the best interest of the Dalits, there were others who got closer to Hindu nationalism and demanded Partition of Bengal at a time when it seemed imminent that the whole of Bengal might go to Pakistan. Many Dalit peasants in Bengal were caught in this politics, and became both victims and perpetrators of violence.

In the immediate post-Partition days, the fate of the Dalit peasants of East Pakistan remained tied, in strange ways, to the plight of the Muslim minorities in West Bengal. Dalit peasants who were beaten up and finally left East Pakistan after the riots of 1950 did not spare Muslims on the other side of the border. Yet these Dalit refugees could not fully identify with higher-caste Hindus either, and their conflicts with Muslim peasants – in the border districts of Nadia and 24 Parganas in the 1950s – cannot be simply explained as communalism. Competition for land and livestock played a significant role in this story of struggle for survival in border strife. Therefore, Dalit politics, and the migration and resettlement trajectories of Dalits, were different from that of high-caste Hindu *bhadralok* refugees. In other words, Dalit experiences represent another level of complexity in the already complicated terrain of Partition and refugee history. In order to explain these complexities in the long history of Partition, let me start with a brief description of Dalit movements in pre-Partition Bengal.

Dalit Movements of the Colonial Period

Social movements that began to assert Dalit identities in Bengal started in the 1870s, and had two very clearly identifiable geographical locations and two communities that were at the forefront. One was the Rajbansi community, which lived mainly in the north Bengal districts of Rangpur, Dinajpur, Jalpaiguri and the princely state of Cooch Behar.[6] The other, the Namasudras of East Bengal, lived mainly in the districts of Bakarganj, Faridpur, Jessore and Khulna, but were also scattered in other eastern and central Bengal districts.[7] When the Scheduled Caste political movement started in the early twentieth century, these two communities provided the majority of its leadership and were its main rural support

base. For both communities their close geographical location was a major
factor behind their successful social mobilization, and both lost their
geographical anchorage as a result of the Partition. As refugees in West
Bengal they had to confront different political realities than what they
had encountered before independence. I will illustrate this with reference
to the Namasudras.[8]

The social movement among the Namasudras started in 1872 as
a protest to claim their social rights after they had achieved limited economic mobility by taking advantage of the reclamation of the marshlands
of East Bengal and the forest tracts of the Sundarbans. By the beginning
of the twentieth century, the movement proceeded along two very distinct
lines. On the one hand, the educated leadership of the community chose
to travel the path of modern constitutional politics, placing emphasis on
the issue of social justice, and demanding and then taking advantage of
reservation in educational institutions, government jobs and finally legislative assemblies. In this modern arena of politics, they actively opposed
Congress-led nationalist movements such as the Swadeshi (1905–08), Non-
Cooperation (1921–22) and Civil Disobedience (1929–32) movements
– the last two being Gandhian movements that are widely known to have
elevated nationalism to its mass-agitational stage. If the Namasudra leaders actively opposed these movements, the Namasudra peasants remained
largely apathetic and silent. This political mood was also reflected in the
1937 election, in which out of thirty-two elected Scheduled Caste candidates, only seven owed allegiance to the Congress.

Side by side with this modern politics, there was also a more
popular mode of assertion of Namasudra identity through the evolution
of a Vaishnava religious sect called Matua, which followed the more
radical *sahajiya* tradition of Vaishnavism that interrogated the notion of
hierarchy and brahmanical domination. The devotional songs of the sect
questioned the very ethos of hierarchy, and if there existed any ritual in the
community, it was the congregational singing of devotional songs. This very
congregational nature of their religious life subverted the hierarchical structure of East Bengal's rural society, although within a limited social space.
However, there is evidence that the Namasudra peasants also participated
in the mainstream Hindu religious life of the villages – the popular Hindu
festival of Durga Puja or Kali Puja, for instance – although this caused,
from time to time, frictions with the high-caste custodians of tradition.

The Namasudra peasantry in East Bengal had two adversaries –
two referral groups – for constructing their adversarial identity politics.
On the one hand, there was the Hindu high-caste rural gentry whose
association with the Congress was the main reason for the Namasudras'

antipathy towards it. In this social relationship the issues of caste and social justice converged. On the other hand, the Muslim peasants were their competitors for land and honour. There were a series of riots between Namasudras and Muslim peasants in East Bengal between 1911 and the 1930s, but in all these riots the Namasudras were involved and targeted as Namasudras and not as Hindus. On the other hand, there were also instances of peasants belonging to the two communities combining against their high-caste Hindu landlords. In other words, there were different layers of social relations that both converged and cut across caste, class and communal boundaries in rural East Bengal at various points of time.

In Bengal politics of the 1940s, the discourse of social justice was gradually overtaken by the discourse of community, which could easily soak up the Namasudras' already competitive relationship with the Muslims. The Dacca riot of 1941 is usually taken as a watershed marking the 'communalization' of politics in Bengal.[9] Namasudras were victims of the riot as well as its main perpetrators. The riot was preceded and followed by an intense Hindu Mahasabha campaign to win over the Dalit peasants of East Bengal. After the riot the Mahasabha soon took over the issue and for the first time, Namasudra peasants were seen openly chanting Hindu communal slogans. Amidst the uncertainties of the period, their relationship with the Muslims became more politicized and linked to the wider provincial politics. At this juncture, as India started drifting uncomfortably towards transfer of power and Partition, Dalit politics in Bengal began to experience tension and rupture.

On the one hand, in 1944, Namasudra leader Jogendra Nath Mandal started the Bengal provincial branch of Dr B.R. Ambedkar's Scheduled Caste Federation. He believed that Dalit and Muslim peasants in East Bengal had similar interests, and that a Dalit–Muslim political alliance was in the best interest of the Dalits. But his pro-Muslim League stance made him unpopular even among fellow Dalits, many of whom were intensely anxious about their future in a Muslim-majority Bengal. Around this time there were two other rival Dalit organizations, both headed by Namasudra leaders. The Depressed Classes League headed by Radhanath Das and Pramatha Ranjan Thakur supported the Congress, and the Depressed Classes Association led by Birat Chandra Mandal was more directly aligned with the Hindu Mahasabha.[10] In the 1946 election, of the thirty reserved seats in the province, the Congress won twenty-six, signalling a complete reversal of the 1937 election results. Mandal was the only Scheduled Caste Federation candidate to win the election in this province. The ruptures in Dalit politics and a decisive worsening of Dalit–Muslim relations in Bengal were clearly visible at this historical juncture.

The 1946 riot brought a further rift in Dalit politics, as Mandal remained the only non-Muslim minister in the Muslim League ministry of H.S. Suhrawardy, widely believed to have been the mastermind behind the Great Calcutta Killings in which Dalits were also among the victims. In the Noakhali riots that followed, a significant number of Namasudras were affected. In a situation like this, when the Hindu Mahasabha launched its campaign to partition Bengal in order to create a Hindu-majority province of West Bengal within the Indian Union, and the Congress endorsed it at the Tarakeswar Convention in April 1947, a very sizeable section of Namasudras became associated with this movement. Their major concern at this stage was to keep their habitat – the districts of Bakarganj, Faridpur, Jessore and Khulna – within the Hindu-majority province of West Bengal. Many of the Rajbansi leaders supported them as well, as they wanted to keep Rangpur and Dinajpur within West Bengal. Despite the geographical absurdity of this claim, the Hindu Mahasabha argued on their behalf before the Boundary Commission.[11] At this stage only a few Dalit leaders like Mandal and Rasiklal Biswas, who led the Bengal branch of the Scheduled Caste Federation, opposed Partition, on the ground that the interests of the Muslims and the Scheduled Castes, both being poor and agriculturists, were identical.[12] Mandal opposed Partition and supported the campaign for an autonomous united Bengal, spearheaded by the dissident Congress leader Sarat Chandra Bose and Muslim League leader Abul Hasem. However, as has now been shown by a number of historians, in the charged atmosphere of 1947, this proposal had very few takers in Bengal.[13]

It will be wrong to conclude, however, that this meant a takeover of Dalit movements by Hindu-nationalist politics. The other strand in the Dalit movement, organized around the demand for social justice, never completely died out. But in the absence of community leadership, it found another outlet: in 1946, when the Communist-led sharecroppers' movement known as the Tebhaga movement started, the Rajbansis in north Bengal and Namasudras in east and central Bengal were its main protagonists. Its impact on the Rajbansi movement was more divisive as it involved direct confrontation – in many areas bitter armed conflicts – between the Rajbansi *jotedars* (large landholding peasants who were the main targets of this movement) and Rajbansi *adhiars* (sharecroppers). It divided their caste movement down the middle, with their caste organization leaders trying in vain to diffuse the tension.[14] As Sugata Bose has observed, in this movement of poor peasants, class clearly overtook caste as a mobilizing force, and divided the identity politics of the Rajbansis and the Namasudras.[15] The Partition dealt the final death blow to their distinctive identity politics.

Partition and Reconfiguration of Identities

As identities are constructed and articulated in specific conjunctures, the Partition represented a significant conjunctural shift that led to a reconfiguration of Namasudra – and, for that matter, also Rajbansi – identity politics, and a redefinition of their relationship with the Muslims. As already mentioned, for representing their distinctive community interests in legislative politics and in the broader public arena, some of their leaders felt that aligning with the Congress and remaining within India offered a realistic prospect of access to political power. Of course, not all Scheduled Caste leaders thought the same way and there was a clearly visible rift within the Dalit ranks on the Partition issue. The Bengal branch of the Scheduled Caste Federation resolved on 14 May 1947 that 'the division of the province into Hindu and Muslim Bengal [was] no solution of the communal problems'. It would

> check the growing political consciousness and ruthlessly crush the solidarity of the Scheduled Castes of Bengal. . . . While the Scheduled Castes of Eastern Bengal . . . [would] be at the mercy of the majority community [i.e. the Muslims] the Scheduled Castes of Western Bengal . . . [would] be subject to perpetual slavery of the caste Hindus. Hence the Scheduled Castes of this province . . . [could] not be a party to such a mischievous and dangerous move.[16]

The anti-Partition campaign of the Dalits was spearheaded by the Paundra-kshatriya leader Anukul Chandra Naskar in south Bengal,[17] while at a wider level the initiative was taken by Jogendra Nath Mandal who opposed the Partition proposal at the Constituent Assembly:

> If Bengal is partitioned, [he argued] the Scheduled Castes will suffer the most. The caste-Hindus of East Bengal are wealthy and many have salaried jobs. They will have little difficulty in moving from east to west Bengal. Poor Scheduled Caste peasants, fishermen and artisans will have to remain in Bengal where the proportion of Hindus will decline and they will be at the mercy of the majority Muslim community.[18]

With the benefit of hindsight Mandal's observations sound prophetic, but there were other Dalit leaders at that time who thought differently. Indeed, many Namasudra leaders believed that the Dalit peasantry in East Bengal was already at the mercy of the majority Muslim community – Partition and the creation of a Hindu-majority province in West Bengal was its only chance of political survival. So Radhanath Das, the Congress Scheduled Caste member of the Constituent Assembly, retorted to Mandal that he would 'not be able to make them [the Namasudra peasants] feel secure under Muslim League rule or Muslim League protection . . . the backward Hindus will be better able than others to leave east Bengal, since they have few possessions besides their tiny huts.'[19] A section of Namasudra leaders and their followers in the East Bengal countryside launched a campaign at this stage in support of the Partition of Bengal, and for the creation of a Hindu-majority province in West Bengal within the territory of the Indian Union. P.R. Thakur, the other Namasudra member of the Constituent Assembly, asserted in a press statement on 28 April 1947 that:

> As such Mr Mandal has no right to say anything regarding the issue of partition of Bengal, which is nothing but an offshoot of anti-Pakistan agitations. Even Dr Ambedkar, who Mr Mandal acclaims as his political 'Guru', does not support Pakistan, what is more Dr Ambedkar is definitely in favour of Bengal partition movement. Mr Mandal's pretension, therefore, to speak on behalf of the Scheduled Caste people of Bengal falls to the ground since his views on this crucial issue are at variance with the considered opinion not only of the Depressed Classes League but also the Depressed Classes Federation, two most representative and recognized organization [sic] of the Scheduled Caste people all over India.
>
> I should rather say that if Mr Mandal had any sympathy for the wishes and sentiment of the Scheduled Caste people of Bengal, he should have persuaded the Muslim League not to insist on Pakistan in Bengal but to work for a United Bengal under the Indian Union.[20]

In another press statement on 1 May 1947, Thakur declared the Partition of Bengal to be a 'settled fact' and told his Scheduled Caste followers in East Bengal that: 'They should not be disturbed by the false idea that they would be doomed for ever after the partition of Bengal. I can assure them that Hindu-India will pay their first and foremost attention of [sic] the solution of their acute problem.'[21]

As his son tells us in a recent article, Thakur had met Lord Mountbatten on the one hand, and Gandhi, Nehru and other Congress stalwarts on the other, to secure their assurance that if Dalit peasants had to migrate from East Bengal after Partition, their rehabilitation would be guaranteed.[22] With their assurance, on 20 June 1947, at the Bengal Legislative Assembly, twenty-five of the thirty Scheduled Caste MLAs, including Thakur, voted for the Congress–Mahasabha-sponsored resolution in support of the Partition of Bengal.

But Mandal was right – for the Dalit peasants, despite their active support for the Hindu-nationalist majoritarian politics at this penultimate stage of colonial rule, the Partition did not solve their problems, as despite their vehement protestations, all the districts they lived in went to East Pakistan.[23] And this probably had long-term effects on their identity and politics. In Bengal, the migration of refugees took place in waves – not as a cataclysmic movement of large bodies of population, as in Punjab. The first wave of refugees mainly consisted of the more wealthy classes, mostly upper-caste Hindu gentry, and educated middle classes with jobs including many Namasudras as well, who could sell their properties or arrange exchange of properties. It has been argued that the Bengali Hindu *bhadralok* migrated at this stage as they felt insecure and alienated from the emerging Islamic state of Pakistan.[24] However, very few Dalit peasants migrated or could afford to move, because migration required resources, which they lacked. Those who took the fateful decision to relocate had barely anything more than the clothes on their backs when they arrived in a land that appeared foreign and hostile to many of them.[25]

Among those who remained in Pakistan, there was now a greater compulsion to live with the 'Hindu' minority identity imposed on them by the growing power of Islamic nationalism of the Pakistani state. Of their leaders, Jogendra Nath Mandal chose to remain in Pakistan, and joined the Liaquat Ali Khan ministry as its Labour and Law Minister. He remained in this position until 1950, and all this time, as Masayuki Usuda's study tells us, he alternated between representing the larger Hindu minority interests on the one hand and championing the specific Scheduled Caste identity on the other.[26] As for the Namasudra peasants, they too had to live more and more with a generalized Hindu minority identity, as both Usuda's and Beth Roy's studies tell us.[27] This was the result of a process of ascription or a process of othering initiated by the Pakistani state as it moved towards greater Islamization of the polity. This policy of exclusion represented all non-Muslims as the projected 'other' of the Pakistani nation and called them 'Hindu'. When the Namasudra peasants fought for social justice, particularly when peasant movements under Communist leadership were renewed in 1948 in various eastern as well as western Bengal districts, the state in Pakistan represented the Namasudra peasant rebels as 'Hindu' miscreants,[28] thus not only excluding them from Pakistani nationhood, but also allowing them to be appropriated by the Hindu communal discourse in India at the time. This situation came to a head in January–February 1950 when at last the Namasudra peasants decided to leave Pakistan in large numbers.

This second wave of refugee influx was occasioned by a particular incident in Bagerhat subdivision of Khulna district in East Pakistan, in December 1949. There are many versions of the story, which differ in nuance and numbers. We may mention here Jawaharlal Nehru's version as presented in the Indian parliament. In the last days of December 1949 a police party came to a Namasudra village called Kalshira in search of a few communists and were offered resistance by the villagers, resulting in the death of a police constable. Two days later a large police force, assisted by Ansars and other elements, attacked not this one but twenty-two other neighbouring villages inhabited by 'Hindu Namasudras'. What followed then may be recounted in Nehru's own words:

> There was arson and looting on a large scale, men were murdered and women ravished. There were also forcible conversions and desecration of places of worship. The residents of those villages could not escape from the scene because of a rigid cordon maintained by the armed police and others. And even news could not come through.[29]

Thus, in the emotive language of India's first Prime Minister, what started as an anti-communist operation soon became a religiously charged incident. The Calcutta press immediately picked it up – the fact that the victims of this incident were communists and Namasudras was lost, and they all became 'Hindus'. The media frenzy resulted in the outbreak of a fierce riot in Calcutta and Howrah for the first time after independence, and Muslims from West Bengal began to flee. This led to retaliatory violence in East Pakistan, where the rioting spread from Khulna to Rajshahi and Dacca, and then to Mymensingh and Barisal districts. And the main victims of these riots were not the high-caste Hindu *bhadralok* who had already left, but Dalit and tribal peasants like the Namasudras and the Santhals who were now forced to leave their homes and migrate to India.[30] Thus, contrary to what Butalia has postulated for Punjab, in East Pakistan Dalit peasants were deliberately targeted in this post-Partition upsurge of violence. At the Bongaon railway station, the first batch of Namasudra refugees of about 500 families arrived in the first week of January 1950[31] – and thereafter thousands of them began to arrive every day. They either came through Bongaon and on to Sealdah station in Calcutta, from where they were despatched to various refugee camps; or they arrived at the border district of Nadia, where they began to settle down as the local Muslims began to flee across the border. By the beginning of 1951, following the disturbances in Khulna, about 1.5 million refugees had arrived in West Bengal[32] – and the majority of them were Namasudra peasants.

Around 1950, in West Bengal, the dominant popular discourse of persecution of 'minority Hindus' in Islamic Pakistan and the predicament of 'Hindu' refugees overshadowed all other discourses of victimhood. While official correspondence from Nehru acknowledged that those who were migrating at this stage were 'mostly belonging to the depressed classes',[33] in popular media reports that distinction was rarely made as all refugees became 'Hindus' fleeing from 'Muslim' atrocities.[34] After the riots of 1950 the media reports became even more aggressive and provocative. 'I regret to say', Nehru noted on 1 April 1950, 'that many newspapers in India are . . . hysterical and also give a completely one-sided picture.'[35] The Congress government at this stage wanted these refugees to go back at an appropriate time, but the Hindu Mahasabha launched a campaign demanding military action against Pakistan. Shyama Prasad Mukherji, who started the Jan Sangh a few months later, demanded an exchange of population as the only solution to this 'Hindu minority' problem and vowed not to allow the refugees to be sent back.[36] In West Bengal's public space the rhetoric of victimhood of the 'Hindu refugees' seemed to have silenced all other discourses of identity at this juncture.

This discourse was further strengthened by the fact that many of those who migrated after the riots of 1950 came with traumatic memories of horrific communal violence, which many had experienced personally.[37] This led to retaliatory violence on Muslims in the districts. Some of the worst cases of violence in 1950 took place in the border district of Nadia, where the Namasudra migrant peasants, driven out of their villages in Faridpur, Jessore and Khulna in East Pakistan, took revenge on Muslim villagers and forced them to migrate to Pakistan, resulting in an almost virtual exchange of populations.[38] Thus, in Bengal, post-Partition violence affected Dalit groups more directly, and their desire for vengeance and strategies of survival, it seems, led to an appropriation of their distinctive Dalit identity by a more overarching Hindu identity arrayed against its oppositional other – the Muslims. But was the Dalit identity completely Hinduized? Let me now move on to what I call the dilemmas of Dalit identity in post-Partition Bengal.

Dilemmas of Dalit Identity

First of all, if we look at the details of what was actually happening at a mass level in the border regions of Nadia in the early 1950s, we will find it difficult to lump all of it into a simple narrative of communalism. The district of Nadia, on the date of Partition, was a Muslim-majority area; but this was reversed soon as many exclusive Muslim villages were evacuated and then repopulated by Namasudra refugees from Jessore. By the middle of 1948, about 200,000 refugees had settled in this district – half in the urban areas and the remainder in various border regions of rural Nadia. However, those who had left their lands and migrated to the other side of the border often tried to return at harvest time to reap the paddy from those lands, and such attempts were violently resisted by the new occupants.[39] Such incidents of violent conflict between Muslim and Namasudra peasants increased manifold after the fresh exodus of refugees following the 1950 riots, when the Namasudras coming to Nadia often tried to force the Muslims still living there to vacate their houses and lands and migrate to Pakistan. Many of them would return at dead of night to harvest paddy on their fields and this inevitably led to violent clashes. The other complicating factor was the Namasudra refugees' need for cattle; they often ventured to the Pakistani side by crossing the river Ichhamati to steal cattle, leading to a series of conflicts between the two peasant communities across the border. The situation was often further complicated by the intervention of the police forces of the two nation-states that zealously tried to protect and support the interests of their citizens.[40]

These conflicts were thus more for land and livestock – for survival – rather than for religion or community. A further complicating factor was that these Namasudra refugees also clashed frequently with locally powerful Hindu groups. There are several recorded incidents of conflict between the Namasudra refugees and the locally entrenched Goalas, who did not like the refugees disturbing the local balance of power and often sided with the retreating Muslims. Again, when the high-caste Hindu refugees who had arranged exchanges of properties with Muslims came to take possession of these lands, they faced violent resistance from Namasudra squatters who had already taken hold of the lands, cultivated them and claimed their harvests.[41] In other words, this history of violent discord on the borderlands of Nadia cannot be easily fitted into a simple narrative of the Hindu–Muslim communal binary.

Such ambiguities and dilemmas were also present among the leaders of the Dalits. On 8 October 1950, Jogendra Nath Mandal migrated to West Bengal after resigning from his ministerial position in Pakistan's central cabinet as a mark of protest against the continuing repression of Hindu minorities in East Pakistan.[42] His long (about 8,000 words) letter of resignation,[43] which he sent to Pakistan's Prime Minister Liaquat Ali Khan, aptly summarized the dilemmas of Dalit identity in post-Partition Bengal. In the opening sentence of his letter Mandal acknowledged 'the failure of . . . [his] lifelong mission to uplift the backward Hindu masses of East Bengal'. Since 1944 he and his colleagues of the Scheduled Caste Federation had collaborated with the Bengal Muslim League, believing that the interests of the Muslims in Bengal were 'generally identical with those of the Scheduled Castes'. In 1946, at the time of the Calcutta riots, he remained in the Suhrawardy cabinet even though his 'life was in peril', and in October he agreed to join the interim government at the centre as a Muslim League nominee.[44] He believed in Qaid-e-Azam's 'solemn assurance of equal treatment' for all in future Pakistan; but he 'always considered the demand of Pakistan by the Muslim League as a bargaining counter'. He therefore 'was opposed to the partition of Bengal', and for that position invited 'unspeakable abuse, insult and dishonour' from the Hindus of Bengal. 'I recollect those days', he writes in a sombre tone, 'when 32 crores [320 million] of Hindus of this Indo-Pakistan Sub-continent turned their back against me and dubbed me as the enemy of Hindus and Hinduism.'

After 1947 Mandal remained in Pakistan and joined the central cabinet. But after Jinnah's death, he ruefully laments, the Scheduled Castes did not get 'a fair deal in any matter'. And then the East Pakistan government started what he calls 'the anti-Hindu policy', of which the Namasudras and other minorities were equal victims. In his letter Mandal then starts listing the 'atrocities by the police and the military', and here he describes the victims using the terms 'Hindu', 'Scheduled Caste' and 'Namasudra', sometimes in parallel references and sometimes interchangeably. He is even critical of the officer-in-charge of recovery of abducted girls in Pakistan for not treating Scheduled Caste women as Hindus. In other words, the othering process initiated by the Islamization policies of the Pakistani state seem to have collapsed the internal social boundaries within its projected other. So Mandal, once condemned as an 'enemy of Hindus and Hinduism', and who once sincerely believed in a Dalit–Muslim political alliance, wrote the final justification for his resignation in the following words:

> When I am convinced that my continuance in office in the Pakistan Central Government is not of any help to Hindus I should not with a clear conscience, create the false impression in the minds of the Hindus of Pakistan and peoples abroad that Hindus can live there with honour and with a sense of security in respect of their life, property and religion. This is about Hindus.[45]

Thus when Mandal left Pakistan he was clearly torn between two identities – the distinctiveness of his Dalit selfhood had not disappeared from his mindscape, yet his enforced location within a broader Hindu social space vis-à-vis Muslims was also a reality of his quotidian existence. But he was soon to find out that his new homeland, which he was forced to embrace two-and-a-half years after Partition, was not prepared to provide him with any political space.

The Dalit–Muslim relationship in Bengal had thus undergone a significant shift by 1950–51. While an aggressive discourse of Islamic nationalism forced the Dalits out of Pakistan, the dominant Hindu discourse in India tended to absorb them into a 'Hindu refugee' identity. But ruptures within that identity remained. Neither were the Dalits fully able to identify with the Hindus, nor was Hindu nationalism willing to offer them full citizenship. Resolutions passed at the annual sessions of the All India Hindu Mahasabha at Calcutta in December 1949 and at Poona in December 1950 endorsed the ideal of Hindu *rashtra*, which was to be based on a brahmanical version of the *varna* system.[46] At the Calcutta session Mahant Digvijaynath even proposed a resolution to create a fifth *varna*, a '*nabinvarna*', to classify the outcastes.[47] Even the Indian state, then governed by a secular Congress, did not offer a fair deal to these Dalit refugees. Let us now turn to that.

We often tend to consider 'refugees' as a homogeneous group united by their shared past of displacement; but not all refugees are the same. While the first wave of mainly high-caste Hindu *bhadralok* refugees in West Bengal were resettled in squatter colonies in and around Calcutta, the Dalit peasant refugees who came after 1950 were despatched to various refugee camps in districts like 24 Parganas, Nadia, Burdwan, Midnapur or Cooch Behar – or rehabilitated in the neighbouring provinces of Assam, Bihar and Orissa, and later transported to the Andaman Islands and the Dandakaranya region in central India.[48] The government persistently argued that there was not enough vacant land in West Bengal to rehabilitate these agriculturists. The Dalit refugee camps, under the leadership of Jogendra Nath Mandal, offered stiff resistance to this rehabilitation scheme by conducting sustained *satyagraha* campaigns between 1959 and 1961. Yet, despite all these protests, the government did not listen to the pleas of the hapless Namasudra refugees, because the larger Bengali society, by 1959–60, had embraced the Dandakaranya plan as a possible way to get rid of these unwanted refugees who were allegedly endangering an already fragile provincial economy. The situation was further complicated by the outbreak of yet another riot in 1964, causing a fresh influx of refugees from East Pakistan. The Namasudra refugees were now forcibly despatched to Dandakaranya where, by 1965, 7,500 refugee families were settled.[49] Mandal, a frustrated but still spirited man, died on 5 October 1968 while on an election campaign. He never won an elected seat in West Bengal.[50]

As a result of this dispersal, tightly knit peasant communities like the Namasudras that were once geographically anchored were dispersed across large parts of eastern and central India. In the unforgiving, hostile physical conditions that prevailed in some of the resettlement camps many of these refugee families perished; others suffered unimaginable hardship and privation.[51] The Bahujan Samaj Party leader Kanshi Ram summarized their conditions most aptly in 1988:

Immediately after the exit of the British in 1947, there was a sharp and steep slump in the Namasudra Movement. The partition of India ruined many people, but those harmed maximum were the Namasudra. Not only the people and the community were ruined, but also their movement was completely destroyed. Today the Namasudra are the rootless people. Divided in two countries, their roots are in Bangladesh and branches in India.[52]

Conclusion

This essay seeks to conclude that the Partition and its aftermath affected the Dalits in some very direct ways in Bengal. They were neither disinterested onlookers nor accidental victims. Partition cannot be understood only in terms of Hindu–Muslim or Muslim–Sikh relations. We need to introduce the category of caste into this discussion, as the Dalits participated actively in the politics of Partition, and were equally victims and perpetrators of violence. However, the Dalit identity was never a homogeneous one. Different Dalit groups at different historical conjunctures used various idioms of community for negotiating identity, and deployed diverse strategies of survival that ranged from collaboration to resistance. Dalit participation in Partition politics, and Dalit–Muslim and Dalit–Hindu relationships will have to be understood in this heterogeneous context of political response to fast-changing historical contingencies.

In Bengal, since the election of 1946, the discourse of caste was overpowered by politically more influential discourses of nation and religion. Then the sharecroppers' movement in the same year wrecked Dalit solidarities in a significant way. The Dalit political leadership tried to realign their positions strategically within this shifting political paradigm – but this led to serious ruptures in their movements. While some leaders opposed Partition, collaborated with the Muslim League and aligned with the pan-Indian Dalit movement of the All India Scheduled Caste Federation led by B.R. Ambedkar, others joined hands with mainstream political parties like the Congress and the Hindu Mahasabha, as that seemed to be the most useful strategy for their survival and empowerment in the emerging post-colonial structures of power.

In pre-Partition Bengal there were two major communities which provided both the leadership and the support base for the organized Scheduled Caste movement in the province, and both these two communities lost their geographical anchorage as a result of Partition. The pre-Partition political realignments did not solve their problems, as they got pushed from both sides. In the immediate post-Partition years, the Dalit peasants were pushed out of their ancestral homes by an aggressive

Islamic nationalism in Pakistan, while a militant Hindu nationalism tried to appropriate them in India but was not prepared to offer them full citizenship. Neither did the Dalit refugees in West Bengal get a fair deal from the Congress or the Communists.[53] While everyone suffered as a result of Partition, Dalit peasants seem to have been the worst victims, as there was ultimately no demarcated space that they could call their homeland. As a result of their dispersal to various refugee camps across India they lost that crucial spatial capacity required to develop horizontal solidarity. An organized Dalit voice consequently disappeared from Bengal's public space, leading to that all-powerful political myth that caste does not matter in Bengal.

An earlier version of this paper was presented at a seminar at Tufts University, Boston, in November 2011. I am grateful to the participants, particularly Ayesha Jalal and Brian Hatcher, for their perceptive comments on the paper.

Notes and References

1. For a fuller discussion of this historiography, see S. Bandyopadhyay, *From Plassey to Partition: A History of Modern India*, Delhi: Orient Longman, 2004, pp. 460–64.
2. U. Butalia, *The Other Side of Silence: Voices from the Partition of India*, London: Hurst & Company, 2000, p. 235.
3. P.K. Chakrabarti, *The Marginal Men: The refugees and the left political syndrome in West Bengal*, Calcutta: Naya Udyog, 1999; T.Y. Tan and G. Kudaisya, *The Aftermath of Partition in South Asia*, London and New York: Routledge, 2000; J. Chatterji, *The Spoils of Partition: Bengal and India, 1947–1967*, Cambridge: Cambridge University Press, 2007; N. Chatterjee, 'Midnight's Unwanted Children: East Bengali refugees and the politics of rehabilitation', unpublished PhD thesis, Brown University, 1992; H. Roy, 'Citizenship and National Identity in Post-Partition Bengal, 1947–65', unpublished PhD thesis, University of Cincinnati, 2006.
4. I. Ahmed, 'The 1947 Partition of Punjab: Arguments put forth before the Punjab Boundary Commission by the Parties involved', in I. Talbot and G. Singh, eds, *Region and Partition: Bengal, Punjab and the Partition of the Subcontinent*, Karachi: Oxford University Press, 1999, pp. 116–67.
5. R. Kaur, *Since 1947: Partition Narratives among Punjabi Migrants of Delhi*, New Delhi: Oxford University Press, 2007, pp. 164–65.
6. This community has been studied in detail in S. Basu, *Dynamics of a Caste Movement: The Rajbansis of North Bengal, 1910–1947*, New Delhi: Manohar, 2003.
7. This community has been studied in detail in S. Bandyopadhyay, *Caste, Protest and Identity: The Namasudras of Bengal, 1872–1947*, second edition, New Delhi: Oxford University Press, 2011.
8. The following account of the Namasudra movement is based on Bandyopadhyay, *Caste, Protest and Identity*.
9. See S. Das, *Communal Riots in Bengal 1905–1947*, Delhi: Oxford University Press, 1991, chapter 5.
10. 'Extract from File 1164–44 Genl.' and 'S.S.1', IB Records, File No. 191/46, West Bengal State Archives, Kolkata (hereafter WBSA).

11. See J. Chatterji, *The Spoils of Partition*, p. 35.

12. M. Usuda, 'Pushed Towards the Partition: Jogendra Nath Mandal and the Constrained Namasudra Movement', in H. Kotani, ed., *Caste System, Untouchability and the Depressed*, New Delhi: Manohar, 1997, pp. 221–74; Butalia, *The Other Side of Silence*, p. 254.

13. For more details on these movements, see S. Bandyopadhyay, *Caste, Culture and Hegemony: Social dominance in colonial Bengal*, New Delhi: Sage, 2004, chapter 5; J. Chatterji, *Bengal Divided: Hindu communalism and partition, 1932–1947*, Cambridge: Cambridge University Press,1994, pp. 240–65.

14. For details, see Basu, *Dynamics of a Caste Movement*, chapter 5.

15. S. Bose, *Agrarian Bengal: Economy, Social Structure and Politics 1919–47*, Cambridge: Cambridge University Press, 1986, p. 258.

16. Quoted in Bandyopadhyay, *Caste, Culture and Hegemony*, p. 228.

17. S.K. Biswas, *Hari-Guruchand: Banglar Chandal o Bharatbarsher Bahujan Abhyuththan* (Hari-Guruchand: The Chandals of Bengal and the Rise of the Indian Bahujan), Delhi: Orion Books, 2004, pp. 178–79.

18. Quoted in Partha Chatterjee, 'The Second Partition of Bengal', in R. Samaddar, ed., *Reflections on the Partition in the East*, New Delhi: Vikas Publishing House, 1997, p. 49.

19. Quoted in ibid., p. 49.

20. *Amrita Bazaar Patrika*, 28 April 1947, quoted in Jagadish Chandra Mandal, *Rupkathar Rupokar Guruchand Thakur*, Kolkata: Author, 1413 BS, p. 16.

21. *Amrita Bazaar Patrika*, 3 May 1947, quoted in Mandal, *Rupkathar Rupokar*, p. 17.

22. Kapil Krishna Thakur, 'Dalits of East Bengal: Before and After Partition', in B. Chatterjee and D. Chatterjee, eds, *Dalit Lives and Dalit Visions in Eastern India*, Kolkata: Centre for Rural Resources, 2007, p. 31.

23. See 'Report of the Bengal Boundary Commission', Government of India, Reforms Office, File No. 68/47-R, National Archives of India, New Delhi (hereafter NAI).

24. N. Chatterjee, 'The East Bengal Refugees: A Lesson in Survival', in S. Chaudhuri, ed., *Calcutta: The Living City*, Vol. 2, Calcutta: Oxford University Press, 1990, p. 72; J. Chatterji, *The Spoils of Partition*, pp. 111–19; S. Bandyopadhyay, 'The Riddles of Partition: Memories of the Bengali Hindus', in R. Samaddar, ed., *Reflections on the Partition in the East*, pp. 66–69.

25. Note by Governor of East Bengal to Nurul Amin, Prime Minister of East Bengal, 24 February 1950, Bourne Papers, MSS.Eur.E.364, Oriental and India Office Collection, British Library, London (hereafter IOR).

26. Usuda, 'Pushed towards the Partition'.

27. B. Roy, *Some Trouble with Cows: Making Sense of Social Conflict*, New Delhi: Vistaar Publications, 1994.

28. A.H. Ahmed Kamal, 'Peasant Rebellions and the Muslim League Government in East Bengal, 1947–54', in D. Chakrabarty, R. Majumdar and A. Sartori, eds, *From the Colonial to the Postcolonial: India and Pakistan in Transition*, New Delhi: Oxford University Press, 2007, pp. 203–04, 217.

29. *Amrita Bazaar Patrika*, 24 February 1950.

30. For details on these riots, see S. Biswas and H. Sato, *Religion and Politics in Bangladesh and West Bengal: A Study of Communal Relations*, Joint Research Programme Series No. 99, Tokyo: Institute of Developing Economies, 1993, pp. 34–44.

31. *The Statesman*, 21 January 1950.

32. J. Chatterji, *The Spoils of Partition*, p. 112, Table 3.1.

[33] Jawaharlal Nehru, *Letters to Chief Ministers 1947–1964*, Vol. 2: 1950–1952, New Delhi: Oxford University Press, 1986, p. 23.

[34] See, for example, *Amrita Bazaar Patrika*, 30 December 1949, 6 February 1950.

[35] Nehru, *Letters to Chief Ministers*, p. 57.

[36] 'Brief History of Sri Ashutosh Lahiry'; also, 'History sheet of Shri Ashutosh Lahiry', IB Records, S. No. 45/1920, F. No. 210/20, WBSA. See also the intelligence report on Ashutosh Lahiry in IB Records, S. No. 158/20, F. No. 210/20, WBSA; FR No. 9 for period ending 4 May 1950, IOR; L/P&J/5/320, IOR; *Amrita Bazaar Patrika*, 27 April 1950; *The Statesman*, 2, 8 and 10 August 1950.

[37] For a retelling of these memories, see A. Basu Raychaudhury, 'Nostalgia of "Desh", Memories of Partition', *Economic and Political Weekly*, 25 December 2004, pp. 5653–60.

[38] See, for details, J. Chatterji, 'Of Graveyards and Ghettos: Muslims in Partitioned West Bengal 1947–67', in M. Hasan and A. Roy, eds, *Living Together Separately: Cultural India in History and Politics*, New Delhi: Oxford University Press, 2005, pp. 228–29. For evidence of widespread anti-Muslim attitudes in Nadia in 1950, also see W. van Schendel, *The Bengal Borderland: Beyond State and Nation in South Asia*, London: Anthem Press, 2005, p. 99.

[39] See: Extract from W.C.R. of Hanskhali P.S. for the week ending 6.9.49; Copy of a report of a A.S.I. of Police of Banpur B.O.P., 24.8.49, IB Records, F. No. 1238–47 (Nadia), WBSA.

[40] Series of reports on such incidents can be seen in IB Records, File Nos. 1238–47 (Nadia), 1809–48 (Nadia) and 1838–48, Part III, WBSA.

[41] See ibid.

[42] *The Statesman*, 9 October 1950.

[43] The letter is reproduced in T. Roy, *A Suppressed Chapter in History: The Exodus of Hindus from East Pakistan and Bangladesh 1947–2006*, New Delhi: Bookwell, 2007, Appendix B, pp. 469–92.

[44] This was a clever move by Muslim League leader M.A. Jinnah to contest the claim of the Congress that it alone represented the Scheduled Castes.

[45] Roy, *A Suppressed Chapter*, p. 490.

[46] Mahant Digvijaynath to the President, AIHM, 15 December 1949, Hindu Mahasabha Papers, F. No. C-180/1949–50, Nehru Memorial Museum and Library, New Delhi.

[47] Ibid.

[48] *The Statesman*, 23 August and 26 September 1950; G. Kudaisya, 'The Demographic Upheaval of Partition: Refugees and Agricultural Resettlement in India, 1947–67', *South Asia*, Vol. XVIII, Special Issue, 1995, pp. 73–94; J. Chatterji, *The Spoils of Partition*, pp. 127–41.

[49] Tan and Kudaisya, *The Aftermath of Partition*, p. 151.

[50] See D. Sen, 'A politics subsumed: the life and times of Jogendranath Mandal', *Himal South Asian*, April 2010, http://www.himalmag.com/A-politics-subsumed_nw4416.html, accessed on 3 April 2010.

[51] R. Mallick, 'Refugee Resettlement in Forest Reserves: West Bengal Policy Reversal and the Marichjhapi Massacre', *The Journal of Asian Studies*, Vol. 58, No. 1, February 1999, pp. 105–06.

[52] Quoted in ibid., p. 109.

[53] See, for details, ibid.; Tan and Kudaisya, *The Aftermath of Partition*.

Bengal Famine of 1943 and the Chittagong Nari Samiti

Gargi Chakravartty

The famine of 1943 ruined rural Bengal: 2 crore people in 29 districts and 90 subdivisions were severely affected;[1] and 35 lakh people perished. It was a man-made calamity that exposed both bureaucratic corruption and the exploitative zamindari system to the world. The Famine Enquiry Commission itself admitted that the famine took place not due to paucity of rice but because of the spiralling rise in the price of rice.[2] This happened because hoarders stocked foodgrains in their godowns. Big merchants made a surplus profit of Rs 150 crore by selling the very rice for want of which 15 lakh people perished.[3]

Even in the year of the famine, Bengal peasants, in spite of starvation and shortage of bullocks, cultivated every available acre of land. Five crore maunds of the *aus* (autumn) bumper crop was enough to feed Bengal's population for at least two months. Once the government announced the price control order, however, the crop suddenly disappeared from the market. Neither the zamindar nor the *jotedar* ever bothered to take care of the peasants; rather, they found it more profitable to sell the rice in the black market. When the rice vanished in 1943, it was these zamindars and *jotedars* who became 'the rulers of Bengal's destiny'.[4] Of 5.5 crore people living in the villages, 1 crore were landless labourers, and 1.5 crore were sharecroppers and poor peasants. Along with the landless labourers and village artisans, sharecroppers and poor peasants also had to quit the villages in search of food. This led to the ruin of the rural economy. Bureaucratic corruption providing support to the blackmarketeers and hoarders created a terrible situation, not seen earlier. Blackmarketeers entrenched themselves among government officials and soon had a powerful position in society. Had the bureaucracy not been so corrupt, blackmarketeers would not have thrived. Not just rice but every commodity – cloth, oil, salt, sugar, medicine – 'passed into the deadly grip of the blackmarketeers'.[5]

The vast ranks of the poor peasantry lost their paddy to the hoarders, and became destitute along with village artisans and labourers.[6] From April 1943, prices began to soar. The General Secretary of the Communist Party of India, P.C. Joshi, after a six-week tour of famine-struck Bengal, wrote about how 'the credulous peasant was defrauded of his stocks by the hoarder and later skinned off his cash too when he came to buy rice. This is how he began sinking to the status of the pauper.'[7] In 1943, poor peasants in famine-struck areas of Bengal sold land worth Rs 10 crore. 'The displacement of peasantry from land had never before taken place on such a large scale as in 1943.'[8]

The role of the Congress and the Communists has been criticized for making no effort to rally the peasants around the food crisis, and the 'lack of revolutionary potential among the famished population'[9] has been noted. This criticism, however, failed to grasp the pragmatic and mature step taken by the CPI. The situation was so volatile that there was every possibility of the rice riots turning into a communal frenzy. P.C. Joshi wrote:

> If the zamindars and jotedars hoard the next crop to make fabulous profits or sell to the hoarder to get blackmarket rates, they will invite the wrath of the hungry millions from the village and the town, they will pave the way for food riots inside villages, civil war between town and village and martial law for the country. This course helps none but harms all.[10]

He was apprehensive that the food crisis could take a communal turn and made this clear when he pointed out:

> Through the horrors of death, disease and degradation, the situation is drifting towards a civil war. If the League Ministry is not able to improve the situation single handed, as it can't, it will go and the way the Muslim masses will understand it will be that the Hindus have overthrown their Ministry. We will have communal riots on the top of food riots.[11]

It was a difficult era full of complexities, emanating from a new international scenario with the emergence of Hitler's Germany. Its attack on the Soviet Union and the threat of fascism changed the Communists' perception about the imperialist war, which they soon termed a People's War. The fall of Singapore was a turning point as the 'danger grew to the extent that the Japanese invasion looks inevitable and becomes only a question of time'.[12] The political line of People's War as a war to fight Hitler's fascism was misconstrued by the people in general. The Congress and the Forward Bloc regarded it as a betrayal of the national movement. This was the period when the Communists were labelled as traitors for not joining the Quit India movement. It was a stupendous task for the Communist Party to break free of its isolation from national politics and come back to the centrestage of the national scene.

The Chittagong Chapter

Two events happened simultaneously – the defeat of the fascists in the glorious battle of Stalingrad and the Japanese air raids on India. Bengal was the frontier province and Chittagong, 'India's bastion in the East', was the gateway to Bengal. Japanese invasion seemed imminent, and 'there was panic, evacuation and general confusion'.[13] Around this time a whisper campaign began, which pointed out that the disappearance of Burma rice would lead to a food crisis. Chittagong was situated nearest to war-ridden Arakan, and soon it had the 'first dose of Japan's liberating mission'.[14] Chittagong was bombed forty-four times and yet it held on. For the Communist Party, it was also a political battle, opposed as it was to Subhas Chandra Bose's political formulation of an alliance with Japan. The Party was more concerned about its fall-out on Bengal. P.C. Joshi felt that Bose was 'fully exploiting the Bengal famine in his Radio broadcasts' and 'repeatedly announcing that he is coming with his puppet army'. Joshi wrote about Bose's announcement of the path of invasion via Chittagong and expressed worry when Bose moved his Provincial Government from Singapore to Rangoon. He was apprehensive that after Bose brought the Japanese to Bengal, they would not remain content with Bengal.[15] Against this backdrop, Chittagong remained an extremely sensitive zone. The Communist Party's weekly journal, *People's War*, reported how Chittagong stood bravely and faced the first assault. It was an opportune moment for the Party to justify its political line. 'The All-People's war against fascism and for world liberation found Chittagong quite prepared. Their brave sons, the Chittagong patriots issued the clarion call that war against Fascism is our road to freedom.'[16]

Nari Samiti

In the midst of all this the Japanese repeatedly bombed Chittagong, and the people were hit by an acute food crisis. Chittagong town itself had a total population of 30,000, of which 3,000 died within five months. Ela Reid (née Sen), general secretary of the Mahila Atma Raksha Samiti (MARS), a radical women's organization formed in the wake of the Bengal famine, wrote in 1944 (about Chittagong) that 'this district has not only been ravaged by famine but has had to face the greatest horror of air raids for the past two years'.[17] Chittagong being a port-city and open to Japanese attacks, the food crisis created havoc and money sanctioned for rehabilitation was squandered by the bureaucracy and contractors. The Japanese air raids roused the women of Chittagong as never before and 'they rallied in a mighty upsurge for self-defence'.[18] This is precisely why the story of Chittagong and the struggle of its women is a distinct one, and the intention of this essay is to unravel the unknown history of the Nari Samiti which was affiliated to the Mahila Atma Raksha Samiti. The Nari Samiti of Chittagong soon turned into a patriotic mass organization which raised the slogan: 'We will fight the Japs to save our honour and defend our motherland.'[19] The Samiti was set up around 1938 at the initiative of a few Congress women and local social workers, much before the central organization of MARS was formed. Many of them subsequently became members of the Communist Party of India. Among its founder members or those who joined soon after, in 1939, were Jyoti Devi, Kalpana Dutta, Nivedita Nag, Arati Dutta, Manikuntala Chaudhury, Pushpa Das and others.[20]

    This was the time when the Communist Party, politically exiled for its strategy of supporting the British war effort as part of its anti-fascist campaigns, gave a national call to observe the first week of November 1942 as National Unity Week. Later all its mass fronts, including its embryonic women's front, started campaigning for the release of the Congress leaders who were imprisoned during the Quit India movement. They clamoured for unity of the Congress and Muslim League, and demanded a national government to check the Japanese threat. Communist women moved from house to house explaining the need for a national government.[21] In fact, the Jana Raksha Samiti (People's Defence Committee) and soon the Mahila Atma Raksha Samiti (Women's Self-protection Committee) were formed to counter the impending Japanese aggression.[22]

    The Communist Party gave categorical instructions to its cadres – men and women – about their task in the affected areas. The first move was to organise the self-help movement in villages in order to expand the relief kitchens. Every patriotic citizen in every home was asked to join the Party squad. P.C. Joshi, in a pamphlet titled '*Bhookha Hai Bangal*' (Hunger Stalks Bengal), directed comrades to organize a countrywide movement to bring together and 'move Patriots of all parties, to which nobody could take objection and in which nobody could refuse to join'.[23] The Party leadership had confidence in its mass fronts that were already working in 700 kitchens and feeding around 1,17,000 destitutes to take up this challenge. By July 1943, the Chittagong Nari Samiti and the Self-Defence Committees had opened 72 independent relief kitchens for the poor and the starving. They also demanded that the government should open many more.[24]

This was the time when MARS had set up units in most of the districts of Bengal and plunged into relief work, though with limited resources. Regular correspondence between the secretaries of the Chittagong Nari Samiti and the provincial leaders of MARS made it clear that the Nari Samiti, as an affiliated organization, was in close contact with MARS. Food conferences were held in different districts as a prelude to the formation of Mahila Samitis. On 17 January 1943, women from Patnikola village in Chittagong district walked three miles in procession, with babies in their arms and posters in their hands, to attend the food conference at Koroikora.[25] Before the First Bengal Provincial Conference of MARS, twelve districts had their respective conferences between the end of April and the first week of May in 1943. For the first time, 2,500 women gathered at one such conference in Chittagong.[26] Among those who played a leading role in the conference were Kalpana Dutta, Jyoti Devi, Arati Dutta, Saudamini Sengupta, Manikuntala Chaudhury, Amiya Sen and Rina Sen. Arati Dutta was elected secretary of the Nari Samiti.[27] Chittagong was a war zone with military camps and these women soon realized the need for a radical women's organization. By this time, the Chittagong Nari Samiti already had 3,600 members, organized in thirty-six primary committees. Ten women's squads took up the campaign for defence and food.[28] Within three months, the number of members rose to 4,600 in thirty-nine primary committees.[29] Soon after the food conference, women launched a campaign for rationing and succeeded in getting it for the town.[30] Later delegates came from Chittagong to attend the first conference of Bengal Provincial MARS, held in Calcutta in May 1943.

As the food crisis worsened, women of the Nari Samiti started moving from village to village, knocking on the doors of every household: 'Mothers! Give rice, cash or whatever you can, to save the honour of Chittagong's daughters and save the lives of its children.'[31] Those women were never turned away empty-handed. With renewed energy, they organized a large number of relief kitchens on their own. Wherever the Nari Samiti existed, its members opened relief kitchens, cooked and served the famished. It was a sight to watch women coming out of their homes to work in those community kitchens. Brittle pages of old issues of People's War are replete with innumerable sketches drawn by none other than Chittaprosad, the remarkable artist from Chittagong. The reality of famine was boldly etched by his brush. One such was the free kitchen in village Noapara, organized by the Nari Samiti and helped by members of the Kishore Bahini (the boys' wing). The sketches were like political reportage. Some of these bear testimony to an otherwise unnoticed activity of those patriotic women. [32]

Keeping in touch with the central leadership of the Bengal Provincial MARS, the Chittagong Nari Samiti carried out its programme and responded to MARS circulars with detailed information. Ela Reid, general secretary of MARS, wrote at length from Calcutta to Kalpana Dutta, the then district secretary of the Chittagong Town Nari Samiti, about the activities and work to be taken up in every district, mainly the building of shelter homes for distressed women.[33] In Chittagong there were five government centres, which could take care of only 150 women.[34] The need to start more work centres compelled the Nari Samiti to set up three more work centres in Satkania to teach the affected women to spin yarn, weave fishing nets and cloth. The Nari Samiti soon set up another thirty-five cottage industry centres to help women weave sarees for themselves, and napkins and towels to be sold in the market to buy grain for their children.[35]

The situation was pathetic. Hoarders were omnipotent and around 2 lakh people died in Chittagong alone. Peasants lost their property and land, and women had to sell themselves in exchange for food. Price rise, closure of government kitchens, and the ravages of epidemics of cholera, dysentery and malaria prevailed everywhere. Faced with starvation, women turned themselves into prostitutes. There was a sense of despair and disappointment among members of the Nari Samiti. [36]

With resolute determination to face this challenge, the Nari Samiti decided to reopen the relief kitchens and to increase their supply, making them more useful. With a view to restore women to family life, it encouraged the growth of cottage industries, established women's homes with working centres for deserted women, and set up orphanages for children. It campaigned to enforce rationing all over the rural areas and politicized cadres to learn the art of agitation.[37] During December 1943, tour committees carried on relief work. On 3 January 1944, the district office of the Nari Samiti was opened and subsequently a 'Babies Hospital' was set up in town; this was the first of its kind in eastern India for destitute children.

Medical relief provided by the British government was inadequate; even the city hospital had hardly fifteen beds for children. The death of a large number of children prompted the Nari Samiti to start a children's hospital in spite of its limited financial resources.[38] Kalpana Dutta, an architect of the idea of this hospital, later described in detail the plight of those famished children. A short excerpt from her report is revealing:

> Some of these children had seen their parents die right in front of them
> and leave them alone in a mad world. Some mothers had gone for a few
> hours to look for food for the children – but the children had not seen

them again. Others had torn themselves away from their starving children in a mad desire to live – all human bonds had snapped.[39]

It was indeed an uphill task and there were initial problems the Nari Samiti had to deal with. Lack of funds was the main obstacle. In September 1944, the Communist Party of India handed over a donation of Rs 800, received from the People's Relief Committee of Calcutta, for relief activity in Chittagong. This was a small beginning and there still remained innumerable impediments, the most serious being non-availability of rooms, because most of the available houses had been requisitioned by the Army or the ARP (Air Raid Precaution) organization. Added to this was the problem of getting medical equipment, medicines and even doctors, as doctors fetched handsome salaries in the Army and the ARP. The response of public men, including leaders of the Congress and the Muslim League, was cynical. Finally a Medical Relief Committee was set up in November 1944, with the support of medical and other public institutions.[40]

The stories of the dedicated women who came to the rescue of the destitute have not been recorded in any history of the Bengal famine. Kalpana Dutta recalled the philanthropic role of those selfless women who went around from house to house collecting donations, and spent two hours every day with the children in the hospital. Mrs Das, the wife of an Army doctor, was one such dedicated soul. Similarly, Sabita Shyam and Kiranbala De, members of the Nari Samiti, Jatin, a student, and Dr Krishnapada Ghosh came forward to help the organizers.[41] A person named Prabodh handed over his Chittagong house for use as a hospital, as he lived in Calcutta. Though it solved the housing problem, sanitation remained a grave concern for the organizers because of the non-availability of scavengers. Finally, Mrs Jasoda took charge of the sanitation of the hospital and three volunteers joined her in this work. The Nari Samiti thus kept the hospital running for over a year. Outpatient treatment was also carried out not only of children, but also of nursing mothers. In all 257 patients were treated in this hospital, of whom 40 died while 215 survived.[42]

In the post-famine period, the Nari Samiti geared up the self-help movement as per the instructions of the Communist Party.[43] The Samiti formed squads, organized group meetings in the villages, collected old clothes and procured as much medical help as possible from local doctors. The Samiti appealed for medicines to big pharmacies and doctors. Its members soon realized that without the cooperation of the government, it would not be possible to succeed fully. So it asked members to 'send deputation and arrange for mass rallies before the DM, CO and influential personel [sic] of the mills.'[44] Famished children below the age of 12 were taken care of in newly set-up centres in different villages – 90 children in Karankhine, 80 in Dhemsa, 75 in Dhalghat, 100 in Chikdavi, 120 in Gujra, 80 in Nishochintapur, 50 in Kharadwip, 80 in Bidgram and 50 in Amirabad.[45] Kalpana Dutta reported about the self-help movement at length:

> We gladly undertook this responsibility and opened our centres, first of all, in those places where we had functioning units of our Nari Samiti. This was the period when the famine had just blown over and our organization was yet in a fluid state, most of our workers being ill. We did not venture to open centres in all places, because our resources at the moment were not adequate.[46]

In fact in this way, along with more relief kitchens, bases of the Nari Samiti sprang up in areas where they did not exist before.[47] Interestingly, the opening of milk canteens in different places was able to draw women who initially remained aloof from the Nari Samiti 'on the plea that it was a branch of the Communist Party'.[48] They took up the relief work of giving milk to underfed babies.[49] Between July 1943 and January 1944, MARS was engaged in opening free and cheap kitchens and milk canteens all over the province. In Chittagong also, 'small centres of cottage industries were linked up with the food canteens to enable women to earn something towards their own upkeep'.[50]

Apart from economic devastation, MARS was also worried about the lack of social security among women. It decided to observe the week of 10–17 June 1944 with the call to 'restore and rebuild social life' in all districts. Chittagong being in the war zone, the problem was much more acute there. In just Chittagong, there were 1 lakh destitutes.[51] The problem of destitution forced 30,000 women from Chittagong to join the Labour Corps. Large numbers of women from families of fishermen, scavengers and others were compelled by the distress and devastation in the wake of famine to join the Military Labour Corps. From these corps, girls were easily lured into brothels, as happened in Dolghat and Kulgan. At Kandakia, there were agents who regularly supplied the military with girls from the age of 12 and upward. At the Kulshahar Labour Corps, girls were picked up for shorter periods for the flesh trade and sent back. MARS leaders complained to the Famine Inquiry Commission that no effort was made by the authorities to prevent this sex trade.[52]

Around 1944, the Nari Samiti carried out a campaign for an increase in the number of workhouses, for providing work to destitute women, and to increase the food rations so that each person could have three full meals a day. It became an agenda for Nari Samiti activists to put pressure on the government to open more workhouses. In February 1944,

137 workhouses were opened by the government throughout the district. Out of over 1 lakh destitutes, only about 6,000–7,000 destitute women could be accommodated in these. Each one of them worked six hours a day to get six *chhataks* of rice per head, and another three *chhataks* for each dependent family member. Meals were provided in the workhouse itself and two annas were paid to each inmate for fuel, oil, *dal* and vegetables. The Nari Samiti continued its campaign for an increase in the number of workhouses with suitable work and at least two full meals a day. Such sustained pressure on the government was essential, for otherwise government schemes were bound to fail.[53] Earlier, government homes provided for a maximum of 10,000 destitutes. On 7 July 1944, a government circular was sent round to all the districts with 'an improved and centralized scheme', which actually meant that whereas in August there were 500 workhouses, in future there would be only 60. Circulars were sent to workhouses in Amirabad, Noapara, Cox's Bazar and Chikadi.[54]

Once the workhouses were closed down, the destitute women could be easily lured with money to join the Labour Corps. Female labour was cheaper than male labour. Subsequently, contractors of the Labour Corps used these helpless women and 'made a flourishing side trade out of their bodies'.[55] Women from fishermen's families were most affected, but there were women from other sections also who were picked up. The story of Charubala Acharya of North Kathali was one such example of a middle-class woman taking up a job in the Military Labour Corps.[56] Pahartali became a centre of this trade. Old men were virtually selling their daughters and daughters-in-law out of pressing need for money.[57] In a village near Dohazari, women from Hindu weavers' families as well as Muslim peasants became victims of this flesh trade on a large scale. It was horrific to find Army contractors making money by selling destitute women and soldiers falling prey to this.[58] In Chittagong, the immoral slave trade became 'a vicious scourge which spared no caste, no community'.[59] Surprisingly, the contractors belonged to *bhadralok* families of both Hindu and Muslim communities.[60]

The problem was aggravated with the closing down of workhouses, and most of the destitute women turned to the Nari Samiti to get them reopened. A self-help movement at the initiative of women in village Chikdair led to the opening of a new workhouse. Twenty of them collected Rs 5 each and gave the money to their leader, Binod Bala, to start this venture. From twenty their number increased to 80, and this helped Binod Bala to organize the Nari Samiti in her area with all the destitute women becoming members.[61]

During 1944 in Chittagong district, of the 1 lakh destitutes who were fed in relief kitchens, only 5 per cent were men and the rest were women.[62] This explains the enormity of the situation that the Nari Samiti had to handle. It is true that members of the Nari Samiti became very popular among the local women in some villages for their tenacious relief work. But the Samiti on its own was 'too weak to help the women of the village whose poverty and destitution was apalling'.[63] The Nari Samiti received very little support from top Congress leaders as they felt there were Communists inside the Samiti; at that time Communists were regarded as untouchables by some Congressmen for their political line.[64]

With the closing down of free kitchens and workhouses, 'greater demand created by the artificial swelling of population by the military', only two options were open to these destitute women – prostitution or death. By October and November 1944, mass prostitution became a prevalent phenomenon among the destitutes in Chittagong town. Thirty thousand women had joined the Labour Corps and from there they were brought to brothels in Dolghat, Kolgan, Dohazari and Kulshahahr. This was not restricted to Chittagong alone, but was common throughout the famine- affected districts in all the provinces of Bengal. About 30,000 women out of Calcutta's 1,25,000 destitutes had gone into brothels.[65] But Chittagong being a war zone, because of the presence of the military camps, the contractors and agents could easily exploit the vulnerable situation. The seriousness of the problem deepened with the air-raids of the Japanese and the extensive presence of the Army.

Added to this were epidemics of various kinds. The first wave of epidemics of cholera and dysentry came in August–September 1943, along with the famine, and the second wave in December 1943 which continued till February 1944; the dominant ailments were malaria and small pox.[66] But incidence of veneral disease in Chittagong was higher than in Calcutta.[67] Many came back from the Military Labour Corps infected with venereal diseases.

Countless people perished due to malnutrition and starvation along with malaria in epidemic form, as their bodies had no power to resist. In May 1944, 30 million out of Bengal's 60 million people were struck with malaria, and, from various estimates, it was clear that more people had died in Bengal from epidemics than in the worst days of food scarcity.[68] In fact, in one *thana* of Chittagong alone, 5,000 had died of cholera. [69]

Epilogue

The famine of 1943 struck twenty-nine districts of Bengal and within two years the entire province was ravaged, families disintegrated and women turned destitute. Kanak Mukherjee, a leading member of MARS, wrote: 'When the women in a family died in the famine – families did not always break up, the menfolk carried on. When the men wage-earners died, their mothers, wives, sisters and children – who were unfit and untrained for any trade – were thrown on the streets.'[70] There were 60 lakh such destitutes who had been waiting for relief in 1944 and the government could provide for no more than 20,295 of them.[71] 'Till the end of 1944, despair and hopelessness prevailed all over.'[72] The Bengal government did sanction some amount for rehabilitation, but there were innumerable examples of money being squandered by government employees, contractors and Union Board Presidents in Chittagong alone.[73] In such a situation of despondency, the intervention of the People's Relief Committee and the Nari Samiti, however limited in scale, was a silver lining amidst the dark clouds hovering over Chittagong.

Chittagong stood unique for its 'marvellous tradition of nationalism'. It was not swayed by the propaganda of the Fifth Column.[74] Chittagong was in the limelight of the nationalist movement in the 1930s when the revolutionary acts of Surya Sen and his comrades shook the entire country; Pritilata Wadedar and Kalpana Dutta became household names for their bravery. After coming out of jail, Kalpana became a Communist and wrote extensively in her memoirs about why and how she transcended from revolutionary nationalism to communism. She wrote: 'Marxism is no magic that could turn everything to gold or bring us the moon. From the grim and bitter lessons of life, we have come to realize that Marxism is the science that helps us to understand society, the life of the people.'[75]

Food crisis, famine and epidemics compelled Kalpana to plunge into relief work. In every Chittagong home she was called 'amader meye' (our daughter). She became an activist in building the Nari Samiti, a MARS unit, in Chittagong. She also worked among the kisans. She explained to them the linkage between the fight for resistance against the Japanese and the struggle for livelihood – land, food, clothing. Kalpana realized that her earlier dream of freedom, during the revolutionary phase of the 1930s, could come true through this new struggle for a better world. This widened her ideological horizon and strengthened her political understanding. In Chittagong, it was easier to rouse anti-Japanese sentiments because the threat of the Japanese menace was visible, unlike in other parts of the country. This was the time when Kalpana worked among the women. She explained to them: 'It is time to get ready for resistance against the Japs in self-defence and for the defence of your honour.'[76] She further wrote: 'We took up the work of building up women's organization for self-defence and at the same time began anti-Jap propaganda.'[77] The Nari Samiti had made arrangements for practice in lathi and dagger-play in several centres, besides starting cottage industries for village self-sufficiency. Women were taught how to crawl under fire, scale walls, etc.[78] From all quarters came a remarkable response to their campaign against the Japanese threat. Kalpana reminisced about those experiences: 'Through this we could rouse the natural patriotism and hatred against slavery in everybody, because the Japanese invasion was a thing which was real and imminent to them. And through all these, the mass organizations grew in strength and activity.'[79]

Chittagong suffered the most, and the devastation of women and children knew no bounds. Worst hit were the families of fishermen, scavengers and peasants. The fishermen's settlement was in complete ruins. There was despair and doubt as to whether these people would be able to resist the onslaught of the Japanese invasion. As Ela Reid wrote, 'Harried by epidemics, want of food, malnutrition – can one expect them to create a formidable defence of their country? And they did.'[80] The quantum of relief work was miniscule compared to the enormity of the devastation. But still there was a movement, small efforts by energetic workers in some areas to move forward. Forty-five huts of the destitute of Katthuli village were raised and rebuilt; brothels at Pahartali were closed down in spite of the presence of the military. Fifteen girls belonging to the fishermen's community were rescued from Chittagong brothels.[81]

When this crisis engulfed Chittagong, women like Kalpana were 'dumbfounded for the time being', overwhelmed by the distress and devastation wrought by famine and air raids. But once the war was over and the famine-struck people's life slowly limped back to normalcy, a realization dawned in the minds of these dedicated workers, that 'patriotism does not mean a superficial and sentimental trust in the people nor blindly following the leaders, but the rousing of that self-confidence in the people which makes them the masters of their own destiny and conscious creators of their own future'.[82] The saga of the women's struggle in Chittagong should not be allowed to be forgotten. The story of the Chittagong Nari Samiti and many of its workers, lesser known and unknown, needs to be woven into the texture of the history of the Mahila Atma Raksha Samiti. It has been a revelation to unearth a treasure-house of people's struggle, a movement by ordinary women against the backdrop of a horrific situation that suddenly destabilized families and their social life. The story of the Chittagong Nari Samiti deserves a special place in gender historiography.

Notes and References

[1] Bhowani Sen, *Rural Bengal in Ruins*, Bombay: People's Publishing House, 1945, p. 16. According to the Famine Inquiry Committee Report (p. 96), Bengal's total area was 82,955 square miles, of which people occupying 21,665 square miles were very severely hit by the famine.

[2] Ibid., p. 5.

[3] Ibid., p. 1: 'Out of this very famine, the big merchants had made a surplus profit of Rs 150 crores by selling the very rice . . .'.

[4] Ibid., p. 4: 'In May 1943 at the time when corpses were found in the streets and the army of destitutes roamed all over, 75 per cent of the peasants had no stock at home, food stock was in the hands of Jotedars and merchants, and of Government agents and factory owners.'

[5] Ibid., p. 26: 'Where distribution is arranged through Food Committees the black-marketeer sneaks into the Food Committee itself. Many of the Food Committees in Bengal have passed into the hands of the black-marketeers. Where Government dealers are appointed for distribution, there too the black-marketeer gets himself installed as the dealer.'

[6] G. Adhikari, *No More Famine for All*, Bombay: People's Publishing House, 1945, p. 15.

[7] P.C. Joshi, *Who Lives If Bengal Dies?* Bombay: People's Publishing House, 1943, p. 4.

[8] Bhowani Sen, *Rural Bengal in Ruins*, p. 6. In fifteen areas alone, 5 lakh kisans sold off Rs 10 crore worth of land in the course of 1943.

[9] R. Paul Greenough, *Prosperity and Misery in Modern Bengal: The Famine of 1943–44*, New York: Oxford University Press, 1982, p. 268.

[10] P.C. Joshi, *Who Lives If Bengal Dies?*, p. 24.

[11] Ibid., p. 28.

[12] Hansraj (P.C. Joshi's underground name), *Foreword to Freedom: India in the War of Liberation*, New Delhi: Anand Press, November 1941, p. 13.

[13] Ela Sen, *Darkening Days: Being a Narrative of Famine-Stricken Bengal*, Calcutta: Susil Gupta Publication, 1944, p. 14. 'It was during this period of confusion that the profiteers went quietly about and began to buy up rice all over Bengal.'

[14] *People's War*, 23 August 1942.

[15] P.C. Joshi, *Who Lives If Bengal Dies?*, p. 10.

[16] *People's War*, 23 August 1942.

[17] Ela Sen, *Darkening Days*, pp. 160–61. 'It lies nearest to the war-ridden Arakan and one hopes that if the Japanese attempt an invasion through this area, it is these people of Chittagong who will help to stem their onslaught.'

[18] Renu Chakravartty, *Communists in Indian Women's Movement (1940–1950)*, New Delhi: People's Publishing House, 1980, p. 24.

[19] *People's War*, 22 August 1943.

[20] Kanak Mukhopadhyay, *Nari Mukti Andolon o Aamra* (in Bengali), Kolkata: Ek Sathe, 2005, p. 50.

[21] Ibid., p. 38.

[22] Renu Chakravartty, *Communists in Indian Women's Movement*, p. 21.

[23] P.C. Joshi, *Who Lives If Bengal Dies?*, p. 23.

[24] *People's War*, 18 July 1943.

[25] Renu Chakravartty, *Communists in Indian Women's Movement*, p. 35.

[26] Ibid., p. 52.

[27] Kanak Mukhopadhyay, *Nari Mukti Andolon o Aamra*, p. 41.

[28] Renu Chakravartty, *Communists in Indian Women's Movement*, p. 24.

[29] *People's War*, 22 August 1943.

[30] Renu Chakravartty, *Communists in Indian Women's Movement*, p. 59. Later, Kalpana Dutta recalled in her reminiscences how everybody said in one voice – 'It is the Communists who really campaigned for rationing.' Kalpana Dutta,

Chittagong Armoury Raiders Reminiscences, Bombay: People's Publishing House, 1945.

[31] *People's War*, 22 August 1943.

[32] *People's War*, 15 August 1943. Chittaprosad, a budding artist, was first spotted by Party comrades in Chittagong during the war years. He used to draw posters and paste them at vantage-points in the port-city. When Bhowani Sen, secretary of the Bengal Communist Party, got a few of these posters that were new both in content and style, he sent them to P.C. Joshi, General Secretary of the Party in Bombay. Promptly came an instruction from Joshi: 'Catch Chitto and pack him off to Bombay.' Then there was no return. Chittaprosad accompanied P.C. Joshi on his tour of the famine-struck areas in Bengal. One finds similar sketches of peasant women from Satkania in the Chittagong Relief Hospital on the pages of *People's War* of 5 December 1943.

[33] Special Branch (SB) Collection, File No. 1340/43, West Bengal State Archives (WBSA): Letter dated 28 December 1943 from Ela Reid to Kalpana Dutta. In this letter it was instructed that 'in every district, maternity homes and shelter houses for the distressed women are to be permanently established with a view to give permanent relief. For this purpose our Provincial Committee will open a Board of Trustees in cooperation with other bodies. With the amount deposited with this Board, shelter houses for the distressed women will first be opened at Barasat, Kakdwip, Chittagong, Noakhali, Rangpur and Barisal.' There were specific instructions regarding propaganda for rationing and self-protection, distribution of clothes and medicines, particularly quinine.

[34] Renu Chakravartty, *Communists in Indian Women's Movement*, p. 57. A destitute centre was run in Barama village by the Nari Samiti; ibid., p. 59.

[35] *People's War*, 22 August 1943.

[36] SB Collection, File No. 1340/43, WBSA; 'Mass prostitution became a reality more in town, far less in villages', P.C. Joshi, *Who Lives If Bengal Dies?*, p. 7.

[37] SB Collection, File No. 1340/43, WBSA: Letter from Arati Dutta, District Secretary of the Chittagong Nari Samiti to Kanak Mukherjee, Secretary of the Bengal Provincial MARS, dated 20 January 1944.

[38] Renu Chakravartty, *Communists in Indian Women's Movement*, p. 46.

[39] *People's War*, 26 August 1945: Kalpana Dutta, 'Story of Who Built It and How? Only Children's Hospital in East Bengal'.

[40] Ibid.

[41] Ibid.

[42] Renu Chakravartty, *Communists in Indian Women's Movement*, p. 47.

[43] P.C. Joshi, *Who Lives If Bengal Dies?*, p. 24. 'The first task inside the village was to organize a Self-Help Movement to be able to continue, improve and enlarge the relief kitchens. We decided to appeal to every patriot inside the villages to come with Party squad to every home with the message: In the name of the honour of your own women, help the destitute women.'

[44] SB Collection, File No. 1340/43, WBSA.

[45] *People's Age*, 23 December 1945.

[46] Ibid.

[47] Ibid.

[48] Renu Chakravartty, *Communists in Indian Women's Movement*, p. 83. In fact earlier, in the wake of anti-communist hysteria, in the middle of the conference of the Nari Samiti, communist-baiters started throwing stones at the meeting place. The volunteers of the Reception Committee kept silent watch and kept them at bay. p. 83.

[49] *People's Age*, 23 December 1945, Kalpana Dutta's report.

[50] Memorandum to the Famine Inquiry Commission, submitted by MARS, Nanavati Papers, National Archives of India (NAI).

[51] *People's War*, 24 September 1944.

[52] Memorandum to the Famine Inquiry Commission, submitted by MARS, Nanavati Papers, National Archives of India, NAI.

[53] *People's Age*, 23 December 1945.

[54] *People's War*, 24 September 1944: Kanak Mukherjee, 'Our Famine – Homeless Sisters' Plight: Bengal Government's Workhouses Closing Down'.

[55] *People's War*, 11 February 1945: Bhowani Sen, 'Slave Trade in Chittagong – Gruesome Picture of Traffic in Women Destitutes'.

[56] Ibid.

[57] Ibid.

[58] Ibid. Bhowani Sen met a British soldier who was shocked to hear these barbaric stories. He told Sen: 'What will happen to England when they go back with their barbaric consciousness?'

[59] Ibid.

[60] Ibid.

[61] *People's War*, 26 August 1945.

[62] *People's War*, 11 February 1945.

[63] Ibid.

[64] Ibid. Bhowani Sen narrated an incident in village Dhalghat. A contractor came into the village and distributed handsome gifts among the poor women and warned them not to be associated with the Nari Samiti. The women, out of desperation to live at any cost, asked the Nari Samiti workers to quit the village and not offend the contractor.

[65] Memorandum to the Famine Inquiry Commission, submitted by MARS, Nanavati Papers, National Archives of India, NAI.

[66] Bhowani Sen, *Rural Bengal in Ruins*, p. 19.

[67] Ela Sen, *Darkening Days*, p. 179: 'Incidence of veneral disease in Calcutta is between 33 and 45%, in Chittagong, it is correspondingly high.'

[68] Ibid., p. 178.

[69] Ibid., p. 164.

[70] *People's War*, 24 September 1944.

[71] Bhowani Sen, *Rural Bengal in Ruins*, p. 33.

[72] Ibid., p. 34.

[73] Ibid., p. 38.

[74] Ela Sen, *Darkening Days*, p. 161. Also see Renu Chakravartty, *Communists in Indian Women's Movement*, pp. 23–24: 'Chittagong's women were in the frontline of attack from Japanese bombing and it was natural that the Japanese attack aroused them as never before and they rallied in a mighty upsurge for self-defence.'

[75] Kalpana Dutta, *Chittagong Armoury Raiders Reminiscences*, p. 98.

[76] Ibid., p. 94.

[77] Ibid., p. 95. This was how it was explained to the kisans: 'The struggle for resistance against the Japs is the struggle in defence of your food and cloth, your property and land.'

[78] *People's War*, 30 September 1945: Kalpana Dutta, 'A report from Inside Chittagong'. In southern parts of Chittagong (Kutubolia and Maheshkhali areas) people (mostly Muslim areas) used to say, 'let Kalpana Dutta give us the order once and we shall plunge into fight against the Japs and lay down our lives in battle.'

[79] Kalpana Dutta, *Chittagong Armoury Raiders Reminiscences*, p. 95.
[80] Ela Sen, *Darkening Days*, p. 161.
[81] Bhowani Sen, *Rural Bengal in Ruins*, pp. 34–35.
[82] Kalpana Dutta, *Chittagong Armoury Raiders Reminiscences*, p. 98.

From Cantoobabu to Dwarakanath

Emergence of a New Commercial Elite in Bengal (1757–1850)

Shubhra Chakrabarti

The turn of the eighteenth century was marked by massive trading activities between the European companies and merchants from Bengal, among others. This business interaction resulted in the growth of a new commercial elite centred on the upcoming port-city of Calcutta,[1] which was to become the future commercial and administrative capital of India under the British.

In 1757, the British defeated the Nawab of Bengal, Siraj-ud-Daula, in the Battle of Plassey, and wrested political control from him. But much before Plassey, from the early years of the eighteenth century, the indigenous merchants of Bengal – popularly known as *banians, diwans, gomashtas, dalals* and *pykars* according to their rank and status in the business hierarchy[2] – had been collaborating with the Europeans, especially with the British, in trade. The profits from this commercial partnership helped turn many of these merchants into business tycoons of their time. This essay is an attempt to establish the story of such business magnates, who not only earned fortunes for themselves and their descendants but were instrumental in ushering in a new age of culture and modernity in Bengal. My study begins with Krishna Kanta Nandi or Cantoobabu,[3] and ends with Dwarakanath Tagore.[4] Between them they capture the developmental sequence of the transformation of the world of indigenous business. While Cantoobabu made use of his position as the *banian*[5] of Warren Hastings, Dwarakanath actually entered into business partnership with the British. The history of this process of development also depicts the extent to which the Bengalis accepted or rejected the 'western' world as they came in close proximity with the British. In this essay I will talk about two different categories of merchants who were the by-products of changed times after the Battle of Plassey. One category comprised independent merchants such as Ramdulal Dey, and the other, Cantoobabu and Dwarakanath Tagore who made their pile through collaboration.

I begin the study by introducing a few representative entrepreneurs who came from diverse backgrounds and lived different kinds of lives, but collectively participated in the making of a specific kind of commercial culture in early nineteenth-century Bengal.

The Making of a Commercial Elite

The earliest merchants to have transacted with the Europeans were the Seths and the Basaks, who have left their legacy as Bengali surnames. They belonged to the traditional *tantubai* or weaver community, and are fabled to be the first dwellers of Calcutta. It is learnt from their family chronicles that Mukundaram Seth, along with a few Basaks, were the first to migrate to Calcutta in the sixteenth century – after the decline of Saptagram, an important trading centre, due to silting of the river Saraswati.[6] They were dealers in cotton, silk and Bengal muslins in various courts of the country before coming to Saptagram and then to Govindapur.[7] The early Seths came to be known as the '*jangal-kata basinda*', or those who had cleared the jungle to become its inhabitants. In the seventeenth century they settled around Bitore near Shibpur, close to Calcutta, and started an extensive cloth trade with Portuguese traders in temporary markets, which disappeared when the ships sailed away. But these markets played a great role in building up the future city of Calcutta. From the late seventeenth and early eighteenth century, English traders began to trade in these markets on both banks of the Ganges river. The latter acted as *dadni* merchants (those who supplied goods on advance payment basis) who took advance or *dadan* from the English merchants, distributed this to the weavers, and then collected cotton piece-goods made according to specifications from the weavers and delivered these. Later, this practice of advance payment was followed by other Europeans as well.[8]

The more enterprising among the Seths and Basaks moved further down the river and colonized its east bank, just above the junction of the Adi Ganga, and founded the village of Govindapur. Soon these cotton and cloth merchants established another market on the north side of Calcutta, which was popularly known as the Sutanuti *haat* (or that which abounded in cotton yarn). In this way the space between Sutanuti in the north and Govindapur in the south were both converted by the Seths and the Basaks into settlements, with the village of Dihi Kolkata in the middle. Calcutta gradually developed into an urban complex around these nuclei of villages.[9] Its first citizens came from among those who made their wealth in trade and business.

Two brothers, Janardan and Banarasi Seth, who had risen from humble beginnings, became the most important and influential brokers for the English in Bengal in the first quarter of the eighteenth century. It is recorded that they were succeeded by Baishnabdas, whose extreme high-handedness in matters of investment made the English Company replace him with his son Shyamsunder in 1732.[10] As is evident, during the first half of the eighteenth century the English could think of replacing one broker with another, but they could not do away with the indigenous system of procuring goods. From contemporary records it appears that the Seths and Basaks were indispensable agents without whose assistance the English Company was helpless. At the same time, as they were leaders of the weaving community of Bengal, the Company preferred not to antagonise them lest their investment be jeopardized.[11] Moreover, young English fortune-seekers were financially dependent upon the Seths, who carried on an extensive banking business in the Bara Bazaar (literally, 'big market') area of Calcutta.

Some historians maintain that the decline of the Seths began after the Company dispensed with the *dadni* system of procuring goods, and took to the agency or direct procurement system. However, this did not mean there was a decline in the Seths' influence over the mode of investment, as the office of the broker was inseparably connected with any kind of purchasing process in Bengal.[12]

The Basaks, who were less prominent in the earlier part of the century, came into the limelight during the latter half of the eighteenth century. Pradip Sinha, quoting from Long's *Selections*, has shown that one member of this community, Shobharam Basak, was second in the list of Indian inhabitants of Calcutta who received restitution money for the sack of Calcutta from the new Nawab after the Battle of Plassey.[13] One section of wealthy Basak traders invested in land, while the rest invested in urban properties and estates in different parts of Calcutta.[14]

This tradition of making a fortune by acting as an intermediary for foreign merchants became a common practice in Bengal as the eighteenth century progressed. Krishna Kanta Nandi, popularly known as Cantoobabu (1720–1794), was another such merchant. In 1754, Krishna Kanta became the *banian* of Warren Hastings for a paltry sum of Rs 15 or Rs 20 a month. His steady rise from humble beginnings to a millionaire was facilitated by the political chaos that prevailed in Bengal at that time. Krishna Kanta's biographer Somendra Chandra Nandy's findings reveal that Cantoobabu could serve as Warren Hastings' *banian* primarily because he could advance him capital for his business.[15] This perhaps cemented the bond between the two in later days. As Hastings reaped profits from his private trade, his *banian* also prospered.

Cantoobabu's case is representative of the gradual rise of a trading family to opulence in eighteenth-century Bengal. He successfully increased his family trade in silk, and by 1787, established two silk filatures, which enabled him to become the biggest indigenous producer of filature silk in Bengal.[16] Not content with the silk trade alone, he became, as early as 1768, the first manufacturer of '*teeka*' salt and later took to wholesale trade.[17] He diversified his business and traded in cotton cloth, lime, metals, and foodgrains and spices as well.[18]

Cantoobabu realized from early experience that it was extremely profitable to stay close to the British. He therefore became the *banian* of Sykes, Resident at the Murshidabad court, in 1765–66, when Hastings was away. This helped him use his political connections to serve in important administrative positions that enhanced his power and political prestige. In 1769 he became the Treasury Daroga of Fuccercoondy in Rangpur.[19] Interestingly, while serving in administrative positions, Cantoobabu started assiduously investing his profits from trade in land purchase, and created an enormous zamindari that was more profitable and less risky than trade. It earned him respectability in society as well and helped him climb the caste ladder with ease, as has been documented in a long poem titled *Kantanama or Rajdharma*, written by his biographer Dewan Manulla Mandal, resident of Fakanda village in the Kasimbazar Raj zamindari.[20] Cantoobabu's son Lokenath never emulated his enterprising father so far as business was concerned, and remained primarily a landed aristocrat.

In 1772 Cantoobabu circulated the *parwana* or deed that established him as zamindar in his landed estate. This he named as 'Kantanagar', after himself. Thus the foundation of the Kasimbazar Raj family was laid.[21] We learn from Manulla's account how exacting and strict Cantoobabu was about tax collections and levying extra cess or *abwabs* that terrorized the ryots (peasants) and filled his coffers.[22] Cantoobabu amassed his fortune by capitalizing on the new commercial opportunities offered by foreign enterprise. He began his career as a mere trader, but was determined to push his image up the social ladder. This became easy as he lived at a time when social mobility was already altering the traditional structure of society by loosening the rigidity of the caste hierarchy, which I shall discuss later. [23]

Another example of wealth acquisition – this time through collaboration with the English in the salt trade – was that of the Ghoshal family of Bhookailash. The family established a virtual monopoly in this business by dabbling in the vulnerable political situation of mid-eighteenth-century Bengal. The first Ghoshal to become prominent was a merchant named Kandarpa, who established himself in the Khidirpur area of Calcutta after the English captured Govindapur from Siraj in 1756.[24] His son Gokul Ghoshal, who served as the *banian* to Harry Verelst, Governor of Bengal

(1764–66), is credited with the founding of the Raj family of Bhookailash in 24 Parganas, West Bengal. It was this political connection, similar to Cantoobabu's, that helped him acquire extensive wasteland, jungles and swamps in Chittagong district. Here he outdid all other indigenous salt traders in competition. Later, in 1762, his nephew Joynarayan obtained a *sanad* (deed) from Mr Verelst, which further strengthened the Ghoshals' monopoly in the salt business. Such was their position and power that the English Collector Charles Bentley complained of their highhandedness, which, he claimed, hindered the Company in realizing land revenue from these lands.[25]

Another prominent business entrepreneur of eighteenth-century Bengal was Akrur Dutta (Dutt in the English Company records) (17??–1809). Like many of his generation, he rose from humble origins to build his fortune by supplying sloops or small country-made boats to the English East India Company. These sloops were easily navigable in shallow waters, thus asserting their value to English traders who required such boats to procure goods of investments from distant *arangs* and factories situated beside rivers. The sloops were also essential for loading and unloading goods from waiting ships which could not sail upstream on shallow river-waters, but had to be anchored in deep waters in the port of Diamond Harbour.

Akrur Dutta was an independent contractor. He began his career as an ordinary *dadni* merchant in the 1740s.[26] One assumes he turned to the sloop business after disbandment of the *dadni* system in 1753. Speaking about him in 1821, his son Rammohun Dutta stated that for thirty years his father had furnished the English Company with river sloops for the transit of goods and merchandise from towns to stations.[27] His sloops moved between Calcutta and Diamond Harbour, to Kedgeree and Cox's Island, constantly loading and unloading the Company's goods.[28] His sloops often transported troops, stores and provisions from one place to another.[29] Akrur Dutta was highly respected by the English, and although his tenders were occasionally high, he was preferred over other competitors such as Madan Mohan Dutt,[30] Durponarain Chatterjee, Mansook Ornab, or even the Englishman Richard Ecroyd.[31] Though Dutta's sloops were more expensive, the Board of Trade always found it 'impossible, embarrassing and risky' to dispense with him.[32]

Akrur Dutta was a seasoned businessman who served the English East India Company for over twenty-five years. We do not know whether he purchased a zamindari like Cantoobabu or the Ghoshals of Bhookailash. What we do know is that he was extremely rich. Successive generations of his family followed him in the sloop business. In the 1820s, when other

sloop owners of Bengal had taken a beating from rival English sloop contractors, Akrur Dutta's family survived by producing heavy copper-bot-
tomed sloops that were in much demand at that time. However, Seppings,
the Marine Surveyor who was appointed by the English Company to
examine Akrur Dutta's son Rammohan Dutta's sloops, rejected all nineteen
that the latter had provided. This did not spell ruin, however. Over time
the Duttas had amassed enough wealth to shift their business away from
the English and join hands with the Americans.[33]

Let us now turn to Krishna Panti (1749–1809), the founder of
the Palchaudhury family of Ranaghat in Nadia district, West Bengal. He
was another business entrepreneur who made his fortune by speculating
in the grain trade.[34] Krishna Panti was originally a Pal who belonged to
the poor *Teli* community, and started off as a vendor of *paan* or betel-leaf
in the local *haat* (market) of Gangapur. It was from *paan* that the family
obtained its surname 'Panti'. It is testimony to Krishna Panti's zeal and
enterprise that he transformed himself from a poor vendor into a successful
businessman retailing on a partnership basis within a short time.

We learn from his biographer that speculation on the price and
availability of grains as fodder for cattle and especially for cart-horses in
Calcutta made him rich. He arrived in Hatkhola in Calcutta, the nerve-
centre of business activities before the emergence of Bara Bazaar, with a
paltry sum of money in hand. Here he speculated on and hoarded goods in
a cheap market, selling them when prices rose. He kept himself informed of
the rapid price fluctuations and intricacies of a rural–urban supply network.
When money started pouring in, Krishna Panti diversified his capital and
invested it in the salt trade. Soon he was recognized as one of the most
important salt merchants by the Salt Board. Krishna Panti's salt *arangs*
were spread all over Bengal. His importance to the English Company can
easily be assessed from a letter by William Berrie, Clerk and Inspector of
Public Granary at Fort William, to George Dowdeswell, Secretary to the
Board of Revenue, where the former asserted that if anyone had a doubt
about the quality of 'rice and paddy', they should have it examined by
'Kissen Panty'.[35]

Like many affluent men of his time, Krishna Panti purchased a
zamindari in Ranaghat, in Nadia district of West Bengal. A contemporary
song by a popular composer, Ramprasad Sen, narrates how Krishna Panti,
once a betel-leaf seller, built his zamindari on the ruins of the once-famous
ruler of Nadia, Maharaja Krishna Chandra, who lost his estates to him in
auction.[36] Warren Hastings conferred the title of 'Pal-Chaudhuri' on the
family after Krishna Panti bought the zamindari.[37]

The history of the Palchaudhuri family is a typical example of the sudden opulence of the first group of men to take advantage of the Permanent Settlement. The following generations 'successfully integrated themselves into the rural world as an influential class of gentry with a well marked out lifestyle'.[38]

Our next case study is of a merchant who was a complete anomaly, for, unlike most of his contemporaries, he carried on an independent business without collaborating with the British. He was Ramdulal Dey (1752–1825) whose biographer Girish Chandra Ghose has recounted the almost unbelievable story behind his rise to fortune and fame. According to Girish Ghose, Ramdulal served as an apprentice to a rich merchant named Madan Mohan Dutt. Luckily, he chanced upon a sunken ship at Tulloh's auction, bought it with his master's money and then offered it to his master. Later, he was gifted this as a prize for his honesty, which completely changed his fortune. He became a Bengali millionaire whose wealth, according to his biographer, was a source of envy to all.[39]

Ramdulal's case is unique, as his trading partners were not the British but Americans who started their eastern voyages after obtaining independence from the British in 1783. Ramdulal secured himself as their *banian* when their ships first touched the distant Bengal shores. The enormous pile of letters exchanged between Patrick Tracy Jackson, a supercargo from Boston, and Ramdulal Dey bear testimony to the good relationship they shared.[40] Ramdulal supplied Jackson mostly with coarse cotton cloth, lines and twine, sugar, stick-lac, gunny bags, goat-skin, cow-hide, turmeric, saltpetre, indigo and other objects. These goods enjoyed a demand both in the American markets and in the European countries of Holland, Germany and France. From there these travelled in European vessels along the coasts of Africa, the West Indies and Latin America.[41]

One may assume the vital importance of this American trade in global maritime history. Ramdulal was a crucial link in this trade, as he informed Jackson of the demand for American goods in Calcutta markets and also about the price of goods that he supplied to the Americans.[42] The following example illustrates the relationship of trust that existed between Jackson and Ramdulal. In 1804, on many occasions, Ramdulal made an invoice of goods loaded on a ship going from Calcutta to America. He put 80 tons of piece-goods worth Rs 40,000 including freight for Jackson, on the understanding that the money would be remitted later in fifteen thousand-dollar bills through Francis Cabot.[43] For the first time in the history of Indian commerce, merchants of the United States dispensed with European agents in Bengal altogether, instead 'transacting direct with a native house, sending ships to its consignments and drafts to its credit, for the purchase of Indian produce'.[44] Ramdulal's popularity is evident from the fact that an American ship plying between Calcutta and Boston was named after him.[45]

Ramdulal simultaneously carried on trade with Britain and China, and was the sole agent of Philippines & Co. in Calcutta. Besides, he was the *banian* of Fairlie Fergusson and Co., the largest English company in Calcutta. His stature was such that a nod from him could unsettle the money market in Bengal. The severe financial crisis of the 1830s, in which he is believed to have suffered a loss of Rs 25 lakhs, a huge sum at that time, hardly made a dent in his acquired fortune. This prompted *The London Times*, to describe Ramdulal's sons as the Rothschilds of Bengal when alluding to this loss.[46]

Ramdulal was a self-made man. The aristocratic lineage left in his wake was due to his own achievements and reputation. He was not born into this aristocracy. In spite of his fabulous wealth, he never purchased a zamindari and also discouraged his sons from purchasing landed estates. Instead, he left behind an enormous amount of urban property.

The story of Motilal Seal (1792–1854) is very different from all the other merchants mentioned so far. He came from a family of established cloth merchants in China Bazar, and belonged to the traditional *Subarnabanik* (gold merchants) caste. Interestingly, his father sent him to English-medium schools for higher education. His education helped Motilal become part of a new generation of entrepreneurs. By learning English and adopting the western culture, men of his generation became business partners of the British instead of serving them as mere collaborators. This new class gained greater social respectability than their predecessors in the eighteenth century, which enabled them to enter into new, profitable business relationships.

In the initial days of his career, Motilal supplied stores to military officers stationed at Fort William; then he graduated to employment as a Customs Daroga at Bali Khal. His knowledge of English helped him get these jobs easily. He caught a break when he decided to supply bottles and corks to Mr Hudson, the most important beer merchant in Calcutta at the time. Soon he became the *banian* to several English agency houses like Messrs Reach Kettlewell, Messrs McLeod Fagan & Co., Messrs Kelsall & Co and Messrs Tulloh & Co. As a *banian* Motilal imported commodities such as rice, wheat, mustard and linseed through his agents spread all over Bengal. He also had agents in Chhapra, Bihar, to collect and deliver saltpetre; in Ghazipur for sugar; and in Rampur-Baolia in Rajshahi district, for silk. His success lay in straddling the eighteenth-century style of business, of collecting commodities through agents, with the nineteenth-century structure of dealing with agency houses.

Motilal's success in the business world reached new heights when he floated his own company with one Mr Oswald on a partnership basis; the company was named Oswald Seal and Co. Through this company Motilal founded and promoted the first indigo mart, named Messrs Hickey & Co. His knowledge of indigo and other country produce earned him a big reputation in the business world. He was the only Bengali merchant who had extensive dealings with up-country business firms. He was quick to grasp the importance of any new trade; he took to shipping and soon possessed thirteen ships of large and small tonnage. He introduced the use of tug steamers, and *Banian* was the first tug owned by him.[47] Motilal built up a huge zamindari, like Cantoobabu and Krishna Panti. Some of these lands he acquired by foreclosing mortgages entered into by old zamindars, who borrowed from him to meet their revenue obligations. He believed that land was the safest mode of investment, and remunerative too.

The nineteenth century for the first time saw an entrepreneur in Ramgopal Ghose (1815–1868), who was essentially an intellectual. He was a member of Derozio's Academic Association and was very close to several distinguished persons like David Hare and Peary Chand Mittra. Ramgopal was an outstanding orator, extremely well-versed in English. He started his career as a *banian* to a Jewish merchant; he then became the *banian* of Mr Kelsall and finally his partner. In 1848, he moved away from Kelsall and founded his own firm styled 'Ramgopal Ghose & Co.'. This is considered to be the first instance of an indigenous business house exclusively established and run by a Bengali businessman, to have had extensive transactions with Europe. Ramgopal is a typical example of an entrepreneur who began his career as a *banian* and later diversified his capital to other businesses. He had extensive transactions both with Europe and other Indian states, with agents posted in different districts of the country to collect and deliver saltpetre, sugar and silk. He thus combined the eighteenth-century style of business of collecting commodities through intermediary agents with the nineteenth-century structure of negotiating business transactions with agency houses working in partnership with English firms.

But the man who stood on top of this commercial pyramid was Prince Dwarakanath Tagore (1795–1846) of the Jorasanko family of Calcutta. Under him 'the age of enterprise' reached its culmination.[48] He succeeded in combining the new technologies introduced by the British with prevailing Indian business practices.[49]

The Tagores were divided into two branches – the affluent Tagores who lived in Pathuriaghata, and the not-so-rich who lived in Jorasanko. Dwarkanath belonged to the latter, less moneyed group. Like Motilal Seal and Ramgopal Ghose, he was a beneficiary of an English education and everything associated with it. His career began as a law agent to several landed proprietors in Bengal and the North West Provinces. He was associated with Mackintosh and Co., an agency house for which he shipped indigo and silk to Europe. In 1822 he became the *sheristadar* (head native officer) of Plowden, the Collector and Salt Agent of 24 Parganas, and later became the *dewan* (finance officer) of the Board of Customs, Salt and Opium. In 1834, along with William Carr, he launched his own Carr Tagore & Co., and was congratulated by Lord William Bentinck for setting up the first indigenous business house in Calcutta on a European model.[50]

An entrepreneur, Dwarakanath set up his own silk filatures in Kumarkhali, which alarmed the English. This fear is evident in a letter that Richardson, the Resident, wrote to the Board of Trade in 1831:

> I think it is absolutely necessary that Dwarakanath Thakoor should be bound down not to erect or cause to be erected any filature or filatures within the Comercolly *aurangs*, for should he at any future period refuse to renew the contract, having possession of all the *aurangs* and under command of all the people engaged in cultivating and rearing cocoons with filatures of his own or under his control, he could raise a competition ruinous to the Company.[51]

He ventured into the indigo business when it showed a promising market abroad and set up factories at Shilaidaha. He believed that cultivation of indigo would lead to a fusion of the entrepreneurial skills of India and Europe, which would ultimately help India develop into a manufacturing country at par with Britain.[52] Dwarakanath speculated on sugar as well, and set up a distillery for producing rum for export. His most important venture, however, was the purchase of a coal mine in Raniganj in 1836, which was a real industrial investment. His American biographer Blair Kling has emphasized that it was this purchase that helped Carr Tagore & Co. to rise from the status of a mere agency house to that of a business company.[53]

Dwarakanath established the Union Bank, which was a joint-stock venture. At the same time he was the managing agent of the Calcutta Steam Tug Association, the Bengal Coal Company and the India General Steam Navigation Company. The dual character of his enterprise – both in land and in business – turned him into a zamindar in the commercial world and a businessman among landed proprietors.[54] His position in the contemporary business world can be assessed by his purchase of Fort Gloster, the largest single industrial complex, from the other shareholders, after Fergusson & Co. collapsed following the financial crisis of 1833.[55]

Dwarakanath decided to follow in the footsteps of other Bengali entrepreneurs and invested his profits in landed estates. He once boasted that the estates of the Tagore family accounted for one-fifteenth of the total land revenue of the Lower Provinces of Bengal.[56] Because of his immense fortune Dwarakanath, like Ramdulal Dey, remained relatively less affected by the commercial crisis of 1830–33 which shook the Calcutta business world.

Dwarakanath was undoubtedly a stalwart among his peers, but there were others, whose history we have narrated above, who were also important figures in the business world. S.N. Mukherjee has remarked that most of these merchants who later accumulated a fortune were initially from an insignificant background: a conclusion arrived at perhaps by studying the lives of Krishna Panti, Ramdulal Dey and their like. His view, however, has been contested by P.J. Marshall who argues that many of these Bengali merchants were already men of substance when they entered the service of Englishmen.[57] Cantoobabu's family was already in the silk business and Cantoobabu himself was an established merchant before he became the *banian* of Warren Hastings. The history of India would have been different had he not bailed out Warren Hastings for Rs 3000 when the latter was imprisoned by Siraj-ud-Daula in Murshidabad in 1756.[58] Similarly, Gokul Ghoshal and the Rays of Bhagyakul in the eighteenth century, and Motilal Seal and Ramgopal Ghose came from established commercial families.

These Bengali entrepreneurs were good at their professions. They studied the nature of demand, both at home and in foreign markets, before they speculated, and then ventured accordingly. Motilal Seal changed his fate by supplying corks and empty bottles to a beer merchant. Krishna Panti rose in business from being a petty betel-leaf and grain vendor to securing for himself the title of 'Raja'. We learn from Ramdulal's biographer how he once stocked up fabulous amounts of glass beads, and later, when the market for beads opened up in Madras, he made a huge profit by selling them there.[59] Ramdulal often stocked black pepper, broad-cloth and sugar in periods of abundance, which he would release when the demand rose in distant as well as home markets.[60] Similarly, Krishna Panti customarily hoarded grain, molasses, salt and many other items as a wholesale dealer, to get a good return later.[61] Once, when there was a reduction in the duty on sugar from 32 to 24 shillings, Motilal Seal sold Banaras sugar worth Rs 12 lakhs in Patna and Ghazipur, and made a solid profit of Rs 3 lakhs, considered a huge amount at that time.[62]

The Cultural Constitution of a Commercial Elite

Scholars such as Kumkum Chatterjee have contended that the eighteenth century should not be characterized as one that witnessed remarkable mercantile activities with the advent of foreigners. Instead, it should be looked upon as a century marked by decadence and misery that came upon the Muslim aristocracy, high-ranking Hindu officers, old zamindars and old banking families who failed to capitalize on the new commercial opportunities. Accordingly, after the Battle of Plassey in 1757, the section of great independent merchants – such as Khwaja Wajed, Amirchand and the Jagat Seths – who comprised the 'princely aristocracy' gradually disappeared from the scene.[63] Chatterjee has observed that 'it is over-simplifying the case to imply that indigenous merchants "survived" in the changed situation'.[64]

It is true that after Plassey, a few aristocratic merchants like Khwaja Wajed and Amirchand, who had earlier reigned supreme in the trading world of Bengal, were no longer active. But their decline did not signal a complete collapse of all commercial enterprises in Bengal. Historians have observed that talk of the economic decline of Bengal 'before Plassey is a myth'.[65] Similarly, observations that Indian merchants were driven out of business by European competition after Plassey also need to be 'treated with scepticism'.[66] I would contend that merchants like Amirchand and Khwaja Wajed belonged to a miniscule group of a commercial elite who were not representative of Bengali merchants as a class or community in the eighteenth century. Those who dominated the business world from the mid-eighteenth century were not these princely merchants but men who took advantage of the new avenues of trade and commerce opened up by European commerce in Bengal. These indigenous merchants began to collaborate with foreign merchants to make their fortune. From the middle of the century one therefore finds the gradual growth of a new commercial aristocracy that was different from the earlier merchant-princes. The new merchants tried to make the best of a volatile situation and became part of a new aristocracy.

Here we shall make a quick distinction between the commercial magnates of the eighteenth and nineteenth centuries. We will revisit the eighteenth century, when indigenous merchants exercised a different kind of power and control over foreigners, who by and large were completely dependent upon their Bengali collaborators. The foreign merchants were unfamiliar with the new terrain, ignorant of the local languages, and unsure of the prevailing customs and practices of commerce. They required specific commodities – cotton and silk textiles – at cheap prices and pertaining to specific standards, for which they advanced money known as *dadan,* as mentioned earlier. Without the assistance of the *banians* and a whole hierarchy of intermediary merchants, this *dadni* system would not have worked. Moreover, the *banians* provided the necessary capital, the technical business know-how, and managed and controlled the teeming millions of lesser intermediaries who collected the commodities.

This picture of indigenous control started to change when the English became rulers of Bengal. They now gradually started to exercise their political authority to restructure the trading pattern in order to dispense with the indigenous merchants. The Company had earlier tried various means to get rid of the petty intermediary merchants. The *dadni* system had already been replaced by the *gomashta* system of procurement even before the Battle of Plassey. But this did not lessen their dependence upon intermediaries. Our study reveals that as long as trade in commodities like textiles, salt, indigo and grain was a priority, the intermediary collaborators were required to procure merchandise. With the establishment of agency houses in Bengal,[67] the East India Company merchants gradually became less dependent on their *banian*s. The agency houses started handling a fairly large volume of trade in commodities such as opium and indigo, over which the Company exercised monopolistic control. Change did take place, but not overnight. It became perceptible only after the 1820s, when the British transformed themselves from traders to rulers.

With the turn of the nineteenth century, the commercial world of Bengal saw new methods of business transactions and the emergence of a new culture. Caste mobility played a crucial role in this. I will cite only a few examples here from among a very large number. Cantoobabu, the founder of the Kasimbazar Raj family, began his career as an ordinary trader, but was determined to push his image up the social ladder. This was easy, as he lived at a time when social mobility was already altering the traditional structure of society by loosening the rigidities within the caste hierarchy.[68] Wealth became an important determinant of one's rank and status in society. When Cantoobabu, who originally belonged to – what was seen at the time – the low-caste *Teli* or oil-pressing community, became a rich zamindar, he was recognized by the scholars of Nabadwip and Tribeni as an aristocrat. This elevated him to the *Nabasak* caste, much higher in rank than the *Teli*s. After he secured this injunction from the pandits of Bengal, the *panda*s (priests) of Orissa allowed him to provide *atkes* or assignments of land for the maintenance of the poor in Puri, and offer gifts to brahmanas. Henceforth, many *Teli*s would cite Cantoobabu's case as a precedent and declare their own status similarly during their visit to the Jagannath temple in Puri.[69] Cantoobabu's successor, Maharaja Mahindra Chandra Nandi, consolidated the status of the upwardly mobile

Telis further, under the common name of *Tili*. These progressive *Tilis* came to be known by and were incorporated within the *Nabasak* caste.[70]

Similarly, Krishna Panti, founder of the Palchaudhuri family of Nadia, belonged to the class of merchants who invested the capital they earned from trade in the purchase of zamindaris. Once again it was financial power that enabled this mercantile family to transform itself into the respectable elite. This was possible, as Hitesh Ranjan Sanyal remarks, because of the social mobility within an individual caste, 'without a corresponding change in the existing ceremonial rank of the caste'. Thus the *Nabasak Gandha-baniks*, who were conventionally the spice and herb-selling druggists and grocers, and the *Tambul-baniks*, traders in betel-leaf, succeeded in promoting themselves to comparatively higher positions than those of their *Barui* (betel-leaf) brothers.[71]

Dwarakanath Tagore also belonged to the *Pirali* caste, considered very low in the brahmanical caste hierarchy. But it was his wealth that elevated him in rank and status over his contemporaries. Money came to dominate society.[72] The example of Raja Nabakrishna Deb, founder of the Shobhabazar Raj family, however, is atypical. He did not make his fortune from mercantile transactions but was amply rewarded by the British, whom he helped become rulers of Bengal. But he was not content with the acquisition of money and power, and aspired for higher social status by raising his family in the caste hierarchy. He therefore changed his grandson's surname from Dey to Deb, which sounded more like the name of a brahman.

This new mercantile generation who began to dominate in the nineteenth century was very different from the earlier generations of Seths and Basaks, and from Cantoobabu or Gokul Ghoshal. They ventured to learn the trading practices of the western world, and became interested in partnership business with European firms and agency houses. Knowledge of English was the most important factor that helped them enter into this partnership business. We have already mentioned that Motilal was sent to English-medium schools; Ramgopal Ghose, an outstanding orator, was equally proficient in English, and Dwarakanath Tagore, the greatest entrepreneur of this age, was an ardent protagonist of Bengali–British partnership.[73] Dwarakanath's biographer Kissory Chand Mittra has observed that he was so well versed in law, and so well acquainted with the Supreme Court as well as Sudder and Zilla courts, that he received 'valuable assistance from Mr. Robert Cutlar Fergusson, a leading barrister of his time'. His knowledge of English and of jurisprudence helped him become the law agent of many indigenous landlords, such as Durga Charan Mookherjee of Bagbazar, Raja Baroda Kanto Roy of Jessore and

Kumar Harinath Roy of Kasimbazar, whose estates he had saved.[74] The examples can be multiplied.

In nineteenth-century Bengal, English thus became the language of the elite, which gave them access to western culture and facilitated communication.[75] One would presume that it was English that enabled P.T. Jackson, the shipping magnate from Boston, to write volumes of letters (later compiled by K.W. Porter) to Ramdulal Dey. I cite from one such letter here to illustrate how language facilitated communication regarding complex business transactions between those who had never ever met and lived in two different parts of the globe. Jackson wrote to Ramdulal:

> By every opportunity let me know the state of your market. I do not mean a common price current, but inform me how many Americans have been out, a list of their names as far as you are informed, the amount of their funds and the kind of goods they bring, this kind of information is very important to me, and if you can give it correct, it will enable me to persuade gentlemen going out, to employ you to transact their business.[76]

English was a sign of a new time, a new culture.

The new commercial magnates were interested in learning English and not for acquiring wealth alone. These entrepreneurs and their descendants adopted a new lifestyle, not visible among their predecessors of the eighteenth century. This nouveau-riche class, considered the harbinger of 'modernity' in Bengal, earned the appellation 'abhijata bhadralok' or respectable elite. Some of them, like Cantoobabu, Krishna Panti and the Ghoshals of Bhookailash, took advantage of the Permanent Settlement and became founders of notable zamindari families. Others like Ramdulal Dey and Akrur Dutta remained rich urban citizens. These elite families tried to imbibe the lifestyle, etiquette and manners of the western world, and to blend these with the oriental customs and rituals of their households. For example, they entertained Europeans in a separate area within the premises of their residences when they celebrated the autumnal worship of the goddess Durga. Reference may be made here to the Durga Puja celebrated by Raja Nabakrishna Deb of Shobhabazar, who is credited with the introduction of baroari or public Durga Puja in Bengal. Nabakrishna invited Clive, the Governor of Bengal, and other contemporary Europeans to his Shobhabazar palace on this occasion. The fusion between the two cultures, the oriental and the occidental, was an important feature in Bengali life from the beginning of the nineteenth century. The most important protagonist of this synthesis, as mentioned earlier, was Dwarakanath Tagore, who organized lavish banquets at his Belgachia villa where he served wine and food in the manner of an English aristocrat, and even crossed the forbidden sea, considered anathema at that time.[77] He was an ardent believer in 'partnership' on equal terms between the European and the Indian, in which both sides had clearly defined parts to play. According to Peter Marshall, while Cantoobabu, Gokul Ghoshal, Motilal Seal and Ramgopal Ghose were content with their positions as *banians*, Dwarakanath was more confident and secure enough to make an offer to the British who had already become masters of the land. He directly invited Prinsep and Carr to join his firms. I would contend that Dwarakanath might have been more progressive than Motilal Seal or Ramgopal Ghose, but the latter were equally formidable in handling the partnership business with the British on equal terms. In this context I will quote Marshall again, who has mentioned in another context: 'there can be no doubt that in many partnerships it was the *banian* who was the senior partner, making the decisions, and merely paying a commission for the use of his master's name and his *dastak*'.[78]

Bengal's commercial encounter with the west bred a culture that opened itself to the west. It was not only a bourgeois lifestyle and taste in their everyday living that the elites absorbed and emulated. Alongside, they came to appreciate the western liberal arts and sciences that promoted liberalism and humanism. The age of reform, ushered in by Raja Rammohan Roy, bears testimony to that. Dwarakanath, a friend and close associate of Rammohan Roy, endeavoured to promote English education in India. He laid the foundation of Hindu College and financially supported the establishment of Calcutta Medical College in its early days.[79] He revolted against the heinous crime of *sati* (burning of widows on the funeral pyre of their husbands) and fought for its abolition. He was a keen advocate of women's education. He was all for freedom of press, setting up of juries in civil courts, and in favour of reforming the police system. He desired a progressive and enlightened India to emerge out of cultural harmony between the two civilizations, Indian and British.[80] Motilal Seal was also known for his charity work and public philanthropy. 'Mutty Seal's Free College', established in 1842 for promotion of English learning, still stands as a testimony to his keen interest in western education. He donated land for the establishment of Fever Hospital in Calcutta.[81]

Likewise, the outstanding entrepreneur Ramgopal Ghose was a social reformer who worked extensively towards propagating female education and the introduction of the grant-in-aid system in educational institutions. Ramdulal Dey's biographer repeatedly mentions the extensive private charity of his 'citizen-king'.[82] The opulent merchants did not rest content simply with giving donations for the promotion of education. Raja

Nabakrishna Deb, Ramdulal Dey and Ramgopal Ghose were instrumental in establishing public libraries, besides owning personal libraries, as was prevalent among wealthy gentry in the west. Some of these are still in existence.

Descendants of the commercial elites became important figures in the political, literary and cultural movements of Bengal. Dwarakanath was the founder of the Landholders' Society. It is recognized as the parent of all future political associations in India, and provided a platform for public opinion and discussion to spread political consciousness among mercantile elite and the landed aristocracy.[83] In course of time it began to encourage literary and aesthetic movements in the country.

The elite played a leading role in promoting public theatre, a forum for expressing one's thoughts and ideas which had been discouraged and looked down upon on moral grounds in the earlier century. It took off from *jatra*, a form of popular theatre of the eighteenth century, but borrowed heavily from European drama and dramatic techniques.[84] To begin with, English-educated landowners and wealthy merchants flocked to the theatres showing British plays, before they started to appreciate indigenous plays. The first Bengali production was *Bidyasundar*, which was enacted at Nabinchandra Basu's home theatre in 1835. It was Dwarakanath Tagore, again, who became one of the founders of the Chowringhee Theatre. A landmark achievement in the world of Calcutta theatre came in August 1848, when 'a "Native Gentleman", Baishnabcharan Adhya, played Othello at Sans Souci theatre, set up in 1839 in Calcutta'.[85] In 1857, Ramnarayan Tarkaratna's *Kulinkula Sarbasya* (published in 1854), a play on contemporary social evils such as the caste system and polygamy, was staged. Another striking example was the staging of Dinabandhu Mitra's *Neel Darpan* in December 1872, a powerful play protesting against the tyrannical exploitation of English indigo planters.[86] The stage thus helped to create awareness among the rich as well as the growing middle class about the pressing need of social reforms. Later, apart from Rabindranath, three other intellectuals from the Jorasanko Tagore family, Ganendranath, Gunendranath and Jyotirindranath, set up private theatres where women were also invited to participate.[87] This is considered a great leap forward in women's liberation and progress.

High levels of luxury consumption and display of wealth became modes of exercising cultural authority. Accumulation of wealth was linked to the development of an indigenous culture, often derogatorily described as '*babu*' culture, 'essentially Hindu dominated and Calcutta based.'[88] Though the word *babu* is supposed to be an equivalent of the English 'Mr' in nineteenth-century Bengal, it referred to the nouveau-riche class that wallowed in luxury, and indulged in a lavish and extravagant life-style, but did not have the aristocratic lineage to claim the status it aspired towards.[89] To the British, the epithet *babu* stood for a petty clerk as well as millionaire.[90] It has therefore been remarked that often 'the word reflected contempt of the ruler for the ruled',[91] and therefore, western-educated Bengalis particularly despised the word. In a pluralistic society like Bengal, *babus* often denoted wealthy landlords who frittered their fortunes over nautch-girls, idle sports like kite and pigeon-flying, and on expensive *sradh* (memorial) ceremonies and religious festivals. Rich Bengali *babus* whose fortunes came from trade and commerce were notoriously extravagant and wasteful. Although Motilal Seal did not belong to this category of *babus*, even he had the reputation of being unnecessarily extravagant. He spent his fortune on expensive marriages and *sradh* ceremonies. And Dwarakanath was referred to as 'prince' for his royal, extravagant and immodest lifestyle. When in England and France, he 'moved in commercial and courtly circles', and is said to have frittered away his wealth on lavish gifts and banquets.[92]

Charity and display of generosity was another means of mobilizing symbolic power. The *babus* were renowned for their generosity and acts of charity. In nineteenth-century Calcutta, it was from their grants that many schools, colleges and religious institutions were established. Raja Radhakanta Deb, Ramdulal Dey and Dwarakanath – all donated towards the foundation of Hindu College in Calcutta. Ramdulal Dey and Krishna Panti gifted Rs 1 lakh each to the famine victims of Madras.[93] Dwarakanath left a provision of Rs 1 lakh for charity in his will.[94]

The *babu* culture is also associated with the propagation of *adda* – a practice of friends getting together for long informal conversations,[95] which were not always 'idle gossip', but a platform for discussing many social and cultural reform programmes. They also contributed to the pub-lication of periodicals and the formation of political institutions. In fact *adda*, oratory, publication of periodicals and founding of organizations for different purposes were integrally associated with the '*babu* culture'.[96]

Essentially Hindu-dominated, the *babus* were greatly influenced by the Persianized *nawabi* culture. Members of the rich Bengali elite, such as Rammohan Roy, Raja Nabakrishna Deb, Rajballabh Ray Rayan and Dwarakanath Tagore – all partly emulated the lifestyle of the *nawabs* and became connoisseurs of the *nawabi* culture. Interestingly, Raja Nabakrishna Deb, an orthodox Hindu, was the Persian tutor of Warren Hastings, who became the Governor of Bengal after Clive.[97]

It was this legacy of the *nawabi* courts that made the urban rich appreciate and nurture the *gharanas* (genres) of classical music and dance.

Raja Nabakrishna invited nautch-girls and *baijis* (courtesans) from the *darbars* (courts) of Murshidabad and Lucknow to perform at Durga Puja ceremonies. The origin of the *tappa* (a genre of semi-classical music), mostly sung by these nautch-girls in Calcutta, the hub of the *babus*, can be traced to this culture. The *babus* also patronized popular enactments of impromptu songs and verses, known as '*kabir-larai*' (repartee), performed by *kabiyals*.

The emergence of this new culture of consumption, display and festivity prompted social censure, which is captured in popular texts and prints. Kaliprasanna Sinha, in his *Hootum Pyanchar Naksha* ('The Owl's Gaze', 1862), offers a scathing critique of these cultural forms. Though most of the *babus* in his sketches were descendants of the commercial elite, they were intrinsically idle and did not strive to expand the businesses they had inherited from their forefathers. They indulged in drink, dance and merry-making, particularly during festive occasions like Durga Puja, *Rathayatra* and *Snanyatra*, to name only a few. Their position in society was determined by the number of mistresses they had and the extent of revelry they participated in. They were ill-mannered, garrulous, and, in the company of crude and worthless 'time-servers', enjoyed lewd verses or *kheud* to entertain themselves.[98] Caste and religion played a vital role in their everyday functioning.[99]

So far we have discussed the career graphs of the Bengali commercial magnates, some of whom transformed themselves into zamindars after they ploughed back their commercial profits into buying up zamindaris. We have traced how they came to inhabit the growing city of Calcutta, the capital of British possessions in India, from the last two decades of the eighteenth century. This mercantile aristocracy, however, suffered a rude shock when the agency houses collapsed in the 1830s and a commercial crisis overtook them in the late 1840s. On both occasions, it was over-speculation in indigo that brought about the crisis.[100] These crises generated uncertainty among the commercial magnates who became wary of risk-prone investments. When the Union Bank failed in 1848, Bengali entrepreneurs began to withdraw their capital from trade and business, and invested in land instead, which they considered a safer mode of investment.[101] 'A distrust of European business became a part of Bengali business thinking.'[102] Nilmani Mukherjee's work on Jaykrishna Mukherjee shows how, after the fall of the agency houses, Jaykrishna withdrew from commerce and invested in land, which resulted in the establishment of the Uttarpara Raj family.[103] This is just one among several such examples. Zamindaris ensured large incomes after the first decade of the nineteenth century, when prices and rents of land soared.

By the 1850s, the British had completely ceased to be traders in the manner they were in the eighteenth and early nineteenth centuries. The Charter Act of 1833 abolished the English East India Company's right to trade in India. Moreover, by then the British had emerged as the supreme political power in India, and Indian administration became more important to them than the kind of trade that had brought them to Bengal. In the eighteenth and early nineteenth centuries, English merchants were primarily engaged in procuring 'investments' with the help of intermediary merchants through a contract system. But now, collaborative ventures with intermediary merchants were no longer required as the British became the masters of the country. The crash of the financial market in 1848 resulted in the collapse of all British agency houses in Bengal, and from the 1850s, trade was conducted through and controlled by the managing agency system. Silk, cotton, cotton piece-goods, indigo, grain and saltpetre, which formed the bulk of the trade till the third decade of the nineteenth century, were now replaced by tea, jute, coal and the railways.[104] As India became a full-fledged colony, her economy was slowly harnessed to the financial interests of Britain.

Under these changed circumstances, it was not possible for the Bengal merchants to thrive in the way they did earlier. It has been remarked that the Bengali entrepreneur became timid and shy of risk. Also, by the 1830s it was difficult for merchant-millionaires like Cantoobabu or Gokul Ghoshal, whose fortunes were linked to the Company's external trade, to emerge any more. Their place was ultimately taken over by the Marwaris, Punjabis, Gujaratis and the Sindhis from the end of the nineteenth century, whose manner of doing business and conducting trade was completely different.[105] The collapse of big business, however, did not spell complete ruin in Bengal's trading world. Merchants who were not in the British export business thrived and prospered for years to come. The Ray families of Bhagyakul, the Dattas of Hatkhola, Ramdulal Dey's family and Akrur Datta's family are a few among many such examples.

Dwarakanath, strictly speaking, was the sole exception. He was partly responsible for the effacement of Bengali indigenous enterprise. His dream of collaboration on a footing of equality with the British was not feasible. He failed to realize that 'a comprehensive Indo–British partnership' was impossible, as India had already been reduced to the status of a colony.[106] He did little to preserve the business empire he so arduously built. His extravagant lifestyle considerably reduced his capital, so much so that his son Debendranath Tagore had to repay a huge debt after his demise. It is a pity that his descendants were indifferent to mercantile activities, which they inherited as a legacy. Later, it was the revenues from the zamindari estates that accounted for their opulence, as was the case with many other business families.[107]

The significant contribution of these Bengali millionaire-merchants lies in not just making the commercial life of the time, but in creating a new commercial culture. The entrepreneurs I have studied made their fortunes by working within spaces opened up by Company commerce, but reworked the channels within which incomes flowed. They collaborated with as well as resisted the East India Company's power in order to make their individual fortunes. They consolidated their commercial power by diversifying investments, and linking control over zamindaris with control over commercial capital.

At the same time, they recognized the importance of asserting symbolic and cultural power. The history of Bengal's peculiar cultural modernity is intimately linked to the constitution of this new class – at the same time zamindars and commercial capitalists, owning *rajbaris* (palatial buildings) and business houses, investing in land and trade, patronizing English as well Persian and Sanskrit literary cultures. They opened themselves to the west but appropriated western cultural norms in ways that constituted something new – melding traditions, fusing norms, producing a local cultural form in early nineteenth-century Bengal that was at the same time both 'western' and 'indigenous', and neither in its pure form.

Notes and References
[1] A.K. Ray, *A Short History of Calcutta, Town and Suburbs*, 1901, reprint, Calcutta: Riddhi, 1982. James Rennell, *Memoir of a Map of Hindoostan*, second edition, London, 1792, pp. 148–50. Also see, Thankappan Nair, 'The Growth and Development of Calcutta', in Sukanta Chaudhuri, ed., *Calcutta: The Living City*, Vol.1, Calcutta: Oxford University Press, 1995. Nair has stated (ibid., p. 11) that before the rise of Calcutta, Hugli (which had replaced its predecessor Saptagram or Satgaon) was a busy port-town where the Portuguese established their trading centre in 1535, the Dutch in1636 and the English in 1651. What later came to be known as Calcutta, which overshadowed Hugli, initially comprised three villages, viz., Sutanuti, Govindapur and Dihi Kalikata. The zamindari rights over these three villages were held by the Sabarna Raychoudhurys of Barisha-Behala. It was in 1698 that Charles Eyre, Charnok's successor, who obtained zamindari rights from the Raychoudhurys for Rs 1,300. Till 1757, the Company paid regular revenue to the Mughal emperor. Pradip Sinha, 'Calcutta and the Currents of History', in Sukanta Chaudhuri, ed., *Calcutta*. Sinha has pointed out (ibid., p. 32) that when Sobha Singh, a feudal lord of southern Bengal, rebelled, it enabled the British to secure permission from the Mughal Governor to erect fortifications at Fort William. Their position was further strengthened when they purchased the zamindari rights of the three villages of Sutanuti, Govindapur and Kolkata. See also Pradip Sinha, *Calcutta in Urban History*, Calcutta: Firma K.L. Mukhopadhyay, 1978. For the planning of the city, see a recent work, Partho Datta, *Planning the City: Urbanization and Reform in Calcutta, c. 1800–c. 1940*, New Delhi: Tulika Books, 2012.

For references on port-cities particularly, see Dilip K. Basu, ed., *The Rise and Growth of Port Cities in Asia*, Lanham: University Press of America, 1985. Howard Spodek has cited after Basu that these port-cities had certain similar characteristics. These cities usually had a mixed population of foreigners and indigenous peoples who came there to earn their fortune. The foreigners created new economic hinterlands here to tap raw materials for their overseas export trade. Further, these cities were governed by foreigners and were places where both indigenous and foreign languages were spoken. The port-cities had architecture which was a synthesis of both Indian and foreign styles. Howard Spodek, 'Studying the History of Urbanization in India', *Journal of Urban History*, No. 6, 1980, p. 260.

[2] See Gautam Bhadra, 'The Role of Pykars in the Silk Industry of Bengal, *circa* 1756–1830', *Studies in History*, Vol. 3 (2), 1987, and Vol. 4 (1 and 2), 1988. Shubhra Chakrabarti, 'Collaboration and Resistance: Bengal Merchants and the English East India Company, 1757–1833', *Studies in History*, 10, 1, new series, 1994.

[3] Somendra Chandra Nandy, *Life and Times of Cantoo Baboo*, 2 vols, Bombay: Allied Publishers, 1978 and 1981.

[4] Kissory Chand Mittra, *Memoir of Dwarkanath Tagore*, Calcutta, 1870. Blair Kling, *Partner in Empire: Dwarakanath Tagore and the Age of Enterprise in Eastern India*, Berkeley: University of California, 1976.

[5] Peter Marshall, 'Masters and Banians in Eighteenth Century Calcutta', in M.N. Pearson and Blair B. Kling, eds, *The Age of Partnership: Europeans in Asia before Dominion*, Hawaii: The University Press of Hawaii, 1979, pp. 191–213.

[6] Nagendranath Seth, *Kalikatastha: Tantubanik Jatir Itihas* (in Bengali), Calcutta, 1930. Pradip Sinha, *Calcutta in Urban History*, Calcutta: Firma K.L. Mukhopadhyay, 1978, pp. 62–66. Benoy Ghose, 'Some Old Family Founders in 18th Century Calcutta', *Bengal Past and Present*, Vol. CV1, Parts I and II, Nos. 202–203, 1987.

[7] Dilip Basu, 'The Early Banians of Calcutta', *Bengal Past and Present*, Vol. XCIV, Part II, No. 179, 1975, p. 31.

[8] Nagendranath Seth, *Kalikatastha Tantubanik Jatir Itihas*, pp. 14–15. Harisadhan Mukhopadhyay, *Kalikata, Sekaler o Ekaler* (in Bengali), Calcutta, 1915, pp. 282–99.

[9] P. Thankappan Nair, 'The Growth and Development of Old Calcutta', pp. 10–21.

[10] Nagendranath Seth, *Kalikatastha Tantubanik Jatir Itihas*. See also Benoy Ghosh, 'Some Old Family Founders'.

[11] For details see ibid., pp. 119–205.

[12] For details see, N.K. Sinha, *Economic History of Bengal*, Vol. 1, Calcutta: Firma K.L. Mukhopadhyay, 1956, Chapter II, pp. 6–33.

[13] Pradip Sinha, *Calcutta*, p. 65.

[14] Ibid.

[15] Somendra Chandra Nandy, *Life and Times of Cantoo Baboo*, Vol. 1, p. 445.

[16] Ibid., p. 94; N.K. Sinha, *Economic History of Bengal*, Calcutta: Firma K.L. Mukhopadhyay, 1970, Vol. III, pp. 93–94.

[17] Somendra Chandra Nandy, *Life and Times of Cantoo Baboo*, pp. 99–280.

[18] Ibid., pp. 445–86.

[19] Ibid., p. 344.

[20] See Gautam Bhadra, 'The Mentality of Subalternity: Kantanama or Rajdharma', in Ranajit Guha, ed., *Subaltern Studies*, Vol. 4, Delhi: Oxford University Press, 1989. Manulla states that between 1765 and 1772, Cantoobabu acquired

various farms worth almost Rs 5 lakhs. Manulla was a *ryot* (peasant) himself. Therefore it was easy for him to say that Krishnakanta used his political connections and manipulated *izara* contracts and *benami* (illegally bought in another person's name) transactions to carve out the huge landed estate, which earned him the appellation of a 'zamindar'; ibid., p. 71.

For a detailed account of Cantoobabu's zamindari, see Somendra Chandra Nandy, *Life and Times of Cantoo Baboo*. He consolidated his position in Dinajpur and in Rungpur first before his estates spread to other areas in east and west Bengal, comprising several *taluqs* such as Coolberia, Bamankabela, Mankor, Samaskhali and Chunakhali in Murshidabad *pargana*; Baharbund in Rangpur district in north Bengal; Santosh in Dinajpur; Jehangeerpur, reckoned to be the highest money-yielding and largest single-unit property; Taherpur and Hatenda in Dinajpur; Futtysingh *taluq* and *thana* Pachete in Birbhum; Seegur and Dyneah in Burdwan; and several other small properties along with these. *Benami* (illegal) properties were also acquired in the names of brothers, nephews and his only son Lokenath. Thus he created the zamindari of Kantanagar, named after him, which, according to F.O. Bell, had 'an illegitimate origin in the obscure depths of eighteenth century politics and intrigues'. From F.O. Bell, *Final Report on the Survey and Settlement Operations in the District of Dinajpur 1934–40*, Calcutta, 1942, cited in Gautam Bhadra, 'The Mentality of Subalternity: Kantanama or Rajdharma', in Ranajit Guha, ed., *Subaltern Studies*, Vol. 4, p. 71.

21 Ibid., p.75.

22 Ibid., p.67.

23 Hitesh Ranjan Sanyal, *Social Mobility in Bengal*, Calcutta: Papyrus, 1981, pp. 102–03.

24 Gyanendranath Kumar, 'Bhookailash Rajvamsha' (in Bengali), *Vamsha Parichaye*, Vol. 5, Calcutta, 1926, p. 1.

25 Proceedings of the Board of Revenue, 5–30 March 1773: Letter dated 13 February 1773.

26 N.K. Sinha, *Economic History of Bengal*, Vol. 1, p. 26.

27 Proceedings of the Board of Trade, 4 August 1821: Letter dated 26 July 1821.

28 Proceedings of the Board of Trade, 19 July 1791: Letter dated 14 July 1791.

29 Proceedings of the Board of Trade, 4 October 1805: Enclosure in letter dated 26 September 1805.

30 Proceedings of the Board of Trade, 1 September 1809: Letter dated 30 August 1809.

31 Proceedings of the Board of Trade, 16 August 1791: Letter dated 16 August 1791.

32 Proceedings of the Board of Trade, No 33, 4 June 1794.

33 Shubhra Chakrabarti, 'The English East India Company and the Indigenous Sloop Merchants of Bengal: Akrur Dutta and His Family, 1757–1857', *Studies in History*, 20, 1, new series, 2004.

34 For details see, Gyanendranath Kumar, 'Mahanubhab Krishna Panti', *Vamsha-Parichaye* (in Bengali), Vol. 18, Calcutta, 1937, pp 34–94; Subodh Chandra Ganguli, *Krishna Panti* (in Bengali), Calcutta, n.d.; Priyanath Singha, *Krishna Panti* (in Bengali), Calcutta, 1911.

35 Board of Revenue (Grain), 15 July 1796: Letter dated 21 June 1797.

36 Subodh Ganguli, *Krishna Panti*, p. 46. In Bengali it reads thus: '*Pyadar Raja Krishna Chandra / tar namete nilam jari / Ar je pan beche khay Krishna Panti / tare dile ma jamindari*' (Oh Mother, Maharaja Krishna Chandra, (of Nadia) who was at the helm of affairs before, has his zamindari put to auction, whereas

that Krishna Panti who used to sell betel-leaf once has now become the zamindar in his place).

37 Gyanendranath Kumar, 'Mahanubhab Krishna Panti', p. 53.

38 Ratnalekha Ray, 'The Changing Fortunes of the Bengali Gentry under Colonial Rule: Palchaudhuries of Mahesganj, 1800–1950', *Modern Asian Studies*, Vol. 21, No. 3, 1987, p. 511.

39 Girish Chandra Ghose, *Ramdoolal Dey: A Lecture on the Life of the Bengalee Millionaire*, Calcutta, 1868. Madan Mohan Kumar, *Bharat Markin Banijyer Pathikrit Ramdool Dey (1752–1825)* (in Bengali), Calcutta, 1976; N.K. Sinha, *Economic History of Bengal*, Vol. III, pp. 110–12.

40 K.W. Porter, *The Jacksons and the Lees: Two Generations of Massachusetts Merchants: 1765–1844*, Vol. 1, reissued, New York: Russell and Russell, 1969. In the letters exchanged between Jackson and Ramdulal, he has often been referred to as 'Du Lall'. Readers have been cautioned against confusing Ramdulal as one being of French origin, as he had been referred to in the American records. Ibid., p. 593.

41 Ibid., pp 594–95.

42 Ibid., pp. 598–99.

43 Ibid., pp. 594–95.

44 Girish Chandra Ghose, *Ramdoolal Dey*, p. 20.

45 Proceedings of Board of Revenue (Customs), Vol. 46: Letter dated 30 May 1817.

46 Girish Chandra Ghose, *Ramdoolal Dey*, p. 26.

47 Kissory Chand Mittra, *Mutty Loll Seal*, Calcutta, 1869, pp. 14–15.

48 For details on Dwarakanath, see Kissory Chand Mittra, *Memoir of Dwarakanath Tagore*, Calcutta, 1870. Kling, *Partner in Empire*.

49 Ibid., p. 250.

50 Kissory Chand Mittra, *Memoir of Dwarakanath Tagore*, p. 12.

51 Proceedings of Board of Trade, 16 Sept 1831: Letter dated 9 September 1831.

52 Kling, *Partner in Empire*, p. 27.

53 Ibid. For details, see Chapter V.

54 Ibid., p. 31.

55 Ibid., p. 66.

56 Ibid., p.32. Dwarakanath started purchasing land at Baharampore, Jessore, Pabna and Kumarkhali. He inherited landed properties in Cuttack in Orissa, in Pandua and Balia *taluqs* (estates). In 1830 Dwarakanath bought Kaligram in Rajshahi district, and in 1834 Shahazadpur in Pabna district. Apart from sole ownership, he enlarged his zamindari through purchase or default on mortgages. He once boasted that the estates of the Tagore family accounted for one-fifteenth of the entire land revenue of the Lower Provinces. Dwarakanath decided to follow the footsteps of other Bengali entrepreneurs and invested his profits in landed estates. Ibid., pp. 31–36.

57 Marshall, 'Masters and Banians', pp. 194–95.

58 Somendra Chandra Nandy, *Life and Times of Cantoo Baboo*, Vol. 1, p. 13.

59 Girish Chandra Ghose, *Ramdoolal Dey*, pp. 26–28.

60 Ibid.

61 Priyanath Sinha, *Krishna Panti*, pp. 164–65.

62 Narendranath Laha, *Subarnabanik Katha*, Calcutta, Vol. 1, pp. 21–22.

63 Kumkum Chatterjee, *Merchants, Politics and Society in Early Modern India, Bihar: 1733–1820*, Leiden: E.J. Brill, p. 151.

64 Ibid.

65 N.K. Sinha, *Economic History of Bengal*, Vol. 1, p. 10.

66 Marshall, 'Masters and Banians', p. 206.
67 For details, see S.B. Singh, *European Agency Houses in Bengal: 1783–1833*, Calcutta: Firma K.L. Mukhopadhyay, 1966.
68 Hitesh Ranjan Sanyal, *Social Mobility in Bengal*, pp. 102–03.
69 Ibid.
70 Sanyal has cited other examples of dissident *Telis* who prospered by leaving their traditional occupation of oil-pressing and taking to trade. These were the Pal family of Daspur in Midnapur, and the Pal family of Kalyanpur in Howrah who flourished in the silk trade. Fortune-seekers such as Gangaprasad, Guruprasad and Baikunthanath of the Bhagyakul Roy family similarly became wealthy through the salt trade. Other examples are Krishna Panti, the founder of the Palchaudhuri zamindari of Nadia and the Dey family of Srirampur – all of whom established sub-monopolies in salt under the East India Company. Ibid, pp. 99–100.
71 Ibid., p. 42.
72 There are many such examples. We have already cited the case of Cantoobabu. Similarly, Ramdulal Dey knew that wealth was the keystone to success. His arrogance becomes evident from this story. Once Kaliprasad Dutta, a reputed citizen of Calcutta, was ostracized by the brahmans during his father's funeral, and they refused to perform the *sradh* (after-death) ceremony because Kaliprasad had a concubine. Ramdulal silenced these brahmans by paying them adequately and made them perform the rites, after which he is said to have remarked, 'society is in my iron-safe'. Girish Chandra Ghose, *Ramdoolal Dey*, pp. 54–55.
73 Partha Chatterjee, 'The Disciplines in Colonial Bengal', in Partha Chatterjee, ed., *Texts of Power: Emerging Disciplines in Colonial Bengal*, Minneapolis: University of Minnesota Press, 1995. Chatterjee has shown that those educated in the English language became the intelligentsia, who were at the vanguard of modernization and later the national movement. Ibid., p. 9.
   Here we can draw a parallel from Norbert Elias's *The Civilizing Process*, where he has analysed how upward social mobility took place in Germany in the eighteenth century. Elias exemplifies the manner in which language plays a dominant role in shaping the culture and sophistication of people. He cites the case of the Germans who imitated the French and spoke their language, considered the language of the cultured and of the court. For details, see Norbert Elias, *The Civilizing Process: Changes in the Behaviour of the Secular Upper Classes in the West*, Vol. 1, reprint, Oxford: Blackwell, Part 1, pp. 5–26. Elias argues that during the time of Louis XIV (mid-seventeenth to early eighteenth century), most aristocrats in the European continent, including the famous German court philosopher Leibniz, wrote and spoke only in French and seldom in German, which was considered the language of the lower and middle classes. Ibid., pp. 11–12. Similarly, knowledge of English was considered honourable and prestigious, and it gradually became the classical language of Bengal. For details, see Aparna Basu, *History of Education in India*, p. 125, cited in Partha Chatterjee, 'The Disciplines in Colonial Bengal', p. 9. The Bengali commercial elites gradually took to this language with more confidence and authority in order to deal directly with their European partners and earn more social respectability. Cantoobabu's biographer Somendra Chandra Nandy has mentioned that as early as the mid-eighteenth century, Cantoobabu could speak in English, Bengali and Persian with equal ease. Somendra Chandra Nandy, *Life and Times of Cantoo Baboo*, p. 6.
74 Kissory Chand Mittra, *Memoir of Dwarakanath Tagore*, pp. 8–9.
75 See Sibnath Shastri, *Ramtanu Lahiri o Tatkalin Bangasamaj* (in Bengali),

Calcutta: New Age Publishers Private Ltd, 1957. pp. 137–60. Sumit Sarkar has also remarked that it was the rapid spread of English education that was responsible for the 'new Renaissance' in mid-eighteenth-century Bengal, and led to the emergence of the '*bhadralok*' (English-educated upper class) community, who were the protagonists of this movement. Some members from among the *bhadralok* were both professional and landed magnates. Sarkar has also emphasized that knowledge of English would breed the *madhyabitta* or middle class in Calcutta, where new schools and colleges and the printing press expedited the process. Sumit Sarkar, 'Calcutta and the Bengal Renaissance', in Sukanta Chaudhuri, ed., *Calcutta*, Vol. 1, pp. 100–02.

[76] Porter, *The Jacksons and the Lees*, Vol. 1, pp. 633–34. Letter from Boston dated 8 December 1808.

[77] Kissory Chand Mittra, *Memoir of Dwarakanath Tagore*, pp. 73–74.

[78] Marshall, 'Masters and Banians', p. 205.

[79] Chitra Deb, 'Jorasanko and the Thakur Family: The Tagore Family of Jorasanko', in Sukanta Chaudhuri, ed., *Calcutta*, Vol. 1, p. 65.

[80] For details, see Kling, *Partner in Empire*, chapter entitled 'Conclusion'.

[81] Lokenath Ghose, *Kalkatar Babu Brittanta* (in Bengali), Calcutta, 1983, p. 36. Kissory Chand Mittra, *Mutty Seal*, p. 29.

[82] Girish Chandra Ghose, *Ramdoolal Dey*, pp. 40–43.

[83] For details, see S.N. Mukherjee, 'Class, Caste and Politics in South Asia', in Leach and Mukherjee, eds, *Elites in South Asia*, Cambridge: Cambridge University Press, 1970, pp. 76–78. Also see Subir Roychoudhury, 'The Lost World of the Babus', in Sukanta Chaudhuri, ed., *Calcutta*. Vol. 1, where he has cited Rajat Sanyal's *Voluntary Associations and the Urban Public Life in Bengal, 1815–1876*, Calcutta: Riddhi Publishers, 1980, where the latter has shown that 119 associations were formed between 1815 and 1876 under twenty-six heads. Interestingly, twenty-five bodies were formed jointly by Indians and the British. Some of these were The Calcutta Public Library (1836), The Landholders Society (1838), The Bengal British India Society (1843–46) and The Bengal Social Science Association (1867). Ibid., p. 71. Also see Chitra Deb, 'Jorasanko and the Thakur Family', p. 67.

[84] For details, see Kironmoy Raha, 'Calcutta Theatre: 1835–1944', in Sukanta Chaudhuri, ed., *Calcutta*, Vol. 1, pp.186–94. Raha has cited Shishir Bhaduri, a pioneer in Bengal's stage-theatre, who had lamented in *Natyalok,* 10 December 1951, that it is a pity that Bengali theatre did not completely evolve from *jatra*, but 'has grown under foreign influences'. As a result, it could never become a true national theatre. Ibid., p. 186.

[85] Ibid., pp.186–87.

[86] Ibid., p.188.

[87] See Chitra Deb, 'Jorasanko and the Thakur Family', p. 66.

[88] For details, see Subir Roychoudhury, 'The Lost World of the Babus', p. 68.

[89] Ibid.

[90] For details, see Chitra Deb, 'The Great Houses of Old Calcutta', in Sukanta Chaudhuri, ed., *Calcutta*, pp. 56–58.

[91] Subir Roychoudhury, 'The Lost World of the Babus', p. 69.

[92] For details see, Kling, *Partner in Empire*, chapter titled 'The Prince at Bay', particularly, pp. 176–83 and pp. 234–35; Kissory Chand Mittra, *Memoir of Dwarakanath Tagore*, p. 113.

[93] Girish Chandra Ghose, *Ramdoolal Dey*, p. 40.

[94] Kling, *Partner in Empire*, p. 188.

[95] For details, see Dipesh Chakrabarty, 'Adda: A History of Sociality', in

Provincializing Europe: Postcolonial Thought and Historical Difference, Princeton: Princeton University Press, 2000, pp. 180–213.

[96] For details, see Subir Roychoudhury, 'The Lost World of the Babus', pp. 71–72. Periodicals became an important mouthpiece of nineteenth-century polemics as well as creative writing. It is on record that as many as 219 periodicals, mostly in Bengali and some in English, were published between 1818 and 1867.

[97] Ibid., p. 71.

[98] Kali Prasanna Sinha, 'Babu Padmalochan Dutta, Alias "Chance Avatar"; "Snanyatra at Mahesh"; "Rathayatra"; and "Durga Puja"', in *Hootum Pyanchar Naksha* (in Bengali), Calcutta, 1862; translated by Swarup Roy into English as *The Observant Owl: Hootum's Vignettes of Nineteenth-Century Calcutta*, Ranikhet: Black Kite, 2008, pp. 119–65.

[99] Ibid.

[100] N.K. Sinha, *The Economic History of Bengal*, Vol. III; S.B. Singh, *European Agency Houses in Bengal: 1783–1833*, Calcutta: Firma K.L. Mukhopadhyay, 1966; H.N. Sinha, *Early European Banking in India*, London, 1927; Amalesh Tripathi, *Trade and Finance in the Bengal Presidency*, revised edition, Calcutta: Oxford University Press, 1979; Sabyasachi Bhattacharya, *The Financial Foundations of the British Raj: Ideas and Interests in the Reconstruction of Indian Public Finance, 1858–1872*, revised edition, Hyderabad: Orient Longman, 2005.

[101] Amalesh Tripathi, *Trade and Finance*, p. 217. N.K. Sinha, *The Economic History of Bengal*, Vol. III, chapter VII entitled 'Failure of Business Enterprise in Calcutta', pp. 105–27.

[102] N.K. Sinha, *Economic History of Bengal*, Vol. III, p. 124.

[103] Nilmani Mukhopadhyay, *Bengal Zamindars: Jayakrishna Mukherjee of Uttarpara and His Times (1808–1888)*, Calcutta: Firma K.L. Mukhopadhyaya, 1975, p. xxv.

[104] For details see, Amalesh Tripathi, *Trade and Finance*, pp. 201–05.

[105] Kling, 'Entrepreneurship and Regional Identity in Bengal', pp. 75–84.

[106] Kling, *Partner in Empire*, p. 251.

[107] Pradip Sinha, *Calcutta in Urban History*, p. 79. Sinha has estimated this income to be over Rs 10,00,000.

SECTION THREE

Tagore estates as well.[9] Repressed quite ruthlessly by the state, it nonetheless alerted the British about peasant problems and prepared the way for
a new rent law. In the mid-1880s, the Permanent Settlement was modified
to reduce the arbitrary powers of landlords over their cultivator-tenants. [10]

Men of the Hindu upper-caste gentry now began to have a distinct
feeling that their economic control as well as their social authority were
slipping away. Worse, their domestic hegemony also faced a challenge as
reformers campaigned hard against child marriage, polygamy and cohabi-
tation with infant-wives. That could have been a reason why the opposition
to the 1891 Act was particularly intense in Bengal under the leadership
of upper-caste elites. Some of the fervour of the revivalist orthodoxy is
captured, and some other aspects shrewdly anticipated, in *Gora*.

At the time of the Swadeshi movement of 1905–08, Muslim and
'low-caste' cultivators defied upper-caste nationalists and refused to burn
stocks of cheap foreign cloth at the behest of the boycott call. The movement, however, gained new recruits among middle-class women who
entered the political world for the first time and played auxilliary roles
from within their domestic interiors. They boycotted foreign cloth and
loyalist kinsfolk.[11] Coming out of these turbulences, *Ghare Baire* focuses
on a woman who is politicized within the home and whose world gets
shattered by a transgressive redefinition of conjugality. The protagonist, a
liberal reformer in the domain of gender politics, is also deeply disturbed
by the violent and manipulative political rhetoric of Extremism, supremely
indifferent to the miseries of the rural poor.

The inter-war years were marked by massive Gandhian and revolutionary movements, waged under the direction of great leaders. They also
saw the emergence of the 'new Indian woman': restricted to the middle
classes, culturally cosmopolitan, and experimenting with bold changes in
lifestyle and gender practices. The 1930s were also the years of the great
agrarian depression which disastrously undermined the security of Bengali
cultivators. The Congress would not let them struggle against eviction by
landlords. There were communist-led working-class strikes in the 1920s
and 30s among jute workers and Corporation sweepers and scavengers
who were mostly untouchables. In a short story, 'Sanskar', written by
Rabindranath at the time of a scavengers' strike in Calcutta, an ardent
nationalist woman refuses to rescue a scavenger, besieged by a mob of
pious temple-goers who suspect that he has touched and polluted them.
'But he is a *methar*', she reprimands her husband who wants to help the
hapless untouchable.[12]

Char Adhyay, written in the midst of these profound social changes
and political turmoil, configures the new woman in a world of refurbished

gender and nationalist politics where she has acquired a great measure
of self-determination. It also reflects on the costs of the new nationalism
which enhances her political participation beyond all expectations, but
which also subordinates her emotional needs and autonomy tragically.
The hero, once a practitioner of secret violence, declares at the end: 'I am
not a patriot in your sense. There is something higher than patriotism
. . . nationalists of the entire world today are roaring like beasts . . . they
think they can save the country by killing off its soul.'[13] The three novels
therefore share important continuities as well as departures in fictional
themes, characters and situations.

Sometimes these broad changes resonated with Rabindranath
Tagore's personal history. In the 1880s, he had been critical about non-
consensual child marriage. His own marriage to a child-bride in this decade, and her early child-bearing, probably made him reflect keenly on the
problem of stolen childhoods. Later, the birth of his daughters deepened his
sensitivity as he tenderly watched over their infancy. He was recently back
from England where he had found much to admire in western domestic
arrangements. In 1891–92, shortly after the Age of Consent agitations, he
wrote a memorable little story: 'Khata' or 'The Exercise Book'. It talked
of the lost worlds of child-wives and lampooned Hindu revivalism with
bitter, though quiet, irony.[14]

By the time the Swadeshi movement began, however, Rabindranath
had moved over to a phase of deep reverence for brahmanical traditions
– as is evident from his efforts to replicate an imagined Vedic ashram in
his Santiniketan school, along with appropriate caste observances. This
was also the time when he married off his first two daughters at a very
early age: something that caused them, and him, immense suffering later.[15]

By the time he wrote Gora and Ghare Baire, he had revised his
political and social positions all over again. In 1909 Myron Phelps, an
American, asked him what he considered to be the most critical problem
of contemporary India. Rabindranath wrote back to say that it was caste.[16]
In 1910 he wrote – over three consecutive days – three passionately angry
poems about untouchability. He arranged the marriage of his eldest son and
heir, Rathindranath, with a child-widow around the time he wrote Gora.[17]
He would, however, temporize about caste once again when Gandhi went
on a fast unto death in 1931 to oppose Ambedkar's demand for separate
electorates for untouchables. Rabindranath too opposed separate electorates in no uncertain terms. Like Gandhi, his was a paternalist resolution
to the problem of caste: encouraging a profound sense of guilt for upper
castes who were expected to initiate self-reform, but not keen on autonomous political struggle against caste abuses by lower castes themselves.[18]

In 1914 a young Bengali girl, Snehalata, committed suicide to save her parents from bankruptcy which would follow from the pressure to provide the dowry for her marriage. The event, much discussed in the press, coincided with Rabindranath's own experience: one of his daughters was cruelly treated by her in-laws over dowry demands. Not only did the problem of dowry feature in his memorable short stories of this decade, like 'Haimanti' and '*Streer Patra*', but, more importantly, a savage indictment of familial relationships and expectations was also prominent. '*Streer Patra*', a short story that Hindu nationalists reviewed most indignantly, imagined a woman who had torn asunder family controls and discipline, and set out to reinvent her life on her own terms.[19]

Ghare Baire is situated in a time when a few men from extraordinarily liberal households no longer feared and repressed the woman's urge to read and to inhabit a wider world; they actively fostered it. The energies of an intense anti-colonial struggle also opened up fresh spaces, bringing to women of such families a taste of active politics even within their domestic confines. The new freedom was heady and unsettling, and it could, conceivably, move the question of freedom far beyond older reformism. *Ghare Baire* raised the possibility of the woman's choice beyond and against conjugality, threatening even reformist versions of masculinity. This was the boldest and most difficult novel that Rabindranath wrote.

The space of the novel evokes intricately interwoven areas of human concerns, whereas political treatises see them as disjunct and incommensurable. It is precisely because literature smudges the boundaries between different orders of experience that it can both capture and refashion a historical structure of sensibilities so successfully.

II

For a number of historical reasons, it has been exceptionally hard for Indian patriotism to find a sure footing for itself. Patriotism requires an enclosed territory as its first condition. Why that land is valued and what the land represents are, however, contentious questions. To secular Indian patriots, land as birthplace is the source of the self. In V.D. Savarkar's Hindu nationalism, in contrast, land is the birthplace, above all, of a home-grown Indian faith. Hindutva alone can claim to be the sole religious culture of the nation. Indian Muslims and Christians do not qualify as full-fledged Indians since their faiths were born outside the land.[20]

That spatial integrity has to be underpinned by a stable map, continuous since time immemorial. The nationalist project thus leans upon both time and space, geography and history: the country, as we know it now, must always already have been there. The temporal–spatial identity

must be culturally reinforced as well. That needs cultural unity and sameness running through the entire land mass, and imparting a common aspect
to people who inhabit it. The conditions have an ideological function:
they make the country appear as a natural organism, a self-evident entity.

When they first began to discourse urgently about patriotism,
Indians adopted the map of British India – which spanned an entire
subcontinent – as their natural and historical habitat. It is very unlikely,
however, that the subcontinental geography ever had a real presence, or a
vivid and shared meaning, in the affective world of Indians in pre-modern
days. There never was a history of comprehensive politico-administrative
unification till well into the colonial era. There were, instead, empires
inside India, several at a time, and many kingdoms perpetually at war
with one another.

Shared cultural traits could have overcome politico-administrative
divisions. But there were far too few of them. Apart from Sanskrit, followed
by Persian in later times, there was no single language that people from
different parts of the country would understand or use. These, too, were
elite languages, used for high literary, sacred or bureaucratic needs. Live
linguistic traditions, on the other hand, were plural and mostly mutually
incomprehensible. So were lived cultural traditions and styles of worship. Of course, there were points of continuous contact: pilgrimage and
trade circuits existed from ancient times, connecting different parts of the
country. But they were specific to a particular community or sect, not a
common point of reference for all.

Pre-modern popular loyalty was directed towards the sovereign
and his realm, not towards a land and a people. The word Ramrajya –
Ram's kingdom – is a good example. Emotions of familiarity and loving
intimacy that we now associate with patriotism were actually reserved
for smaller places. The *Ramayana* had declared that the mother and the
birthplace are superior to heaven. The birthplace, in this case, would literally be that – the ancestral homestead where a person is born. Associations
of personal history, property and space gave a piece of land its peculiar
affective claim. A similar felt closeness was conveyed by the word *desh*,
of Sanskrit origin and common to many Indian languages, and also by the
Persian word *mulk*.[21] Both originally meant one's personal address. Both
came to acquire a highly reified aspect when enlarged and strenuously
reinscribed upon a subcontinent which could only abstractly be imagined
as one's own. One of the characteristics of modern patriots like Swami
Vivekananda and, later, Gandhi, was to travel across the length and breadth
of the country. Obviously, being an Indian involved conscious effort. It
was acquired knowledge, not an instinct.

A regional patriotism had, however, emerged simultaneously with pan-Indian or subcontinental patriotism in the nineteenth century. This incorporated the earlier meanings of *desh* more successfully, a region being a more familiar land and people, often unified by a shared language. There was an outpouring of patriotic Bengali songs from the late nineteenth century which expressed love for Bengal more immediately and vividly. India, in contrast, appeared as a project of power and glory. We may contrast two patriotic songs of Rabindranath himself. In one he evokes ancient 'Bharatbarsha' as the cradle of human civilization: 'The dawn first appeared on these skies, here the first holy chants were recited / From these forests, for the first time, faith and knowledge spread across the world along with poetry and tales.'[22] The civilization is unmistakably Hindu. The other is a song about the land of Bengal, which is now the national song of Bangladesh: 'My golden Bengal, I do love you so / For ever and ever, your skies, your winds, make music in my soul / . . . in spring your mango groves enchant me with their fragrance / Late autumn fills your paddy fields with sweetly smiling bounty.[23] (All translations in the essay are mine.)

If the spatial imagination about a region was both precise and sensual, the subcontinent, in contrast, was best conceptualized as history rather than as familiar land. When a strong cartographic imagination emerged from late colonial times, it was the shadowy, vaguely feminine shape of the contours of the map of British India that became familiar in popular representations. India was preferred as an idealized form rather than as concrete geography.[24]

But things do change. In 1888 John Strachey, a senior colonial official, had confidently assured Cambridge University undergraduates in a speech: 'There is not, and never was an India . . . no Indian nation, no people of India of which we hear so much That men of the Punjab, Bengal, the North West Provinces and Madras should ever feel that they belong to one Indian nation, is impossible.'[25] This was a remarkable instance of famous last words. Even as he spoke, the very thing he strenuously denied an existence was already coming to life, provoked by the system of governance that he himself was a part of. The Indian empire, inaugurated with much fanfare a little more than a decade back, was transfiguring fast into a nation of Indians who came to feel with increasing conviction that they were one people. That this was a modern beginning in no way subtracted from its intensity.

History, after all, is not destiny. Indian patriotism as felt emotion was the unintended product of colonial rule which bestowed political unity, and which tied up dispersed spaces and people into a whole. And

which, moreover, through largely similar racial, economic and administrative policies, stirred up very similar grievances, aspirations and emotions
among people across the subcontinent. It was, finally and supremely, anti-
colonial popular movements that melded very large, disparate populations
into a strong, affective people. One may even say that it was patriotism
that gave birth to India as a country. This origin, however, could not be
enough: it was too recent and contingent. It became necessary, therefore,
to imagine other, more enduring and organic bases to justify and propel
the emergent patriotism.

III

All this suggests something very curious for our modern times:
patriotic emotions in search of a country. But what can we find in our history that is old enough, strong enough and generalized enough to provide
a persuasive basis for that?

For a large number of modern Hindus, the answer was simple
and obvious. Hinduism alone could bear the weight of that requirement.
Hindus, they claimed, are the most numerous of Indian people, and they
supposedly provide an unbroken historical continuity that is older than
what other Indian communities can offer. However, there are very old
and extremely populous non-Hindu communities in the country whose
contributions to cultural and political traditions are rich, diverse, massive. To call India Hindu would exclude those critical masses: not only
at the cost of crippling Indian lives, cultures and histories unimaginably,
but also by leaving non-Hindus stranded in their homelands without real
entitlement. Hindus, moreover, are profoundly stratified by caste, region,
language and sect. The one practice all Hindus have held in common is
some variant of caste hierarchy. To invoke it, however, risked alienating
an increasingly self-assertive 'low-caste' politics and leadership. In *Gora*,
the hero's efforts to imagine an eternally unified Hindu India repeatedly
stumbles against the cruel divisions of caste.

Undeterred by these problems, nineteenth-century Hindu reviv-
alists often located cultural continuity and civilizational singularity for
Hindu-Indians in ancient brahmanical texts: in mythological, philosophical
and metaphysical systems, legal statutes, and classical Sanskrit literature.
These, compiled and published by nineteenth-century Indologists, Indian
and western, became internationally renowned. The colonial state itself had
bestowed upon parts of it a great visibility and sanction. It had declared
that in all areas of belief, ritual, marriage, divorce, dowry, adoption, succession, inheritance and caste, Hindus and Muslims would be governed
by their scripture and custom, and the state could only intervene if present

practice contravened more ancient and pristine tradition. Non-interference in intimate spheres, they thought, would reconcile and pacify a subjugated people. But together with political expediency, there was also an element of genuine admiration. When a compilation was made from Hindu scriptural traditions, Bentham, the great Utilitarian, read it in translation and decided that aspects of it should be included in the universal legal code that he planned to write.[26]

Throughout the nineteenth century, liberal reformers and Hindu orthodoxy quarrelled about what uses should be made of this freedom. Should it be a source of introspection and self-reform? Or should it reinforce tradition?

Coming close to ideas that are associated with the conservative parliamentarian Edmund Burke but which actually go back to late medieval English writings, especially of Fortescue, Indian conservatives creatively transfigured certain cornerstones of western conservatism. Their arguments went thus: If certain institutions and traditions have survived through the ages, then their content had to be axiomatically good. That even foreign invaders had not disturbed them, doubly proves their worth. Even if their logic or ethical properties are no longer clear, their historical persistence demonstrates their relevance for modern times. Reformers cannot judge them by their own time-bound reason that is the product of a single generation's thinking – whereas these laws and customs contain the wisdom of past generations.[27] In its own way, the argument invoked what Pocock has described in another context as the democracy of the dead.[28]

There was a second string to the argument. Do not apparently problematic traditions about caste and gender come enfolded within a larger cultural tradition that even the west admits to be civilized: our profound philosophical systems, our wonderful classical literature? If we now question them, do we not undermine the entire tradition, the obviously great and the good, along with those few elements that now appear to be problematic? This form of cultural nationalism thus admitted of grave disorders in the Hindu world, which were far too blatant and had been too obviously exposed by generations of liberals, to deny. At the same time, it offered a rationale for forgetting them. So, with great ingenuity, it acknowledged and denied Hindu social injustice in the same breath.

Such arguments pervade *Gora* where we find some of their most passionate articulations as well as their most effective refutation. If all patriotic projects demand adoration, the patriotism of a colonized people demands it in ways that are more than usually fierce, compelling and poignant.[29]

IV

Rabindranath was the cultural face of the early phase of the Swadeshi movement. Along with other nationalist leaders, he freely used Hindu rituals and symbols for mass mobilization, and he defended Hindu social institutions and statutes, even describing caste as a consensual and rational division of labour that secured social harmony. In the same vein, he also endorsed brahmanical gender practices like widow immolation.[30] He wrote in *Swadeshi Samaj* in 1904: 'Will not Hinduism be able to bring every one of us day by day into bonds of affinity and devotion to this Bharatbarsha of ours – the abode of our gods, the hermitage of our rishis, the land of our forefathers?'[31]

There are such strong recurrences of these themes and even these words in *Gora* that it seems undeniable that Rabindranath of the Swadeshi era provided the model for the patriotic language of the early Gora – the protagonist of the novel. The novel is, therefore, autobiographical in a split mode. The early and the later Gora reflect two different political moments in Rabindranath's own life.

Even in the Swadeshi phase, however, Rabindranath was different from other Hindu nationalists. The differences grew over time, increasingly isolating him from the movement until he turned into its most outspoken critic. He saw Muslims as equal compatriots.[32] Violence horrified him, whether directed against state officials or against Muslims. He insisted that Indian civilization had always been nourished by many cultures. Some of them originally arrived with foreign conquests but then found a home in this country. This included the west whose intellectual and cultural resources cannot be spurned, even in the age of colonialism, without a fatal cultural self-impoverishment.[33] Above all, he – like Nikhilesh of *Ghare Baire* – valued rural uplift and peasant welfare, only too acutely aware of perennial peasant poverty and ignorance for which Indian landlords were to blame as much as colonial depredations. At his own estates at Selaidaha and Kaligram, he experimented with rural cooperatives and banks. As the movement progressed, he became increasingly critical of the upper-class, upper-caste Hindu nationalist leadership which coerced low-caste and Muslim peasants to burn cheap foreign cloth but did nothing to improve their lot.[34]

In the course of the Swadeshi movement, people from the 'low castes' and Muslims began to oppose the enforced boycott of foreign goods, and this soon turned into violent communal clashes: the first rural riots of a communal nature in Bengal. Rabindranath now decisively turned away from the movement. He concluded that untouchability and communalism were no less important than colonial injustice; that as long as the problem of peasant exploitation remained, elite nationalists had no right to command villagers to boycott cheap foreign cloth.[35]

Though *Gora* contained many insights from his own involvement with the movement, he located the fictional situation some time around the 1870s – and here I go by internal evidence that Gora was born in 1857. A conservative Hindu nationalism now stridently opposed liberal thinking and social reform in the name of the cultural distinctiveness of Hindus.[36] Gora, a young man from an educated, orthodox brahman family, towers over his friends and family with his patriotic vision, his uncompromising opposition to colonial racism. He loves all Indians, Muslims and untouchables included, but the one category he abhors are liberal reformers. They are cultural renegades to him, pale mimics of their colonial masters, trying to destroy something in the name of reform for which they have neither understanding nor sympathy. To declare his own distance from them, he demonstratively adheres to every orthodox form of behaviour, especially in areas of gender and caste pollution taboos. He does not eat the food his beloved mother cooks because she takes water from Lachhmia, a low-caste domestic help. Interestingly, Gora's physical description reminds us of Bankimchandra's portrait: 'the forehead is broad . . . the lips are thin and pressed together, the nose overhangs them like a scimitar: the eyes are small but brilliant'. Bankimchandra, rather like Gora, had made a move between liberal reformism and orthodoxy, but in a reverse direction. Of course, Gora is also immensely tall, with powerful limbs and an amazingly fair complexion. Early in the novel we are told that he was born of Irish parents killed during the Mutiny and brought up by a brahman family. He does not know this himself and that adds to the narrative tension.[37]

Bengali literary historians think that Vivekananda provided the model for Gora's character. There is some truth in this, although I think that Rabindranath's own ideas at two different phases constitute the two phases of Gora more accurately. Gora, like Vivekananda, was an agnostic before he embraced revivalism. Both tried to improve lower-caste conditions with upper-caste social welfare; both developed a powerful patriotic prose; both organized middle-class Hindu youth into missionaries; and both equated patriotism with Hindu pride. There may be yet another shared trait. Gora has to constantly repress his doubts about Hindu social institutions in order to inculcate Hindu pride. Sumit Sarkar argues that there was a split between Vivekananda's private utterances and correspondence on the one hand, where he freely mocked Hindu norms, and his public speeches and writings on the other, where he sang their glories. There were also moments of oscillation between confidence and despair about his Hindu missionary project.[38]

There are several counterpoints to Gora. His mother Anandamoyee is remarkably clear-eyed. She despises no one because of their birth or faith, and her love goes out irresistibly to all. The indivisible nature of humanity is something she learnt when she first held the baby Gora in her arms: her maternal love immediately transcended purity–pollution taboos and she would never again return to these divisions. Gora comes in touch with a liberal Brahmo family, argues with the gentle, introspective father, Paresh, and, reluctantly, falls in love with his adopted daughter Sucharita, just as his friend and disciple Benoy comes to love Sucharita's adoptive sister Lalita. There are interesting divergences in speech patterns. Anandamoyee speaks with great emotional depth and clarity. Paresh speaks gently but logically, in measured intellectual cadences. Lalita, who would later marry Gora's friend Benoy, reshapes her father's logicality into an impatient, even shrill argumentativeness. Gora himself speaks in hyperbolic rhetoric, the passion of his language, metaphors and images sweeping away the effects of calm reasoning, logical arguments, the gentle words of love. Speech patterns are intercutting and ungendered, Paresh and Anandamoyee sharing strong features while Gora and Baradasundari use an authoritarian language. Likewise, both Brahmos and Hindus have their tolerant representatives as well as narrowminded bigots.

Sucharita wavers between her father and Gora, as does his friend Benoy – her intellect responding to the social and historical arguments that Paresh assembles to reply to Gora's Hindu nationalism. At the same time, Gora conjures up with his memorable rhetoric, a vision of the country with such force that she is captivated; for her, the country is entirely an effect of his words. She falls in love with both at the same time as Gora casts, Othello-like, the powerful magic of words.

Rabindranath had put his finger on a very important source of the power of Hindu nationalism when he showed the effects of Gora's rhetoric. Verbal images defeat historical evidence and logic: simultaneously displacing the living with an abstraction, a reification and, in the same move, investing the abstract with compelling human qualities – making it more real than the experienced or the historical. Hindu nationalism transacts in the currency of the imagined, made real with words: the imagined and the idealized then overwrite the world we live in. Strangely for a poet, Rabindranath distrusted the reality-transfiguring power of words, the ease with which they create a felicitous web that appears more real than the actual.

Hating himself for his un-Hindu act – pre-marital love being anathema for a non-consensual Hindu marriage system and Sucharita is a woman from another community – Gora hardens his orthodoxy, harshly represses his love for Sucharita and his own doubts about caste divisions and domestic laws. As the rift is about to become final, Gora discovers that he is actually an adopted child born to Irish parents who were killed by Indian rebels. The discovery, at one stroke, removes him from his family, his Hindu and brahmanical ancestry. Being a European by birth, and a Mutiny orphan, he also loses his affiliation to anti-colonial movements.

The brahmanical Gora represents a past of Rabindranath that the author had only recently discarded. But Rabindranath knew well its compelling power. Gora, even as a Hindu hardliner, represents a bright light; he articulates the majesty of a subjugated people rising up to confront injustice and racism. Some aspects of Hindu patriotism did embody the proud defiance of Indians, humiliated and stigmatized as they were by the British. Gora is its strongest self-expression. What makes him especially compelling, however, is that he himself is torn: he admires Muslim social solidarities, he is furious when he sees the low-caste Hindu exploited and insulted by the high caste. On such occasions, he breaks caste taboos to stand with them against the sahib or the brahman.

Early in the novel, Benoy asks: Tell me, Gora, is Bharatbarsha something real to you? Do you see her clearly? How do you see her? Benoy is uncertain about the reality of the icon for whose sake Gora asks him to turn away from a Brahmo girl who attracts him. Unless he too can experience the reality as an actual presence, he cannot abandon his new romantic emotions. Gora replies:

> My country is real and clear to me all the time, but you will not find her in Marshman Sahib's History of India, she lives in my heart. . . . I may lose my way, I may drown and die . . . but that blessed refuge still exists, my country, always filled with wealth, knowledge, faith. Falsehood surrounds us and what we seem to see is no reality . . . this Calcutta of yours, these mercantile offices, these courtrooms, these concrete bubbles . . . can this be my Bharatbarsha? Here we live false lives, do meaningless work, this Bharatbarsha is a magician's trick, it has no real life. . . . There is a true Bharat, we need to search her out, go there, draw out our lifeblood, our souls, our wisdom from that place. . . . We have weakened ourselves with self-loathing, once we embrace pride for the entire country, the truth of India will become manifest.[39]

Gora asserts that the reality of the country is something different from and opposed to its actual appearance. Its inner truth must be seized as an act of faith, a mystical realization, as a project. It is really a future that must masquerade as a past and a present in order to come into being.

He also admits that the apparent India is suffused with misery.

But she is still a goddess. He feels confident that a movement will arise to confront humiliation. But that will arise out of our faith in the goddess:

> Benoy, I see my goddess, she is not bathed in beauty, I find her in the midst of famine, poverty, suffering, she is insulted. She is not to be worshipped with songs and flowers, but with lives and blood. I can see against the bloodshot sky, the birth of a new, radiant dawn of freedom.[40]

The goddess, thus, is a political necessity. The present misery of India is simultaneously invoked and abolished. At one level it is a false cover, masking the real with *maya* or divine enchantment, filled with fleeting evanescence that overwrites Truth which is constant. But at another, simultaneous level it is also a necessary adornment of the goddess because the perception of her misery is also a call for battle against her enemies.

When Sucharita presses him to clarify the precise location of the real country, Gora invokes the ancient past, the historical continuity of its culture. History is destiny, history is country, the past is our real place.[41] Benoy vacillates. At times he is entirely persuaded by Gora's overpowering presence. Away from the charismatic inspiration, however, the power vanishes and he is once more beset with doubts and his own needs. Ultimately, he decides to follow the latter, telling Gora that he can see the country that Gora wants him to see only through Gora's speech, not through his own experience. Before he leaves Gora, however, he talks about his own love to his friend. He also talks about women who must live in freedom to acquire an independent and creative identity that Hindu laws deny them. His words, in turn, strengthen and thrust up to the surface Gora's own need to love, his own appreciation of the potential that women have and are made to hide. Though he represses these thoughts immediately, Benoy's words work within Gora, counterposing the image of fulfilment to the bleak aridity that his own project involves.

Sucharita is compelled by Gora's sheer physical presence that sweeps her off her feet. Gora's convictions also tumble when he looks at her, and, against his will, is enchanted by her tender physical appeal, her calm, bright intelligence. Sudipta Kaviraj points out that unlike Bankimchandra or earlier Bengali Vaishnav poets, Rabindranath's physical descriptions of protagonists is minimal.[42] This is not entirely true of *Gora*. We know Lalita is tall, dark and slim; Binoy is slender and handsome in a delicate mould; and, of course, we know exactly how Gora looks, for his looks betray his origins. But Sucharita and Anandamoyee do remain hazy physical presences; they are physical embodiments of mental and spiritual qualities: gentleness, intelligence, luminous serenity.

Out of her great love for Gora, Sucharita forces herself to accept the Hindu discipline that he thrusts upon her as patriotism. But it means that she must kill her love for Gora and accept a non-consensual marriage with a man of the proper caste and lineage. It is finally her love for her sister Lalita who marries Benoy, defying religious divisions and social stigma, that makes her turn away from Gora's path.

Sucharita asks Gora why the country should be identified with a faith. Isn't faith larger than the country? Gora retorts: Our faith is our history, it is what the country has always had; this is true of all countries, each of them lives through a faith that expresses its essence. For India, that faith is Hinduism. That alone can establish a link between our pasts and presents, can make our country as one.[43] 'Whatever exists here, we need to embrace without qualifications. . . . If we are different from the west, that does not matter.' He admits that caste may seem apparently unjust and irrational. Many problems do flow from it. Yet it is a part of our faith which has produced so much that is eminently rational and humane. The whole must surpass the part and justify it.[44]

Paresh argues that even if there is a higher purpose in Hindu caste, we cannot see it. All we see are walls of loathing for human beings who are not considered human. Gora rebuts: If we see no reason for some elements but can still see that the entire thing is nonetheless marvellous, then we must accept the whole and admit that those elements too must have a higher reason. We cannot see that because we have mortgaged our own vision, we now see with foreign eyes which are critical and sceptical. Once we take on the entire thing with love, the meaning will be made clear. If we discard and change the part, we will destroy a whole, wonderful civilization, we will kill our own selves, our identity. As he says: 'Reform? That will come later. The immediate need is for wholehearted love, to adore the country, to be one with her. Once you try to reform, you pull her down, you degrade her with criticism, you set yourself above her.'[45]

So what is past, what is memory and ideal, what is hidden and opaque, is more real than what is experienced, present and visible. He has only contempt for his orthodox disciples who love to despise the non-Hindu, the low caste, the woman. Yet, they are his only possible companions. He realizes that love has no place in his Hindu Bharat where divisions are more meaningful. His dejection only strengthens his conviction. He must ruthlessly suppress his doubts and needs to reach out to his Bharat. He prepares to build a cocoon of high brahmanical practices around himself. He decides to repress his love for Sucharita for it is a sacrifice that Hindu India deserves. He abandons Benoy whom he adores and chooses the companionship of the mindlessly orthodox Abinash whom he secretly despises. But all this comes at a crushing cost to his soul. In a sense, he stands at the crossroads even before he comes to discover his origins.

The discovery of his Irish origin introduces two critical departures. First, in an instant, Gora is bereft of his past. Is it possible to break away from the past and yet lay claim to a human identity that is worth living for? Can we dispense with the meanings that our pasts had prepared for us? Can patriotism develop an identity that is not derived from the past? Second, his love for Bharatbarsha had been a very real experience for him, the most vivid and powerful identification and emotion that stood higher than his more immediate and personal commitments. Even if it was built on false premises, it was nonetheless a true love. What does he now do with this love of his?

Gora chooses to love the actual people of India: in the present, just as they are, and in the name of a universal good that they must have access to. In the same measure, he develops a new understanding about freely chosen love as the basis for all commitments and identifications: personal and collective. If one can love the country only in the freedom of self-determination and not out of an inherited obligation, then freedom should become a value in all spheres of life: a value that the country herself must respect and which she must never abolish or qualify in the name of patriotism. He turns to Sucharita and, for the first time, holds out his hand to her.

In the novel, the origin of Gora functions as the narrative device for the incorporation of western cultural resources within Indian history. In his subsequent writings like the 'Nationalism' essays, Rabindranath would warn urgently against an indiscriminate expulsion of western values from Indian lives. Gora can be both European and Indian. In fact the naming is significant. The word means a fair complexion, but it also signifies both the white race as well as the beloved Vaishnav saint of early modern Bengal, the great Chaitanya who was called Gouranga or Gora.

The accident of birth releases him from the burden of caste purity which had oppressed him and distanced him from his own people. He knows: 'From north to south, from east to west, all the temples of India are closed to me. I can no longer dine with any caste. In an instant, my whole life has disappeared, I am left without an identity.'[46] What does he make of this loss? He goes to Paresh with joy in his heart – not because he is a white man but because he is now truly an Indian. It is not his Indian identity that he must foreswear, it is his caste and religious identity. He can choose to be an Indian, but he could never have chosen his caste which is a function of birth and faith.

I have tried so long and so hard to merge myself in India but something

would obstinately stand in the way. . . . I tried to reconcile the obstacles
to love with what I love but I could never do it. That is why I never
dared to look at Bharat as she is, I feared to do that. I built up a perfect
ideal and I enclosed it within a fortress . . . now the fortress has disappeared and I have escaped into the lap of my real country. I no longer
need to gild and embellish what I love more than my life and I can begin
my real work at last – the welfare of twenty crores of my people. At last I
become what I have always wanted to be but never could be – an Indian.

The real and the actual, the experience and the desire, are finally
reconciled. Gora is released from his brahman and Hindu identity, and he
is set free among all Indians.

What about faith and country – how are they to be reconciled?
Gora turns to Paresh: 'Now introduce me to that God who belongs to all,
Hindus, Muslims and Christians, whose temples are not closed to any,
who is not the god of Hindus but is the god of all Indians.'

If a particular faith no longer defines the country, what, then, is
the country? Gora returns to his mother in the evening: 'Mother, you are
that mother of mine. I searched for her everywhere and all the time she
sat at home, waiting for me . . . you have no caste, no laws, no hatred,
you are the image of love. You are my Bharatbarsha.'[47]

As he returns to his mother and asks the untouchable Lachhmia
for a glass of water, he returns to another definition of the country. The
goddess disappears as the mother returns.

V

The patriotic resolution in *Gora* – humane and heroic – is not,
however, entirely seamless and internally coherent. If pride in Hindu history cannot be an ingredient of patriotic love, then on what basis does he
identify exclusively with the specific people of a designated territory? Gora,
moreover, tells Anandamoyee that she is the real face of the motherland
because she has no hatred in her. The vision of the just and egalitarian
country is life-affirming, but does it describe an actual past or present? Or,
does an ideal future masquerade as eternal past here too? The new vision
triumphs over the old because it turns to actual people and commits Gora
to their welfare. But now a new problem appears. Why should mutual care
and concern for justice be confined arbitrarily to only one people and not
embrace the entire humanity? There does not seem to be a strong reason
for this overflowing love to contract itself into a particular love, unless
the accident of birth in a designated country is revived again, with all its
attendant problems.

In a poem written soon after the novel, Rabindranath tried to find a way of merging universal love with love for Bharatbarsha. In 'Bharat Tirtha', he describes India as the confluence of all civilizations, the concourse of all the peoples of the world. Here God in Man is realized. Since India has historically been open to all cultures – being so densely marked by so many as to reach the status of being unmarked by any particular one – to love her is to love the entire world. India, then, is more than a country; it is a microcosm of the world itself, it is a symbol of the universal. The condition for this great distinction is to accept all that comes from all sources, to abolish the boundaries between authentic-indigenous and foreign-alien.

This was a courageous vision to proclaim in a colonized situation when anxieties about identities were acute: when the lines between cultural openness which signified self-confidence, on the one hand, and acculturation by an imperial culture, an abject surrender of identity, on the other, were so finely drawn as to be almost non-existent. At the same time, this humane patriotism still straddles an ambiguous and unstable ground. It too uses the past, albeit in a transformed way, to overcome the narrowness of the present. That historical characteristic, that inherited trait of the Indian past – its openness to all cultures – equally ethnocentrically claims exclusively for itself something that should be available to all humanity: love for all humanity, unrestricted by territorial borders. Indian openness had been a consequence of a series of historical conjunctures. It is translated in the poem and in the novel as her innate characterological trait.

Gora's vision thus fails to resolve the intractable problem of finding a convincing locus for patriotism. In it, the particular comes too close to the universal, patriotism threatens to dissolve into love for all the world. In order to escape ethnocentricities that pervert patriotism as Hindu nationalism, it has reached the vanishing point of patriotism itself. In this self-contradiction lies its real strength.

VI

In many ways, *Gora* ends on a happy note – unlike the two later political novels, which are dark, brooding, pessimistic. It has a hopeful approach to love. Love, eventually, conquers all, albeit with painful wrenches and problems of identity definition. It is directed at marriage and is hence acceptable within the framework of liberal individualism. So is the notion of an inclusive, non-discriminatory patriotism that provides justice and dignity to all. In *Ghare Baire*, in painful contrast, love and patriotism throw up far more stringent challenges to the liberal model. Patriotism – even the Extremist hero Sandip's – is now secular and non-

orthodox, even if its strategies and ends callously crush the livelihoods of poor Muslims and low-caste peasants. Significantly, Sandip's India is not a mother-goddess, she is the lover. Patriotism is nonetheless a project of power and self-aggrandizement at individual and national levels, imperial in its arrogance and in the lust for conquest. Sandip continues to weave the magic of words as Gora did in his early phase. But while Gora was entirely honest about what he said, Sandip is entirely manipulative. Gora's love of justice, his love for the poor and the helpless, was unwavering. Sandip has no concern for them at all. Gora had no thought for himself, and Sandip deliberately identifies the country with himself. The critique of nationalism has come very far, indeed. As a consequence, Sandip is a rather hollow fictional character, lacking the interior complexities and struggles of early Gora.

Nikhilesh, a liberal and concerned landlord, continues the benign and rational aspects of Paresh; their languages are very similar, and so is their use of evidence and logic. They distrust rhetoric and they believe in experience, rationally and honestly analysed. Nikhilesh loves his country which he identifies with an actual land and people: a people not idealized as heroic or glorious, but as embodied in the poor, helpless, ignorant, deluded peasant. For him, Panchu – the exploited cultivator – is the true face of the country. As for his love for Bimala, his wife, he needs no verbal or imaginary embellishments. He loves her even when he sees her flaws, her disastrous follies. Sandip cannot love woman or country without inflated words, inflamed imagination. Nikhilesh needs no hyperbole to transfigure the love-object. As Gora approximated the two phases of Rabindranath's politics, so Nikhilesh represents 'constructive Swadeshi'[48] or the welfarism that Rabindranath subscribed to.

At the same time, Nikhilesh's calm truths have no compelling power with which he can combat Sandip's transformation of the young and idealistic Amulya into a revolutionary terrorist, nor can they stop the waves of communal violence that Sandip unleashes on his estate. If Bimala turns away from Sandip's fatal fascination, it is because she cannot accept the way he plays with the life and values of innocent Amulya. It is not because she is persuaded by her husband's reasoning. So, the more positive patriotic alternative is clearly doomed in the novel. If we combine this failure with Rabindranath's stance on secret revolutionary violence in *Char Adhyay*, it seems that nationalism of all hues appears to him as a dead end, unless dedicated to and redeemed by universally valid human values, which would also include opposition to foreign rule.

In an excellent essay on Rabindranath, Martha Nussbaum acknowledges the truth of Nikhilesh's ideals and aspirations. But she does not find his masculinity convincing. He is too cerebral and humourless, too non-assertive to arouse passion in women. Sumit Sarkar, on the other hand, finds the new masculinity a difficult but immensely powerful alternative: its unexpected gentleness and non-possessive individualism suggest, actually, a stronger male person.[49]

Love – chosen in freedom and fulfilled within marriage – now moves towards dangerous terrain. It challenges the control of the husband – by the husband himself, as Nikhilesh admits that he has no real entitlement to compel Bimala to return to him. It admits that the woman is entitled to love a man who is not her husband: even when the husband is a superior human being whereas the lover is scheming in his political and emotional strategies, and even when she is clearly making disastrously wrong decisions. Freedom – the cardinal value in *Gora* that eventually brings narrative release – is upheld in *Ghare Baire*; but its appalling costs are made absolutely clear.

Ghare Baire deliberately evades a firm resolution to any of the questions that the novel asks. Just as Bimala, once disillusioned about Sandip and her political life, can only think back to her mother and to traditional gender as a sanctuary for her tormented self, modernity is not given a form that brings satisfaction and release. Nor is the novel a throwback to past values, to orthodoxy. Bimala may briefly want to move back into the womb of the past, but the way is clearly blocked by her own hard-won maturity of consciousness. Nikhilesh, in a rare moment of nostalgia about his childhood, is sharply reprimanded by her widowed sister-in-law who had shared his childhood days. For her, it had been the bitter time of a humiliating and loveless marriage. Neither past nor present, then, is unalloyed comfort zone. But the present, the modern, at least allows greater self-reflexivity, self-understanding; it can make its own decisions in larger freedom, however fraught they may be.

This, then, is the most radical, the most wrenching, unsparing moment in Rabindranath's entire literary history. The storm of criticism and controversy that it aroused in its times remains a testimony to the boldness of its heroic non-resolution, its unhappy commitments.[50]

Notes and References
[1] All three are included in *Rabindra Rachanabali*, Centenary edition, Vol. 1, Calcutta: Visva-Bharati, 1961.
[2] First published in London in 1917, they are included in Sisir K. Das, ed., *English Writings of Rabindranath Tagore*, New Delhi: Sahitya Akademi, 1996.
[3] Baridbaran Ghosh, ed., *Sabujpatra: Nirbachita Prabandha Sangraha*, Kolkata: New Printers, Kolkata, Introduction.
[4] *Rabindra Rachanabali*, Vol. 13, Calcutta: Visva-Bharati, 1961.

5 On the context of the novel, see Prasanta Kumar Pal, *Rabijibani*, Vol. 6, Kolkata: Ananda Publishers, 1992, pp. 93–112.

6 See Perveez Mody, 'Love and the Law: Love Marriages in Delhi', *Modern Asian Studies*, Cambridge, 36, 1, 2002.

7 See Tanika Sarkar, 'Conjugality and Hindu Nationalism: Resisting Colonial Reason and the Death of A Child Wife', in *Hindu Wife, Hindu Nation: Community, Religion and Cultural Nationalism*, New Delhi: Permanent Black, 2001.

8 Sekhar Bandyopadhyaya, *Caste, Protest and Identity in Colonial India: Namashudras of Bengal, 1872–1947*, London: Curzon Press, 1997.

9 K.K. Sengupta, *Pabna Disturbances and the Politics of Rent*, Delhi: People's Publishing House, 1974.

10 For an excellent review of the contexts behind agrarian laws, see B.B. Chaudhuri, 'Agrarian Economy and Agrarian Relations in Bengal', in N.K. Sinha, ed., *The History of Bengal*, Calcutta: Calcutta University Press, 1967; also Asok Sen, 'Agrarian Structure and Tenancy Laws in Bengal', in Sen *et al.*, eds, *Three Studies on Agrarian Structure in Bengal, 1859–1947*, Calcutta: K.P. Bagchi, 1947.

11 Sumit Sarkar, *The Swadeshi Movement in Bengal, 1903–1908*, New Delhi: Permanent Black, 2009.

12 'Sanskar', in *Rabindra Rachanabali*, Vol. 7, Calcutta: Visva-Bharati, 1961.

13 *Char Adhyay* (1934), in *Rabindra Rachanabali*, Calcutta: Visva-Bharati, 1961, p. 914.

14 'Khata' (1891–92), in *Rabindra Rachanabali*, Vol. 7.

15 Prasanta Kumar Pal, *Rabijibani*, Vol. 5, Kolkata: Ananda Publishers, 2011.

16 Prasanta Kumar Pal, *Rabijibani*, Vol. 6, Kolkata: Ananda Publishers, chapter 1, 2011.

17 On the different phases of his political and social thinking, see Sumit Sarkar, *The Swadeshi Movement in Bengal*. On his life at this time, see Prasanta Kumar Pal, *Rabijibani*, Vol. 6.

18 See Tanika Sarkar, *Bengal 1928–1934 : The Politics of Protest*, Delhi: Oxford University Press, 1987.

19 See Sumit Sarkar, 'Ghare Baire in Its Times', in P.K. Datta, ed., *Rabindranath Tagore's The Home and the World: A Critical Companion*, New Delhi: Permanent Black, 2003, pp. 243–73.

20 V.D. Savarkar, *Hindutva*, Bombay, 1923.

21 Both Subol Chandra Mitra's *Saral Bangla Abhidhan* (third edition, Calcutta, 1909) and Haricharan Bandyopadhyaya's *Bangiya Shabdakosh*, Vol. 1 (Calcutta, 1930) define *desh* as a specific region with personal connotations. Najaf Haidar advises me that *mulk* has similar associations.

22 'Bharat-tirtha', in *Rabindra Rachanabali*, Centenary edition, Vol. 1, p. 281.

23 'Oi Bhubanamonomohini' and 'Amar Shonar Bangla', in *Gitabitan*, Calcutta: Visva-Bharati, 1973, pp. 257 and 243.

24 In this regard, Sumathi Ramaswamy's recent work on the cartographic imagination in popular representations is illuminating, though the points she makes are somewhat different, since she focuses on the icons of the Bharatmata as it appeared on the maps.

25 John Strachey, *India*, London, 1886.

26 Cited in Rosane Rocher, *Orientalism, Poetry and the Millennium: The Checkered Life of Nathaniel Brassey Halhed, 1771–1830*, Delhi: Motilal Banarsidass, 1983, p. 35.

27 See, for instance, extracts from *Bangabashi* and *Dainik Samachar Chandrika* in *Report on Native Papers, Bengal*, between 1889 and 1881; also Chandranath

Basu, *Grahasthya Path*, Calcutta, 1872; Ishanchandra Basu, *Streediger Prati Upadesh*, Calcutta, and many other late nineteenth-century Bengali tracts. Outside Bengal, the great Hindi literary figure, Bharatendu Harishchandra of Benaras, developed this theme in his *Dushan Malika*. See Vasudha Dalmia,*The Nationalization of Hindu Traditions: Bharatendu Harishchandra and Nineteenth Century Banaras*, Delhi: Oxford University Press, 1996. On nineteenth- and early twentieth-century Hindu neo-orthodoxy, see Kenneth W. Jones, *Socio-Religious Reform Movements in British India: The New Cambridge History of India*, Vol. 111:1, Cambridge: Cambridge University Press, 1989, chapter 3.

[28] J.G.A. Pocock, *The Machiavellian Moment: Florentine Political Thought and the Atlantic Republican Tradition*, Princeton, NJ: Princeton University Press, 1975, chapter 1.

[29] Reformers often cited *bhakti* traditions of spiritual egalitarianism. Those, however, had restricted histories and limited acceptance in their own times, and never had the power to seriously challenge mainstream caste or gender norms for most Hindus.

[30] On this, see Sumit Sarkar, *The Swadeshi Movement in Bengal*.

[31] *Swadeshi Samaj* (1904), translated by Sumit Sarkar in *The Swadeshi Movement in Bengal*.

[32] See, for instance, 'Bijoya Festival' (1905), cited in S.C. Sarkar, *Bengal Renaissance and Other Essays*, Delhi: People's Publishing House, 1970.

[33] Rabindranath Tagore, *Nationalism*, London: Macmillan & Co., 1917; also in Sisir K. Das, ed., *English Writings of Rabindranath Tagore*, New Delhi: Sahitya Akademi, 2004

[34] *The Swadeshi Movement in Bengal*; also my 'Questioning Nationalism: The Difficult Writings of Rabindranath Tagore', in *Rebels, Wives, Saints*, Ranikhet: Permanent Black, 2009.

[35] Sumit Sarkar, *The Swadeshi Movement in Bengal*.

[36] Gora was born in 1857. He seems to be a young man in his early 20s in the novel. I conclude, therefore, that the 1870s would be the novelistic time-span, when the first flush of Hindu revivalist nationalism appeared as a force.

[37] *Gora*, in *Rabindra Rachanabali*, Centenary edition, Vol. 1, p. 8.

[38] Sumit Sarkar, 'Kaliyug, Chakri and Bhakti: Ramakrishna and His Times', in *Writing Social History*, Delhi: Oxford University Press, 1997.

[39] *Gora*, in *Rabindra Rachanabali*, Centenary edition, Vol. 1, pp. 17–18.

[40] Ibid., p. 65.

[41] Ibid., p. 101.

[42] Sudipta Kaviraj, *The Invention of Private Life*, Columbia: Columbia University Press, 2015, pp. 160–88.

[43] Ibid., pp. l00–01.

[44] Ibid., p. 263.

[45] *Gora*, p. 46.

[46] Ibid., p. 346.

[47] Ibid., pp. 348–50.

[48] See Sumit Sarkar, *The Swadeshi Movement in Bengal*.

[49] Sumit Sarkar, 'Ghare Baire in Its Times'.

[50] See Jayanti Chattopadhyaya on the many critical observations in P.K. Datta, ed., *Rabindranath Tagore's Home and the World*.

The Best of Nationalism and Beyond

Rabindranath's *Swadesh*

Anuradha Roy

In a sense, Rabindranath Tagore was not a nationalist, and a number of scholars have pointed this out. According to Ashis Nandy, Rabindranath knew of an Indian culture, and although this generated in his mind a love for India, his country, it also led to a rejection of the nation, the very concept of which he found alien and hence unacceptable.[1] Partha Chatterjee has shown how Rabindranath privileged society over the nation, which he found unsuitable for the huge, multilayered and multicultural subcontinent of India.[2] Indeed, we also know how Rabindranath became quite voluble in denouncing nationalism when he saw its dangerously selfish and aggressive manifestation during the First World War.

I tend to agree with these scholars. Yet, in this essay, I am going to give an exposition of Rabindranath's nationalism. This is because I approach the matter from a different angle. I ask this question: 'Even if Rabindranath discarded the ideology of nationalism, can the history of our nationalism dispense with Rabindranath?' The answer is clearly, 'No'. Any cultural history of Indian nationalism has to feature Rabindranath Tagore prominently. His reflections on his country evidently germinated in the context of the nationalist movement going on in India in the second half of the nineteenth century, particularly because his own family was deeply involved in it. As this nationalism went on expanding its agenda, adjusting its current programme and future goals, he not only kept pace, but also voiced its most advanced and progressive thoughts. Thus Rabindranath represented our nationalism at its best, thanks to his sensitive mind that responded powerfully to contemporary currents of thoughts.

And then came a time when he went beyond that, thanks to the remarkable originality of his mind. Thus, in the post-Swadeshi years, his relationship with the mainstream nationalist movement altered decisively and permanently. And then the First World War led to his denunciation of nationalism itself. But even while denouncing nationalism he continued to respond to the vibrancy of the national movement of his country.

Indeed, to a student of history, Rabindranath's nationalist credentials appear pretty strong.

What is interesting is that even in his Swadeshi days, i.e. his most intense nationalist phase, Rabindranath expressed clear reservations about nationalism. On the other hand, even when he vehemently denounced nationalism during the First World War, he remained bound to it. He had problems with certain modules of nationalism that he saw at home and abroad. Another problem for him was the close association between state and nation – he had a deep-seated distrust of the authoritarianism of the state.[3] But had Rabindranath known that he had the liberty to fashion his own nation rather than cling to any particular modular form – that is, had he thought of nationalism in terms of imagination and creativity, as we do today thanks to Benedict Anderson's seminal book,[4] and also, had Rabindranath been able to dissociate the nation from the state, perhaps he would not have been so impatient with nationalism. Indeed, as Partha Chatterjee has perceptively noted, Rabindranath's *swadesh*, a word that occurred frequently in his writings, was not very different from what we know as the nation today. Rabindranath had started thinking of the country in terms of imagination since his Swadeshi days. Much later he wrote in an essay included in *Kalantar*:

> In 1905 I called on the Bengalis to tell them this – create your coun-
> try inwardly with the help of *atmashakti* (self-prowess), because it is
> through creation that the truth is realized. Viswakarma finds himself in
> his own creation. To find one's country means to feel one's own soul on
> a broader basis. When we create our country with our own thoughts,
> deeds and love, we truly see our own soul in our country. Man's country
> is the creation of man's mind.[5]

Atmashakti may be regarded as a keyword in the entire life and works of Rabindranath. It was his most fundamental ideology. In the words of Shankha Ghosh:[6]

> *Atmashakti* searches itself within itself. This leads to a paradox. For the
> more it looks inward, the more it moves outward. The more it discovers
> its own identity, the more it breaks away from its ego. From the confine-
> ment of its 'I', it gets connected with a world-wide non-'I'. And this is
> called liberty.[7]

Thus the liberty of the individual and that of the country became one in Rabindranth's ideal of *atmashakti*. In fact, the entire world could be accommodated in this ideal.

Apart from *atmashakti*, another essential component of

Rabindranath's nationalism was his concept of *manush-bandha* (binding human beings). In an essay titled '*Bharatbarshiya Samaj*'('The Indian Society', 1901),[8] Rabindranath asserted that the greatness of civilization (*sabhyata*) lies in its constructive capacity of unifying the diverse – 'whether you call it "national" or by any other name does not really matter, *the point is to bind human beings (manush-bandha)*' (emphasis mine). And in another famous essay titled '*Swadeshi Samaj*' written a few months later,[9] he upheld '*manusher sange manusher atmiya sambandha sthapan*' (binding humans as relatives) as the principal effort of India from time immemorial. When I talk of Rabindranath's nationalism, I go by this assertion of his, and not by this or that technical definition of nationalism.

Evidently, what Anderson puts forward as a theory for the purpose of an academic analysis of nationalism was upheld by Rabindranath as an ideal for the practical purpose of nation-making. Indeed, if the nation is an imagined community, who can imagine it better than a visionary poet like Rabindranath who was excellent in literary craftsmanship too? It is true that like all true nationalists, he did often try to invest his nation with the 'poetry of primordiality'. But at the back of his mind he must have known that if the nation was to be imagined, there was nothing primordial about it. In fact, at times he did try to demystify the nation in a rather realistic way, as in his novel *Ghare-Baire* (1915),[10] where he showed different conceptions of the nation battling with each other in a fractured world of politics, and where in a mood of stark pessimism, he could not identify with any of these wholeheartedly. But I think, on balance, Rabindranath meant to strengthen the nation by demystifying it.

In this essay I would situate Rabindranath's nationalism in the history that produced it. He had a fairly long life, throughout which his perspectives constantly changed in response to specific historical experiences and due to the maturation of his own mind. And I want to emphasize the processuality of the whole thing. We find roughly three phases in his nationalist thinking. First, the formative phase in the nineteenth century; Second, the turn of the century that saw a new turn in his nationalism too, culminating in the enthusiasm of Swadeshi. During these first two phases, even while keeping pace with the prevalent nationalist thinking, he also stood apart, sometimes criticizing major nationalist trends and sometimes trying to give the movement interesting innovative thrusts, the most remarkable of which is of course the notion of *atmashakti*. Then, third, came the doubting post-Swadeshi years, when he tried to open up a new trajectory of the national movement. The later years that saw his response and reaction to Gandhian nationalism and other developments are of course important, but they will be dealt with rather sketchily in this essay. Anyway, I think Rabindranath's nationalism had attained a certain maturity by the time Gandhi started his experimentation with the Indian national movement, and hence the time-frame chosen for this essay is more or less adequate for making the points I wish to make.

We will see many shifts and even contradictions in Rabindranath's nationalist thinking. For example, sometimes he would look like a Hindu nationalist, sometimes a liberal nationalist and sometimes an anti-nationalist. Sometimes he would look stridently anti-British and sometimes perhaps a little pro-British. Sometimes he would talk like a traditionalist and sometimes like a modernist. But we will also notice that he was always a nationalist with a difference, and hence none of the above categories is actually adequate and fair as his description. Finally and most importantly, we will see that from beginning to end, his entire nationalist thinking revolved around some pivotal values. We have already hinted at a couple of such values – one was *atmashakti* (self-prowess) and the other was *manush-bandha* (human bondage). Associated with them was *mukti* (roughly translated as liberty), which is a sort of spiritual experience to be attained at the individual level, but only by opening oneself up to the world.[11] It is *atmashakti* that makes *mukti* possible. *Mukti* is perhaps more than freedom (*swadhinata*), which sounds comparatively mundane. However, unless one is free from external bondages in the world one cannot attain *mukti* inwardly. These underlying values provide Rabindranath's nationalism with a thread of consistency through all shifts and ambiguities.

The Earliest Phase

In his early years Rabindranath imbibed the nationalist ideology of his day that treated the nation as something given and static, to be conveniently evoked from the past. He subscribed to the historicism of contemporary nationalists. The history that Indian nationalism of those days gave itself was based on the myth of a glorious Hindu–Aryan millennium. Not only that, the notion of Muslim tyranny was an important component of this Hindu–Aryan nationalism. It was a time when the main enemy of the nation was not the British but Muslims, denounced by the repeated pejorative *Yavan*. The abiding theme of the heroic annals of this nation was resistance to Muslim invaders during the medieval era by Hindu chiefs like Prithviraj, Rana Pratap, Shivaji and others. Young Rabindranath began as a Hindu nationalist too. He wrote a historical ballad on Prithviraj at the age of eleven. He prided in the idea of a glorious Hindu–Aryan past in songs like 'Oi Bishadini Bina'('Oh, melancholy lyre', presented at the Hindu Mela, 1877) and in his poem 'Hindu Melay Upahar' ('A Gift to the Hindu Mela'). However, unlike many, he never indulged directly in *Yavan/*

Muslim-baiting, even while extolling a glorious Hindu past. He was one of those liberal Hindu nationalists who stressed *Hindutva* for the nation just to claim authenticity for it – to establish it on the basis of a strong internal principle traceable in history – and not out of any hatred for the Muslims. And we may also recall in this connection how Rabindranath savagely ridiculed the mischief and hypocrisy of Aryanism in a few poems of *Manasi* (1890): for instance, 'Max Mueller has called us Aryans and on hearing this we have stopped working.'[12]

Rabindranath was also a clear exception to the predominant sentiment of loyalty to the colonial masters which was an essential component of nineteenth-century nationalism. Poems of express loyalty were numerous in the nineteenth century, but not a single one of them was penned by him. In 1877, when Queen Victoria assumed the title 'Empress of India' and a Grand Durbar was held in Delhi on that occasion, poets of India filled the sky with the queen's glory. A few regarded the pomp and grandeur of the Durbar undesirable amid the terrible famine raging in India at that time. But Rabindranath, a teenaged boy at the time, found the very idea of submission and royalism unacceptable. He stood up on the platform of Hindu Mela and dared to declare:[13]

> Whoever sings the glory of the British
> We are not going to join him.
> We shall sing another tune.

Mostly, however, the young Rabindranath echoed the nationalist discourses of his time. But here I am hurriedly pointing out only his distinctiveness. Like many others, he addressed the country as mother, and gave idealized descriptions of the beauty and bounty of her natural features. But this mother of Rabindranath had nothing to do with the image of any Hindu deity (Durga or Kali), and was more often than not a loving and giving human mother. Even if she looked gorgeous like a goddess, it was due to the natural beauties and bounties of the land. For example, the poem '*Sharat*' ('Autumn', included in *Kalpana*, 1900):[14]

> Oh! What a lovely appearance you have before my eyes
> Today, in the autumn morn!
> Oh Mother Bengal, your lush green body is dazzling in unblemished
>   beauty
> The rivers are overflowing
> The paddy-fields are more than full
> The doyel twitters and the koyel sings
> In the gathering held in your magnificent garden

> And amid all this you stand, my mother
> In this autumn morn.

Or '*Oi Bhubanamanomohini*' ('O, you charmer of the entire world'), addressing Mother India.[15]

As the century drew to a close, a gradual change was discernable in the atmosphere. The passive, backward-looking nationalism was being infused with a forward-looking, activist spirit. The foundation of the Indian National Congress was a milestone in the process. The method of mendicancy pursued by the early Congress is well known. But in the flush of awakening this method soon came to be criticized. And Rabindranath of course spearheaded the attack, in 1887 – though he also welcomed the Congress as a platform for all-India unity:

> Clever words and crying without tears,
> Hunchbacked by carrying the platter of prayers and petitions on the shoulder.[16]

About the same time, he also expressed his annoyance at the preoccupation with the past all around him, and called his countrymen to move forward instead:

> Move forward, brother
> There is no point in falling back and lying lifeless –
> The memory of the past, the dream of it
> All this is a mere excuse for slumber.
> The pleasure of dream, in fact an illusion of pleasure,
> Oh, we don't need it any more.[17]

And he gave a number of awakening calls to his countrymen towards the end of the nineteenth century – 'Call out "Ma" just once' (1885), 'We have assembled today at the call of mother' (occasioned by the Congress session of 1886), 'Raise a joyous cry to the sky' (1892), etc.[18] Such calls became more and more common towards the end of the nineteenth century not only from Rabindranath but from many others – particularly nationalist poets of the young generation.

The late nineteenth-century awakening made the nationalists work out a programme for the nation oriented to the present and the future.[19] One important item on its agenda was boycott of foreign goods and manufacture of indigenous goods. Rabindranath became a distinguished proponent of this too:

> Mother, never let me forget that
> Your poverty is my glory.

Fie on our pride in other people's wealth,
And our habit of begging alms of them with folded arms.
Give me a simple dish of rice and spinach with your own sacred hand
I shall relish it.
Give me some coarse cloth woven with your own hand
It will remove my shame.[20]

But more importantly, Rabindranath advocated *atmashakti* for the nation about this time. And with this came a new turn in his nationalism, initiating its second phase.

A Transitional Phase at the Turn of the Century

Atmashakti involved boycott of foreign goods, practice of traditional culture and an Indian-type education (Rabindranath had already started his educational experimentation at Santiniketan), but actually its programme was much broader – an efflorescence of the auspicious and noble 'wealth of the soul'. It meant the building of character and upliftment of soul of every countryman. This ideology of inner strength flowered in a distinguished form in his collections of poems, *Utsarga* and *Naibedya*, as well as his book of essays entitled *Atmashakti* at the turn of the century.[21] He wanted to counter the west's 'endless vanity', 'crude bragging' and 'pompous luxury at the price of the poor' with the programme of *atmashakti*. He rejected the war-mongering western civilization and instead asked his countrymen to inculcate courage, self-restraint, self-sacrifice, forgiveness, tolerance, dispassionate performance of duty and other qualities. To him these comprised a rare and precious treasure lying hidden in the poverty of his country. He wanted to see India awakened in that heaven, 'Where the mind is without fear, and the head is held high / Where knowledge is free, where the world has not been broken up into fragments into the narrow domestic wall.'[22] The myth of the superiority of western civilization, both epistemic and moral, had so long acted as a major prop to the nationalists' allegiance to British rule. Rabindrantath now challenged this myth quite powerfully, thus paving the way for the nationalists' first plunge in an anti-British agitation, which was soon to be occasioned by the Partition of Bengal.

Rabindranath probably received the inspiration for *atmashakti* from within himself, but under the overwhelming influence of the historicist nationalist ideology of those days, he pointed to ancient India as the source of this inspiration. But, of course, his perception of ancient India was his own. Though in *Chaitali* (1896) he had glorified the great valour of the kshatriyas of ancient India, in *Naibedya* (1901) he was silent about

it and preferred to talk only about the hermitage of ancient sages where
the ideals of plain living and high thinking had flourished. This was surely
the good old myth of Hindu–Aryan glory, but in a new form.

For the cultivation of *atmashakti*, Rabindranath pinned his faith
on the society, and not on the nation in the European sense of the term. I
have already referred to his '*Bharatbarshiya Samaj*' ('The Indian Society',
1901), propagating '*manush-bandha*'. Here he said that the process of
unification varies from country to country and that traditional Hindu
society had done it differently from Europe. In this essay and some others like '*Swadeshi Samaj*' and '*Brahman*', written about the same time,[23]
he wanted his country to follow this Hindu social mode and the sense of
unselfish human bondage facilitated by it, and not to emulate the nation-
states of Europe. The traditional Hindu social mode he talked about
was of course the caste system, the innate human inequality of which he
chose to ignore. The premium on society was clearly pushing him away
from the idea of the European nation. But it seems that the very idea of
his *swadeshi samaj*, particularly its Hindu character, was rooted in the
nationalist thought of that time.

Of course, it must be made clear that Rabindranath's Hinduness
was not *Hindutva* in today's sense or in the sense of his contemporary
Savarkar. Rabindranath's was a very liberal ideology intending to integrate even Muslims and Christians. When, in 1902, he wrote the poem
'Shivaji Utsav' by way of an introduction to Sakharam Ganesh Deuskar's
booklet, *Shivajir Diksha*, and put into Shivaji's mouth the words, 'I shall
bind the fragmented India in a single *dharma-rajya*', it must have been a
similarly liberal Hindu *dharma* that he had in his mind. This *dharma* was
not a narrow religious system but a binding force for society, which, in
his imagination, Shivaji upheld and exercised. His was not a Shivaji who
aimed at destruction of Muslims but, rather, would accommodate them.[24]

Hinduness was indeed becoming quite strong for some years, and
at the same time becoming liberal enough to accommodate non-Hindus
(Muslims in particular) in the nation. The dichotomy between the Hindu
mainstream and Muslim 'others', however, remained even in the most liberal unitary impulse. Rabindranath was yet to go beyond this. Of course,
today we find the claim of essential Hindu tolerance and inclusiveness
hypocritical and a mask of self-aggrandizement. But those ancestors of ours
were genuinely looking for ways of accommodating Muslims in the Hindu
nation. Today, *Hindutva* hubris speaks in the language of inclusiveness.
Those days inclusiveness spoke in the language of Hinduness.

This phase of nationalism of the Bengali literati in general, and
of Rabindranath's nationalism in particular, merged with the Swadeshi

movement. Rabindranath's role in the Swadeshi movement, the first big anti-British movement of colonial Bengal, is well known.[25] He was in the forefront of the movement, supplying it with its cultural symbols, its ideal of *atmashakti*, and his numerous songs expressing the richness and promise of the time. But this movement also saw an intensification of Hindu revivalism. For the first time, Rabindranath juxtaposed the image of Durga, the Hindu goddess of power, with the image of Mother Bengal, as is evident in his song, *'Aji Bangladesher hriday hote'*.[26]

However, when one strives for *atmashakti*, *Hindutva* or any other narrow and restrictive ideology is bound to get de-emphasized. In his book of essays, *Kalantar*, written much later, Rabindranath looked back on this phase of awakening of *atmashakti* in the national life and commented:[27]

> The call to make the country one's own with the help of one's own creativity is indeed vital. It is not just a demand of external rituality. Because, unlike bees, man does not construct beehives, sticking to a fixed size and shape, and unlike spiders, he does not weave cobwebs according to a fixed pattern.

Once this is realized, there remains neither any urge to construct the beehive of the nation according to the pattern of the imaginary glory of an ancient Hindu India, nor any need to weave the cobweb of the nation according to any other module, say, the one provided by European nationalism. Thus, though *atmashakti* was overlaid with an ideal of *Hindutva* during the Swadeshi era, it necessarily tended to expand the scale of human existence beyond all narrow confines. In fact it tended to merge patriotism with a very liberal universalism that reached out to the entire world. We may recall *Utsarga*'s verse – 'O, you God of the world! How you have been manifest in my good old swadesh!' Or the very popular song composed during the Swadeshi movement – 'O the soil of my country, I bow down to your feet / Over you Mother Earth herself has spread the border of her *sari*.'[28]

It should also be remembered that the turn of the century was the phase of his life when Rabindranath discovered the real, the ordinary and the everyday nation in the rural surroundings of his zamindari estate, and developed a great empathy and sympathy therewith, as is evident in some of his short stories written about this time, his adaptation of folk-tunes for his *swadeshi* songs, and his initiative in rural reconstruction. All this contained the seeds of his later demystification of the nation. This was the ultra-nationalist phase of his life. And at the same time, quite paradoxically, he was moving away from nationalism.

A Fresh Ideological Operation of Nation-Making:
The Post-Swadeshi Phase

It is well known that Rabindranath soon got disillusioned with
the Swadeshi movement, particularly its Hindu character, and sharply
repudiated it. The novel *Gora* was the first major step in this critique.[29]
The caste system that Rabindranath had admired in 'Swadeshi Samaj' for
its tolerance and all-embracing character was shown in *Gora* as an instrument in the hands of the neo-orthodox for social oppression, leading to
social fragmentation. Ultimately, *Gora*'s patriotism transcended Hinduism
to take on a liberal humanitarian colour.

But mere criticism could not solve the problem. The vision of a
multicultural and yet singular Indian society seemed fraught with difficulties, and Rabindranath's search for it continued. Now he visualized India's
swadeshi samaj somewhat differently. He wanted to believe that India as
a microcosm of humankind had already evolved a culture of diversity and
synthesis. Yet, his was not just a static historical picture of synthesis but
a dynamic vision of constant cultural recharging informed by the ideal
of *atmashakti*. His newly-found India representing a composite culture
was presented in the song '*Bharat-Tirtha*' ('The pilgrimage that is India',
1910)[30] as 'a shore of the ocean of great humankind', where everyone
is engaged in a process of give-and-take and nobody goes away empty-
handed. What is more, he felt that this picture of the composite culture
of popular India was to be continuously created in our everyday life. '*He
mor chitta punya tirthe jagore dhire / Ei Bharater mahamanaber sagartire*'
('Oh my soul, wake up slowly in this sacred place of pilgrimage – this shore
of the ocean of great humankind, that is India'). I remember Professor
Ashin Das Gupta asked us once, during an informal discussion: Why did
Rabindranath use the word '*dhire*' (slowly) in the very first line of this
song? Only to rhyme it with '*tire*'? Was he that inept and crude a poet,
or thinker, for that matter? The answer is an obvious 'no'. Rabindranath
definitely meant it very much. A nation is not a readymade object, but has
to be made slowly – over days, months, years, centuries and even millennia
– through the imagination and efforts of its people. When Rabindranath
had advocated *atmashakti* some years back, he had had such a hunch, but
now he realized it more clearly.[31]

But this Bharat was still sanctified as a *tirtha* or a pilgrimage centre. It was something sacred and based on a singular historical principle.
Moreover, perhaps unconsciously, the poet used some Hindu symbols
like *mangalghat* (a consecrated pitcher for winning divine favour) and
omkardhwani (the mystic sound denoting the Hindu Trinity) in this song.
I do not want to read too much into all this. After all, every language has

a distinctive cultural heritage, and that of the Bengali language has many 'Hindu' religious associations which can be easily used by non-Hindus too. But one wonders if this composite culture of India is not still centred on a Hindu core. We must remember that even after this Rabindranath admired the Hindu social system for its spirit of tolerance and inclusiveness, as in the essay '*Atmaparichay*' (1912),[32] though of course this was the very liberal Hinduness of Rabindranath. Here he talked about 'Hindu Muslims', Hindu being the adjective of Muslims – and yet about the same time he also expressed reservations about the naming of Banaras 'Hindu' University, for fear that in this case the word Hindu stood in danger of very narrow interpretation by some people. He was still in two minds about the Hinduness of the nation.[33]

Possibly, Rabindranath realized soon that any stress on the compositeness of Indian culture, a singular Indian culture, would willy-nilly privilege Hinduness, which would not be quite desirable. In 1911 he wrote the song '*Janaganamana*',[34] where the country is evoked as an entity made up of many peoples, many landscapes, many histories and many cultures. In this song we do not have a composite nation but a federal nation. National unity is ensured by dedicating the land to a god called '*Bharat-bhagyabidhata*' ('the god who decides India's destiny'), but who is evidently above all nations. Maybe for a huge and multicultural land such as India, this is the only practical and healthy solution. And indeed, having been adopted as the national anthem of India, the song has provided a workable basis for the nation. However, I am always uncertain in my mind about my comparative evaluation of the two songs, '*Bharat-Tirtha*' and '*Janaganamana*'. After all, a federal nation is never as strong as a composite one, it does not evoke as much emotion as the latter. I often wish that '*Bharat-Tirtha*' instead of '*Janaganamana*' was our national anthem, of course with some modifications. If '*Tapasyabale eker anale bahure ahuti diya*' ('Sacrificing many in the fire of One by an ascetic force') sounds a little hegemonic, I would surely like to feel '*Tara mor majhe sabai biraje, keho nahe nahe dur / Amar shonite royechhe dhwanite tar bichitra sur*' ('I can feel all of them in myself – no one is distant / Hence my blood sings such varieties of music').

Evidently, Rabindranath was getting increasingly uncomfortable about how to ensure a singular Indian-ness. In '*Bharat-Tirtha*' the pluralities of India get somewhat synthesized; in '*Janaganamana*' they harmonize. In the novel *Ghare Baire*, written in 1915, they are evidently contentious. The novel explored alternative modes of nationalism associated with different ways of living.[35] The nationalism of Sandip elevated the nation to the level of a god, subordinated morality to its worship and treated it as a bounded territory he could use for fulfilling his own desires – all this involving too much of hyperbole. His was an aggressively masculinist, coercive and morally dubious character. Through this character Rabindranath showed the predicament of a nation goaded on by agitational extremism with its violent rhetoric and its encouragement of terrorism among young people. He also showed its distance from the rural masses – particularly how its cultural and political symbolism caused alienation among Muslims. The nation of Nikhilesh, on the other hand, is based on the everyday life of its people and their relationships. But this counterpoint character remains ineffectual and his failure is constantly underlined in the novel. Even while seeking mutuality with the poor peasant Panchu, this paternalist zamindar suffers from a sense of distance from the peasantry. He fails not only in his relation to his social subordinate, but also to his own wife, and thus cannot fashion a proper gender relationship for the national movement. Perhaps at that moment Rabindranath saw the difficulty of choices and found himself utterly helpless in negotiating the extremely fractured political reality.

I do not think Nikhilesh of *Ghare Baire* was anti-nationalist. He gave a strong warning of the corruptibility of nationalism and spoke for an alternative nationalism, though this alternative was evidently not satisfactory to his creator. Two years later, however, in his book *Nationalism*,[36] Rabindranath denounced nationalism globally and completely. He found now that nationalism had sprung from the greedy and unbridled pursuit of wealth that defined the industrial culture of the west. He not only criticized the nationalism of the west that had thrived long upon mutilation of humanity and led to destructive wars, but also expressed his fear of the nationalism of the east, 'for the temptation which is fatal for the strong, is still more so for the weak, and I do not welcome it in our Indian life'.

Rabindranath's demystification of the nation was now complete. But his patriotism remained as strong as ever. And he continued to lend qualified support to the nationalist movement of his country, though his relationship with it continued to remain troubled.

The Later Years

As I have already said, it would not be possible for me to deal with Rabindranath's last twenty years adequately in this paper. His critics accused him of condoning imperialism during the *Ghare Baire* phase. But he soon returned to a sustained criticism of British rule from 1917, first by condemning the internment of Annie Besant, then by renouncing his knighthood in protest against the Jalianwallabagh massacre. When Gandhi promised to give a new turn to the Indian nationalist movement, Rabindranath could not but welcome him. Basically, both of them perhaps wanted the Indian national movement to be a battle for the mind of the nation and not just a political exercise. Rabindranath had already anticipated much that was novel and distinctive in the Gandhian programme of social reform and political resistance. But then he began to feel uncomfortable about the way the concept of *satyagraha* was being used as a mere stratagem in politics and the *charkha* as a mindless *mantra*, thus strengthening bigotry and inertia all around. He found the Gandhian movement sharing the same historical and ideological impasse as the Swadeshi movement.

However, till the end Rabindranath remained always on the side of whatever dynamic, humane, freedom-loving and courageous aspects he found in the national movement. He showed ample sympathy for its activists in different streams – even for extremists and communists, with whom his differences were greater than those with Gandhi. And of course, he found the growing communal separatism lamentable.

Some Political Limitations

There are many important questions related to Rabindranath's nationalism which are beyond the scope of this paper. For example: (1) How strong was his anti-colonialism? (2) Was he a traditionalist or a modernist? (3) How did he view the question of domesticity and gender in connection with nationalism. A recently published volume of essays on *Ghare Baire* has raised all these questions in inter-related and insightful ways, and created scope for debate.[37] But I refrain from responding to it right now. I would say only this much:

(1) Why should all thoughts about the country and its national movement be preoccupied by a single colonial/anti-colonial binary? To my mind, Rabindranath's anti-colonial credentials are above any doubt. But sometimes he surely found some other things more important than anti-colonial resistance, which led him to serious introspection. And, of course, he dissociated his criticism of the Raj from any downright denigration of the British or western people and their culture.

(2) I think he was neither wholly traditionalist (and I think Ashis Nandy is wrong in regarding him so) nor an unqualified modernist in the western sense. Perhaps he wanted a modernity in indigenous and ultimately on his own terms. Because that was not easily attainable, he had a love–hate relationship with modernity till the very end.

(3) Similarly, a tension between modernity and traditionalism always

remained in Rabindranath's mind in regard to the women's question.

So Rabindranath's nationalism cannot really be understood in terms of stereotypical binaries that feature in most discussions of nationalism. Rather, we have to understand it in terms of its process. It travelled a long way through many shifts, and even involved quite a few confusions and contradictions. This was due to his positional limitations. For example, his Hindu-nationalist milieu made him a sort of Hindu nationalist too, though very briefly and in a somewhat different sense. He was not invariably well-informed about everything that was going on, sometimes certain aspects of reality did elude his understanding, and yet he was obliged to express his opinion about them. In admiring the social harmony of the *swadeshi samaj*, he indirectly supported the hierarchical logic of the caste system, though later he openly criticized the inequities involved in it.

Then, Sumit Sarkar is probably right in saying that the ineffectuality of Nikhilesh in *Ghare Baire* largely emanates from Rabindranath's own position as a paternalistic zamindar. It made him unable to understand the changes in the world around, which made the binary framework of evil politician/paternalistic landlord insufficient for grasping its complexities.[38]

Amartya Sen has pointed out another positional limitation of Rabindranath.[39] He questions Rabindranath's fond belief that the effort to establish unity amidst diversity was a dominant feature of Indian culture and furthermore an exclusively Indian tradition. Sen first interrogates such a systematic attempt to focus on unity rather than discord, and then asks: Even if the tendency towards unity is seen as the Indian reality, was this really a special feature of India? Haven't many other countries also seen diversity, invasion and absorption? Sen seems to be very right. The synthesizing tendencies of India may be seen as being overshadowed by diversities from another point of view. And indeed, we have instances of absorptive cultures in history other than India. The history of Great Britain readily comes to mind in this connection.

However, I would like to point out that Rabindranath actually thought that this unity amidst diversity was a feature of the entire human civilization, which was manifest in India too. That he did not claim this to be an essentially Indian virtue is clear from his essay, '*Bharatvarsher Itihaser Dhara*'.[40] At the same time, I would not deny that India had a specially privileged place in his heart in this regard. And Sen is not perhaps wide off the mark when he says that such a prejudice for India was natural for Rabindranath as a subject of a colonial empire. He held to the position of a practical commitment to national cohesion and was engaged in the task of making an Indian nation out of a pre-nationalist entity named 'Bharat' – a nation for which he demanded the right of self-determination. In this task he found the uniting features of Indian culture more important than diversity and discord. Moreover, he had to take on the challenge of British cultural superiority in this exercise. He had to counter the British claim that whatever little unity India had was due to the *Pax Britannica*. In this situation, such a prejudiced view of Rabindranath did have much practical value.

We may add to this. Even though Rabindranath acknowledged and respected the diversity of Indian culture, on the question of language, he refused to consider Oriya and Assamese as distinctive languages independent of his own Bengali.[41] This was due to his positionality as a Bengali-speaking person, particularly a Bengali litterateur.

It is well known that Rabindranath was misinformed about the rising ideology of fascism, and therefore admired Mussolini's fascist variety of nationalism during his visit to Italy in 1926. However, on realizing its true nature he recanted. Indeed he was not infallible and I am not trying to iconize him.[42] On the whole, however, his nationalism was self-reflexive and introspective. So his limitations could not keep him tied down for long.

The Legacy

Partha Chatterjee has questioned the relevance of Rabindranath's legacy in his essay on Rabindranath's nationalism.[43] He argues that Rabindranath knew that to bind men on a plane bigger than a small village of face-to-face contact, some sort of mechanism or '*kal*' (in Rabindranath's language) was needed, and that he distrusted any kind of mechanism as artificial and hence contrary to the spirit of human bondage. Binding social exchanges through a technology of power was not his cup of tea and thus he showed no interest at all in the '*kshamatatantra*' of the modern era that was making its way into Indian politics in his lifetime – a system of diffused power that we call democracy. So, says Chatterjee, Rabindranath's social thoughts are no longer relevant for us. For today, we are not concerned with abstract morality but with a 'strategic morality' required by democracy, where the common and the average have a big role to play. Chatterjee admires Rabindranath's urge for *atmashakti*, but says that it is imperative we formulate the mantra of *atmashakti* ourselves.

On the last point, I fully agree with Chatterjee. Let us look up to Rabindranath, and for that matter all other thinkers of the past (e.g., Gandhi, Karl Marx), as part of an inspiring tradition to be cherished and not to be blindly emulated. Ultimately, such people are relevant to us as *byakti-bhabuks* (inward-looking individual thinkers) only, and not as practical guides in today's vastly changed situations. However, I would have to protest that calling Rabindranath anti-democratic is a bit unfair to him. Recently, Asok Sen and Abhra Ghosh have taken on Chatterjee on this issue and I am not going to repeat their arguments here.[44] But what I find important is that for an ordinary individual like me, Rabindranath's nationalism seems to have some relevance in another sense too. It has a moral centrality and an ethical imperative which, even if they cannot guide a political scientist in fashioning a big political project, help us restore the human essence in our individual lives. I find the moral premises it was based on and the human values associated with it very relevant to us even today. In fact Rabindranath's nationalism, if any such thing existed at all, did so because of some fundamental human values, which seem very valuable to us even if we take them away from their nationalist moorings. We have already identified three such values – *atmashakti, manush-bandha* and *mukti.*

In this increasingly fetishized world dominated by multinationals and media, with the state acting as their instrument and human beings increasingly turning into automatons, the ideal of *atmashakti* can meaningfully connect the dignity and creative power of the self with that of a bigger collectivity. It can unfold our human capacities, draw us towards humanity and on the whole have a defetishizing effect. The precise application of *atmashakti* is of course a matter of strategy that has to be worked out on the basis of concrete study of the concrete situation. Rabindranath did it in his own way.

The ideal of *mukti*, which is closely associated with *atmashakti*, and which means liberty both within oneself and in the outside world, made him question all forms of domination of man by man, and all forms of congealed, constricting and authoritative frameworks of thought. This made him a critic of British rule, of Hindu orthodoxy, of Swadeshi nationalism, of Gandhian nationalism and a critic of nationalism itself.

Rabindranath's ideal of *manush-bandha* or human bondage has some very interesting aspects. Let me elaborate. First, it means a concern with what one sees around oneself rather than with things remote and abstract. Elsewhere I have called this '*kachha-kachhibad*' (near-ism),[45] for lack of a better term. Rabindranath himself showed concern for the *kachha-kachhi* or the 'near' again and again. His concern for *kachha-kachhi* is manifest in the essay titled '*Byadhi o Pratikar*'(1907),[46] where he vehemently denounced the animosity between Hindus and Muslims just on the ground of their living close to each other – 'We live on the same land amid the same joys and sorrows. If we do not become one, it is shameful, it is irreligious!'[47] Rabindranath was not an abstract philosopher or poet detached from the real life.

In a very different context, he wrote about the dangerous implications of metaphysical thoughts that take man away from his immediate surroundings and deny the immediate reality. While flying to Persia (Iran) in 1932, he came to know that Baghdad was being bombed from the sky. He was aboard a plane himself, which gave him a rare insight into what was happening in Baghdad, and he painfully reacted:

> The creation is manifest in particular structures of concrete time and space. As the outlines of that structure get blurred, the creation tends to dissolve. Its existence then becomes intangible, its hold on the mind becomes weak – when the reality that a man is attached to gets blurred, the attachment loses its moorings.[48]

Hence, he said, it was so easy to drop a bomb from an aircraft and kill people far below. He added that the abstract theorization in the *Gita* was like an aircraft. Krishna used it to take away the mind of Arjuna to a distant land, where who kills and who gets killed do not matter.

Indeed, Rabindranath's love for life was of a very intimate nature – the kind that takes great pleasure in saying, '*ghase ghase pa phelechhi baner pathe jete*' ('I have trodden upon every blade of grass on my way through the forest').[49] This kind of intimacy with life is surely a safeguard against alienation. It helps ordinary individuals to live their lives meaningfully.

Secondly, his urge for human bondage was related to the ideal of universal humanism. If it wants to tread upon every blade of grass, it also responds to '*bishwa-bhara pran*' ('the life that pervades the entire world'). It is not just a matter of joy for a handful of individual hearts, as Chatterjee somewhat sarcastically says. It is an urge to open oneself up to the entire humankind – its joys, sorrows, struggles for existence and of course its cultural wealth.

One may ask whether this ideal of universal humanism negates nationalism. To some extent it does. But despite being a strong universal humanist, Rabindranath did recognize certain cultural barriers that largely regulated one's capacity to reach out, though not entirely. To him, humanism was indeed universal and very much accessible in its basic ethos. But the coating of culture does create some problems. In his *Europe Jatrir Diary* (*The diary of a traveller to Europe*), a young Rabindranath wrote:[50] 'Now I desperately want to go home. There I know everyone understands everyone. There, overcoming all outer barriers, I can taste humanism easily.' In this connection he retold the famous tale of Aesop about the fox inviting the crane and serving food to the latter on a saucer, and the crane inviting the fox and serving food in a pitcher. Rabindranath ended the story with the comment – 'In any national feast, this is the plight of a foreigner.' Not that Rabindranath regarded the problem as insurmountable. But he knew that some conscious effort and systematic training were required to overcome the problem.[51]

I find all these values that gave structure to Rabindranath's nationalism very relevant even today. I am not talking of any big social or political project of *nirman* (construction), but of *srishti* (creation).[52] And I am talking primarily of individual lives. These values may help many of us live our individual lives in a meaningful, confident and dignified manner.

Notes and References

As I have tried to show the process of Rabindranath's thought regarding his *swadesh* in this essay, I have to give the original dates of all his works I have cited. But for the actual citations, unless otherwise mentioned, I have relied heavily on the volumes of *Rabindra-Rachanabali*, Calcutta: Visva-Bharati, which has a total of twenty-seven volumes plus two volumes titled *Achalita Samgraha*. For the songs I have mostly used *Geetabitan* (three volumes), again a Visva-Bharati publication. All translations are mine, unless otherwise cited.

[1] Ashis Nandy, *Illegitimacy of Nationalism: Rabindranath Tagore and the Politics of Self*, Delhi: Oxford University Press, 1994.

[2] Partha Chatterjee, 'Rabindrik Nation Ki?' and 'Rabindrik Nation Prasange Aro Duchar Katha', in *Praja o Tantra*, Kolkata: Anushtup, 2005. Here I refer to the first essay in particular, published in the journal *Baromas*, which generated some interesting reactions and prompted Chatterjee to write the second essay by way of a rejoinder.

[3] Usually Rabindranath used the word 'nation' even in his Bengali writings, as he could not think of an equivalent Bengali word. Bengalis often use the word 'jati' for 'nation'. 'Jati' is a very pliable word, which can denote several human units (based on species, gender, religion, caste and so on) at the same time. But Rabindranath was reluctant to add the nation to its usage. However, in a letter to Rebati Barman dated 22 January 1932, he wrote that the term 'rashtrajati' could be used for 'nation' in Bengali. This letter has been cited in Chinmohan Sehanavis, *Rabindranath o Biplabisamaj*, Calcutta, BS 1392/1985. It is evident that Rabindranath could not dissociate the nation from the state. This, of course, is true of most people. But can we not think of a world which will have nations in a very loose sense, but no states? In fact, in socio-linguistics there are two different words for distinguishing nationalism as self-identity from nationalism related to the state. The former is called nationalism and the latter, 'nationism' (a term coined by Joshua A. Fishman).

[4] Benedict Anderson, *Imagined Communities: Reflections on the Origin and Spread of Nationalism*, London: Verso, 1983.

[5] 'Satyer Ahvan', written in BS 1328/1921. It was later included in the book of essays entitled *Kalantar* (BS 1344/1937), *Rabindra-Rachanabali*, Vol. 24, Calcutta: Visva-Bharati, 1970.

[6] Sankha Ghosh, 'Ami', included in his book of essays, *Nirman o Srishti*, Kolkata: Papyrus, BS 1399/1992.

[7] In the French tradition of liberty, this is called *amour de soi*, as distinct from

amour propre. Amour de soi is natural self-love, living within oneself independent of the will and judgment of others. This means freedom for original thinking, love and creativity. This is unsullied sovereignty of man's self, innate to his original nature. *Amour propre*, on the other hand, is liberty that is defined in other people's terms, i.e. freedom to acquire money, fame, etc. This is living outside oneself, in the opinion of others. It means egoistic self-interest and vanity that corrupts one's original nature and eclipses one's natural self-regard. Paradoxically, *amour propre*, despite being dependent on others in a sense, is actually selfish; while *amour de soi* is the flourishing of the self but outside of the self. See Paul M. Cohen, *Freedom's Moment: An Essay on the French Idea of Liberty from Rousseau to Foucault*, London: The University of Chicago Press, 1997.

8. *'Bharatvarshiya Samaj'*, written in 1901, was included in the book of essays *Atmashakti* (BS 1312/1905), *Rabindra-Rachanabali*, Vol. 3, Calcutta: Visva-Bharati, 1969. (First published BS 1346.)

9. *'Swadeshi Samaj'* was included in *Atmashakti*, ibid.

10. *Ghare Baire* was published serially in *Sabuj Patra* during 1915. It is available in *Rabindra-Rachanabali*, vol. 8, Calcutta: Visva-Bharati, 1967. (First published BS 1348.)

11. Now one may protest – 'The world is surely much more than the nation or *swadesh*!' But I would argue that in Rabindranath's world his *swadesh* did have a primacy. He was deeply rooted in his *swadesh* and can never be called denationalized. A contrast with Frantz Fanon will perhaps help us understand this better. Fanon, the famous post-colonial philosopher and a champion of human liberty, had a basic similarity with Rabindranath in his world view. But he did not have his roots in any particular land. He was born in the Caribbean island of Martinique. Later he migrated to France, and then to the French colony Algeria, where he participated in the struggle for liberation of the Algerians. His widely acclaimed book *The Wretched of the Earth* emerged from his Algerian experiences. His country or nation was not important for Fanon. This cannot be said of Rabindranath.

12. The poem *'Bangabeer'*, written in 1888, was included in the book of verses *Manasi* (BS 1297/1890), available in *Rabindra-Rachanabali*, Vol. 2, Calcutta: Visva-Bharati, 1966 (first published BS 1346). In fact, the urge to accommodate the Muslims in the nation even after harrying them out as 'others' was a general feature of the nineteenth-century nationalism of Bengal. This urge became increasingly powerful towards the end of the century. See my *Nationalism as Poetic Discourse in Nineteenth Century Bengal*, Kolkata: Papyrus, 2003, especially the chapter entitled 'Foreign Tyrants or Foster Brothers? Muslims in the Eyes of Hindu Nationalists'.

13. The poem *'Dillir Darbar'* written for Hindu Mela, cited in Jogesh Chandra Bagal's *Hindu Melar Itibritta*, Calcutta: Talpata, BS 1375/1968.

14. The poem *'Bange Sharat'* included in the verse-book *Kalpana* (BS 1307/1900), available in *Rabindra-Rachanabali*, Vol. 7, Calcutta: Visva-Bharati, 1965 (first published BS 1348).

15. The song *'Oi Bhubanamanomohini'* was composed in BS Poush 1303/1896 and included in *Kalpana*, under the title *'Bharatlakshmi'*. It has been included in the section 'Swadesh' in the collection of Tagore songs entitled *Geetabitan*, Vol. 1, Calcutta: Visva-Bharati, 1968 (first published BS 1348).

16. The first line of this song is *'Tabu parina sampite pran'*; it was written in BS 1294/1887 and included in the section *'Jatiya Sangeet'* in *Geetabitan*, Vol. 3, Calcutta: Visva-Bharati, 1969 (first published BS 1357).

[17] Composed in BS 1294/1887. Included in the section '*Swadesh*' in *Geetabitan*, Vol. 1.

[18] In the original Bengali, '*Ekbar tora ma bolia dak*', '*Amra milechhi aaj mayer dake*' and '*Anandadhwani jagao gagane*', respectively. The first song is available in the section '*Jatiya Sangeet*' in *Geetabitan*, Vol. 3; the other two are in the section '*Swadesh*' in *Geetabitan*, Vol. 1.

[19] In *Nationalism as Poetic Discourse*, I have discussed several aspects of the cultural nationalism of the Bengali *bhadralok* of the nineteenth century. The mood of activism in the late nineteenth century has been discussed too. See the chapter titled 'Working out a Programme for the Nation', in particular.

[20] Published in *Bharati*, BS 1305, included in *Kalpana*, available in *Rabindra-Rachanabali*, Vol. 7, Calcutta: Visva-Bharati, 1965 (first published BS 1348).

[21] *Naibedya* was published in BS 1308/1901, available in *Rabindra-Rachanabali*, Vol. 8, Calcutta: Visva-Bharati, 1967 (first published BS 1348). *Utsarga* was published much later, but most of its poems had been included in Mohitchandra Sen, ed., *Kabyagrantha*, published in BS 1310/1903. *Utsarga* is available in *Rabindra-Rachanabali*, Vol. 10, Calcutta: Visva-Bharati, 1971 (first published BS 1348). *Atmashakti* was published in BS 1312/1905. It contained '*Nation Ki?*', '*Bharatvarshiya Samaj*', '*Swadeshi Samaj*' and other essays. *Atmashakti* is available in *Rabindra-Rachanabali*, Vol. 3.

[22] The original poem is titled '*Prarthana*' and it appeared in *Naibedya*. Tagore translated it into English and included it in *Geetanjali (Song Offerings)*, London: The India Society, 1912.

[23] '*Brahman*' was included in the book of essays entitled *Bharatvarsha* (BS 1312/1905), available in *Rabindra-Rachanabali*, Vol. 4, 1965 (first published BS 1347). The essays of *Bharatvarsha* had been originally published in *Nabaparyay Bangadarshan*.

[24] '*Shivaji Utsav*' was written in 1904, in *Rabindra-Rachanabali*, Vol. 3 ('*Parisishta*'), Calcutta: Visva-Bharati, 1961. In this connection one may mention the poems of his book *Katha o Kahini* (BS 1306/1899), written towards the end of the nineteenth century. Quite a few poems describe struggles of Hindus and Sikhs against Muslim aggressors during the medieval period ('*Bandi Beer*', '*Prarthanatit Dan*', '*Horikhela*', etc., are well known among them). But on the whole the book seems to evoke just the ideal of death-defying courage for the sake of honour and dignity. The poem '*Mani*' even shows the generosity of Aurangzeb towards a rebel Rajput prince. The book also describes struggles other than Hindu–Muslim conflicts, e.g., that of Dumraj, the Rajput owner of a fort, against the Maratha dacoits. The poems mentioned above are in the section '*Kahini*' of *Katha o Kahini*, and '*Kahini*' is available in *Rabindra-Rachanabali*, Vol. 5, Calcutta: Visva-Bharati, 1967(first published BS 1347).

[25] See Sumit Sarkar, *The Swadeshi Movement in Bengal 1903–1908*, Delhi: Peoples' Publishing House, 1973.

[26] The song has such lines – 'Your right hand is flashing a falchion and your left hand is assuring us of safety / Two smiling eyes are full of affection, but the third eye on the forehead is emitting fire.' The song is in the section '*Swadesh*' in *Geetabitan*, Vol. 1.

[27] The essay entitled '*Satyer Ahvan*' is in *Kalantar*.

[28] This line – '*Mile gechho ogo bishvadevata mor sanatan swadeshe*' – occurs in poem no. 16 of *Utsarga*, written just before the Swadeshi movement. The song '*O amar desher mati*' was composed in the course of the Swadeshi movement. It is included in the section '*Swadesh*' in *Geetabitan*, Vol. 1.

[29] *Gora* was published serially in *Prabasi* during 1907–08. It is available in

Rabindra-Rachanabali, Vol. 6, Calcutta: Visva-Bharati, 1969 (first published BS 1347).

[30] '*Bharat Tirtha*' was written in BS 1317/1910. It is song number 106 in the '*Swadesh*' section of *Geetabitan,* Vol. 1.

[31] The essay '*Bharatvarsher Itihaser Dhara*', written in 1912, is included in the book of essays *Parichay,* available in *Rabindra-Rachanabali,* Vol. 18, Calcutta: Visva-Bharati, 1966 (first published BS 1351). It identified unity in diversity and a cohesive efflorescence transcending all conflicts as the hallmark of the culture and civilization of the whole world, and noted its manifestation in Indian culture as well – 'It is not the nature of India to disperse itself among the diverse. India strives for the One and thus tries to make all diversities cohere in a unified whole.'

[32] The essay '*Atmaparichay*' was published in the journal *Tattvabodhini,* BS 1319/1912. It was included in the book of essays *Parichay* (BS 1323/1916), which is available in *Rabindra-Rachanabali,* Vol. 18.

[33] The essay '*Hindu-Vishwavidyalaya*' was published in *Prabasi,* BS 1318/1911. It was included in *Parichay, Rabindra-Rachanabali,* Vol. 18.

[34] '*Janaganamana*' was written in 1911 and sung for the first time at the Calcutta session of the Indian National Congress on 27 December of that year. It is included in the section '*Swadesh*' in *Geetabitan,* Vol. 1.

[35] For some thoughtful essays on *Ghare Baire,* see P.K. Datta ed., *Rabindranath Tagore's The Home and the World: A Critical Companion,* New Delhi: Permanent Black, 2003.

[36] Rabindranath Tagore, *Nationalism,* London: Macmillan Company, 1917.

[37] P.K. Datta, ed., *Rabindranath Tagore's The Home and the World.*

[38] Sumit Sarkar's essay in ibid.

[39] Amartya Sen, 'On Interpreting India's Past', in Sugata Bose and Ayesha Jalal, eds, *Nationalism, Democracy and Development: State and Politics in India,* Delhi: Oxford University Press, 1997.

[40] '*Bharatvarsher Itihaser Dhara*', *Rabindra-Rachanabali,* Vol. 18.

[41] Lakshminath Bezbaroa, an eminent writer of Assamese literature and nephew-in-law of Rabindranath, sounds very aggrieved about this. Not only Rabindranath, educated Bengalis in general were very proud that the neighbouring Assamese and Oriya languages were mere dialects of Bengali and also inferior to it. For a trenchant criticism of this superiority complex of the Bengalis, see Debaprasad Bandyopadhyay, '*Banglar Khoabnama*', in Debabrata Chattopadhyay, ed., *Bangabhanga Pratirodher Satavarsha,* Kolkata: Pustak Bipani, 2006.

[42] The period that we have marked as the third phase of Rabindranath's *swadesh*-related thinking has earned him considerable criticism from his contemporaries as well as later-day academics. One example is Bikash Chakravarty, 'Tagore's Idea of Culture and Arnoldian Context', in Jashodhara Bagchi, ed., *Literature, Society and Ideology in Victorian Era,* New Delhi: Sterling Publishers Pvt. Ltd., 1991, pp. 294–313. What Chakravarty says is roughly as follows. Since 1907, Rabindranath withdrew from nationalist politics, started spending most of his time at Santiniketan, away from the din and bustle of Calcutta, and took an aesthetic way out of the historical contingencies of the time, turning away his face from the burning colonial issues. He now insisted on disengaging the social and moral from the political questions. Politics was viewed as merely an external thing, over which the 'life of the mind' should be prioritized and in its turn would rouse the life of the society. According to Chakravarty, from about this time Rabindranath forcefully and urgently pleaded for an 'ideology of culture' comprising some timeless universal truths and free from the pressures of his-

torical necessities. Drawing largely on Mathew Arnold's cultural arguments, it was culture where Rabindranath now sought beauty, spiritualism and liberty (though sometimes he quoted the *Upanishadas,* too, in support of his stand). For creating and nurturing this culture, he used a clerisy argument and riveted his faith on a few culturally-minded leaders of society. Furthermore, he placed the mantle of this culture mainly on the Brahmos and took the initiative in unifying the fragmented Brahmo society of Calcutta for this purpose. Also, instead of blaming the British for the growing communal tension, he now questioned the role of his Indian compatriots ('*Byadhi o Pratikar*', 1907) in this matter. He presented the typical Victorian argument of 'prematurity' in this connection, contending that the English had come to India to draw the Indians towards humankind, that this would do India good, and until this happened the English would continue to govern the Indians, and also beat and injure them (the lecture entitled '*Purba o Paschim*', 1908). This argument of Rabindranath minimized the tyranny of colonialism. When he did protest against the internment of Annie Besant and also against the Jalianwallahbagh Massacre, he presented the argument of 'small English and big English' thereby blunting the edge of his protest. His rural reconstruction programme was aimed at 'co opting the discontent of the masses'. To weaken the militancy of political extremism, he tried to divert its energy to moral and cultural activities. All this was to help restore the wounded self-respect of the Bengalis, and at the same time to remain politically innocuous. Chakravarty adds that in this ideology of culture, the stress was not so much on ethics as on aesthetics. The same ideal of aesthetics rather than ethics guided Rabindranath's notion of unity among diversity too. Hence the ethical efforts of Nikhilesh in *Ghare-Baire* appears rather artificial to Chakravarty. To him, this character is based on a sense of aesthetics determined by its own inner greatness rather than practical experiences in the external world. The character is imbued with a lot of dramatic elements too, for the sake of aesthetics and nothing else.

Needless to say, my understanding of Rabindranath's nationalist thoughts is very different from that of Chakravarty's. The present article has hopefully made this clear. I do not want to enter into a full-fledged argument with Chakravarty in this respect. Of course, Rabindranath had his positional limitations, which I have briefly discussed in the body of my text. The myth of 'big/good and small/bad English' dichotomy had been there in the collective mind of the nationalist *bhadralok* since the nineteenth century and Rabindranath could not escape it too. I have no problem in agreeing with Chakravarty here. But I would not agree with his most fundamental criticism – that Rabindranath escaped from the reality of the time and tried to create an illusion centring on the country. And I find Chakravarty's explanation of Rabindranath's rural reconstruction very uncharitable. Above all, I think that despite all its limitations, Rabindranath's nationalist thinking provides us with notions of some basic human values, which one can pick up and practice.

However, I am grateful to Chakravarty for drawing my attention to the fact of Mathew Arnold's influence on Rabindranath at this point of time. But I see it producing a very different result – the Arnoldian paradigm of culture ('all the love of our neighbour, the impulses towards action, help, the beneficence, the desire for removing human error, clearing human confusion, and diminishing human misery, the noble aspiration to leave the world a better and happier than we found it') perhaps helped Rabindranath to present the notion of a composite humane culture as the basis of his country in the place of a Hindu culture, and also to view this culture not as something given but to be continuously nurtured in the everyday life of people.

[43] The two essays of Partha Chatterjee, '*Rabindrik Nation Ki?*' and '*Rabindrik Nation Prasange Aro Duchar Katha*', in *Praja o Tantra*.

[44] See Asok Sen, '*Rajnitir Pathakrame Rabindranath*', *Bangadarshan*, January–December 2005 and January–December 2006. Sen has discussed democracy in the second installment. Also see Abhra Ghosh, *Ganatantrer Rabindrik Paradigm o Unnayan*, Kolkata: K.P. Bagchi, 2009. Both Sen and Ghosh argue that Rabindranath was not against democracy and that rather some of his thoughts can be used to enrich the concept of democracy. Here I will try to summarize their contentions very briefly, at the risk of oversimplification. Rabindranath, who talked about creating the country through all-pervasive social efforts and took actual initiative in this direction, can hardly be called anti-democratic. Through his rural reconstruction work, he tried to construct an ideal India in a miniature form in his own zamindari estate, because that was the only area where he could realize his ideal. He gave considerable thought to work out the details of rural development. And in this respect, he did not always avoid 'kal' or machine. He showed considerable concern for the institutional aspects of rural reconstruction – right from its constitutional code to the division of *mandals*, allocation of duties, and establishment of cooperative banks. His objection was to '*kal*' as a source of dehumanization and alienation factor. He resented the loss of human control to '*kal*', '*kal*' robbing man of his creativity. The '*kal*' that was likely to promote well-being of people was welcome to him. It is also to be remembered that in planning the rural reconstruction he hoped that the raiyats would soon give up their dependence on the zamindar and assume the organizational responsibility themselves. It is not true that Rabindranath held the elitist view that only one or a few big leaders could guide the country properly. He never neglected the common people. After all, it is he who demanded political lectures to be delivered in Bengali to reach out to the people in an age when lectures in English were the usual norm. His aim in this case was formation of public opinion that would facilitate self-rule. It is, however, true that he did not believe in the *kshamatatantra* embedded in the state. The adverse effects of *kshamatatantra* were too obvious to him. Also, he had no taste for the process of apportionment of power within *kshamatatantra*. He wanted even the Hindu–Muslim problem to be solved not through such calculated apportionment, but through constructive work on a collective basis at the rural level. Rabindranath cannot really be blamed if he did not take much interest in the democracy that he saw in India during his time. Its appearance was not very inspiring indeed. It was just an electoral system which allowed voting rights to 10–12 per cent of the population only. In any case, even today, democracy is just a vehicle of greedy capitalism. In his book *Samabayniti* Rabindranath said quite insightfully that in a situation of conflict between capital and labour, democracy could not really thrive (a contention that reminds us of Karl Marx!). It is true that democracy has pushed this conflict under the carpet and constructed a durable power structure behind the optimistic rhetoric of 'governmentality' and 'development' where subjugation becomes possible with support from the subjugated and oppression is carried out with support from the oppressed (here Asok Sen has used the theory of Michel Foucault). Should not the real democrats give their primary attention to the fundamental principle of democracy rather than its tactical details? Rabindranath was not disinterested in democracy, but could not tolerate its deceitful manifestation that was quite evident. He wanted a deeper efflorescence of democratic consciousness – not only at the level of the state, but in society, family, everywhere. He had no faith in democracy in its western form, which was a mere politics of number. He was more interested in the spirit of democracy.

45 'Swadesh Swadesh Koris Kare', in Debabrata Chattopadhyay, ed., *Bangabhanga Pratirodher Shatavarsha*, Kolkata: Pustak Bipani, 2006.
46 'Byadhi o Pratikar', published for the first time in *Bangadarshan*, BS 1314/1907. Included in the collection of essays titled *Samaj* (reprinted as *Gadyagranthabali*, Vol. 13, BS 1315/1908). The essay is available in *Rabindra-Rachanabali*, Vol. 12, Calcutta: Visva-Bharati, 1960 (first published BS 1349).
47 Ibid.
48 *Parasye* was first published in the twin travelogue *Japane-Parasye* in BS 1343/1936. *Parasye* is available now in *Rabindra-Rachanabai*, Vol. 2, Calcutta: Visva-Bharati, 1966 (first published BS 1346).
49 The first line of the song is '*Akashbhara suryatara, biswabhara pran*', in the section '*Prakriti*', *Geetabitan*, Vol. 11 (2).
50 This particular letter of *Europe Jatrir Diary* was written on 6 October 1890. It is included in *Rabindra-Rachanabali*, Vol. 1, Calcutta: Visva-Bharati, 1968 (first published BS 1346). The original book was published in two volumes, in BS 1298/1891 and BS 1300/1893 respectively.
51 In the same diary Rabindranath said that he already had the requisite training in the field of literature to be able to appreciate European literature. However, so far as European music was concerned, he was gradually beginning to derive pleasure from it by paying it proper attention. Of course, we know that as days went by, he became more and more equipped to scale the 'national' barriers.
52 See Sankha Ghosh, *Nirman o Srishti*.

SECTION FOUR

The Concept of Poverty in Colonial India

Sabyasachi Bhattacharya

How was 'poverty' conceptualized in colonial India? It is argued in this essay that there are three distinct discursive traditions in this regard. A certain approach to the issue of 'poverty' was brought from Europe by British colonial administrators. The ideas of Jeremy Bentham and the Poor Law in England contain a tradition of thinking on poverty. Under the influence of capitalist ethics, poverty was regarded in nineteenth-century England as a mark of economic inefficiency, and the poor were regarded as a burden on the national economy in so far as they, being inefficient in a competitive world (and in the case of the unemployed poor and vagabonds, totally unproductive), caused consumption of a part of the national wealth which they did not create. Bentham's *Pauper Management Improved* (1798) provided the blueprint for a new Poor Law, which was given its final shape by his former secretary Chadwick in the Poor Act of 1834. This trend of managing poverty, and its discontents and problems, deeply influenced Indian colonial thinking, as evidenced in the Famine Laws from 1888 onwards (a point ignored by Eric Stokes in his otherwise perceptive history of Utilitarianism in India).

The idea of poverty appears in a different form in the nationalist discourse, most typically in the writings of Dadabhai Naoroji, author of *Poverty and Un-British Rule in India* (1901). Naoroji made a departure from the colonial bureaucratic approach in rejecting the palliative approach and addressing himself to the causative aspect of poverty. Another significant departure was his macro approach towards national income estimation, in contrast to the bureaucratic tendency to generalize from isolated instantiation. On the basis of Naoroji's private papers, now in the National Archives of India, this essay argues that his quantitative method was influenced by his acquaintance with Thorold Rogers, professor of political economy at Oxford. Moreover, Naoroji brought into the discourse of poverty in India an international comparative approach, constantly comparing metropolitan Europe with colonial India. Above all, nationalist thinking on India's poverty had a strong historical content, and probed the link between the impact of British rule and India's impoverishment. Thus there developed a critique of the colonial approach to poverty, and eventually an agenda of political action.

Finally, there is a question rarely asked in academic writings: How did the poor in India look at poverty? Was there a notion of poverty prevalent among the labouring poor in India different from the two above? While we do have a few studies of the cognitive map of the peasantry as a whole, there has been scarcely any attempt to understand the peasant's notion of poverty, as distinct from that of colonial administrators and the nationalist intelligentsia. Unfortunately, historians have neglected this crucial question. They depend mainly on the oral traditions and folk literature. In this essay, a new source brought to attention is a manuscript of a rural poet who wrote about the Orissa famine of 1866.

I

What was the intellectual lineage of what I propose to call the 'colonial paradigm' of poverty and the management of poverty? It has been demonstrated by a series of authors from R.H. Tawney[1] to Gertrude Himmelfarb[2] that in England poverty was conceptualized in a totally new way since the advent of modern capitalism. The substance of their findings is that under the influence of capitalistic ethics, poverty is increasingly regarded as a mark of economic inefficiency; failure to act efficiently in a competitive world being identified as the cause of poverty, the poor were regarded as a burden on the national economy in so far as their being inefficient (and, in the case of the unemployed poor or vagabonds, totally unproductive) caused the consumption of a part of the national wealth by a class which did not contribute to the creation of that wealth. From Mercantilists to Utilitarians, it has been argued, this approach to poverty was retained.

First, let us look at the idea of poverty in the colonial bureaucratic discourse. Perhaps the vantage point of entry into that question is to look at the official pronouncements on the developing art of management of poverty and stress in famine periods.

What were the basic ideas concerning poverty behind the so-called famine policy of the British Indian government? I will argue that an ideological lineage can be traced through the Poor Laws of nineteenth-century England to Bentham. This connection may appear remote and implausible at first sight. Eric Stokes,[3] in his highly perceptive analysis of the impact of Utilitarianism on Indian policies, did not look into this aspect – he concentrated on the connections between Utilitarianism, and Indian legislative and land revenue policies, which were more overt. Historians of famines in India have been equally silent on the question of the idea of poverty and the impact of Benthamite 'Panopticism' (Foucault's phrase) in British India. Yet when one reads the Poor Laws of nineteenth-century England, and the Famine Codes and Famine Commission Reports of nineteenth-century India, the continuities and parallels become obvious. That is not the least surprising, for the new English Poor Law (1834) owed much to Bentham, and Bentham likewise influenced makers of famine policy in British India (e.g., Strachey, chairman of the 1880 Famine Commission which framed the Famine Code). Once we discover this ideological lineage, working out the genealogy is not too difficult.

Gertrude Himmelfarb has shown in her recent work how Bentham's *Pauper Management Improved* (1798) offered the first blueprint for disciplining the poor. Elsewhere, in his more well-known *Panopticon*, Bentham claimed to have 'the Gordian Knot of Poor Laws not cut but untied'. The tract of 1798 was a fuller plan for 'the burdensome poor', including a 'national chanty company' on the model of the East India Company, 'Industry houses' or poor houses, a Commissioner or Governor to administer all poor relief, etc. This tract on pauper management was reprinted several times up to 1831. In 1832 the Royal Commission on Poor Laws was appointed. This was a decision made by Lord Grey's Cabinet before the passage of the 1832 Reform Act, but it was not wholly unconnected with the political reorientation signalled by parliamentary reforms; and it was certainly connected in a direct way with the recent experience of unrest of the rural poor in the form of the 'Captain Swing Riots' of 1830, which Eric Hobsbawm has chronicled in detail.

As for the outcome of the efforts of the Poor Law Commissioners, the Act of 1834, there is an extensive literature that need not concern us here. What we are interested in is the Benthamite core of the Poor Law, which is transmuted in the Indian Famine Code. It appears that the carrier of the Benthamite lymph in the Poor Law Commission of 1832–34 was Edwin Chadwyck, former secretary to Bentham. While Chadwyck and the economist Senior in the Commission rejected the Malthusian prescriptions, having made that concession, they brought into existence a regime of poor relief which applied eligibility conditions that would deter the poor from drawing relief, confine the pauper in work houses, and systematize a state-controlled machinery in place of charity on the lines Bentham recommended.

Some of these basic concepts are in evidence in the Famine Code in India from 1880 till the end of the Raj, and even beyond. This is where new research needs to be done, to connect the colonial discourse on pov-

erty and distress with the thinking in England on Poor Law. First, consider
the Famine Commission's concept of 'test of relief-worthiness' of those
in distress. Forms of relief other than gratuitous relief 'are appropriately
regulated by a *self-testing test*, a labour test, a distance test, a residence test'
(emphasis in original).[4] This meant that any person starving in a famine-
affected area would have to perform a certain amount of labour in public
works and/or travel a certain distance (up to 15 miles), or accept com-
pulsory residence in a special area away from the home village. This was
expected to deter those who did not really need the wages in government
works programmes for the famine-affected. This idea was first put forward
in 1877 by Lord Lytton during a famine in south India: 'The obligation
to do a full day's work at a low rate of wage, and to go some distance to
work, keeps from seeking relief those who can support themselves otherwise.'[5] The idea was to distinguish the poor from the really destitute,
in the same manner as the English Poor Law of 1834 distinguished 'the
indigent' entitled to relief from the ranks of the poor. The Secretary of State
endorsed this principle of discouraging 'relief of applicants not in want'
and the requirement of a distance test which can 'without undue hardship
be used as a *test of destitution*'.[6] The Famine Commission of 1880 under
the Utilitarian Strachey devised a Famine Code in which 'the fact of his
(i.e. relief seeker) submitting to the test of giving a reasonable amount of
work in return for a subsistence wage is considered to be sufficient proof
of his necessity'.[7]

These discussions about eligibility were a re-run of what England
witnessed in connection with the Poor Law. The British Commission on
Poor Law of 1832–34 spent a great deal of its time distinguishing the common poor from the 'indigent'. In their report they observed that even those
earning wages sometimes were incorrectly classed as indigent and were
thus entitled to poor funds. The Commission now redefined indigence as
'the state of a person unable to obtain, in return for his labour, the means
of subsistence'. This was the concept that the Famine Commissioners in
India extended to those who, under famine conditions, were unable to
find subsistence and thus became entitled to subsistence wages in government public works. As for the mechanism for enforcing this principle,
the English Poor Law Commission used a 'self-acting test of the claim
of the applicant' – the very same words the Famine Commissioners used
in India; public works in India was the mechanism in place of the work
houses in England, and the 'work house test' in England was replaced by
various relief tests in India relating to distance, rigour of work demanded,
etc., mentioned earlier. Compliance with work house terms of relief in
England was itself a test of entitlement, just as the severity of conditions

under which the famine-stricken Indian native was employed in 'famine works' was meant to filter out those not truly in distress.

As regards the 'poor houses' in India, these were not meant to be permanent institutions like the English work house. They were really temporary institutions to 'collect and relieve paupers sent adrift by the contraction of private charity'. They were also used at a late stage in the famine 'for contumacious idlers', i.e. 'contumacious persons fit to work who refused to labour'.[8] The condition in the poor house being unattractive, to say the least, 'a certain amount of pressure may be required to induce people to remain in poor houses', or else they revert to vagrancy. It was the Commission of 1880 which suggested that suppliants for relief, 'in case of doubt as to eligibility', could be sent to poor houses. The centuries-old English laws against vagrancy have an obvious relevance to the policy of British Indian administrators, going well beyond Bentham to Tudor times.

The third form of famine relief in India, gratuitous relief to the villages, corresponds to 'outdoor relief' under the old Poor Law in England. According to Benthamite principles such relief was undesirable, and the Poor Law Commission of 1832–34 disrecommended it. However, in view of the public outcry and local-level opposition to the abolition of outdoor relief, it was retained on a reduced scale in England. In India this form of relief was sometimes totally unavoidable under famine conditions, though the famine officers were uncomfortable with it. They were uncomfortable because of their awareness of 'that most dangerous popular vice – the disposition to force the government to grant public charity'.[9] The famine officers were expected to play it by the ear and 'hit the happy mean', i.e. to avoid gratuitous relief as much as possible.

Richard Strachey, who headed the Famine Commission of 1880, was well-known for his Utilitarian sympathies along with his brother John Strachey. The authority they cited was John Stuart Mill. They quoted Mill with approbation on the need to resort to active state interventionism in backward economies. Mill was also a strong supporter of the Poor Law of 1834.[10]

To sum it up, through the medium of Mill's writings and the experience of the Poor Laws in England, Bentham's ideas left a clear impress upon the thought and action of the upper echelons of India's colonial bureaucracy. Some of the basic categories of thought, I have argued, are common in the Indian Famine Code, the Poor Laws in England and Bentham's original blueprint. Apart from the specific terminology and notions, it was the approach towards *management* of poverty that was Benthamite. There are many other aspects in which contemporary British economic thinking touched upon Indian questions, which we need not go into here since an authoritative study is already available.[11]

II

The nationalist thinkers in colonial India were able, in the teeth of mainstream British discourse of the day, to put forward an independent and markedly different approach to poverty. We shall focus on Dadabhai Naoroji, because, through his *Poverty and Un-British Rule In India*,[12] he was in advance of the rest of the nationalist economists in so far as the poverty question was concerned. Romesh Chandra Dutt also wrote extensively about poverty in India, especially in the context of deindustrialization. (We find Mahatma Gandhi writing in *Hind Swaraj* in 1909 that Dutt's description of the destruction of India's artisanal industries moved him to tears.) Dutt was rich in empirical data and description, while Naoroji's writings offered something more: a distinct break from the contemporary British bureaucratic discourse of poverty.

How was Naoroji's framework of analysis different from the colonial bureaucratic outlook?

(1) First, Naoroji's was a historical approach unlike that of the bureaucracy, which by and large limited its interest to the 'here and now' with a view to pragmatic management of the problem in times of intense impoverishment and food insecurity such as famines. In this historical approach, I think, there is an interesting parallel with the work of his contemporary Rogers, professor of political economy at Oxford for a while.

Now that the private correspondence of Dadabhai Naoroji is available to researchers, much new information on his intellectual interests and contacts is accessible. One of these contacts that probably influenced Naoroji was his acquaintance, revealed in his private letters, with James E. Thorold Rogers (1829–1890). Naoroji met him in London in 1887 and wrote to his friend in Bombay, Dinshaw Wacha.[13] Wacha urged Naoroji to 'cultivate his acquaintance' because, Wacha said quite correctly, Rogers was 'the one great authority on statistics of the kind you have unaided collected'.[14]

Indeed, the kind of quantification Naoroji had begun in his study of India's economy and poverty in India had, as Wacha said, a close parallel in Rogers' work on English economic history. Thorold Rogers published from 1866 till his death in 1890, in eight stout volumes, a history of prices and wages in England. He devoted himself to this work soon after completing his education at King's College, London and Magdalen Hall, Oxford, and eventually his research won him the professorship of political economy at Oxford. He was also active in politics for a while as a Liberal Member of Parliament in 1880–86. It is interesting to note that his contemporary, Karl Marx, noticed his work favourably and used it in *Capital*. Marx praised Rogers' work, 'the fruit of patient and diligent labour', as the 'first authentic history of prices'.[15] Marx particularly endorsed his study in respect of the increasing poverty of the agricultural labourer class in England.[16] Rogers was generally associated with the trend of statistical compilation in economic studies, and his was an approach and methodology shared by Naoroji. However, Naoroji's first exposition of Indian economics was published about a decade before he became personally acquainted with Rogers.

(2) In Naoroji's *Poverty and Un-British Rule in India* (1901), the second major difference between his approach and the colonial paradigm emerges. Naoroji rejected the palliative approach to poverty and addressed himself to the causative aspect of poverty in India. Poverty in India attracted British official attention only when it took the acute form of famine and hence attracted action under the Famine Code. Naoroji, like other nationalist economists, dug deeper into the causes of poverty and causally linked the political status of Indians as a subject race to their economic well-being.[17] He was critical of the famine policy *ab initio*.

> The so-called Famine Relief Fund is nothing more or less than a subterfuge of taxing the starving to save the dying. . . . If the government spends say five million on the present famine they will simply squeeze it out of the poverty-stricken surviving tax payers, who in turn would become the victims of the next drought.[18]

He argued that not famines alone but the endemic condition of deprivation, leading to diminution of nutrition, merited attention; his favourite example of this was the fact that the nutrition available to prisoners in jails was higher than that available to the average native of India, judged by the records of jails and medical departments.

(3) This line of argument led Naoroji to the most significant departure from the colonial discourse on poverty. He adopted a macro approach, aiming to calculate the wealth or poverty of India through national income estimates. He contested the practice of officials who generalized from examples or areas known to them or suited to their argument. For example, while refuting Grant-Duff, former Governor of Madras, Naoroji made the point that the argument is about 'the income of *all* British India' and not that of isolated instances of a town or a district.[19] Official admission of poverty 'in many parts of India' was as meaningless as claims of prosperity in some other parts.[20] Naoroji thus elevated the discussion to the level of estimation of national income as a whole, since the generalizability of

poverty and prosperity could be founded on that method alone. He was followed in this regard in Parliament debates by Grant-Duff in 1880, Viceroy Curzon in 1901, F.J. Atkinson in 1902, and others.

(4) The fourth notable feature of Naoroji's aproach to the question was that he framed his enquiry in the international comparative scale. How much of poverty there is in India was established by him through international comparisons. With great insight he focused attention on the income inequality between nations and then to the inequality between strata within nations. 'Poverty in the countries of Western Europe is not from want of wealth or income, but from unequal distribution. But British India has her whole production or income itself most wretched.'[21] The international comparison of economic well-being was developed with particular acuteness in comparing governmental income through taxation as a ratio of national incomes.[22] We are concerned here not with the accuracy of his calculations but with his conceptual framework. By distinguishing between poverty due to unequal distribution of national income and poverty due to overall level of national income, Naoroji answered naive disputants who pointed out the existence of poverty-stricken sections in other countries. The point of posing the issue in terms of international comparisons was, evidently, to highlight the contrast between the poverty of a colonized country and the wealth of the imperialist nations of Europe.

In these four ways – adopting a historical and quantitative approach, replacing the palliative approach with a search for deep-seated causative issues, putting forward a macro approach to the national income question, and positing a scale of international comparison – Naoroji made a departure from the colonial bureaucratic discourse and raised the level of analysis to a higher theoretical plane, to contest established notions about poverty.

Naoroji and his contemporaries, such as Romesh Chandra Dutt and, a little later, Sakharam Ganesh Deuskar, offered a full-scale analysis of the economic exploitation India was subject to under British rule. They perspicaciously pointed to the influence of British business, but did not adopt the approach that was just beginning to be influential in Europe in the early twentieth century postulating an intrinsic connection between capitalism and imperialism. J.A. Hobson (1858–1940) focused on that in his famous work *Imperialism* in 1902, and of course, earlier to that, Karl Marx had pointed to the same connection though his emphasis was on other mediating factors.[23] However, one cannot trace an influence of their theory that economic imperialism was an inevitable outcome of the nature of capitalism. While Dutt as well as Naoroji successfully established the fact that British business interests had a hegemonic role in determining imperial economic policies in India, to the detriment of India's prospect of development, the theory of an intrinsic link between capitalism and imperialism was not a part of their approach.

III

A question that needs to be addressed but has rarely been addressed is: How was poverty looked at by the labouring poor themselves in colonial India? This question has not received academic attention because the usual sources are silent on the subject. In the literature of those times we see descriptions of the life of the poverty-stricken multitude, we sense the discontentment that occasionally found expression in popular resistance movements such as the Indigo Rebellion in Bengal or the Deccan peasant uprising of the 1860s – but if you ask how the poor themselves thought of poverty and wealth, there is scarcely any clue in the usual sources. For the present I can only attempt an outline of research in progress.

To begin with, what were the values in the moral economy of the poor peasantry? What was the difference, if any, between the notion of poverty prevalent among the labouring poor in India and the pattern of thinking of the British bureaucracy who ruled over them? One can only surmise on the basis of folk literature. Scholars of pre-modern literature have drawn upon that source to depict traditional peasant society.[24] The lives of the unfortunate victims of poverty are described in great detail in the *baramassyas* in *Mangal Kavyas*; abject poverty is depicted in these, but the poor are not perceived as lesser men. In the *gajan* songs as well as the many literary depictions of the deity Siva, we see a divine glory attributed to his poverty. As Dinesh Chandra Sen, Asutosh Bhattacharya and other authorities on pre-modern Bengali literature have pointed out, Siva is imagined as if he is an impoverished vagabond and yet the highest among the gods. Poverty does not diminish his glory. This suggests that dignity, human or divine, was not inconsistent with poverty in the traditional imagination.

Secondly, authoritative studies in the area of Bengal's social and cultural history attribute to the Bengali peasant till the early twentieth century, a world outlook that is communitarian and not individualistic. A common stereotype is that of the peasant, though poor in terms of worldly goods, being happily ensconced in familial or communitarian bonds in his village, and devoid of the competitive spirit that is born of economic individualism. The eminent anthropologist Nirmal Kumar Bose, in his *Hindu Samajer Gadan* (translated by Andre Beteille under the title *The Structure of Hindu Society*), is an exponent of this view.[25]

These broad generalizations about the dignity ascribed to poverty, and about the salience of communitarian and familial bonds as opposed to economic individualism, are difficult to prove or disprove on the basis of historical evidence. While one must be careful not to exaggerate the cast of mind thus postulated, or to project it as unique and somehow morally superior, there seems to be some point in an implicit contraposition. This indigenous conception of poverty is markedly different from that of contemporary economics and the utilitarian approach of the state. From the latter point of view, poverty was almost an economic crime; it was to be punished by putting the poor in the work house or poor house. Poverty was not only distressing to those affected by it, it was much worse: it was evidence of failure to be productive enough to be sustained by the market. Therefore, the poor who depend on charity need to be forced to work in the work house in England. In India, the corresponding system was to force famine-affected and poverty-stricken people to engage in very rigorous labour in order to be entitled to receive famine relief under the Famine Code. In contrast, in indigenous thinking poverty was looked upon as a misfortune but not a crime.

Another difference between the British and the indigenous outlook was in respect of the attitude towards social redistribution. To the British bureaucracy taxation was the appropriate means of redistribution, if such redistribution was at all desirable. In fact there was a strong resistance among policy makers in nineteenth-century England and India to the very idea of redistribution, because it was against the *laissez faire* principle. For instance, on this ground progressive income tax was opposed when income tax was accepted as a *pro tem* measure to tide over financial deficit.[26] From the same point of view, charity was a totally objectionable means of social redistribution because it would maintain economically unproductive people and reduce the rate of accumulation of capital. Famine Commission Reports from 1877 to 1898 contain many passages arguing that private charity was dysfunctional and inconsistent with the system of public relief for the indigent. In the years after the 1898 Famine Commission, charity from landed magnates and the like was declared to be acceptable, chiefly as a means of enhancing the government's funds for famine relief. The generally adverse attitude to charity on theoretical grounds by the Utilitarians and members of the 'Manchester school' may be contrasted not only with the now discarded idea of 'Christian charity', but also with the value ascribed to charity in Indian belief systems. Charity in India was traditionally regarded as a virtue and a means of earning *punya* or merit. This was one belief that the poor and the rich shared. The Famine Commission Reports of the late nineteenth century, in reporting census of the famine-affected population, indicate that a fairly substantial section of both the rural and urban population – variously named as beggars, vagabonds, religious preachers, itinerant *sanyasis*, etc. – were regular recipients of charity in normal times, i.e. even when there was no sign of a famine. To the poverty-stricken or those who did not earn a regular income, living on charity was no cause for shame. The wide prevalence of charity matches with the notion that there was a spirit of sharing the surplus within a community bound by a sense of mutuality.[27]

Historians usually look for sources that are contemporary and first-hand observations, of known authorship and provenance. If one is asking how the poor looked at poverty, such sources are rare. I propose to make use of one such rare source that I have found. This is a manuscript on the famine of 1866 in Orissa and the western part of Bengal. This manuscript, now in the Calcutta University manuscript collection (manuscript no. 4870), was written by a rural poet by the name of Dwija Nafar. According to the colophon at the end of the manuscript, he wrote this account of the famine in 1867, and he seems to have been a resident of the present district of Medinipur in West Bengal. The rural poet was, judging by the manuscript and its orthography, somewhat literate although not educated, and he consistently identifies himself with the poor victims of famine. He writes of how the stability of the moral economy of the poor peasantry is destroyed by the famine: '*Paiya jathar kashto / kolir manab nashto / dharma karma sab parihori*' ('Pangs of starvation / lead men to the wrong path / abandoning dharma and duty'). In times of famine, the poet laments, the wealthy are untouched by distress though distress is widespread, and they think themselves to be the masters of the world. In times of famine the wealthy, with paddy in their hands, lord it over others: '*Akale jar chilo dhanya / tar oti holo manya / ahankare paripurno tar*' ('He who had paddy in his hands in famine times / was on top of the world / and bursting with self-pride'). The famine destroys fellow-feeling and charity, and profiteering flourishes. The poet witnesses a collapse of the traditional value system which accorded respect to the respectable in rural society. '*Guru thake dware baishye / dhanya kinibar ashe / tare bole dhanya nahito ghare. / Guru jaye baimukh hoyya / Chor ashe paisa loyia / tare dhanya daye besi dare*' ('The Guru waits in vain at the door / in the hope of buying paddy / and he is told there is no paddy in this house. / The Guru leaves disappointed / the thief comes with cash / and he buys paddy at a high price').[28]

Nafar nurses the faith which has sustained poor people in all societies at all times, that the sins of the exploiting wealthy will be punished: '*papir dhon shunye uribek*' ('the sinful profits will not last'). Some day, the bad times will be over. The famine will not last forever and dharma will reassert itself: '*Ei durbhikhee akal / na rohibe chirokal / sukal haibe punascho / eha bujhe karo karma / ei kahilam mormo / jate grihasther dharma roy*' ('These are times of famine / such times do not last forever / good times will come again / do your duty bearing that in mind / mark my words / let the dharma of the household prevail'). The poet is keenly aware of inequity, the difference between poor and being rich, but it seems that Nafar's ethics do not prescribe expropriation of the wealthy: '*Purbarjita dhan jar / purbamato robe tar*' ('Earnings of normal times / will remain with those who earned it').

In this folk poet's imagination the misery suffered by the poor, especially in times of famine, is an inevitability. It is inevitable in the era of *Koli*: '*Kolir bhog / purba haite ishwar adesh*' ('The sufferings of the *Koli* era / are foreordained by god'). He depicts the famine as *Koli avatara*. The bottom line seems to be that, although in times of famine the dharma of the householder may be flouted and the market may favour the profiteer, the poet declares his faith that ultimately moral values rooted in traditional beliefs will survive the bad times. The social and moral values of normal times, this village bard believes, would prevail when normal times return. And *grihasther dharma*, the values and norms the householder should uphold, are simple: it is immoral to make profit when others in the community suffer *jathar kashto* or pangs of hunger; give due respect to the *guru* (preceptor, teacher or an elder in the community) and eschew dealing with thieves; wealth from sinful profit in the market does not last; it is a divine dispensation that men will suffer in the *Koli* era, but good times will come again; *dharma* may be defeated for the time being, but it will ultimately prevail. There is something touching in these simple beliefs one notices in the poet Nafar's ballad, of the bad times the poor went through in Orissa and Medinipur in 1866.

To sum it up, in the latter half of the nineteenth century we have seen three discursive traditions: that of (i) the colonial bureaucracy drawing upon the fund of ideas Utilitarianism provided; (ii) the nationalist intelligentsia who departed from conventional economic theory of the day to develop a critique of British rule; and (iii) the labouring poor in terms of their own reflections on their experience of poverty. These discourses of the state, of the political leadership and the victims of poverty among the subject-people in colonial India are of more than historical interest. Arguably, there has occurred in our times a resuscitation of the colonial bureaucratic approach to poverty since the installation of neo-liberalism in government policy in the 1990s, and the contestation of that policy brings to mind the early nationalists' understanding of poverty, as well as an indigenous discourse of poverty which upheld values other than the market value of commodities and labour. That perhaps imparts to the historical issues discussed above, a contemporary relevance.

Notes and References

1. R.H. Tawney, *Religion and the Rise of Capitalism* [1938], reprint, New York, 1947.
2. Gertrude Himmelfarb, *The Idea of Poverty: England in the Early Industrial Age*, New York, 1984.
3. Eric Stokes, *The Utilitarians and India*, Oxford, 1959. He notes that the Famine Commission of 1880 justified an increase in land revenue on the basis of their opinion that economic distress or famine in the 1870s in north India was unrelated to land revenue demand (ibid., p. 138); that is his only reference to famine or poverty.
4. *Report of the Famine Commission 1901* (Chairman: A.P. MacDonnell), Calcutta, 1901, p. 45; also see India Office, HMSO, *East India (Famine) Papers*, London, 1902.
5. *Report of the Famine Commission* (Chairman J. B. Lyall), Calcutta, 1898, Vol. I, p. 239.
6. Ibid., p. 84.
7. *Report of the Famine Commission 1878–1879* (London, 1881) is to be read along with the earlier report put out by India Office, HMSO, *East India (Madras and Orissa) Famine* (London, 1867) to appreciate the difference the Famine Code made.
8. *Report of the Famine Commission 1901*, p. 18.
9. Ibid., p.45.
10. John Stuart Mill, *Principles of Political Economy* [1848], reprint, London, 1902, p. 584.
11. S. Ambirajan, *Classical Political Economy and British Policy in India*, Cambridge, 1978.
12. Dadabhai Naoroji, *Poverty and Un-British Rule in India*, London, 1901. Since I was unable to access this edition published by Sonnenschein, I refer to the reprint: New Delhi, 1962. Also see Naoroji, *Speeches and Writings*, edited by C.Y. Chintamani, Allahabad, 1905.
13. Private Papers of Dadabhai Naoroji, National Archives of India: Naoroji to Wacha, 21 October 1887.
14. Ibid.: D.Wacha to D. Naoroji, 11 November 1887.
15. *Capital*, Vol. I, Moscow, 1956, Chapter XXV, p. 673.
16. Ibid., p. 678.
17. Bipan Chandra, *Economic Nationalism in India*, New Delhi, 1969.
18. Naoroji, *Poverty and Un-British Rule in India*, p. 367.
19. Ibid., p. 229.
20. Ibid., p. 226.
21. Ibid., p. 232.
22. Ibid., p. 55.
23. J.A. Hobson, *Imperialism* [1902], reprint, Ann Arbor, 1965.
24. David Arnold ('Famines in Peasant Consciousness and Peasant Actions: Madras 1876–78', in Ranajit Guha, ed., *Subaltern Studies III*, New Delhi, 1984) has used Tamilian proverbs to understand the peasant mentality in respect of famine.
25. Nirmal Kumar Bose, *The Structure of Hindu Society* (*Hindu Samajer Garan*), translated by Andre Beteille, New Delhi, 1975.

[26] Sabyasachi Bhattacharya, *Financial Foundations of the British Raj: 1858–1872*, New Delhi, 2007, pp. 261–73.

[27] In the following pages I have drawn upon an earlier publication of mine, discarding the theoretical discussion in that paper: Sabyasachi Bhattacharya, 'The Labouring Poor and their Notion of Poverty: Late Nineteenth and Early Twentieth Century Bengal', *Labour and Development*, Vol. 3, No. 2, July 1999, pp. 1–23.

[28] Manuscript No. 4870, 'Akal Charit' by Dwija Nafar, *c.* 1867, stanza no. 23, Bengali Manuscript Archive of Calcutta University.

Revisiting the 'Drain', or Transfers from India to Britain in the Context of Global Diffusion of Capitalism

Utsa Patnaik

Introduction

The West European powers transferred economic surplus from their colonies on a very large scale, and this substantially aided both their domestic industrial transition from the eighteenth century and the subsequent diffusion of capitalism to the regions of recent European settlement. The literature on economic imperialism, however, reveals little awareness of even the *fact of the existence of transfers*, let alone the sheer *scale* of the transfers involved, or the specific real and financial *mechanisms* through which these transfers were effected. In India, the largest colony of the first world capitalist leader, Britain, a rich discussion dealing with transfers, termed the 'drain of wealth', has been taking place from the time that the phenomenon was pointed out over a century ago by Dadabhai Naoroji and R.C. Dutt.[1]

The literature on industrial transition in the core countries in the eighteenth–nineteenth centuries ignores almost completely this existing discussion on the drain of wealth, or transfers from the colonies.[2] The mainstream interpretation posits a purely internal dynamic for the rise of capitalist industrialization, and some authors argue that the colonies were a burden on the metropolis which would have been better off if they had been 'given away'.

In this essay I intend to put forward some basic propositions without entering into the complex ramifications of the subject. The *concept* of 'drain' as put forward by pioneers in India is theoretically correct and can be depicted readily in terms of present-day open-economy macroeconomics; the *scale* of the drain was very large, looking at historical statistics on global trade; and the *importance* of the drain from colonies was immeasurable in financing the diffusion of capitalism to Europe, North America and other regions of recent European settlement via capital exports from Britain using the exchange earnings drained from its colonies. Two of the more important balance of payments estimates for India will also be

discussed briefly, especially in relation to the hitherto unsatisfactory treatment of gold flows. The terms 'drain from colonies' and 'transfers from
colonies' are used synonymously.

How Is 'Drain of Wealth' to Be Conceptualized?

As developed by its originators, the concept of 'drain' is quite simple, but its actual estimation can be carried out in different ways. Knowing
the conceptual basis of a country's gross domestic product allows us to see
that it can be measured both from the side of production and from that
of incomes. Similarly, once the conceptual basis of the drain of wealth is
clear, we see that it can be measured either from the colony's budget or
from its external accounts, and a similar order of magnitude for the drain
will be obtained in either case.

We cannot do better than to go to the classical pioneers, Dadabhai
Naoroji and R.C. Dutt, who wrote over a century ago.[3] Far from being
outdated, their works show a deep qualitative insight into the economic
processes underlying the drain, which is missing from much of present-day
writing. Without going into lengthy quotations, which are otiose since
reprints of the classic works are easily available, we see that their concept
of drain turned on the fact that *a substantial part (up to one-third) of the
total tax and other revenues raised within the colony was not spent in the
normal way within the country, but set aside for sterling expenditure by
Britain on its own account abroad. But how did the transformation of
rupees in the Indian budget into sterling with Britain take place? By using
that part of revenues to reimburse colonized producers of export goods
(the very same producers who had paid in the taxes in the first place!),
while the financial gold and foreign exchange (forex) earned through their
global net commodity exports was appropriated by the metropolis for its
own use.* Hence, the particular part of the Indian budget set aside for such
abnormal use could be a measure of the drain. Alternatively India's global
commodity export surplus – whose forex proceeds were not credited to
the producers and who were fobbed off by being 'paid' out of their own
taxes (hence the classic term *unrequited* export surplus) – could be the
measure of drain adopted. A similar value of drain would be obtained in
either case, because India's rising export surplus earnings were completely
offset – usually more than offset – on its external account by imposing
the same liabilities, but now expressed in sterling, of the similarly rising
sums set aside in the rupee budget under numerous items of expenditure
abroad, gifts to Britain and so on.[4] This classical concept of the drain was
absolutely correct and can be expressed in terms of modern macroeconomic
theory, by suitably modifying the identity linking the external balance,

the savings–investment balance and the budgetary balance, as we show in the fourth section.

The only matter Naoroji and Dutt did not write about, because it took place mainly after their time, was that the Indian peasantry and workers produced *the second largest merchandise export surplus in the world* for at least four decades from the 1890s.[5] But India was never permitted to show current account balance, leave alone current account surplus. These enormous exchange earnings, appropriated by the then world capitalist leader, Britain, allowed it to export capital to develop Europe and the regions of European settlement, despite its running large and rising current account deficits with these same regions. The rapid diffusion of capitalism was ensured thereby to what constitutes today's advanced countries.

Let us consider the beginning of the transfer process. The East India Company's trade monopoly started from 1600; it had to pay for its import surplus from Asia with silver, arousing the ire of the early mercantilists. The Company acquired tax revenue-collecting rights in Bengal province in 1765, and the substantive drain started precisely from that date. Some form of drain was already taking place through underpayment for goods by using coercion on petty producers, but this was nothing compared to the bonanza after 1765, when free acquisition of export goods by using local taxes started. Bengal's population, at about 30 million, was nearly four times that of Britain; but the rapacity of the Company, which more than trebled tax collections over five years, helped to decimate one-third of that population in the great 1770 famine. Slow recovery took place; the land revenue fixed under the 1793 Permanent Settlement in Bengal exceeded the British government's taxes from land in Britain. In the next 80 years revenue collection grew steadily as, using Bengal as its economic base, the Company fought to acquire political control over the north Indian provinces, the Bombay Deccan, Madras, Punjab and Awadh. The Burmese fought three wars before their land was fully occupied by 1885. Land revenue collection systems were promptly put into place – the very term for the British district administrator was 'Collector'. Britain saw a steadily increasing and completely costless inflow of tax-financed commodities – textiles, rice, saltpetre, indigo, opium, raw cotton, jute – which far exceeded its own requirements, the excess being re-exported. While indigo and opium were produced under state-imposed monopoly and coercive conditions, as B.B. Chaudhuri has documented,[6] the growth of later commercial exportable crops was mainly under the pressure of rising rent and revenue demands.

In what sense did the inflow of tropical goods become costless for

Britain? Suppose that a peasant-cum-artisan producer in India paid Rs 100 tax to the state, and sold 10 yards of cloth and 2 bags of rice worth in total Rs 50 to a local trader. This sale would be a normal market transaction and not connected in any way to his tax payment, since the trader would advance his own funds for the purchase in the usual way, expecting to sell the cloth and rice, and recoup his outlay with a profit. Now, suppose not a local trader but an agent of the Company bought the 10 yards of cloth and 2 bags of rice for export from the peasant-cum-artisan producer by 'paying' him Rs 50 of the same producer's own money, out of the Rs 100 tax taken from him. This means the producer was not paid at all. The producer might have smelled a rat if the agent of the Company who collected his tax also, at the same time, bought his goods out of that money. But the two agents were different, and the two acts – collecting tax and buying produce – took place at different times by different agents, so the producer did not connect them. Purchase by the Company's agent would appear to the producer as a normal market exchange no different from purchase by the internal trader, but in fact it was qualitatively quite different, since a part of his own tax payment came back to him – a fact he did not know – while his cloth and rice were taken away. In this transaction, the *form* of half of the total tax of Rs 100 he had paid changed from Rs 50 cash to 10 yards cloth and 2 bags rice. In effect he handed over these goods for export completely free to the Company, as the commodity equivalent of Rs 50 tax, worth say £5 (at the current exchange rate of Rs 10 to £1).

When the Company exported the cloth and rice, the final consumers in England and in other countries paid for them in sterling and their own currencies. The cloth and rice worth £5 at the Indian port (export *f.o.b.*) would be sold at roughly £7 to £7.5 in England to cover cost of transport, insurance and trader's margin (import *c.i.f.*). In fact only the rice would be sold and the cloth re-exported to Europe since there was a ban on consumption of Asian textiles in England (on which more later). Some scholars have periodically muddied the conceptual waters by saying that since final consumers paid in full at the going high prices, the goods were not 'costless' and the benefit went only to the monopoly trading company putting a high mark-up and making profit: tropical goods prices were higher in Britain than in France, and Britain would have been better off if the colonies had been 'given away'.[7] These authors have missed the point completely: the Company's trade would not have existed at all if final consumers in England and Europe did not demand the products and were not prepared to pay the going price. The question of high traders' margins and high prices is irrelevant, it is not germane to the core issue of transfer. Indian consumers today who choose to import expensive German automobiles with a high dealer's mark-up are not obtaining transfer from that country in any way.

The transfer or drain consisted in the fact that export surplus was the product equivalent of taxes paid in by colonized producers, so its external sale value did not come back to these producers. The high propensity of foreign consumers to consume tropical goods, which appeared as a merchandise import surplus, namely, a trade deficit of Britain vis-à-vis India (up to the 1840s), *did not create any external payment liability for Britain,* as its trade deficit with a sovereign partner, like say France, did. Britain's perpetual trade deficit with France had to be settled in the normal way through outflow of specie (precious metals), or borrowing, or a combination of the two, and this was true of its deficits with all other sovereign regions. It was also true of its trade with India up to 1765 which involved silver outflow. After that date, when local tax collection began, the situation changed completely.

On Britain's external account the cloth and rice import from India now created zero payment liability since Indian producers had been 'paid' already out of their own tax contribution – namely, not paid at all. *This clever system of getting goods free as the commodity equivalent of economic surplus, extracted as taxes, was the essence of the drain, of transfer.* It did not merely benefit the Company as trader by raising its profit rate to dizzying heights, since its own outlay on purchasing the goods became zero; it benefited Britain as a country, because on its external account, its growing trade deficit, namely, import surplus of Indian tropical goods and textiles, created no payment liability for it, and re-exports of these free goods also bought it goods from other sovereign countries like France, reducing its trade deficit with them. (Some silver inflow continuing after 1765 had to do with paying for the Company's deficit on the China trade, before sufficient Indian opium could be grown and thrust on China.) For balancing external accounts, India's export surplus earnings were fully offset by imposing the sterling value of the very same total of invisible debit items comprising the politically determined tribute, that was already set aside in the Indian budget as 'expenditure abroad'. This procedure, peculiar to the system of colonial exploitation, is dealt with in the third section.

Had the colony remained a sovereign country, its foreign exchange earnings would have accrued entirely to its own government, boosting its international purchasing capacity, while the local producers of export surplus would have been issued the local currency equivalent of these forex earnings as a normal expansion of the money supply, not connected in any way to taxes they might or might not pay. The taxes they did pay would have been spent entirely under normal budgetary heads. British economists, when writing of the drain, obfuscated the actual position, for they were careful not to connect the colonial taxation system with trade in their textual and algebraic formulations, though they must have had a shrewd idea of what was happening.[8] A simple diagrammatic exposition showing how the production of economic surplus, the fiscal system and the trade system were linked to effect the drain has been presented earlier by this author.[9]

The colonizing power always needed to establish *property rights* in some form over the local population since this was the necessary condition for surplus extraction and transfer. In India it was the sovereign right of tax collection, but in the West Indies plantation slavery meant that the extraction of surplus by British owners took the form mainly of *slave-rent* namely the excess of net output (net of material costs) over the bare subsistence of the enslaved workers. In Ireland, English settler landlords took over the land of the local peasantry, and economic surplus was extracted as land rent as well as taxes. In all cases goods were obtained free as the commodity equivalent of economic surplus – whatever the specific form, in which this surplus might be appropriated – as slave rent, land rent, taxes or a combination of these methods.

'Rent of land' is used in this paper always in the sense discussed by Adam Smith and Karl Marx: those who concentrated property right in land, could extract surplus as land rent from the producers merely by virtue of this right, without necessarily making a single penny's worth of outlay in production. The term 'rent' of land is never used here in the completely opposite sense specified by Ricardo who tied it to production, mislabelled surplus-profit in production as 'rent' and de-linked the concept from property concentration.[10]

Tax-financed transfer by the Company from India was direct and transparent. About one third of the annual tax revenues net of collection costs, was used for purchasing export goods, of which cotton textiles and food items made up the major part. Thereby the metropolis imported a vast flow of goods, far in excess of its own requirements; it retained a part of the imports within the country and re-exported the remainder to other countries, against the goods it needed from them. Cotton textile imports were entirely re-exported. Parliament in England had passed a law in 1700 banning the consumption of imported pure cotton goods from India and Persia at the insistence of the jealous woollen industry, and had enforced the ban in 1721 with heavy fines on those found to violate it.[11] All textiles imported by the Company from India were warehoused in English ports and re-exported, mainly to Europe and the Caribbean. Once cotton yarn could be spun and woven in England itself, using the new spinning jenny,

Arkwright petitioned Parliament successfully in 1774 and the ban on the consumption of pure cotton goods was lifted.[12] But the restriction on Asian textiles' entry into the British market continued in the form of tariffs that were sharply raised in 1813, the last tariffs not going until 1846.[13]

In the *Cambridge Economic History of India* (1985) there is not a single word or reference in its 1073 pages, to Britain's stringent protectionist policy against Asian textiles, maintained for nearly 150 years from 1700 to 1846. Nor do the historians of Britain's industrial revolution and technical change in cotton textiles refer to it anywhere,[14] while more recent authors on India's economic history continue to write in the same blandly amnesic Cambridge tradition.[15] Much of the make-believe 'history' of the first industrialization that emanates from these sources suffers from such truly heroic acts of omission, from deafening silences. We have to read List, Dutt, Mantoux and Baran to obtain the true picture regarding Britain's mercantilist policies of discrimination against manufactures from Asia beginning from 1700, long before colonization.[16]

Under the Navigation Acts dating from the 1650s, every important colonial or tropical good, whatever its final destination, had to first come to Britain's ports and then be re-exported. (Re-exports must not be confused with transit goods; the goods were warehoused and a 15 per cent trader's mark-up added before being re-exported.) All colonial imported goods had to be carried only in British bottoms staffed by British officers.[17] There is a misconception that the most important import from the colonies was raw materials, but in fact the foodstuffs group was the most important all through the eighteenth century and remained so even at the height of the Industrial Revolution when raw cotton imports were growing fast.[18]

Phyllis Deane had discussed how important re-exports were in the eighteenth century, allowing Britain to purchase strategic materials from Europe (bar-iron, pitch and tar, timber).[19] This discussion was cut out completely by Deane and Cole.[20] Further, they eliminated re-exports entirely by subtracting these from both the import and the export figures; they estimated what they called 'the volume of British trade' by taking *retained imports plus domestic exports*. But their concept is not found in any macroeconomics textbook discussing trade, nor is it ever applied by the international organizations presenting trade data for different countries (United Nations, World Bank, International Monetary Fund). These sources always present *total trade*, namely total imports plus total exports, inclusive of re-exports if any. This is the correct concept, since re-exports financed imported inputs for domestic production and import of final consumption goods, just as a country's domestic exports did.

Calculating from the same data-series as Deane and Cole but using the accepted trade concept, namely total imports plus total exports, this author found that Britain's trade to GDP ratio had reached 56 per cent by the three years centred on 1800, compared to only 34 per cent estimated by Deane and Cole.[21] Many development economists have been misled by Deane and Cole's incorrect figures. The confusion was further compounded by S. Kuznets, who reproduced an early version of the Deane–Cole figures without mentioning that their estimates for Britain could not be compared with trade data of any other country he presented, which were all based on the accepted concept of total trade.[22] A critique of these misleading estimates by this author is available.[23]

Asymmetry of Production Capacities between the Global North and the Global South

A country located in the cold temperate region of Europe, controlling a tropical region, in effect sat over an inexhaustible gold mine. Gold-seams might eventually run out, but the surplus-producing and taxable capacity of the colonized peasants and artisans did not – as long as they were not entirely decimated through overexploitation. They could be set to produce more tropical crops like cane sugar, stimulants like coffee, tea and tobacco, drugs like opium, raw materials like indigo, jute and cotton, and to cut more tropical hardwoods (teak, mahogany, ebony) from the forest or from timber plantations. None of these goods could be produced in cold temperate lands.

Northern populations in Europe could not then – or for that matter in present times – ever 'import-substitute' in these goods. But they developed an increasing appetite for these goods that they could never produce and, for that very reason, prized greatly. On the other hand, there was no particular temperate-land good which the larger colonized countries voluntarily wished to import in any substantial way, since they could produce all their traditional requirements, and could also produce if needed in their winter, all the summer season crops that cold temperate lands produced. (The Chinese emperor's famed remark that the Middle Kingdom already had the best drink and the best clothing in the world held for India as well.) This very important material reality of *asymmetric production capacities*, that actually explains the historic drive by European countries to colonially subjugate more productive tropical areas, was not only ignored by David Ricardo, but this real reason was explicitly assumed away by him.

Ricardo assumed in his two-country, two-goods model that 'both countries produce both goods' – indeed his assumption was that 'all countries produce all goods' – while arguing that specialization and exchange according to comparative cost advantage led to mutual benefit.

The material fact was ignored that unit cost of production *could not be defined* for tropical goods imported by cold temperate European countries, where the output of such goods was, and always will be, zero. What is the 'cost of production' per unit of coffee in Germany, or of cane sugar in England? Where a good cannot even be produced, no cost of production exists. 'Comparative cost', to be comparable at all, requires that we know for each trading country, the number of units of good B producible by redirecting to it the labour released by reducing the output of good A by one unit. Thus it is essential for the theory to hold that both goods can actually be produced in both countries, but this was, and continues to be, impossible for temperate countries with regard to tropical products. Since the assumption that 'both countries produce both goods' is not true, the inference of mutual benefit does not follow.[24] On the contrary, historical evidence shows that the less powerful country obliged, for non-economic reasons, to specialize in export crops loses out through area diversion leading to falling domestic foodgrains output, and as it is kept compulsorily open to imports of manufactures, sees domestic deindustrialization. Modern economics textbooks continue to carry Ricardo's argument for free trade, ignoring the glaring fallacy that makes the theory incorrect.

Compared to the demand for Britain's own goods, the demand for tropical goods by Northern populations was higher and more income-elastic. Re-exports boosted the purchasing power of Britain's domestic exports by as much as 55 per cent during the period 1765 to 1821.[25] Four-fifths of goods re-exported by Britain were from tropical regions, and the re-exports went mainly to Continental Europe. Re-exports from the Netherlands actually exceeded exports of its own domestically produced goods in the eighteenth century.[26] The metropolis enjoyed a double benefit – not only did it get prized tropical goods free for its own use, but it got them free to exchange for temperate land products in which it was deficient.

Calculating from data in Davis,[27] we find that Asia, West Indies and Ireland taken together contributed half of all British imports during 1784 to 1826. We had earlier estimated from constant value trade data that the transfer, measured by import surplus into Britain from its tropical colonies in Asia and West Indies – which embodied taxes and slave rent, hence created no external liability – ranged from 5.3 to 6.1 per cent of Britain's GDP during 1801 to 1821. As a proportion of capital formation out of domestic savings, the same transfer ranged from 66 per cent to 86.4 per cent on an underestimated basis.[28] The current value data in Davis[29] similarly show the trade deficit of Britain with these colonies ranging from 4 to 6 per cent of its GDP during most triennia between 1784–86 and 1824–26, but, as explained, this created no external liability.

Can we arrive at a rough estimate of the drain for the early period? Using the available time-series from 1765 to 1822 in Mitchell and Deane,[30] and price indices from Imlah,[31] we had earlier estimated the import surplus into Britain from Asia as the measure of drain. Using the data from Davis we can bring the estimate up to 1836, after deducting the value of the China trade.[32] The current value import surplus for 1765 to 1836 was £316.247 million. *Compounding at a low 5 per cent interest rate from the mid-point of the period to date, the sum amounts to £8,226.771 billion.* We will come back to this figure in the last section.

Metropolitan Transition from Costless Direct Import Surplus to Appropriating the Colonies' Global Exchange Earnings

By 1833 the East India Company's already eroded trade monopoly finally ended owing to demands from English manufacturers who, having displaced Indian textiles from European markets, wanted free access to the Indian market. India's exports to Britain declined, imports grew fast, and, by about the late 1840s, India's trade with Britain showed a deficit as deindustrializing imports, mainly of yarn and cloth, poured in. But Indian exports to the world continued to rise and exceed the new deficit with Britain, so that an overall rising global export surplus was always maintained (see Table 1 and Figure 1). The current value annual merchandise export surplus rose from Rs 3.4 crore during 1833–35 to Rs 87.2 crore by 1917–19, at a compound growth rate of 3.94 per cent. Owing to rupee depreciation from the 1870s, in terms of sterling the growth rate is lower at 3.5 per cent. From 1833 onwards, British India's exports to the world were no longer routed exclusively through Britain's ports but increasingly were sent directly to foreign destinations, the most important being the European Continent, China (the opium trade), later the Americas, and Japan.

The drain increased as internal revenue collections rose, but it was now effected in a more roundabout manner than the earlier *direct* unrequited merchandise export surplus to Britain, since the latter no longer existed as English manufactures were dumped on India. The ensuing problem of 'the realization of the tribute', as Irfan Habib termed it,[33] was tackled by promoting Indian exports to countries with which Britain ran trade deficits. The drive to expand opium exports to China, where the trade was illegal, and to forcibly open up its ports in the Opium Wars was part of this process of promoting triangular trade patterns. In India, local peasants were coerced under state monopoly into growing opium for a very low price,[34] were 'paid' out of taxes as before while the silver *tael* proceeds of their exports to China were used to cancel Britain's deficits.

TABLE 1 *India's global merchandise export surplus, 1833 to 1940* (three-year annual average in Rs 10 million)

Period	X – M	Period	X – M
1833–35	3.35	1887–89	29.14
1836–38	6.82	1890–92	35.77
1839–41	5.37	1893–95	35.42
1842–44	6.74	1896–98	30.85
1845–47	6.37	1899–01	32.24
1848–50	7.12	1902–04	52.6
1851–53	8.73	1905–07	50
1854–55	8.81	1908–10	55.34
1857–59	8	1911–13	73.74
1860–62	16.23	1914–16	61.9
1863–65	38.08	1917–19	87.21
1866–68	15.41	1920–22	–14.62
1869–71	23.84	1923–25	141.23
1872–74	21.56	1926–28	71.58
1875–77	22.18	1929–31	51.09
1878–80	23.55	1932–34	18.57
1881–83	32.38	1935–37	39.77
1884–86	27.49	1938–40	35.62

Source: Calculated from annual series of Exports and Imports, three tables from K.N. Chaudhuri, in D. Kumar, ed. (with the editorial assistance of Meghnad Desai), *The Cambridge Economic History of India, Vol. II: c. 1757 – c. 1970*, Delhi: Orient Longman in association with Cambridge University Press, 1984. Current values.

After India's governance passed to the Crown, the problem of the British rulers continued to be that of promoting India's merchandise exports to maximize gold and exchange earnings from the rest of the world, while ensuring that these earnings remained with Britain and were not credited to Indian producers. The objective was to 'pay' Indian producers as before out of their own taxes, in short not to pay them at all, while their earnings from merchandise surplus in the form of specie, sterling and other currencies were to be intercepted in London and siphoned off by the metropolis for its own needs.

The solution that was worked out was, in principle, both simple and effective: the Secretary of State for India in Council, based in London, would issue rupee bills of exchange to foreign importers of Indian goods, against deposits with him of gold, sterling and their own currencies, as

FIGURE 1 *Merchandise exports surplus, India, 1833 to 1919*

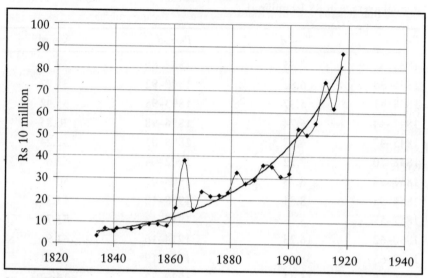

Source: Table 1.

payment for their imports from India. The rate (rupee relative to sterling, the latter being fixed with respect to gold) at which the bills were sold was carefully calibrated down to the smallest fraction of a penny, so that foreign importers would never find it cheaper to send gold as payment directly to Indian exporters, even when that gold might come from nearby Egypt or Australia, compared to using the London Council Bill route. These Council Bills could be cashed only in rupees and the exporters in India who received the Bills (by post or by telegraph), on submitting them through the exchange banks, *were paid by the Indian Treasury out of the rupee budgetary funds already set aside for the purpose as expenditure incurred abroad.* Exporters in turn paid the actual producers while retaining a hefty commission for themselves.

Thus the essential feature of the earlier transfer, or drain, was retained – producers were apparently paid but not actually paid for their export surplus, because the payment continued to come out of taxes raised from the very same producers. The export surplus continued to be merely the commodity form of tax revenues, while its gold and sterling value remained with Britain. However, some internal redistribution of incomes did take place from the producing classes to the Indian and foreign exporters, since these agents took a fairly large cut out of the producer's price.

Sunanda Sen faults Naoroji and Dutt as follows:

... it is not logical to argue that India's export surplus remained unpaid.

> Revenue against such surpluses were duly remitted under the Council
> Bills schema . . . and actually paid out via the intermediation of exchange
> banks to exporters in India. Revenue earmarked in the domestic budget
> as 'Expenditure Abroad' was however effectively transferred abroad
> with home charges met in sterling without the necessity of an actual
> sterling remittance to England.[35]

This lone critical reference in an otherwise valuable study posits an
untenable distinction between Council Bills paid out to exporters and
Expenditure Abroad. It is perhaps best ignored by readers, for the author's
own repeated statements throughout the entire book contradict this one
statement, and make it clear that the distinction did not exist:

> The CBs provided a route for retaining in England the entire amount
> of India's export surplus . . . the budgetary sources of revenue in India
> provided for the entire payments to exporters on account of their net
> export earnings abroad. . . . *Funds earmarked in the annual budget as
> 'Expenditure Abroad' were used to honour the Council Bills in India.*
> (Emphasis added)[36]

To repeat, all Council Bills, amounting to the rupee equivalent of
India's annual commodity export surplus earnings (in gold and forex, kept
by Britain), were paid out to exporters in India out of the annual budget,
under the general head of Expenditure Abroad (this head included both
Home Charges and other items; it varied from 26 to 36 per cent of gross
expenditure). Paying out Council Bills did not increase liquidity, since the
payment was *not* via a complete and equivalent expansion of money supply against forex earnings at the going exchange rate, as would happen
in a sovereign country. It took the abnormal, deliberate form of payment
out of taxes, and Sen herself documents very effectively the stringency of
liquidity arising from this. The paper currency reserve and the gold standard reserve were also sometimes utilized. Because the entire net earnings
of gold and forex of Indian producers were appropriated by Britain, and
even their rupee equivalent was not paid to the producers in the normal
way but out of their own taxes, it was perfectly logical and entirely correct
for Naoroji and Dutt to call it 'unrequited' export surplus.[37]

Some financial gold as payment by foreigners for India's exports
may have evaded this tight system of economic control and reached India,
perhaps through ports in the 'native states'. But this is likely to have been
negligible and is impossible to estimate. The overwhelming bulk of the
rest of the world's payments for India's commodity export surplus was
successfully intercepted and appropriated by the metropolis, and was never

permitted to reach the people who had earned it, either as physical gold for financial payment purposes (as opposed to commodity gold, which was imported like any other good) or as foreign exchange denoted as a final net credit for India. On India's external account, her large and rising commodity export surplus earnings were shown as *completely offset,* and usually somewhat *more than offset,* by the total of politically determined, state-administered invisible debits (the tribute), which included all the rupee 'drain' items of the budget, now expressed in sterling, but which were not necessarily confined to the usual budgetary drain items alone – on which more later.

R.C. Dutt's annual data-series in sterling, one on 'Export Surplus' and the other on 'Expenditure in England', covering the period 1837 to 1900, were spread over several separate tables in his second volume. These have been summarized by this author as two continuous series in Table 2. The export surplus series was reworked by A.K. Banerjee for the same period in his *Aspects of Indo-British Economic Relations.*[38] On comparing the two series, we find that they are near-identical: Banerjee obtained as the total figure only £10 million less than R.C. Dutt did.

India's Export Surplus earnings from the world were precisely what Britain appropriated *in toto,* while the earners of this gold and forex continued to be defrauded of their earnings by being reimbursed out of their own rupee tax contributions. Table 2 shows the remarkable long-term near-equality of India's total export surplus (£617.6 million) and the sterling expenditures in England on account of the sum of 'drain' items (£621 million) over the 65 years.[39] But as Figure 2 depicting these two series makes clear, export surplus earnings fluctuated greatly, affected by internal upheavals and external demand conditions, while the tribute rose steadily. We can distinguish three sub-periods.

During the turbulent period 1837 to 1860 – which saw the Opium Wars to open up China's ports to Indian opium as well as the Great Rebellion of 1857–58 in India – sterling expenditures charged to India exceeded export surplus earnings by £19 million. The cost of the Opium Wars, of suppressing the Rebellion and generously indemnifying the Company as governance passed directly to the Crown was shown as India's debt. The next sub-period, 1861 to1880, saw a raw cotton boom as supplies from North America were affected by its Civil War. There was a steep rise in export surplus earnings, which exceeded the regular sterling expenditure in England by a massive £47 million. Under what heads this large sum was appropriated by Britain needs further research, since as usual India was not permitted to show current account balance, leave alone surplus. The last sub-period, 1881 to 1901, saw a reversal:

TABLE 2 *India's global export surplus and expenditure in England, 1837 to 1901*
(three–year annual average in £ million)

	Expenditure in England	Global export surplus		Expenditure in England	Global export surplus
1837–39	2.499	3.779	1873–75	10.257	15.673
1840–42	2.64	3.684	1875–77	12.458	13.239
1843–45	2.024	4.613	1878–80	14.281	13.932
1846–48	3.03	4.826	1881–83	14.488	18.108
1849–51	2.658	3.809	1884–86	14.151	11.892
1852–54	2.99	4.941	1887–89	15	10.914
1855–57	4.317	−2.146	1890–92	15.892	14.305
1858–60	7.484	−2.096	1893–95	15.681	15.234
1861–63	7.257	8.115	1896–98	16.069	14.913
1864–66	6.919	11.158	1899–01	16.988	12.415
1867–69	9.757	4.969	TOTAL		
1870–72	10.161	19.593	SUM	621	617.6

TOTAL VALUES in £ million for sub-periods

Sub-periods	Expenditure in England	Global Export Surplus	Difference (2 – 1)
	1	2	3
1837 to 1860	82.93	64.23	−18.7
1861 to 1880	213.27	260.04	46.77
1881 to 1901	324.81	293.34	−31.47

Source: R.C. Dutt, *Economic History of India*, Vol. 2: *In the Victorian Age 1837–1900*
[1905], second reprint, Delhi: Government of India, by arrangement with Routledge and
Kegan Paul. Total Export Surplus is Merchandise Export Surplus minus net Gold Imports.
The figures above underestimate, as do all official figures, the actual commodity export
surplus especially for the last period, because financial or monetary gold imports are wrongly
included in the current account along with commodity gold imports. Eight separate tables
of annual values have been combined to give the continuous series above. For the period
1878 onwards, the trade data in Dutt are in rupees. The annual exchange rate is provided
and has been used to convert the rupee values to pound sterling.

sterling expenditures in England charged to India exceeded the latter's
export surplus earnings by £31.5 million, very likely owing to the large-
scale purchase and import of monetary gold as backing for India's gold
exchange standard, against a background of a depreciating rupee and
unremitting transfer (see the last section discussing Y.S. Pandit's estimate).

FIGURE 2 *India's export surplus and expenditure in England, 1837–38 to 1900–01* (in £ million, three-year annual averages)

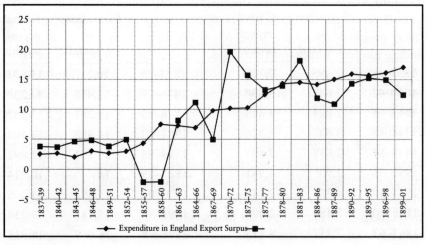

Source: Table 2.

Clearly, it was not possible for the colonial government to match exactly, year by year, the invisible tribute demands to commodity export surplus earnings, since the latter fluctuated and could not be predicted precisely. But over a run of years the total of drain items making up the colonial tribute was always pitched somewhat *higher* than India's ability to meet the demand through her large, rising global gold and forex earnings from commodity export surplus, no matter how fast the latter might grow. India's rising external earnings not only magically disappeared into the yawning maw of the Secretary of State's account in London, but she was shown to be in perpetual deficit, despite running the second largest merchandise export surplus in the world for decades on end. The data for 1898 to 1913 in Pandit[40] show commodity export surplus of Rs 551.4 crore (equal to Council Bills to this value paid out from the budget). But this was more than offset by imposing invisible debits of Rs 625.4 crore, leaving a current account deficit of Rs 74 crore (see Table 4).[41] The estimate by A.K. Banejee[42] for 1922 to 1938 shows commodity export surplus earnings of Rs 905.5 crore, substantially less than invisible demands imposed, totalling Rs.1433 crore, entailing a large current account deficit of Rs 527.5 crore (see Table 5).[43]

If India's own gold and forex earnings from global commodity export surplus had been actually credited to it, or even partially credited and not entirely siphoned off, then, given the very large size of these earnings especially in the twentieth century, India would have enjoyed a current account surplus and could have imported technology to build up a modern industrial structure as Japan was doing at that time, or exported capital itself. But colonial exploitation made for an *Alice through the Looking Glass* world: India, the country with the second largest global export surplus for decades, had more than its entire forex earnings taken away and was reduced to enforced borrowing. With its iron grip over Indian internal and external finances, the metropolis kept an entire colonized people as 'perpetually indebted' to it, as any bonded labourer to his landlord. Conversely, the metropolis, though it incurred the largest trade deficits globally, through such appropriation of its colonies' earnings, could become nonetheless the world's largest capital exporter.

India's annual net exchange earnings from commodity trade, termed NX1 in the next section, were appropriated by Britain via a number of arbitrary invisible liabilities ostensibly owed to it by India in sterling, which we term NX2. This included all the regular annual drain items mentioned in rupees in the budget (Home Charges, dividends and so on), but could also include additional items such as 'gifts'. Within Home Charges, interest payments exceeded other items by far, not because there was much of productive loans – the entire subcontinent had received hardly one-tenth of total British foreign investment by 1913 – but because the cost of all Britain's imperial wars of conquest outside Indian borders had been charged always wholly or mainly to Indian revenues. So was the cost of maintaining several of Britain's legations in foreign countries, and the cost of telegraph lines – first the Red Sea line and later the Mauritius–Cape Town line. These and other expenses were shown as a cumulating, artificially created debt.

The government in Britain, working in tandem with its colonial counterpart, adjusted the tribute to actual, realized export surplus earnings, *in an asymmetric manner*. When India's export surplus earnings rose to an unusual extent, or when Britain needed more gold and forex, additional debits including munificent 'gifts' from India to Britain were imposed. Bagchi points out that an astonishing *additional £100 million* over and above the regular transfer (this sum exceeded the entire annual budget) went as a 'gift' from British India to Britain after World War I, a gift no Indian knew about.[44] Japan used its wartime forex boom to build up reserves and its industry; India's earnings were always siphoned off.

But if India's global exchange earnings happened to falter, owing say to world recessionary conditions, the sum demanded as sterling tribute was never lowered, and any gap between it and actual earnings was covered by showing (enforced) borrowing by India which raised its future interest burdens. *Such manipulation of invisibles liabilities by government ensured that over a given run of years India's current account was always*

*made to remain in deficit, no matter what heights were scaled by its com-
modity surplus.* The only notable exception was 1907–08 which marked a
global crisis, and the abnormal two years of import surge after World War
I when there was net sale of Reverse Councils. (Gold outflow during the
Depression years was not commodity gold but financial gold, as explained
in the last section.) The mechanism of drain is spelt out in symbols in the
next section and the data are summarized in the last section.

*If we take the mid-point of Dutt's period, 1869, and compound the
total drain of £620 million at a very low 5 per cent interest rate (the present
interest rate is 8 per cent), the resulting sum comes to £848.025 billion.
This amounts to two-thirds of India's entire GDP at factor cost for 2016,
and to 45 per cent of United Kingdom value GDP in 2015.* (A sympathetic
observer, Montgomery Martin, had compounded the drain at 12 per cent,
the prevalent Indian interest rate. This would give us £11,930.54 *trillion*
as the present value of £620 million, over six thousand times the 2015
GDP of the United Kingdom!) Let us bear the grossly underestimated first
figure in mind until the last section, where we present similar deliberate
underestimates of transfer for 1901 onwards.

Both Naoroji and Dutt were acutely conscious of the fact that
when monies raised from producers in India were not spent in their entirety
within the country under normal budgetary heads, it meant a severe squeeze
on the producers' incomes. Insightful British administrators said the same;
Dutt supported Major George Wingate's remarks:

> . . . the tribute paid to Great Britain is by far the most objectionable
> feature in our existing policy. Taxes spent in the country from which
> they are raised are totally different in their effects from taxes raised in
> one country and spent in another . . . they constitute no mere transfer
> of a portion of the national income from one set of citizens to another,
> but an absolute loss and extinction of the whole amount withdrawn
> from the taxed country. As regards its effects on national production,
> the whole amount might as well be thrown into the sea as transferred
> to another country.[45]

They were quite right for, in effect, *surplus budgets* to an unimaginably large extent were being operated with a strongly *deflationary
impact* on mass purchasing power. The crucial fact to be added to Wingate's
remarks was that for the foreign ruler, this portion of taxes transferred
was not 'thrown into the sea' – rather, it was embodied in vast volumes
of completely free goods, sea-borne in British bottoms for use in the home
country and for re-export. Since getting goods free, thanks to its control
of taxation, was one major reason the British were in India at all (the

other reason was markets on tap for their manufactures), they were never going to give up defrauding local producers by operating surplus budgets to acquire costless goods. The last section of this paper shows that in the five decades before independence, the budgetary surplus (or expenditure abroad) ranged from one-third to nearly four-fifths of total expenditure. This meant drastic *income deflation* – this was the 'necessary' economic mechanism for imperialists (since there was no overt use of force after the 1860s) – to reduce the producers' own consumption of basic staples, and so squeeze out more export crops from the same area. How successful this was can be seen from the virtual stagnation of estimated per capita income and the steep decline in per capita foodgrain absorption in British India from 200 kilograms per capita in 1900 to 157 kilograms per capita by1938.

While the pre-British rulers including invaders had also raised taxes, they had become a permanent part of the domiciled population, spending all public funds within the country. There were no systematic surplus budgets, no income-deflating impact on producers as under British rule, nor was there any drain. Naoroji and Dutt pointed out that the very existence of the large number of specific heads of spending *outside* the country, which constituted the drain items in the budget, arose solely from India being a colony, run for the maximum benefit and imperial aggrandizement of the metropolis. In the 'Home Charges', the major part was military spending abroad – the cost of imperial wars of conquest outside India was always put on the Indian revenues, supplemented by enforced borrowing.[46]

Sterling companies were given full freedom to take out without limit dividends generated within the country, and very large sums went as interest payments on growing public sterling debt. The parasitic habit of putting large extraneous charges on India was to be repeated, for the last time, to disastrous effect from 1941 to 1946. The enormous burden of financing the Allies' war spending in South Asia was put on the Indian revenues. Forced savings were extracted through a profit inflation which reduced mass consumption in India, and in Bengal, where the Allied forces were located, reduced it to such an extreme extent that 3 million civilians died of starvation.[47]

Some authors have said, and this author agrees entirely with the point, that the merchandise export surplus *understated* the true adverse impact. First, many imported goods were demanded only by the rulers, followed imitatively by the tiny local elite, and not by the population. These included such items as marble statuary, crystal chandeliers and grand pianos. However, we do not try to adjust the recorded export surplus upwards by any estimated amount of luxury imports as it is preferable to underestimate the drain given our contention that it was very large. Second, mass consumption goods like machine- made cotton yarn and cloth from Britain entered India displacing local production, solely owing to discriminatory colonial policy which kept the Indian market completely open to dumping for over a century while protecting the British market. Such deindustrializing imports constituted an adverse impact on employment of such extreme importance that it has always been analysed separately. It cannot be subsumed under the drain discussion here.

Macroeconomic Basis of Colonial Transfers, or the Drain of Wealth

The assumption underlying standard open-economy macroeconomics is that all countries are sovereign and trade voluntarily. For the metropolis and colony, this assumption did not hold. While some authors had earlier expressed the metropolis–colony relation in symbolic terms, they did not modify the standard formulations to take account of the specificity of this relation.[48]

The essence of the internal-cum-external drain discussed so far can be captured, we believe, by modifying the identity linking the budgetary balance, the external balance and the savings–investment balance, for both colony and metropolis. This has been shown earlier by this author.[49] Here we recapitulate briefly only the part dealing with the colony. The drain can be measured either by that part of the colony's rupee budget which was set aside for spending outside the country, or by its merchandise export surplus, since these forex earnings covered these items of spending. Either measure would do as a minimal approximation to the actual drain.

In a sovereign country, the identity linking the savings–investment balance, the budgetary balance and the external balance is expressed as follows:[50]

$$(S - I) = (G - T) + NX \quad \dots\dots\dots\dots (1)$$

where S and I refer to private savings and investment; G is government expenditure; T is taxes and other forms of revenue so that $(G - T)$ is the budgetary balance; NX is net exports, the short form of $(X - M)$, namely the excess of exports of goods and services over imports of the same. Given savings–investment balance, a budgetary surplus would be reflected in a current account surplus, and the converse would hold: a current account deficit accompanies a budgetary deficit. Given a balanced budget, a current account deficit would be reflected in an excess of private investment over savings, and a surplus budget, with balanced trade, in an excess of savings over investment.

In a colony the matter is quite different owing to the *direct link* between the fiscal and trade parts, whereby export surplus earnings were paid to local producers out of their own taxes deposited with government. The budget *appeared* to be balanced as a measure of 'sound finance', because $G = T$ so that $(G - T) = 0$. But effectively, the budget was kept in large surplus every year, since only a part of tax revenues T was spent in a normal manner. Total public spending G was divided by the government itself into two parts, which we designate as GD for the part spent domestically and GA for the part spent abroad. GA constituted the total of 'drain' items: these were either administratively imposed, like the Home Charges, or as interest on an external debt whose size arose from public policy. Even when private investors were involved, as in remittance of interest and dividends by sterling companies, it was aided by favourable state policies and dividend outflow was permitted without limit. Thus the budget, though apparently balanced, was perpetually in surplus when we consider heads of normal internal spending, leaving out the 'drain' items GA.

$$T = G = (GD + GA)$$
$$(T - GD) = GA > 0 \qquad \ldots\ldots\ldots\ldots\ldots (2)$$

This division of the budget was reflected in a corresponding division of net exports NX into two parts. We define NX1 as the colony's total earnings from the world including Britain on account of its commodity export surplus, namely taking merchandise and commodity gold; it is a large positive figure and these earnings are kept by Britain. NX2 is the balance of invisibles imposed on the colony, arising solely from its colonial status and politically manipulated to be a large negative figure. This includes all the 'drain' items GA of the internal budget, now expressed in sterling, but is not confined to GA and may in some years include additional items. Since all of the colony's global export surplus earnings NX1 are siphoned off by imposing an equivalent value of invisible liabilities NX2 equal to GA, the current account NX will sum to zero. But if *more* than exchange earnings NX1 is demanded by the metropolis so that NX2 > NX1, the current account will be negative and entail borrowing. The latter was generally the case, as the data show. Borrowing could be private or public. If the budget is balanced, this implies that the private savings–investment balance will be negative to the same extent.

$$NX = (NX1 + NX2) \leq 0 \text{ since } NX1 \leq NX2$$

$$NX2 \geq GA \qquad \ldots\ldots\ldots\ldots (3)$$

The trade surplus NX1 grew especially fast from the early 1890s onwards, aided by the depreciation of silver relative to gold. This greatly increased the GA requirement in rupee terms to meet the same level of downwardly inflexible sterling demands as before. Hence it meant increased taxation T on producers. When the limits of tax extraction was reached, the adjustment to increased demands by the metropolis was made through enforced borrowing by the colony.

Payments made by foreigners to Indians for a large, positive NX1 were in Council Bills, including telegraphic transfers cashable only in rupees – as no other mode of remittance was permitted, the value of the Council Bills was identically equal to the export surplus of India with the world on commodity account NX1. We define the commodity export surplus NX1 as Exports *f.o.b* minus Imports *c.i.f.* The producers of this export surplus were paid out of the part of budgetary revenues earmarked as GA, so NX1 would equal GA. The total of the invisible demands on India NX2 would, however, be more than NX1 as well as GA, by the amount of long-term borrowing.

The drain can be approximated as an underestimate by the budgetary expenditures set aside for spending abroad, namely GA, or equivalently by NX1, namely the actual exchange earnings which made possible this spending abroad. Alternatively, the drain can be approximated at a more accurate and higher level by the sum of NX1 and long-term borrowing, which would give us NX2, the actual total of invisible liabilities imposed on India.

The Gold Question

The above framework combined with actual trends enables us to see that while foreigners made payment in full for their import surplus from India, namely NX1, this payment was retained in London since invisibles summing to more than these payments, namely NX2, were demanded by the metropolis, leaving India's current account NX in deficit (over a run of years). Looking at the data on trade surplus in the next section from the United Nations,[51] and the estimates of balance of payments from Pandit and Banerjee,[52] we see that no matter how fast the commodity surplus earnings grew, the administered invisible demands on India were made to grow even faster: with such a managed current account deficit, borrowing was forced on India, increasing future interest burdens.

In all this, *gold movements* play a large part. India was a net importer of gold for the period before the Great Depression, in substantial part as commodity gold for individual use for ornaments and as a preferred means of wealth-holding (along with land) in the absence of a developed financial assets system. The persistence of gold preference in recent times was underlined dramatically when the global financial crisis from 2008 saw a surge of gold import by Indians. However, during the period under discussion, a large part of gold (and silver) movements was on account of government, and clearly comprised financial gold and not commodity gold. We use the term gold here to cover precious metals.

It is standard practice by authors to treat all net gold inflow and outflow as *commodity gold*, and put it in the trade account along with other goods. But this is not a correct procedure, for under the gold standard, the accepted means of settling imbalance in international payments was gold flows. Further, gold was imported by the colonial government for the reserve requirements of India's gold exchange standard, and this definitely constituted monetary gold and not commodity gold. India's merchandise export surplus has tended to be substantially underestimated in the literature,[53] or the current account deficit has been underestimated,[54] by treating all gold inflow and outflow as commodity gold on par with other merchandise imports. The official trade statistics collected at that time could have made the distinction between commodity gold and non-commodity gold, but they did not do so explicitly. In the last section we reclassify Pandit and Banerjee's estimates with respect to roughly estimated financial gold flows (see Tables 4 and 5).

The United Nations and the International Monetary Fund (IMF) recently held a series of discussions by the Balance of Payments Technical Expert Group (BOPTEG), because even the modern system of national accounts and balance of payments needed to be modified. Merchandise trade estimates of many countries were seriously distorted by treating all international gold flows as commodity gold, thus not taking account of monetary gold or other types of financial gold. Three types of use of gold in international transactions have been distinguished by two members of the BOPTEG, Wright and Brown: 'Commodity gold . . . if held for industrial use or as a valuable; non-Monetary Financial Gold, if held by financial institutions and/or bullion traders for market making purposes; Monetary gold (a subset of Financial Gold) if held by Central Banks as a reserve asset.'[55]

The demand for gold historically, as a commodity for industrial or private use, had to be distinguished from its purchase by government for the purposes of building up reserves and for coinage. While the concepts of commodity gold and of monetary gold have been in use for long, the recent proposals included a third category, gold trade by bullion dealers for 'market making purposes', as a subset of financial gold.

These distinctions should have been implemented a century earlier at least: in the era of the gold standard there was lack of clarity by governments on the treatment of different types of gold movements, precisely when gold played a more important role than today as a means of settling external imbalance. As India made the transition to a version of the gold exchange standard in the last two decades of the nineteenth century, the colonial government imported substantial values of gold into India to build up a reserve, using India's export surplus earnings for that purpose and obliging it to borrow to discharge the 'drain' liabilities. This was monetary gold and not commodity gold. Similarly, gold outflow during the crisis of the Depression was a means of payment and hence financial gold outflow. Yet all writers at that time and recently have treated these quite incorrectly as commodity gold flows.

Continuing to Appropriate India's Export Surplus Earnings during the Period of High Imperialism

J.K. Galbraith, in his review of Keynes's *Collected Writings*, wrote impatiently that 'he [Keynes] became concerned with the trivial [*sic*] intricacies of currency and banking in India. . . . On this he wrote a monograph, *Indian Currency and Finance* . . . any scholar of moderate capacity [*sic*] could have learned all that was useful to know about the subject in about three months, perhaps less'.[56]

Galbraith could not have been more wrong. Ripping off India (and smaller colonies) by appropriating year after year, in the pre-World War I period, at least £35–50 million of gold and forex earnings for imperial ends, was not a 'trivial' matter but a very serious business indeed. On it depended the smooth functioning of the international gold standard and on it also depended Britain's undisputed position as the world capitalist leader, with the pound sterling being considered 'as good as gold' and the dollar nowhere in the picture.

The question for imperialist rulers was one of devising the most efficient monetary and exchange rate system for maximizing and appropriating India's external earnings, and to do so without killing outright the goose that laid the golden eggs: the peasant producers and wage workers. This question engaged some of the best English minds of the time (though, naturally, they did not put the matter in quite such blunt terms). Not only did Keynes study the Indian financial system, which he found 'exceedingly difficult to understand',[57] for many years he gave courses of lectures to students in Cambridge on the subject, and he was asked to give evidence to nearly every official Commission on Indian finance and currency (the Chamberlain, Babington–Smith and Hilton Young Commissions).

The main reason that there were so many Commissions on Indian financial matters was that, as European countries dumped their silver for gold in transiting to the gold standard, there was a sharp decline in the global silver price relative to gold during the two decades after 1873. This created specific problems of maintaining the transfer from India to Britain, and World War I introduced questions of relative rates of inflation affecting Indian export competitiveness and hence the transfer. The fall in silver price over two decades from the 1870s made Indian goods cheaper in gold standard countries, and export surplus grew well as did the export surplus of Japan, which also had a silver currency. But unlike Japan, India was subject to the drain: with a given, downwardly inflexible sterling demand as drain on exchange earnings, when the rupee depreciated much more rupee taxes had to be raised from local producers.[58] This got converted to a larger volume of exported commodities in order to obtain the unchanged sterling value of export surplus.

Say India had to pay £15 million of drain items to Britain at least equal to its global export surplus NX1 come what may, which meant that Rs 150 million of tax revenues GA had to be set aside in the budget for this purpose at the initial rate of Rs 10 to £1, to pay out against Council Bills tendered. When the silver rupee depreciated by 60 per cent, to Rs 16 to £1, the same £15 million drain now required Rs 240 million in tax revenues, 60 per cent higher than before. The very idea of reducing sterling demands on the revenues below £15 million would not even occur to imperialists – their solution was always to extract more from the colonized population. The annual sterling expenditures in England charged to Indian revenues in fact actually rose by 17 per cent during the two-decade period up to 1898–99. To finance this higher demand given the fast-depreciating rupee meant that taxes had to be raised greatly, or a larger share of the total budget had to go as drain items GA, exercising a correspondingly greater income-deflating effect. A combination of the two seems to have taken place – new indirect taxes like the salt tax (1885) were imposed, gross revenues rose a whopping 62 per cent over the two decades, and the share of the budget going as GA also went up. With increased exactions and even greater income deflation, an unusually large number of famine deaths marked the 1890s.

Indian 'public opinion' seems to have always agitated for the wrong objective, for rupee depreciation and more exports, seemingly unaware or more likely uncaring that the more export surplus earnings there were, the greater was the tax squeeze on the peasantry to defray these earnings out of the budget. A higher rupee as advised by the Herschell Committee at the old rate of Rs 2 per shilling could have obviated the increased burden on the peasantry. The only class in India that benefited from more exports were the intermediaries or *dalals* of the export–import trade, who took a large cut as commission/profit from the monies paid out to the peasants from their own taxes. Many Indian business houses had started life as agents of the Company in the notorious opium trade to China; the Tatas had made their initial money from *dalali* in the opium trade as had Dwarakanath Tagore, grandfather of the poet Rabindranath Tagore. The business leaders were inclined to bring the *dalal* viewpoint to the issue of the exchange rate while completely ignoring the interests of peasant producers. Dadabhai Naoroji, in his usual insightful manner, had noticed and regretted this class bias.

Returning to the inapposite remarks by Galbraith[59] about the 'trivial' nature of Indian finance, they also showed that he had not read Saul,[60] and had no idea that the large capital exports from Britain from the 1870s onwards, which built US roads, railways and factories, depended crucially on Britain's ability to siphon off India's forex earnings. These earnings not only offset the deficits that Britain was running on its current account with the US, but helped to offset also the additional deficits owing to its capital exports to that country. By the 1920s, over two-thirds of India's global export surplus earnings came from Continental Europe and North America.

Saul did not talk explicitly of 'drain' or transfer from India,[61] because he seems to have had no knowledge of the tax-financed nature of India's export surplus. His main concern was tracing Britain's balance of payments with different regions of the world from the 1880s onwards, which showed a very striking picture. Britain incurred large, rising current account deficits with the European Continent, North America and regions of recent European settlement, while it posted a huge nominal current account surplus only with its tropical colonies, pre-eminently with India. Further, Britain exported capital to the very same developing regions with which it ran current account deficits, leading to capital account deficits. The two deficits summed to large balance of payments deficits. In 1910, Britain's deficit on its balance of payments with the USA plus the European Continent had reached £120 million; India earned that year a massive merchandise export surplus from the entire world of £57.8 million, but a somewhat higher sum, £60 million, was shown as Britain's credit with India,[62] which was set off against Britain's deficit.

In terms of our notation, NX2, the sum of invisible liabilities £60 million politically imposed by Britain and shown as its credit with India in 1910, was pitched a little higher than NX1, India's £57.8 million actual global export surplus earnings that year; the balance, £2.2 million, would have been shown as addition to India's debt to Britain. Such a managed 'perpetual indebtedness' was useful, for any later forex earnings by the colony could be absorbed via 'repayment' of the artificially created 'debt'.

During 1940 to 1944, when food imports were badly needed especially in Bengal, and India had the required forex earnings totalling Rs 396 crore (about £264 million), this exact amount was taken by Britain under 'repayment of debt'.

Saul's study documented the important 'balancing role' that India played in the multilateral trade system centred on Britain during the period of the gold standard. However it was not simply a balancing role, since such a role could also exist if Britain actually had a legitimate surplus to the extent required with India. But it did not have a legitimate surplus, and manipulated invisibles were imposed, defrayed out of taxes as earlier explained, to siphon off India's global forex surpluses to offset Britain's deficits on its balance of payments. Saul could not be expected to enter in detail into the question of how Britain arrived at a 'surplus' in its external account with India, which, taking a run of years, always seemed magically either to equal India's *total* gold and forex earnings from the entire world or be somewhat larger. He certainly realized that Britain treated Indian export earnings as its own, since he pointed out that in effect Indian goods, which were largely duty-free on the Continent and North America, were used by Britain to jump tariff barriers which its own export goods faced.

Saul pointed out that 'The key to Britain's whole payments pattern lay in India, financing as she probably did more than two-fifths of Britain's total deficits'. Further: 'But this was by no means all, for it was mainly through India that the British balance of payments found the flexibility essential to a great capital exporting country.'[63] He went on to say, 'The importance of India's trade to the pattern of world trade balances can hardly be exaggerated.'[64]

In fact Britain would not have been a capital exporting country at all, great or otherwise, if it did not have complete control over colonial exchange earnings – as well as control over taxes enabling it to defraud local producers of their forex earnings – since with the rest of the world it ran current account deficits of such a magnitude that it would have needed to borrow capital. The present-day world capitalist leader, the USA, also has been running large current deficits with the world for the last three decades, but without access to colonial transfers in the old form that Britain enjoyed, it is not an exporter of capital but the world's largest debtor.

Changing Magnitude of the Drain and Corresponding Fiscal Compression

The trade data submitted to the League of Nations (1942) by the colonial government inflated India's merchandise imports, and included only interest payments on government account, as Banerjee points out.[65]

The data presently available online from a later UN study on the matrix of global trade appear to be more reliable,[66] and on checking, we find that these data are broadly consistent with the series built up by Indian scholars from primary sources. The exchange rates for converting the data in dollars to pound sterling, and to different countries' currencies, are given for each year of the series from 1900 to 1960; we focus on 1900 to 1938.

Tables 3a and 3b show that between 1900–01 and 1924–26, India's

TABLE 3a *India's trade balance with the world, 1900 to 1913* (million US dollars, three-year annual averages)

	Exports	*Imports*	*Balance*
1900–01	367.5	313	54.5
1902–04	467.7	349.3	118.4
1905–07	547.3	449.7	97.6
1908–10	584.3	456.3	128
1911–13	765.3	590.7	174.6

Note: Three-year averages calculated from annual series, except the first period which is a two-year average. India includes present-day Bangladesh, Pakistan and Burma. Current values.
Source: Calculated from United Nations, *International Trade Statistics 1900–1960*, Table XIII, 1962, available at www.unstats.un.org/unsd/trade/imts/Historicaldata1900–1960.pdf

FIGURE 3a *India's merchandise trade balance, 1900–1913* (million US dollars, three-year annual averages)

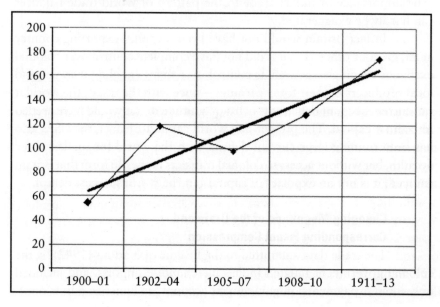

TABLE 3b *India's merchandise trade balance with the world, 1924–1938* (million US dollars, three-year annual averages)

Year	Exports	Imports	Balance
1924–26	1238	909	329
1927–29	1182.3	993	189.3
1930–32	558	485	73
1933–35	566.7	469	97.3
1936–38	668.5	590.3	78.2

Source: Same as Table 3a. Data for 1914 to 1922 are not available in the source.

FIGURE 3b *India's merchandise trade balance, 1924–1938* (million US dollars, three-year annual averages)

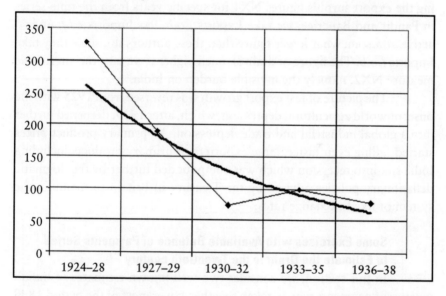

export earnings on merchandise account grew at a spanking pace of 7.5 per cent annually; export earnings scaled their highest level of $1.24 billion by the triennium 1924–26 while export surplus reached $0.33 billion. India posted the second highest export surplus globally from 1900 to 1928 (the USA had the highest) and this is likely to have been true during the 1890s as well, judging from Saul's data. However, India had an import surplus in two years following World War I. There was much sharper import compression than export compression (the belligerents needed Indian jute for sand-bags), and a compensating import surge took place in 1920 and 1921. In the next triennium, 1922–24, export surplus bounced back to an all-time high of Rs 1,410 million or £94 million annual average.

Many economic historians of the period have assumed that liquidity within the country fluctuated directly with the movement of trade. However the actual picture was rather more complicated owing to the effects of the drain. The central plus state revenues roughly doubled from just under Rs 100 crore in 1900–01[67] to Rs 210 crore by 1925,[68] but over the same period the export surplus more than trebled. A higher share of the budget went to 'pay' producers for their export surplus out of their own taxes, making the income-deflating impact even more severe. An important item of drain, the Home Charges, rose as a share of the budget from 18 per cent in the 1860s to 26 per cent by 1928,[69] and additionally there was dividend outflow.

We consider freight, insurance and commission to be charges that India would very likely have paid even as a sovereign nation. In calculating the export surplus figures NX1 for specific years from the time-series in Pandit and Banerjee, we take Exports *f.o.b.* less Imports *c.i.f.* and so arrive at a somewhat lower figure than these authors do, since they take Imports *f.o.b.* The figure of drain is much higher if we take the alternative measure NX2, namely the invisible burden on India.

The picture of fast export growth was reversed from 1925 with the onset of world agricultural depression, which, after 1929, deepened further into a global industrial and trade depression. All primary product prices started falling even faster; large exporters of primary products including India slid into recession which was compounded further by the dogmatic deflationary policies advised by the Treasury in Britain to maintain the system of fixed exchange rates.

Some Exercises with Available Balance of Payments Series to Estimate the Drain in the Twentieth century

In this section, we consider two well-known estimates of India's balance of payments which, taken together, cover most of the period 1898 to 1940 – namely, Y.S. Pandit in *India's Balance of Indebtedness 1898 to1913*[70] and A.K. Banerjee in *India's Balance of Payments: Estimates of Current and Capital Accounts from 1921–22 to 1938–39.*[71] Although neither author mentions the drain explicitly, we can certainly approximate the magnitude of the drain from their data by applying the concepts of NX1 and NX2 as measures.

In Table 4, the aggregate values for the sixteen years from 1898–99 to 1913–14, from Pandit,[72] are set out with respect to the important variables. While Pandit estimates and deducts the freight, insurance and commission from imports every year in order to get a pure trade balance, we retain his original figures of Imports *c.i.f.* for both merchandise and gold

TABLE 4 *Balance of payments aggregates, 1898 to 1913 (Pandit 1937): data reclassified with respect to estimated financial gold*

Summary of Balance of Payments Aggregates, 1898 to 1913
Y.S. Pandit (1937), Rs 10 million

		Total	*Annual*
Balance of Merchandise	(X – M *c.i.f.*)	803.88	50.2
Balance of Gold	(X – M *c.i.f.*)	–408.06	–25.5
Council Bills = Balance of Merchandise and Commodity Gold		551.37 (NX1)	34.5
So, Commodity Gold = Council Bills less Balance of Merchandise		–252.51	–15.8
Total Debits on account of Invisibles		–625.44 (NX2)	–39.1
Current A/c Balance	NX1 less NX2	–74.07	–4.6
Monetary Gold Inflow = Total Gold less Commodity Gold		–155.55	–9.7
Secretary of State's Balances drawn down		29.91	1.8
Import of Capital		199.71	12.5
Additional Merchandise Balance – non-British India		13	0.8
Adjustment for excess Interest Payment		30	1.9
	Sum of Adjustments 43		
Adjusted Capital Import	(199.71 – 43) =	156.71	9.8

Source: Y.S. Pandit, *India's Balance of Indebtedness 1898 to 1913*, London: Allen and Unwin, 1937. Note that I have: (a) separated from commodity gold, the estimated non-commodity gold, so to that extent there is a larger positive balance of commodity trade equal to Council Bills value, compared to the source. (b) Imports are taken here at *c.i.f.* values, so to the extent of freight, insurance and commission amounting to Rs 155.35 crore the balance of commodity trade inclusive of gold is smaller. The same sum is deducted from the Invisibles balance. The last three rows show the two adjustments suggested by Pandit, which would bring his capital import estimate of Rs 199.7 million, which here is a balancing residual, closer to his direct estimate of capital import, Rs 149.6 million.

to obtain a smaller positive balance for merchandise at Rs 8,038.8 million and a larger negative balance for gold at Rs 4,080.6 million. Payments were made for their net imports by foreigners through Council Bills, since directly shipping gold was less paying. The value of Council Bills may be assumed to equal the overall commodity trade balance NX1, namely the surplus on merchandise account plus the deficit on commodity gold account, and this enables us to derive a rough estimate for commodity gold.

The total value of Council Bills being Rs 5,513.7 million (equal to NX1) and the surplus on merchandise account Rs 8,038.8 million, the deficit on commodity gold is derived as the difference, Rs 2,525.1 million. Since we know the deficit for all gold, which was Rs 4,080.6 million, the monetary or, more generally, non-commodity financial gold balance can be derived, and comes to Rs 1,555.5 million or about 38 per cent of the total net inflow of gold over the period. The invisible liabilities put on India or NX2 at Rs 6,254 million, compared with NX1, gives a current account deficit of Rs 741 million. The borrowing required to cover this deficit plus the monetary gold import of Rs 1,555.5 million thus amounts to Rs 1,997 million – an unusually large extent of borrowing.

The interpretation is that, despite the transition to a gold exchange standard which mandated considerable gold purchases (Rs 1.56 billion worth) out of Indian exchange earnings for building reserves, there was no let-up on the huge invisibles tribute to Britain of Rs 6.25 billion, as usual pitched somewhat higher than the total export surplus earnings of Rs 5.51 billion, so only substantial enforced borrowing of Rs 2 billion could balance India's external accounts. In average annual terms the total invisibles tribute NX2 was kept so large at Rs 391 million so as to leave a deficit Rs 46 million, after absorbing the whole of India's fast-rising global export surplus earnings (inclusive of commodity gold imports) of Rs 345 million. This deficit, plus imports of monetary gold by government for coinage and reserves, had to be financed through borrowing to the extent of around Rs 125 million annually, if we take Pandit's initial estimate.[73]

The gold purchased for India's gold standard reserve was physically shifted to London in 1902 and absorbed by the British government (needing funds after the Boer War) that issued securities against Indian gold. De Cecco points out that further, the India Office lent funds out of the gold standard reserve at 2 per cent to a number of City firms, that then leveraged the funds to lend at a higher rate and made hefty profits on the London money market.[74] Manifold and ingenious were the ways in which Indian public resources were diverted for British public and private profit.

Calculating the aggregate drain taking NX1, we find that it is Rs 5,513.7 million over the sixteen years in Pandit's study, 1898 to 1913, with mid-point in 1905. Compounded at a low 5 per cent interest for the 112-year period since 1905, the sum is Rs 1,302.087 billion or £86.805 billion.

Eliminating the years 1898 to 1900 as these have been counted already as the last three years in Dutt's series, and adding the years from 1914 to 1919, the total export surplus is Rs 8,974 million from 1901 to

1919. Compounded from 1910 to date, the sum comes to Rs 1,581.44 billion or £105.4 billion.

Turning to A.K. Banerjee's estimates for the eighteen-year inter-war period, 1921–22 to 1938–39, Table 5 shows that the export surplus on merchandise account was only Rs 13,014 million compared to Rs 9,061 million during Pandit's pre-war sixteen-year period. (Again, we take Imports *c.i.f.* unlike these authors, so both our trade surplus and the invisibles total are smaller.) While India's exports registered unprecedented growth up to 1928, the decline was equally dramatic after that (see Figure 3b) as the global fall in primary product prices from the mid-1920s changed into crashing prices from 1931, and global trade contracted to one-third of the 1929 level within four years.[75]

Net gold inflows over the entire period were much smaller at Rs 1,220 million, less than one-third compared to Rs 4,081 million during 1898 to 1913, because while there was net commodity gold *inflow* from 1921–22 to 1930–31, this was reversed as the impact of the Depression was felt. Very large, unprecedented net gold *outflow* to the tune of Rs 3,072 million during 1931 to 1937 took place owing to deepening agrarian distress, and the insistence of Britain on maintaining the drain from India to the full extent despite the forex crisis induced by the Depression. This gold outflow cannot be treated as commodity gold as is done universally – and quite incorrectly – in the literature. It was financial gold, part payment for the unusually large current account deficit which emerged because India's export earnings plunged during the Depression years, but Britain's demands on India did not.

Continuing with our partial reclassification of Banerjee's data, the (negative) commodity gold balance of Rs 4,293 million is arrived at by treating all the net gold inflow from 1921–22 to 1930–31 as commodity gold. Since no official gold import for reserves took place during this period, the assumption may not be too off the mark. The commodity surplus NX1 amounts to Rs 9,055 million, smaller than Banerjee's estimate, since we treat the distress gold outflow from 1931–32 onwards as financial gold. The sum of all invisible liabilities NX2 heaped on India was Rs 14,330 million. Comparing with Pandit's period, while total NXI was 64 per cent higher, the total NX2 was 129 per cent higher. The resulting *current account deficit* of Rs 5,275 million was thus unusually large owing to the impact of the Depression on India's trade, combined with unrelenting transfer. The deficit was liquidated through the financial gold outflow of Rs 3,072 million, combined with borrowing to the extent of Rs 2,203 million. The estimate of borrowing remains unchanged with our reclassification because our exercise involves merely shifting part of the gold flows out from the

TABLE 5 *Balance of payments aggregates, 1921–22 to 1938–39, A.K. Banerjee (1963): data reclassified by estimated financial gold*

Summary of Balance of Payments Aggregates, 1921–22 to 1938–39
Data reclassified from A.K. Banerjee (1963), Rs 10 million

		Total	Annual
Merchandise Export Balance		1301.8	72.3
Total Gold Balance		−122.12	−6.78
Gold Outflow 1931–37	(Financial, Non-Commodity Gold)	307.22	17.06
Commodity Gold balance = Total Gold balance less Non-Commodity Gold balance		−429.34	−23.85
Balance of Merchandise and Commodity Gold		872.46	48.5
*Adjusted Balance of Merchandise and Commodity Gold		905.46 (NX1)	50.3
Balance of Invisibles		−1432.95 (NX2)	−79.6
Current A/c Balance		−527.49	−29.3
Financial Gold Outflow	1931–37	307.22	17.07
Long-term Capital Import (Borrowing)		220.27	12.2

Source: A.K. Banerjee, *India's Balance of Payments: Estimates of Current and Capital Accounts from 1921–22 to 1938–39*, Bombay: Asia Publishing House, 1963. Note that I have: (a) separated from commodity gold the gold outflow during the 1930s, treating it as monetary gold, so to that extent there is a smaller positive balance of trade and a larger negative current account balance compared to the source. (b) Imports are taken here at *c.i.f.* values, so to the extent of freight, insurance and commission, the balance of commodity trade inclusive of commodity gold is smaller than in the source. The same figure is deducted from total Invisibles, Gold outflow is now in the capital account as means of settling deficit. Thus the estimate of capital import remains the same.
* Adjustment of Rs 330 million is made in the source.

current account, thus affecting the size of the commodity balance NX1 and hence the magnitude of drain using this measure.

A misleading interpretation of events occurs when financial gold is treated as commodity gold and put in the current account, as by Balachandran,[76] who says that from 1931 gold outflow 'enabled India to run a current account surplus until 1936–7, discharge a part of her foreign debt and lend abroad'.[77] A most difficult period of India's history is presented in a favourable light, although the agrarian economy was in deep crisis; the current account, far from being in surplus, was in much larger deficit than usual; and both financial gold outflow and short-term capital flight were taking place. India had the sixth largest gold loss in the world during these years: Triantis,[78] quoted also by Kindleberger,[79] shows that globally there were only five other smaller countries which had a sharper fall in export earnings than did India. All were forced to lose gold, as was India, before they devalued their currencies.

The aggregate drain from Banerjee's estimate taking NX1 is Rs 9,054.6 million (Table 5). Compounded at 5 per cent interest rate over the 87 years from 1930–31 to date, this amounts to Rs 63.145 billion or £4.21 billion. We now need to add up the estimates of present value of transfer or drain for the four periods – 1765 to 1836, 1837 to 1900, 1901 to 1919, 1922 to 1938. The values in billion pound sterling are as follows:

Estimated Drain, 1765 to 1938

1765–1836	*£8226.771 billion*
1837–1900	*£848.025 billion*
1901–1919	*£105.400 billion*
1922–1938	*£4.210 billion*
Total	*£9184.406 billion*

The drain for the entire period comes to £9,184.41 billion, on a highly underestimated basis since the interest rate applied is much lower than the market rate and enforced borrowing is not taken into account. Nevertheless, this sum amounts to ten times the United Kingdom's entire annual GDP for 2015.

These estimates of the drain are merely crudely indicative; the actual impact was incalculable, of withdrawing through taxes much more than was spent within the country. Every single year, Rs 100 taxed and Rs 33 to Rs 36 not spent normally meant the reverse operation of the Keynesian multiplier. Every rupee thus taxed but not spent, if spent, would have generated at least four to five times the income and corresponding employment. But the impact was the negative of this, a severe depression of income and employment. The cumulative effects of this over the years may only be imagined; realistic quantification is simply not possible.

In Lieu of a Conclusion

Branko Milanovic,[80] discussing the necessity and ethics of transfers from the advanced world to the less developed, and referring among others to this author's paper 'The Free Lunch',[81] proposed that Britain should return the money it drained from India. While the idea is an honourable one, it is not practicable for Britain to do so, for it is not rich enough to repay even a fraction of what it extracted from India over nearly two centuries. It used so much of its colonies' earnings to export capital to Europe, North America and regions of recent white settlement, that the entire industrializing world throve on the drain. The drain from smaller tropical colonies was not so small (Malaya was earning £20 million annually at one stage from its export surplus based on rubber) and needs to be estimated by their scholars. Further, we have not even touched here upon the £2.55 billion of war-time spending by Allied forces in South Asia, which was unjustly charged to the Indian revenues, was raised by rapid profit inflation, and claimed 3 million civilian lives in Bengal through extreme demand compression. Nothing can compensate for that loss of lives.[82]

It is practicable for the industrial nations as a whole to repay the transfers which they took, or from which they benefited, in the past. But to do this, their scholars have to come to terms with the real drivers and the real history of imperialism,[83] and show a much greater degree of informed and honest scholarship in writing the history of the rise of industrial capitalism than has been evident to date.

Notes and References

[1] Dadabhai Naoroji, *Poverty and Un-British Rule in India* [1901], Delhi: Government of India, reprint, 1962; R.C. Dutt, *Economic History of India*, Vol. 1: *Under Early British Rule 1757–1837* [1903], Vol. 2: *In the Victorian Age 1837–1900* [1905], Delhi: Government of India, second reprint, by arrangement with Routledge and Kegan Paul, 1970. The literature discussing the drain, whether directly or tangentially, includes: A.K. Bagchi 'Some International Foundations of Capitalist Growth and Underdevelopment', *Economic and Political Weekly*, Vol. 7, 1972, pp. 31–33; A.K. Bagchi, *The Presidency Banks and the Indian Economy, 1876–1914*, Delhi: State Bank of India and Oxford University Press, 1989; A.K. Bagchi, *Perilous Passage: Mankind and the Global Ascendancy of Capital*, Delhi: Oxford University Press, 2005; A.K. Banerjee, *India's Balance of Payments: Estimates of Current and Capital Accounts from 1921–22 to 1938–39*, Bombay: Asia Publishing House, 1963; A.K. Banerjee, *Aspects of Indo-British Economic Relations*, Bombay: Oxford University Press, 1982; D. Banerjee, *Colonialism in Action: Trade, Dependence and Development in Late Colonial India*, Delhi: Orient Longman, 1999; S. Bhattacharya, *Financial Foundations of the British Raj* [1971], Delhi: Orient Longman, reprint, 2005; K.N. Chaudhuri, 'Foreign Trade and the Balance of Payments 1757–1947', in D. Kumar, ed. (with the editorial assistance of Meghnad Desai), *The Cambridge Economic History of India*, Vol. II: *c. 1757 – c. 1970*, Delhi: Orient Longman, in association with Cambridge University Press, 1984, pp. 804–77; B.N. Ganguli, *Dadabhai Naoroji and the Drain Theory*, New York: Asia Publishing House, 1965; J.M. Keynes, 'Review of T. Morison's *The Economic Transition in India*', *Economic Journal*, 22, 1911; A. Maddison, *The World Economy*, Vol. 1: *A Millennial Perspective*, Vol. 2: *Historical Statistics*, Paris: OECD Development

Centre, 2006; T. Morison, *The Economic Transition in India*, London: Murray, 1911; Y.S. Pandit, *India's Balance of Indebtedness 1898 to 1913*, London: Allen and Unwin, 1937; P. Patnaik, *Accumulation and Stability under Capitalism*, Oxford: Clarendon Press, 1994; U. Patnaik, 'Tribute Transfer and the Balance of Payments in the *Cambridge Economic History of India Vol. II'*, *Social Scientist*, 12 (12), 1984, reprinted in U. Patnaik, *The Long Transition: Essays on Political Economy*, New Delhi: Tulika Books, 1999, pp. 305–22; U. Patnaik, 'The Free Lunch: Transfers from the Tropical Colonies and their Role in Capital Formation in Britain during the Industrial Revolution', in K.S. Jomo, ed., *Globalization under Hegemony: The Changing World Economy*, Delhi: Oxford University Press, 2006, pp. 30–70; D. Rothermund, *The Global Impact of the Great Depression, 1929–1939*, London: Routledge, 1996; S. Sen, *Colonies and the Empire: India 1890–1914*, Delhi: Orient Longman, 1992.

[2] The exceptions include P.A. Baran, *The Political Economy of Growth* [1957], London: Pelican, reprint, 1973; Maddison, *The World Economy*, Vol. 1 and Vol. 2; H. Heller, *The Birth of Capitalism*, London: Pluto Press, 2011; and B. Milanovic, 'Ethical Case and Economic Feasibility of Global Transfers', 2007, available at mpra.ub.uni-muenchen.de/2587/1/MPRA-paper-2587.pdf, accessed on 16 April 2016.

[3] Naoroji, *Poverty and Un-British Rule in India*; R.C. Dutt, *Economic History of India*, Vol. 1 and Vol. 2.

[4] R.C. Dutt in particular provided complete time-series from 1837 to 1901 of India's domestic revenues, exports and imports, and expenditure in England.

[5] India is also likely to have produced the second largest commodity export surplus, namely merchandise export surplus adjusted for trade in gold as commodity; but to establish this requires data on gold flows for all countries.

[6] B.B. Chaudhuri, 'Growth of Commercial Agriculture in Bengal (1757–1900)', *Indian Studies Past and Present* (Calcutta), 1964.

[7] P. Thomas, 'A Quantitative Approach to the Study of the Effects of British Imperial Policy upon Colonial Welfare: Some Preliminary Findings', *Journal of Economic History*, 25, 1965, pp. 615–38; P.R.P. Coelho, 'The Profitability of Imperialism: The British Experience in the West Indies 1768–72', *Explorations in Economic History*, 10, 1973, pp. 253–80; P.K. O'Brien, 'The Costs and Benefits of British Imperialism, 1846–1914', *Past and Present*, 120, 1, 1988, pp. 163–200.

[8] See Keynes, 'Review of T. Morison's *The Economic Transition in India*'.

[9] See U. Patnaik, 'Tribute Transfer and the Balance of Payments', pp. 305–22.

[10] See U. Patnaik, 'Classical Theory of Rent and Its Application to India: Some Preliminary Propositions', *Journal of Peasant Studies*, 10, 1983, pp. 2–3, reprinted in T.J. Byres, ed., *Sharecropping and Sharecroppers*, London: Cass, 1983, and in U. Patnaik, *The Long Transition*, pp. 109–30. Also, U. Patnaik, 'Introduction', in U. Patnaik, ed., *The Agrarian Question in Marx and His Successors*, Vol. 1, Delhi: Leftword Books, 2008, pp. 9–51. In both these works U. Patnaik briefly discusses the Smith–Marx concept of rent, which Marx called 'absolute ground rent', and in what way it differs radically from what Ricardo mislabelled as 'Rent'.

[11] See P. Mantoux, *The Industrial Revolution in the Eighteenth Century* [1928], translated by Marjorie Vernon, London: Methuen, reprint, 1970, pp. 200–01.

[12] Ibid., pp. 224–25.

[13] R.C. Dutt, *Economic History of India*, Vol. 1, p. 203.

[14] See E.J. Hobsbawm, *Industry and Empire*, Harmondsworth: Penguin, 1969; D. Landes, *The Unbound Prometheus: Technological Change and Industrial*

Development in Western Europe from 1850 to the Present, Cambridge: Cambridge University Press, 1969; and P. Deane and W.A. Cole, *British Economic Growth 1688–1969: Trends and Structure*, Cambridge: Cambridge University Press, second edition, 1969.

[15] B.R. Tomlinson, *The New Cambridge History of India: The Economy of Modern India 1860–1970*, Cambridge: Cambridge University Press, 1993.

[16] F. List, *The National System of Political Economy*, translated by George A. Matile, Philadelphia: J.B. Lippincott & Co., 1856; R.C. Dutt, *Economic History of India*, Vol. 1; Mantoux, *The Industrial Revolution in the 18th Century*; Baran, *The Political Economy of Growth*.

[17] C. Hill, *Reformation to Industrial Revolution*, London: Pelican, 1967; R. Davis, *The Industrial Revolution and British Overseas Trade*, Leicester: Leicester University Press, 1979.

[18] Davis, *The Industrial Revolution and British Overseas Trade*.

[19] P. Deane, *The First Industrial Revolution*, Cambridge: Cambridge University Press, 1965.

[20] Deane and Cole, *British Economic Growth 1688–1969*.

[21] See ibid.; and U. Patnaik, 'New Estimates of Eighteenth-Century British Trade and Their Relation to Transfers from the Tropical Colonies', in T.J. Byres, K.N. Panikkar and U. Patnaik, eds, *The Making of History: Essays presented to Irfan Habib*, Delhi: Tulika Books, 2000.

[22] S. Kuznets, 'Foreign Trade: Long-term trends', *Economic Development and Cultural Change*, Vol. 15, No. 2, Part 2, January 1967, pp. 1–140.

[23] U. Patnaik, 'Misleading Trade Estimates in Historical and Economic Writings', in P. Patnaik, ed., *Excursus in History: Essays on Some Ideas of Irfan Habib*, Delhi: Tulika Books, 2011, pp. 249–70.

[24] See U. Patnaik, 'Ricardo's Fallacy', in K.S. Jomo, ed., *The Pioneers of Development Economics*, Delhi: Tulika Books, 2005, pp. 31–41, for a critique and numerical example. The material fallacy in Ricardo's theory is termed the converse fallacy of accident. The incorrect theory continues to serve a very useful apologetic function for advanced countries by obfuscating the reality of adverse welfare outcome for the less developed country obliged to trade for extra-economic reasons. I.B. Kravis, in 'Availability and Other Influences on the Commodities Composition of Trade', *Journal of Political Economy*, Vol. 64, 2, April 1956, pp. 143–55, had provided a sensible alternative theory based on local availability, but he did not critique Ricardo's theory.

[25] U. Patnaik, 'The Free Lunch', using data in B.R. Mitchell and P. Deane, *Abstract of British Historical Statistics*, Cambridge: Cambridge University Press, 1962.

[26] Maddison, *The World Economy*, Vol. 1 and Vol. 2.

[27] Davis, *The Industrial Revolution and British Overseas Trade*.

[28] See U. Patnaik, 'Bina Paisar Bhoj: Oupanibeshik sampader hastantar o Britainer shilpayan' (in Bengali), in *India and Indology: Professor Sukumari Bhattacharji Felicitation Volume*, edited by B. Mukhopadhyay, D. Bhattacharya, M. Hassan, K. Roy and S. Bhattacharya, Kolkata: National Book Agency, 2004; and U. Patnaik, 'The Free Lunch'.

[29] Davis, *The Industrial Revolution and British Overseas Trade*.

[30] Mitchell and Deane, *Abstract of British Historical Statistics*.

[31] A.H. Imlah, *Economic Elements of the Pax Brittanica: Studies in British Foreign Trade in the Nineteenth Century*, Cambridge: Cambridge University Press, 1958.

[32] See Davis, *The Industrial Revolution and British Overseas Trade*, and U.

Patnaik, 'The Free Lunch', Table 2.5: estimated China trade is deducted for the period 1822 to 1836 using the information in Davis's Appendix tables.

[33] Irfan Habib, 'The Colonialization of the Indian Economy 1757–1900', in *Essays in Indian History: Towards a Marxist Perception*, Delhi: Tulika Books, 1995.

[34] B.B. Chaudhuri, 'Growth of Commercial Agriculture in Bengal'.

[35] S. Sen, *Colonies and the Empire*, p. 45.

[36] Ibid., pp. 21, 22.

[37] The exporters (including British-owned firms) referred to in S. Sen, *Colonies and the Empire*, p. 45, were mere intermediaries in the circulation process and not productive principals. Their profit was a cut out of the monies due to the peasant and artisan producers from whom they sourced the export goods. For every Rs 100 of Council Bills that they cashed the exporters kept, say, Rs 30 and paid out the remainder to producers; but these very producers were obliged to contribute the bulk of the budget revenues – as land revenue, cess and indirect taxes – out of which they were being 'paid'. Exporters hardly paid any taxes. The author does not refer either to actual producers or to their tax payment (the diagram on p. 22 remains incomplete), hence the core feature, the drain – namely, 'paying' producers out of their own taxes while keeping their export surplus proceeds in London – is never mentioned directly.

[38] A.K. Banerjee, *India's Balance of Payments*.

[39] However, all gold inflow was treated as commodity gold, whereas some part was financial gold inflow. In reality, 'expenditure in England' would have exceeded the correctly measured commodity export surplus, to the extent of long-term indebtedness thrust on India.

[40] Y.S. Pandit, *India's Balance of Indebtedness*.

[41] Note that gold inflow for reserves and coinage is treated by this author as monetary gold and not commodity gold, while deriving the above figure for commodity export surplus.

[42] A.K. Banerjee, *India's Balance of Payments*.

[43] Note that gold outflow during the Depression was not commodity export but a means of payment (financial gold), so the figure of commodity export surplus given here is smaller than in Banerjee (ibid.) by the value of distress gold outflow.

[44] A.K. Bagchi, The Evolution of the State Bank of India, Vol. II: The Era of the Presidency Banks, 1876–1920, New Delhi: State Bank of India and Sage Publications.

[45] Wingate, quoted in R.C. Dutt, *Economic History of India*, Vol. 2, pp. 154–55.

[46] S. Bhattacharya, *Financial Foundations of the British Raj*.

[47] A.K. Sen, *Poverty and Famines: An Essay on Entitlement and Deprivation*, Delhi: Oxford University Press, 1987; U. Patnaik, 'Food Availability and Famine: A Longer View', *Journal of Peasant Studies*, 19, 1, 1991, reprinted in U. Patnaik, *The Long Transition*, pp. 323–50.

[48] B.N. Ganguli, *Dadabhai Naoroji and the Drain Theory*; S. Sen, *Colonies and the Empire*.

[49] U. Patnaik, 'The Free Lunch', Appendix.

[50] Any standard textbook dealing with open economy macroeconomics gives the derivation of the identity. See R. Dornbusch and S. Fisher, *Macroeconomics*, New York: McGraw-Hill, 1990; P.R. Krugman and M. Obstfeld, *International Economics: Theory and Policy*, New York: Harper Collins, 1994.

[51] United Nations, *International Trade Statistics 1900–1960*, 1962, available at www.unstats.un.org/unsd/trade/imts/Historicaldata1900-1960.pdf

[52] Y.S. Pandit, *India's Balance of Indebtedness*; A.K. Banerjee, *India's Balance of Payments*.

[53] Y.S. Pandit, *India's Balance of Indebtedness*.

[54] A.K. Banerjee, *India's Balance of Payments*.

[55] C. Wright and S. Brown, 'Non-Monetary Gold', *Report of Balance of Payments Technical Expert Group (BOPTEG)*, 2006, available at Unstats.un.org/unsd/nationalaccount/aeg/papers/m4Gold.pdf, accessed on 16 April 2016. Also available at www.imf.org/External/NP/sta/bop/pdf/bopteg27.b pdf.

[56] J.K. Galbraith, 'John Maynard Keynes', Review of *The Collected Works of John Maynard Keynes*, *New York Review of Books*, 22 November 1984; reprinted in *A View from the Stands*, Boston: Houghton Mifflin, 1986, pp. 315–16.

[57] Quoted in A. Chandavarkar, *Keynes and India: A Study in Economics and Biography*, London: Macmillan, 1989, which also provides some very interesting facts regarding Keynes's four-decade-long engagement with Indian economic affairs.

[58] B.E. Dadachanji, *History of Indian Currency and Finance*, Bombay: Taraporevala Sons and Co., second edition, 1931.

[59] Galbraith, 'John Maynard Keynes'.

[60] S.B. Saul, *Studies in British Overseas Trade*, Liverpool: Liverpool University Press, 1960.

[61] Ibid.

[62] Ibid., Table 10.

[63] Ibid., p. 62.

[64] Ibid., p. 203.

[65] A.K. Banerjee, *India's Balance of Payments*.

[66] United Nations, *International Trade Statistics 1900–1960*.

[67] S. Bhattacharya, *Financial Foundations of the British Raj*.

[68] Ibid. for the first figure, and D. Kumar, ed., *The Cambridge Economic History of India*, Vol. II, for the second.

[69] D. Kumar, ed., *The Cambridge Economic History of India*, Vol. II.

[70] Y.S. Pandit, *India's Balance of Indebtedness*.

[71] A.K. Banerjee, *India's Balance of Payments*.

[72] Y.S. Pandit, *India's Balance of Indebtedness*.

[73] Pandit adjusts the figure to Rs 98 million after taking account of the trade surplus of non-British India and correcting for possible overestimation of interest payment.

[74] M. De Cecco, *The International Gold Standard: Money and Empire*, London: F. Pinter, 1984.

[75] C.P. Kindelberger, *The World in Depression 1928–1938*, Harmondsworth: Pelican, 1987.

[76] G. Balachandran, *John Bullion's Empire: Britain's Gold Problem and India between the Wars*, Richmond: Curzon Press, 1996; G. Balachandran, 'The Depression Years', in G. Balachandran, ed., *India and the World Economy, c. 1850–1950*, Delhi: Oxford University Press, 2003, pp. 266–306.

[77] G. Balachandran, *John Bullion's Empire*, Table 7.1 and G. Balachandran, 'The Depression Years' (in G. Balachandran, ed., *India and the World Economy*), pp. 274–75 repeatedly reproduced the highly underestimated Indian trade data submitted by the colonial government to the League of Nations, available as an Appendix in A.K. Banerjee, *India's Balance of Payments*, but cut out the first three years and the last year, giving twelve years' figures from 1926–27 to 1937–28 although the official series is for sixteen years from 1923–24 to 1938–39. Comparing the same twelve-year subset taken from Banerjee with Balachandran's table, in the latter the merchandise balance is 52 per cent, the gold balance 142 per cent, the invisibles balance 58 per cent and the (nega-

tive) current account balance only 21.6 per cent of Banerjee's figures. Although Banerjee and the official estimates did treat all gold as belonging to the current account, they were cautious in not drawing conclusions that were at variance with the prevailing situation of economic distress.

[78] S.G. Triantis, *Cyclical Changes in the Trade Balances of Countries Exporting Primary Products 1927–1933*, Toronto: University of Toronto Press, 1967.

[79] Kindelberger, *The World in Depression*.

[80] Milanovic, 'Ethical Case and Economic Feasibility of Global Transfers'.

[81] U. Patnaik, 'The Free Lunch'.

[82] U. Patnaik, 'Food Availability and Famine'; U. Patnaik, 'Mr Keynes and the Forgotten Holocaust in Bengal – or, the Macroeconomics of Extreme Demand Compression', paper presented at the Aligarh Historians Panel, Indian History Congress, 29 December 2016, Thiruvananthapuram.

[83] Utsa Patnaik and Prabhat Patnaik attempt to do this in *A Theory of Imperialism*, New York: Columbia University Press and Delhi: Tulika Books, 2016.

Contributors

DIETMAR ROTHERMUND is Professor Emeritus of South Asian History, Heidelberg University, Germany.

DAVID LUDDEN is Professor of History, New York University, New York.

RAJAT DATTA is Professor of Medieval History, Centre for Historical Studies, School of Social Sciences, Jawaharlal Nehru University, New Delhi.

SHINKICHI TANIGUCHI is Professor Emeritus, Graduate School of Economics, Hitotsubashi University, Japan.

NEELADRI BHATTACHARYA is Professor of Modern History, Centre for Historical Studies, School of Social Sciences, Jawaharlal Nehru University, New Delhi.

GARGI CHAKRAVARTTY taught History in Maitreyi College, University of Delhi, Delhi.

SEKHAR BANDYOPADHYAY is Professor and Head, School of History, Philosophy, Political Science and International Relations, Victoria University of Wellington, New Zealand; and Director, New Zealand India Research Institute.

SHUBHRA CHAKRABARTI teaches History in Dyal Singh College, University of Delhi, New Delhi.

UMA DAS GUPTA, a Tagore biographer, is retired Research Professor, Social Science Division, Indian Statistical Institute, Calcutta; she has taught History at Jadavpur University and Visva-Bharati University, Santiniketan.

TANIKA SARKAR is retired Professor of Modern History, Centre for Historical Studies, School of Social Sciences, Jawaharlal Nehru University, New Delhi.

ANURADHA ROY is Professor of History, Jadavpur University, Calcutta.

SABYASACHI BHATTACHARYA , currently Tagore National Fellow, Ministry of Culture, Government of India, was Professor of Indian Economic History, Centre for Historical Studies, Jawaharlal Nehru University, New Delhi, and Chairman, Indian Council of Historical Research (2007–11).

UTSA PATNAIK is Professor Emeritus, Centre for Economic Studies and Planning, School of Social Sciences, Jawaharlal Nehru University, New Delhi.

Publications by
Binay Bhushan Chaudhuri

1956   'Some Problems of the Peasantry of Bengal after the Permanent Settlement', *Bengal Past and Present*, Jubilee Number, July–December.

1957   'Problems of the Peasantry of Bengal before the Permanent Settlement', *Bengal Past and Present*, July–December.

1958   'Agrarian Relationships in Bengal after the Permanent Settlement, 1793–1819', unpublished Ph.D. thesis, Calcutta University.

1960a   'A Chapter of Peasant Resistance in Bengal after the Permanent Settlement', *Enquiry* (New Delhi), Vol. 3.

1960b   'The Denajpore Report of Buchanan Hamilton', *Indian Studies Past and Present*, October–December.

1963a   'The Cultivation of Poppy under Monopoly Control in Bengal and Bihar: 1757–1900', *Indian Studies Past and Present*, April–June.

1963b   'The Problem of Indigo Cultivation in Bengal, 1757–1900', Part 1, *Indian Studies Past and Present*, July–September.

1963c   'The Problem of Indigo Cultivation in Bengal, 1757–1900', Part 2, *Indian Studies Past and Present*, October–December.

1964a   'Growth of Commercial Agriculture in Bengal, 1757–1900', *Indian Studies Past and Present* (Calcutta).

1964b   'The Structural Changes in Land Rights in the Early Nineteenth Century and Their Impact on the Village Economy', *Readings in Indian Economic History*, Delhi: Vikas.

1968a   'Agrarian Economy and Agrarian Relations in Bengal, 1859–85', unpublished D.Phil. thesis, Oxford University.

1968b   'Agrarian Economy and Agrarian Relations in Bengal, 1859–85', in N.K. Sinha, ed., *History of Bengal, 1757–1905*, Calcutta: University of Calcutta.

1968c   'Political History of Bengal, 1757–72', in N.K. Sinha, ed., *History of Bengal, 1757–1905*, Calcutta: University of Calcutta.

1969a   'Rural Credit Relations in Bengal, 1859–1885', *The Indian Economic and Social History Review*, September.

1969b   'Agricultural Production in Bengal and Bihar: Coexistence of Decline and Growth, 1859–1885', *Bengal Past and Present*, July–December.

1970a   'Growth of Commercial Agriculture in Bengal, 1859–1885', *The Indian Economic and Social History Review*, March–June.

1970b   'Impact of the Growth of Commercial Agriculture on the Peasant Economy of Bengal', *The Indian Economic and Social History Review*, June.

1972   'Agrarian Movements in Bengal and Bihar, 1919–39', in B.R. Nanda, ed., *Socialism in India, 1919–39*, New Delhi: Vikas.

1973a   'Peasant Movements in Bengal and Bihar, 1850–1900', *Nineteenth Century Studies* (Calcutta).

1973b   'The Story of a Peasant Revolt in a Bengal District', *Bengal Past and Present*, July–December.

1975a   'Land Market in Eastern India: Movement of Land Prices, 1790–1930', *The Indian Economic and Social History Review*, March.

1975b   'Land Market in Eastern India: Changing Composition of the Landed Aristocracy, 1793–1930', *The Indian Economic and Social History Review*, June.

1975c   'The Process of Depeasantization in Bengal and Bihar, 1885–1947', *Indian Historical Review*, July.

1976a   'Agricultural Growth in Bengal and Bihar, 1770–1860', *Bengal Past and Present*, January–July.

1976b   'The Agrarian Question in Bengal and the Government, 1850–1900', *Calcutta Historical Journal*, July.

1977   'Movement of Rent in Eastern India, 1793–1939', *Indian Historical Review*, July.

1979 'The Transformation of Rural Protest in India, 1783–1930', Presidential Address, Modern Section, Indian History Congress, Waltair.

1982 'Perspectives on Bengal Agrarian Structure', *Indian Historical Review*, New Delhi, July–December.

1983a 'Agriculture: Eastern India, 1757–1857', in Dharma Kumar, ed. (with the editorial assistance of Meghnad Desai), *The Cambridge Economic History of India, Vol. II: c. 1757 – c. 1970*, Cambridge: Cambridge University Press, 1983.

1983b 'Agrarian Relations: Eastern India, 1757–1947, in Dharma Kumar, ed. (with the editorial assistance of Meghnad Desai), *The Cambridge Economic History of India, Vol. II: c. 1757 – c. 1970*, Cambridge: Cambridge University Press, 1983.

1983c 'Perspectives on Peasant Movements in India', *Indian Historical Review*, 10, July–December.

1984a 'Rural Power Structure and Agricultural Productivity in Eastern India, 1757–1947', in Meghnad Desai, Suzanne Hoeber Rudolph and Ashok Rudra, eds., *Agrarian Power and Agricultural Productivity in South Asia*, Delhi: Oxford University Press.

1984b 'A Tribal World in Transition: Interaction of the Munda and Santal Agrarian Structures and the External Pressures on Them, 1765–1920', *The Journal of the Bihar Puravid Parishad* (Patna), *Dr K.K. Datta Commemoration Volume*.

1985– 'Subaltern Autonomy and the National Movement', *Indian Histo-*
1986 *rical Review*, 12, July–January.

1986a 'Trends in the Recent Studies in Agrarian Social Structure in Colonial India', in T. Banerjee, ed., *Indian Historical Research Since Independence*, Calcutta: Naya Prokash.

1986b 'The Peasant Movement in Tushkhali, 1858–75', in S.A. Hossain and H. Mamun, eds., *Armed Resistance Movement in Bangladesh* (in Bengali), Dhaka: Bangladesh Asiatic Society.

1987a 'Agricultural Commercialization and the Agrarian Social Structure in Colonial India: A Critique of Some Recent Writings on their Interaction', *Economic Studies*, Department of Economics, Jadavpur University, Calcutta.

1987– 'Tribal Society of India', *Calcutta Historical Review*, July–June.
1988

1988– 'Peasant Insurgency and Organized Politics: Role of the Bengal
1989a Provincial Kisan Sabha in the Tebhaga Movement in Bengal,
1946–47', *Calcutta Historical Journal*, July–June.

1988– 'Religion and Peasant Protest Movements in Eastern India, 1825–
1989b 1920', serialized in eleven issues of the Bengali journal *Chaturanga*,
September–July.

1989 'The Story of a Tribal Revolt in the Bengal Presidency: The Religion
and Politics of the Oraons, 1900–1920', in *Aspects of Socio-
Economic Changes and Political Awakening in Bengal*, Calcutta:
West Bengal State Archives.

1989– 'The Chotanagpur Tribal Revolt, 1831–32: Some Methodological
1990 Issues', *Calcutta Historical Review*, July–June.

1992 'Commercialization of Agriculture in Bengal', *History of Bengal*,
Vol. 1, Dhaka: Asiatic Society of Bangladesh.

1993 'Tribal Society in Transition: Eastern India, 1757–1920', in
Mushirul Hasan and Narayani Gupta, eds., *India's Colonial
Encounter: Essays in Memory of Eric Stokes*, New Delhi: Manohar.

1994a 'Towards an Understanding of the Tribal World of Colonial
Eastern India', in S. Taniguchi, H. Yanagisawa and F. Oshikawa,
eds., *Economic Changes and Social Transformations in Modern
and Contemporary South Asia*, Tokyo: Hitotsubashi University.

1994b 'The Myth of the Tribe? The Question Reconsidered', *The Calcutta
Historical Journal*, 16 (1), January–June.

1994c 'Hindu–Tribal Cultural Contacts in Colonial Eastern India' (in
Bengali), serialized in six issues of *Chaturanga*, (Bengali years)
Magh 1401– Sravan 1404, BS.

1994d 'The Tribal Society in Colonial Eastern India: Examination of
Some Recent Concepts' (in Bengali), *Visva Bharati Patrika*, New
Series, First Issue, August.

1994e 'Growth of Commercial Agriculture in Bengal, 1859–1885', in
David Ludden, ed., *Agricultural Production in Indian History*,
reprint, Delhi: Oxford University Press.

1994f Review article, 'S.B. Cook's *Imperial Affinities: Nineteenth Century Analogies and Exchanges Between India and Ireland*', *Calcutta Historical Journal*.

1996a 'The Tribal Village Organization in Colonial Eastern India' (in Bengali), Suniti Kumar Chattopadhyay Memorial Lecture, December 1994, in *Pashcimbanga Bangla Academy Journal*.

1996b 'The Process of Agricultural Commercialization in Eastern India During British Rule: A Reconsideration of the Notions of "Forced Commercialization" and "Dependent Peasantry"', in Peter Robb, ed., *The Meanings of Agriculture: Essays in South Asian History and Economics*, Delhi: Oxford University Press.

1996c 'Petty Peasant Production and Agrarian Capitalism: A Recent View on their Relationship in Colonial India', in P.K. Misra, ed., *Aspects of Indian History and Historiography*, Professor Kalyan Kumar Dasgupta Felicitation Volume, New Delhi: Kaveri Book Service.

1996d 'Reopening the Question of Bonded Labour in Colonial India', *Calcutta Historical Journal*, July–December.

1997 'Tribe–Caste Continuum? Some Perspectives from the Tribal History of Colonial Eastern India', in Dev Nathan, ed., *From Tribe to Caste*, Shimla: Indian Institute of Advanced Study.

1997–   Characterizing the Polity and Economy of Late Pre-Colonial

1998 India: The Revisionist Position in the Debate over "The Eighteenth Century in Indian History"', *Calcutta Historical Journal*, combined issue.

1999a 'Ideology and Organization of Millenarian Protest Movements in the Tribal World of colonial Eastern India', in J.T. O'Connell, ed., *Organizational and Institutional Aspects of Indian Religious Movements*, Shimla: Indian Institute of Advanced Study.

1999b 'Tribal Village Organization and Mobilization in Tribal Protest Movements in Eastern India, 1820–1922', *Studies in Humanities and Social Sciences*, 6 (1), Indian Institute of Advanced Study, Shimla.

2001 'Peasantry as a Category in Indian History', in B. Roy *et al.*, eds., *Politics and Identity in South Asia*, Calcutta: K.P. Bagchi & Co.

2002   'Society and Culture of the Tribal World in Colonial Eastern India: Reconsidering the Notion of "Hinduization' of Tribes', in Hetukar Jha, ed., *Perspectives on Indian Society and History: A Critique*, Delhi: Manohar.

2004   'Adivasi and Aranyaka: Reconsidering Some Characterizations of their Polity and Economy in Precolonial and Colonial India', in B.B. Chaudhuri and Arun Bandopadhyay, eds., *Tribes, Forest and Social Formation in Indian History*, Delhi: Manohar.

2005   (edited volume), *Economic History of India from Eighteenth to Twentieth Century*, Vol. VIII, Part 3, Project of History of Indian Science, Philosophy and Culture series (General Editor: D.P. Chattopadhyaya), Delhi: Pearson Longman.

2008   (edited volume), *Peasant History of Late Pre-Colonial and Colonial India*. Vol. VIII, Part 2, Project of History of Indian Science, Philosophy and Culture series (General Editor: D.P. Chattopadhyaya), Delhi: Pearson Longman.

2011   'Radical Adivasi Movements in Colonial Eastern India, 1856–1922: Origins, Ideology and Organization', in *Proceedings of the Indian History Congress*, Patiala session.